STUDY GUIDE TO ACCOMPANY **Wonnacott/Wonnacott**

ECONOMICS

STUDY GUIDE TO ACCOMPANY **Wonnacott/Wonnacott**

ECONOMICS

Peter Howitt
University of Western Ontario

McGraw-Hill Book Company

New York St. Louis San Francisco Auckland Bogotá Düsseldorf
Johannesburg London Madrid Mexico Montreal New Delhi
Panama Paris São Paulo Singapore Sydney Tokyo Toronto

Study Guide to Accompany Wonnacott and Wonnacott: ECONOMICS

ISBN 0-07-071573-4

3 4 5 6 7 8 9 0 WCWC 7 8 3 2 1 0 9

This book was set in Caledonia by Intergraphic Technology, Inc.
The editors were Bonnie E. Lieberman, Michael Elia, and J. W. Maisel;
the designer was Merrill Haber;
the production supervisor was John F. Harte.
The drawings were done by Intergraphic Technology, Inc.
Webcrafters, Inc., was printer and binder.

To Pat

Contents

Preface

This study guide is intended to help the student who is taking an introductory economics course using the textbook *Economics* by Paul Wonnacott and Ron Wonnacott. It makes no attempt to be self-contained: students will find that it can be used effectively as a supplement to, not as a substitute for, the textbook.

Each chapter is designed to be read and worked through after the student has read the corresponding chapter in the textbook. Each study-guide chapter contains seven sections:

1. *Learning objectives.* This section consists of a list of tasks that the student should be able to accomplish after having studied the chapter in the textbook and in the study guide. The purpose of this section is twofold. First, it should help to give the student direction and purpose while studying the rest of the chapter. Second, it should serve as a checklist to test the student's comprehension after the chapter has been read.

2. *Chapter highlights.* This section contains a summary of the important points of the chapter. Its purpose is mainly to reinforce the textbook by going over these main points from a somewhat different perspective and adding illustrative examples. To a student learning a subject for the first time, everything is likely to appear equally important. This can be a source of great confusion. The chapter highlights should help students sort out the important from the incidental by focusing more narrowly than the text upon the important points, and by drawing the students' attention to the particularly important material by such phrases as "Be sure you understand. . . ."

3. *Important terms.* Any new terms introduced in the chapter are defined in this section. The section is intended mainly to provide a source of reference for the student who is working through the chapter, but the student may also benefit from going down the list to make sure that he or she understands each term before proceeding.

4. *True-false questions;* **5.** *multiple-choice questions;* and **6.** *exercises.* These three sections are meant to help the student learn by doing. As well as providing reinforcement through repetition, many of the questions and exercises are designed to guide the student toward discovering ideas that will be explicitly introduced only later in the textbook. Each section starts with easy questions that get progressively more difficult. Particularly difficult questions are marked with an asterisk. Even students who believe they understand the chapter in the textbook well enough to proceed without using the study guide are advised to spend a few minutes going over the true-false and multiple-choice questions as a self-test. Answers to all questions in these sections are provided at the back of the book.

7. *Essay questions.* This section begins with relatively simple questions and works toward more involved ones for which clear-cut answers cannot easily be given. Again, particularly difficult questions are marked with an asterisk. The questions are meant to help the student recognize and use important concepts that have been developed in the text, as well as to stimulate the student's imagination. No answers have been provided for this section. Thus the questions may be used as material for classroom discussion.

The material from the boxes and optional sections of the text has generally been excluded from the study guide, with a few exceptions. Where such material has been included it is marked with an asterisk, as with the more difficult questions, and a footnote.

In preparing this study guide I was greatly aided by the detailed comments and suggestions of Paul and Ron Wonnacott. I also benefited from the comments of three reviewers, Ronald G. Reddall, Allan Hanock College, and Heidemarie C. Sherman, and Allen R. Thompson, University of New Hampshire, and Mike Elia of McGraw-Hill. I also wish to acknowledge the assistance of Marg Gower and her typing staff in the Economics Department of the University of Western Ontario, whose fast and efficient typing of the manuscript did more than anything else to lighten my load.

Peter Howitt

Special note for those studying only the soft-cover volume "*An Introduction to Microeconomics*"

For students studying the microeconomics soft-cover volume, use the first six chapters of this study guide and then skip to Chapter 17, which corresponds to Chapter 7 in the soft-cover volume. The key for the balance of both books is as shown in the following chart.

Numbers referred to in this study guide	Numbering in microeconomics soft-cover volume	Key
Chapter 17, Figure 17-1, 17-2, etc.	Chapter 7, Figure 7-1, 7-2, etc.	Subtract 10 from any chapter number in this study guide. Similarly, treat any figure, appendix, box, or table number in the same way.
Parts 4 and 5.	Parts 2 and 3.	Subtract 2 from Part number in this study guide.
Pages 373-376 (ignore any references to pp. 377-379).	Pages 120–123.	
Page 380 to the end.	Page 124 to the end.	Subtract 256 from page number in this study guide.

Part One
BASIC ECONOMIC CONCEPTS

chapter 1
Economic Problems and Economic Goals

Learning Objectives

After you have studied this chapter in the textbook and the study guide, you should be able to

Explain the distinction between economic theory and economic policy
State the difference between Adam Smith and J. M. Keynes on the issue of whether or not the government should intervene more in economic affairs
List the five major goals of economic policy
Enumerate four serious problems that can be caused by inflation
Explain the distinction between technical efficiency and allocative efficiency
State how inequality is usually measured and why this measure is not ideal
State one argument for economic growth and two against

CHAPTER HIGHLIGHTS

Economics—like physics, chemistry, biology, and psychology—is a science. Just as the other sciences do, economics helps us to understand the world we live in. The particular aspect of the world that economics deals with, which we may call economic life, is the daily activity of making a living.

Economic theory is the pure science of economics. It attempts to discover and explain the basic laws and principles that govern economic life. It helps us to understand why some prices are higher than others, why some people are richer than others, what the underlying causes of inflation are, and so forth.

The applied science of economics is the study of economic policy—or of how governments can solve economic problems and achieve economic goals. It addresses such questions as: Can the government reduce the level of unemployment? If so, what are the various techniques that can be used? What are the side effects of these various techniques?

Economic theory and economic policy go hand-in-hand. Just as the physician, in order to heal patients, must know how the human body works, so the applied economist must understand economic theory in order to prescribe economic policies that will work. Likewise, just as the pure scientist who is interested in science for science's sake has learned a great deal from applied research on such problems as how to build nuclear weapons or how to cure cancer, so the economic theorist finds it helpful to study economic policy. However, most people become interested in economics initially because of their concern with policy issues rather than out of pure scientific curiosity. This introductory chapter discusses some of the policy issues that people find most interesting.

Probably the greatest and most hotly contested of all the issues of economic policy has been the broad question of whether or not the government should intervene more in private economic affairs. This question motivated Adam Smith, the great eighteenth-century economist who advocated laissez faire, to conceive of the "economic system" as a self-regulating mechanism that needs little guidance by the government. Much of modern economic theory still relies on this original conception of Smith's. On the other hand, J. M. Keynes argued in *The General Theory* (1936) that more government intervention was necessary to prevent massive unemployment. Keynes' position on this question is not accepted by all economists; nevertheless, his theoretical analysis still lies at the core of modern macroeconomic theory (the branch of economic theory concerned mainly with explaining what determines the behavior of aggregate variables like national income, unemployment, and inflation).

Most of this chapter is devoted to a discussion of the major goals of economic policy: (1) a high level of employment, (2) price stability, (3) efficiency, (4) an equitable distribution of income, and (5) economic growth. Some economists would add other goals to this list, such as economic freedom, economic security, national independence, or the conservation of economic resources. However, most disagreement and controversy concerns the question of how best to attain these goals and whether or not any particular goal can be pursued without having to sacrifice one or more of the other goals.

The first two goals come under the heading of maintaining a stable equilibrium to the economy. Throughout United States history there has been a great deal of instability. During the 1930s, for example, the Great Depression produced a substantial drop both in the level of employment and in the cost of living. However, both employment and living costs rose dramatically during World War II. Since then, we have maintained a reasonably high level of employment, at least up until the last four or five years. The problem of inflation has been particularly acute during the 1940s and 1970s.

While everyone agrees that unemployment is a serious problem, it is more difficult to agree on the seriousness of inflation. When employment falls, we have less output to enjoy. When inflation occurs, we don't necessarily have less output; we have to give up more money to buy the things that we consume, but we also receive more money when selling the things that we produce. However, inflation does give rise to some serious complications:

1. There is always the danger that it will turn into hyperinflation, in which prices rise so quickly that the entire monetary system breaks down.

2. It hurts those living on fixed incomes.

3. It can lead to wasteful speculation in real estate, antiques, wine, and other goods.

4. It can also interfere with economic decision making because of the difficulty of keeping track of how much different goods cost when prices keep changing all the time.

The problem of efficiency is twofold. *Technical* efficiency simply means getting the most output out of a given combination of inputs. On the other hand, *allocative* efficiency involves the problem of allocating scarce resources (such as time, machines, land, etc.) among different uses (such as the production of different kinds of goods) so as to avoid the kind of waste that would occur if baseball stars taught economics and were replaced on their teams by professors of economics.

The goal of an equitable distribution of income is becoming even more important as society grows richer. Many people believe that the economic pie should be divided up more evenly than it is. But the more we try to do this the smaller the pie becomes. For example, if we were all guaranteed an equal income, there would not be much incentive for anyone to work. How to measure inequality is also a problem. One common measure is the percentage share of national income earned by the poorest 20 percent of families. However, the economic well-being of these families doesn't depend only upon their incomes; it depends also upon family size, age, whether they are city or farm dwellers, and so forth. In addition, we must remember that even when the fraction of the pie going to the poorest 20 percent doesn't grow, the *size* of that pie may grow, so that their standard of living improves. In other words, the degree of inequality may remain constant while the incidence of poverty has fallen.

The problem of economic growth has recently sparked a great deal of controversy. When total output is growing, the additional output can be used to alleviate poverty and achieve greater equity. However, faster growth requires people to sacrifice current consumption, just as a person normally can make a bank account grow faster only by sacrificing current consumption. Also, growth uses up scarce natural resources; this may work to the detriment of future generations.

IMPORTANT TERMS

Invisible hand A catch phrase used by Adam Smith, the eighteenth-century economist, who argued that if we were all left free to pursue our own selfish interests, we would be led as if by an "invisible hand" to promote the interests of others.

Laissez faire Literally "allow to do" in French. This is the doctrine, also promoted by Adam Smith, that the best government policy is not to interfere with the private economy.

Unemployment The situation of someone who is willing and able to work but unable to find a job. The rate of unemployment is the percentage of the total labor force that is unemployed.

Depression A disease of the national economy, characterized by a high rate of unemployment existing over a long period of time.

Recession A disease similar to depression, but not so severe. We say that a recession has occurred if total output declines for two or more consecutive quarters.

Inflation A rise in the average level of prices.

Deflation A fall in the average level of prices.

Hyperinflation Another disease of the national economy, in which the rate of inflation accelerates so rapidly that the country's monetary system breaks down. Hyperinflations are usually associated with wars.

Technical efficiency The use of efficient methods to produce a particular good. Technical efficiency does *not* exist if the same quantity of output could be produced using less of any given input.

Allocative efficiency The allocation of scarce resources among different uses so as to avoid waste. Notice that an economy can be technically efficient without having allocative efficiency; this may happen because the wrong combination of outputs is being produced or because some goods are being produced with inputs that would have been better allocated to producing other goods.

Equitable distribution of income A fair and not too unequal sharing of the total national income among the different individuals in society. Most people believe that equity requires a reduction of inequality but not complete equality.

Economic growth An increase in total national output resulting from technological improvement and additional factories, machines, and other equipment. The *rate* of economic growth is usually measured as an annual percentage increase in total output.

Complementary economic goals Two economic goals are complementary if the pursuit of one promotes the attainment of the other. For example, anything that reduces the level of unemployment will usually reduce poverty also.

Conflicting economic goals Two economic goals are conflicting if the pursuit of one makes it more difficult to attain the other. For example, attempts to reduce the rate of unemployment often make inflation increase.

True-False Questions

(T) F **1.** Output per person in the United States was higher in 1975 than it was in 1900.

T (F) **2.** Output per person in the United States rose every year from 1900 until 1975.

(T) F **3.** The length of the average work week in manufacturing in the United States was lower in 1975 than in 1900.

T (F) **4.** The length of the average work week in manufacturing in the United States has been falling more rapidly since 1940 than it did from 1900 until 1940.

T (F) **5.** *The General Theory* of John Maynard Keynes is famous for its advocacy of laissez faire.

(T) F **6.** Karl Marx was an economist.

(T) F **7.** In the United States during the period from 1931 to 1940, the rate of unemployment was never less than 14 percent.

T (F) **8.** When the level of prices rises during an inflation, everyone suffers from that rise.

T (F) **9.** Hyperinflation has never occurred in North American history.

(T) F **10.** Homeowners with large mortgages tend to benefit from inflation.

(T) F **11.** Technical efficiency can exist even without allocative efficiency.

T (F) **12.** In order to escape poverty, you need a higher income if you are living in the country than if you are living in the city.

(T) F **13.** From 1950 until 1969 in the United States, the fraction of national income going to the poorest 20 percent of families rose.

(T) F **14.** Economic growth and an equitable distribution of income are generally regarded as complementary economic goals.

Multiple-Choice Questions

1. If total output per person in the United States in 1975 was 100, then in 1900 it was closest to
(a) 10
(b) 30
(c) 75
(d) 100
(e) 125

2. Keynes' *General Theory* argued for a larger role for the government in order to promote the goal of
(a) A high level of employment
(b) Price stability
(c) Efficiency
(d) An equitable distribution of income
(e) Economic growth

3. In 1933 in the United States, the rate of employment was
(a) 5 percent
(b) 10 percent
(c) 25 percent
(d) 40 percent

4. The housewife who works full time at home is counted as
(a) Unemployed
(b) Employed
(c) Part of the labor force
(d) **(b)** and **(c)**
(e) None of the above

5. Inflation can
(a) Hurt people on fixed incomes
(b) Lead to wasteful speculation
(c) Cause business mistakes
(d) All of the above
(e) None of the above

6. Suppose that every factory worker in the economy was in the job best suited for him or her, that they were working as productively as possible, but that they were all employed producing Edsels, which no one wanted to buy. This would be a situation of
(a) Technical efficiency and allocative efficiency
(b) Technical efficiency and allocative inefficiency
(c) Technical inefficiency and allocative efficiency
(d) Technical inefficiency and allocative inefficiency

7. Suppose that the average income of the poorest 20 percent of families were to rise from $4,000 per annum to $5,000, while the average income of the other 80 percent rose from $16,000 to $24,000. Then, if the cost of living didn't change, we would probably say that
(a) The incidence of poverty rose and the degree of inequality rose.
(b) The incidence of poverty rose and the degree of inequality fell.
(c) The incidence of poverty fell and the degree of inequality rose.
(d) The incidence of poverty fell and the degree of inequality fell.

8. The phrase "a rising tide lifts all boats" refers to the complementarity between the economic goals of
(a) High employment and price stability
(b) Efficiency and high employment
(c) Growth and price stability
(d) Growth and equity

9. Economic growth generally tends to
(a) Help reduce poverty
(b) Increase the amount of pollution
(c) Increase the rate of depletion of natural resources
(d) All of the above
(e) **(a)** and **(b)**

Essay Questions

1. In the textbook it was said that economics is a policy study. This is not true of other sciences, like botany. Why not? Would you call the other social sciences, such as psychology, sociology, or political science, policy studies in the same degree as economics?

2. Inflation is sometimes defined informally in the newspapers as "too much money chasing too few goods." What do you suppose would happen to the average level of prices if the quantity of money were to increase drastically? Why? What would happen to the average level of prices if there were the same quantity of money but a drastic decline in the output of goods? Why? With this in mind, do you think that the two goals of economic growth and price stability should be regarded as complementary or conflicting?

3. During wartime, governments are usually hard pressed to pay the cost of their military expenditures. They often resort to printing new money in order to pay the bills. What do you suppose this has to do with the fact that most hyperinflations are associated with wars?

4. If you decide to save more, what must you sacrifice in order to do so? What would you hope to gain from this sacrifice? If the total amount of saving in the whole economy increases, what must be sacrificed? What does the economy as a whole gain? During the 30 years following World War II, Japan had the highest rate of economic growth of all developed countries as well as one of the highest rates of saving. Do you think that these two facts about the Japanese economy are related? What is the connection?

5. Why do you suppose that the rate of unemployment fell so much during World War II?

***6.** While economics and physics are both sciences, there are some fundamental differences between them. One can learn from controlled experiments in physics, but this is not practical in economics. Can you think of any natural sciences in which experimentation is impossible? Are there any social sciences in which controlled experiments are performed? (For example, sociology, politics, anthropology, psychology?) Economics also deals with the human factor, which is absent from physics. Do you think that this requires a fundamentally different approach than the one used in physics? Many have also argued that physics deals with an unchanging physical world, whereas economic life proceeds in an environment of ever-changing institutions and political organizations. What do you think of the prospects of discovering general laws and theorems in economics when everything appears to be changing so drastically? Is there a sense in which the physical world surrounding you is also changing?

Answers

True-False Questions: **1 T 2 F 3 T 4 F 5 F 6 T 7 T 8 F 9 F 10 T 11 T 12 F 13 T 14 T**
Multiple-Choice Questions: **1 b 2 a 3 c 4 e 5 d 6 b 7 c 8 d 9 d**

chapter 2
Scarcity: The Economizing Problem

Learning Objectives

After you have studied this chapter in the textbook and the study guide, you should be able to

Explain why scarcity requires us to make choices
State the problem of scarcity in terms of opportunity costs
Explain why the PPC slopes downward to the right
Explain why the PPC is bowed out from the origin
Explain why the choice between consumption goods and capital goods is fundamental for the process of economic growth
Explain why economic theory deliberately distorts reality with simplifying assumptions

CHAPTER HIGHLIGHTS

Scarcity is one of the most fundamental concepts of economics. The purpose of this chapter is to introduce you to this concept. The basic problem of scarcity is that *material wants are unlimited, but this is not true of the resources available to satisfy these wants.* Hence we cannot have everything we want, and we need to economize on our resources. Some people actually define economics as the study of scarcity.

Scarcity requires us to make choices. Since we cannot satisfy all our wants, we must choose among the limited options available to us. The most important proposition concerning choice is as follows: Whenever we choose one thing, we have to sacrifice some other thing. To use the example given in the text, when we choose more food, we give up some clothing.

Another fundamental concept is that of opportunity cost. The opportunity cost of producing any good is the amount of some other good (or goods) that must consequently be given up. In the example in the text, the opportunity cost of more food is measured by the amount of clothing that must be given up. Another way of expressing the problem of scarcity is to say that every choice has an opportunity cost.

These ideas are neatly summarized by the production possibilities curve (the PPC). The PPC represents the range of options from which it is possible to choose. In the example in the text, the PPC depicts the various combinations of food and clothing that are possible, ranging from the extreme combination of no food and the maximum amount of clothing to the opposite extreme of no clothing and the maximum amount of food. If there were no problem of scarcity, then we could choose any combination of food and clothing we wanted. However, with scarcity, we cannot choose a combination outside the boundary formed by the PPC (although we may, through sheer waste or unemployment of resources, end up inside that frontier).

There are two important aspects of the PPC to remember. The first is that it slopes downward to the right. This is a direct consequence of the existence of opportunity costs. If a choice is made to increase the amount of clothing produced (that is, to move to the right in the diagram), then there must be a decrease in the amount of food produced (that is, a move downward in the diagram). Indeed, the slope of the PPC is a precise measure of the opportunity cost of more clothing, because it indicates the size of the downward movement required for each movement to the right.

The second feature is that it is "bowed out" from the origin. This illustrates the important principle of *increasing* opportunity cost. The greater the production of clothing (the further to the right along the PPC), the greater is the opportunity cost of each additional unit of clothing (the greater is the slope of the PPC). As the text explains, this principle of increasing opportunity cost reflects the specialization of resources.

There are many different kinds of choice. This chapter discusses one of the most important ones, the choice between consumer goods and capital goods. This choice is fundamental to the problem of economic growth. Growth can result from various underlying causes, including technological change and population growth. Perhaps the most important cause is the accumulation of capital goods. If we choose to produce more capital goods this year, the economy will grow faster, because next year those extra capital goods will be available to produce more output.

Consider the PPC with consumption goods on one axis and capital goods on the other (as in Figure 2-4 in the textbook). As growth occurs, this curve shifts out from the origin because our capacity to produce increases. The choice between consumption and capital goods is really a choice between consumption now and consumption in the future. If society devotes most of its resources to the production of consumption goods, then its stock of capital goods cannot increase rapidly and its potential for consumption in the future will not expand greatly. If a significant fraction of its resources go into producing more capital goods, its possibilities for consumption will be much greater in the future. But the only way to do this is to devote fewer resources toward the current production of consumption goods. In other words, the rate at which the PPC expands outward in the *future* is determined by the point chosen on the *present* PPC.

The final major point made by this chapter concerns the nature of economic theory. It is that if theory is to be helpful, it must make simplifying assumptions that strip away the inessential complications of a problem and allow one to see the important relationships. Like a road map that shows only the important features of a landscape, theory should not be dismissed because it fails to account for everything. But—because of these simplifications—theory must be used with caution. Just as a weather map is useless for planning an auto trip, the theory that helps to explain one aspect of economic life may be quite useless for explaining other aspects.

IMPORTANT TERMS

Economic resources Anything that can be used to produce goods or services. These are also referred to sometimes as factors of production. They are generally classified as land, labor, or capital.

Land The resources given by nature. This generally includes more than the common notion of land, also taking in such resources as minerals and the environment.

Labor The services of human effort.

Capital Any economic resource that has been produced. This is to be distinguished from the popular definition of capital, which includes financial assets that are not factors of production. We should also note that some economists speak of "human capital," which consists of the talents, skills, and knowledge built up through pratice, education, or other training. However, we shall generally refer to capital as consisting simply of physical capital, such as machines, buildings, and materials.

Investment The accumulation of capital over time. Once again, investing in the stock market isn't included in this definition, since it does not involve the accumulation of what we are defining as capital.

Production possibilities curve (PPC) The graphical representation of the possible combinations of different goods that can be produced.

Opportunity cost The opportunity cost of a choice is the sacrifice that has to be made because, in order to make that choice, something else is *not* chosen. The opportunity cost of producing one good can be represented as the slope of the production possibilities curve drawn between it and another good.

Economic growth The outward movement of the production possibilities curve. Growth can result from (*a*) technological change, (*b*) increase in the labor force, or (*c*) the accumulation of capital.

Positive economics The study of "what is" in economic life, as opposed to normative economics, which is the study of "what ought to be."

True-False Questions

T F **1.** The problem of scarcity is one that applies only to less developed countries.

T F **2.** Any factor of production is an economic resource.

T F **3.** Consumption goods are usually factors of production.

T F **4.** If, for some reason, wants were not unlimited, the production possibilities curve would not have a downward slope.

T F **5.** The production possibilities curve is bowed out from the origin because of increasing opportunity costs.

T F **6.** Just as it is possible to select a combination of goods inside the PPC, so it is possible to choose a combination that lies outside the PPC.

T F **7.** A movement from a point lying *inside* the PPC toward a point *on* the PPC is an example of economic growth.

T F **8.** Since economic growth shifts the PPC out from the origin, it allows us to produce more of all goods in a given year than in the previous year.

T F **9.** Economic theory is intended to provide an exact description of a real-world economic system.

T F **10.** The statement that the current rate of inflation is higher than it should be is a statement of normative economics.

T F **11.** The statement that the current rate of inflation could be reduced by restricting the rate of growth of the economy's money supply is a statement of normative economics.

Multiple-Choice Questions

1. The problem of scarcity arises because
- **(a)** Wants are limited and resources are unlimited.
- **(b)** Wants are limited and resources are limited.
- **(c)** Wants are unlimited and resources are unlimited.
- **(d)** Wants are unlimited and resources are limited.

2. As economic growth occurs
- **(a)** A point will eventually be reached when all wants are satisfied.
- **(b)** Some wants begin to be satisfied, while others seem to become more urgent.
- **(c)** The PPC shifts outward over time.
- **(d)** **(a)** and **(b)**.
- **(e)** **(b)** and **(c)**.

3. An ice cream cone would be classified as
- **(a)** Land
- **(b)** Labor
- **(c)** A capital good
- **(d)** A consumption good

4. A government post office building would be classified as
- **(a)** Land
- **(b)** Labor
- **(c)** A capital good
- **(d)** A consumption good

5. A PPC between food and clothing shows
- **(a)** How much food we ought to sacrifice in order to acquire clothing
- **(b)** How much food and clothing will actually be produced in the economy
- **(c)** How much potential food production would have to be sacrificed in order to produce any given amount of clothing
- **(d)** How much of both food and clothing would have to be sacrificed in order to produce more capital goods

6. A combination of goods lying outside the PPC
- **(a)** Can always be produced
- **(b)** May eventually be produced if the labor force grows rapidly enough
- **(c)** May eventually be produced even if no economic growth occurs
- **(d)** Can presently be produced if there is some unemployment of resources
- **(e)** All of the above

7. Suppose that you were to give up the prospect of a summer job that paid $1,500 in order to take a vacation in Europe and that the cost of transportation and all other expenses of the trip amounted to $1,100. Then the opportunity cost, measured in dollars, of your vacation would be
- **(a)** $400
- **(b)** $1,100
- **(c)** $1,500
- **(d)** $2,600

8. In Figure 2-1, suppose that the PPC has shifted from the one labeled 1 to the one labeled 2. Then
- **(a)** The opportunity cost of food but not that of clothing has increased.
- **(b)** The opportunity cost of clothing but not that of food has increased.
- **(c)** The opportunity cost of both food and clothing has increased.

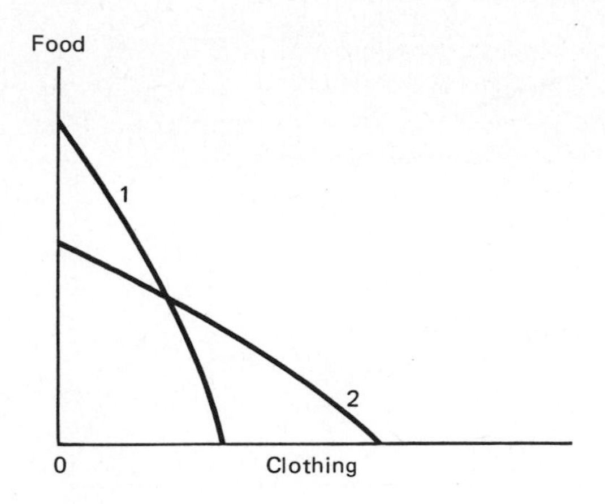

FIGURE 2-1

(d) The opportunity cost of both food and clothing has decreased.

9. Technological improvements that allow us to produce more efficiently
   - **(a)** Cannot shift the PPC outward unless the labor force grows
   - **(b)** Cannot occur in a less developed country until the "takeoff point" has been attained
   - **(c)** Can shift the PPC outward even if there is no investment occurring
   - **(d)** None of the above

10. In Figure 2-2 suppose that the PPC shifts from the one labeled 1 to the one labeled 2 because of a technological

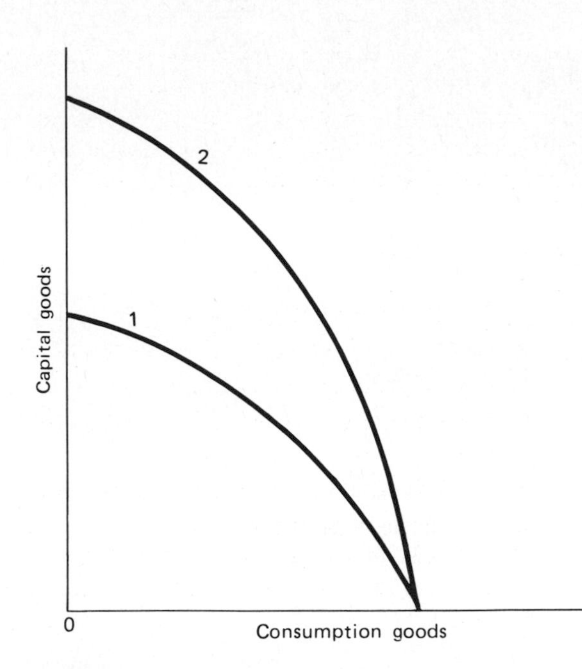

FIGURE 2-2

improvement. This technological improvement
   - **(a)** Allows the economy to produce capital goods at less cost
   - **(b)** Allows the economy to produce consumption goods at less cost
   - **(c)** Reduces the level of unemployment
   - **(d)** Increases the total production of capital goods

Exercises

1. Consider a hypothetical economy with a labor force of 10,000 workers, each of whom can be put to work either building houses or building roads. Each worker provides 2,000 hours of labor services during each year. Thus the economy has available a total of 20 million labor-hours during each year to produce houses and roads. Table 2-1 shows how many labor-hours it takes to build various quantities of houses. For example, in order to build 18 thousand houses, 15 million labor-hours are needed. Likewise, Table 2-2 indicates how many labor-hours it takes to build various quantities of roadway. In Figure 2-3, only one point, A, on the PPC has been plotted out. It shows that one possible combination of houses and roadway is 1,000 miles of roadway and no houses, which is what could be produced if all 20 million of the available labor-hours were used to build roads. Using the data in Tables 2-1 and 2-2, plot four other points on the PPC. Join these points with a smooth curve.

2. Figure 2-4 represents the PPC between wheat and corn. At point *A*, the output of corn equals ______ million bushels and the output of wheat equals ______ million bushels. At point *B*, the output of corn equals ______ million bushels and the output of wheat equals ______ million bushels. In going from *A* to *B*, the opportunity cost of the extra 4 million bushels of wheat is ______ million bushels of corn. At point *C*, the output of corn equals ______ million bushels and the output of wheat equals ______ million. The opportunity cost of the extra 4 million bushels of wheat produced by going from *B* to *C* equals ______ million

Table 2-1

Millions of labor-hours	Thousands of houses
20	20
15	18
10	14
5	8
0	0

Table 2-2

Millions of labor-hours	Hundreds of miles of roadway
20	10
15	9
10	7
5	4
0	0

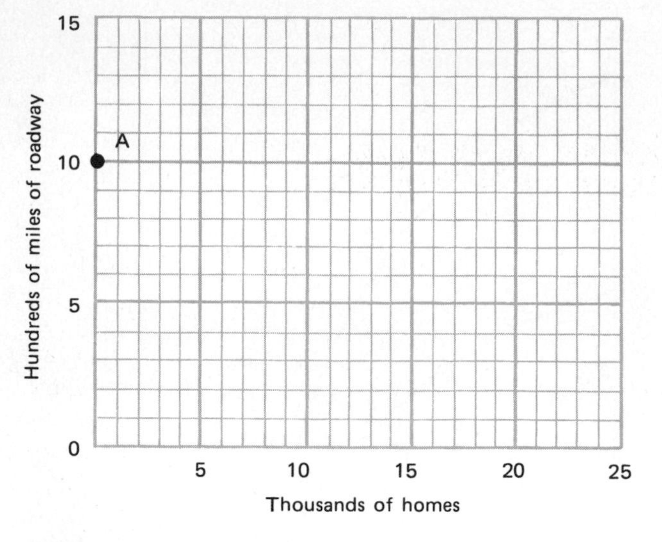

FIGURE 2-3

bushels of corn. When this opportunity cost is compared with the one in going from *A* to *B*, what general principle is illustrated?

Essay Questions

1. Some people have argued that the patent system fosters technological change. Their argument is that the system encourages people to devote their efforts to discovering better ways of doing things by guaranteeing to inventors and innovators that the fruits of their labor cannot legally be stolen. On the other hand, some have argued that the patent system inhibits technological change because it gives a monopoly power to those who develop new techniques, preventing others from being able to copy them. What do you think about this issue?

2. The Reverend T. R. Malthus, writing almost 200 years ago, argued that economic growth was fruitless because population tends to grow faster than the food supply, so that the amount of food per person is inevitably doomed to fall to a minimum subsistence level. What role has technological change played in preventing this Malthusian fate from occurring? Part of Malthus's argument was that if our food supply began rising faster, this would simply accelerate the growth

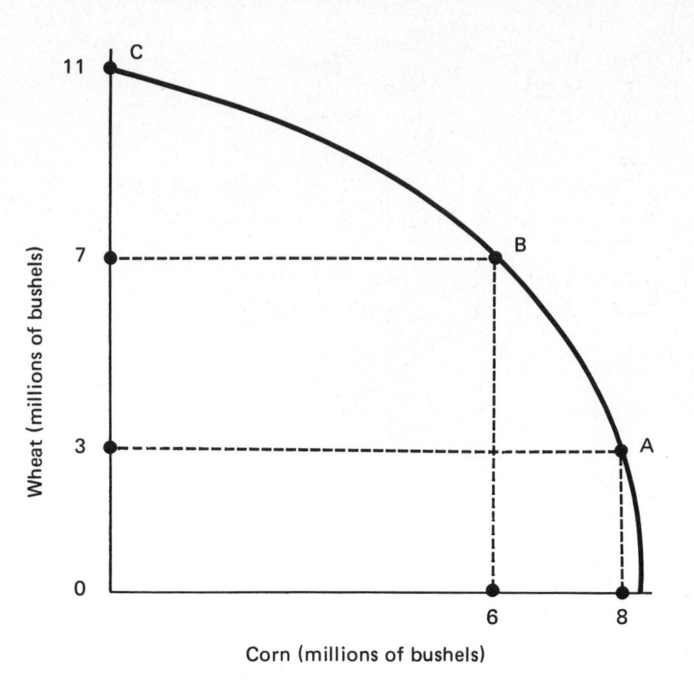

FIGURE 2-4

of population, since fewer people would starve. What do you think of the realism of this argument in light of the fact that, during the present century, the population growth rates of rich, developed nations have been much lower than those of poor, underdeveloped nations?

3. Prof. John Kenneth Galbraith has argued that our economy produces too many private goods (cars, cosmetics, color television sets, etc.) and not enough public goods (parks, clean air, government-supported symphony orchestras, etc.). Is this contention an example of positive or normative economics or are there elements of both? Explain your answer. Draw a PPC between public and private goods and show (*a*) where our economy is currently producing and (*b*) where Professor Galbraith would like the economy to be producing. Professor Milton Friedman has argued that we produce too few private goods. Show where on the PPC Professor Friedman would prefer us to be producing. Show in terms of this PPC how economic growth can help to reduce the conflict between those who agree with Galbraith and those who agree with Friedman.

Answers

True-False Questions: **1 F 2 T 3 F 4 F 5 T 6 F 7 F 8 T 9 F 10 T 11 F**
Multiple-Choice Questions: **1 d 2 e 3 d 4 c 5 c 6 b 7 d 8 a 9 c 10 a**
Exercises: **1.** The four other points are the four columns in this table:

Hundreds of miles	9	7	4	0
Thousands of hours	8	14	18	20

2. 8, 3, 6, 7, 2, 0, 11, 6, increasing opportunity cost.

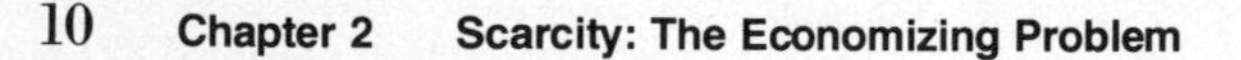

chapter 3
Specialization, Exchange, and Money

Learning Objectives

After you have studied this chapter in the textbook and the study guide, you should be able to:

Explain why specialization requires exchange
Describe two kinds of disorder that can interfere with a monetary system
List five properties that the ideal money commodity should possess
Give two reasons why specialization promotes efficiency
Explain the distinction between absolute advantage and comparative advantage

CHAPTER HIGHLIGHTS

In the last chapter, we mentioned that some people have defined economics to be the study of scarcity and choice. These problems of scarcity and choice arise even in an individual's private life. Yet, as we noted in the very first chapter, economics is a social science—one that deals with problems of interactions among different individuals. How is it that the study of scarcity, which appears to be a private affair, leads to the study of social interactions? The answer has to do with specialization. As society has progressed over the generations, people have tended to become more specialized and less self-sufficient. Rather than producing things for which we have a direct need, we each produce something quite special; we acquire the various goods and services that we need from those who, in turn, specialize in producing those items. Thus, specialization is the basis for *exchange*, the basic form of economic interaction. Economic progress has required us to become increasingly specialized, which has in turn required us to rely more and more upon the process of exchange. This is why we live in such a highly interdependent economy, in which each of us depends so much for our material well-being upon the labors of others and each of us specializes in an increasingly narrow range of activities.

Although different societies have organized their exchange activities in a variety of ways, almost all economies have relied upon the use of money. We sell our specialized output for money, with which we purchase our various items of consumption. It is easy to imagine the sorts of difficulties that would arise without the use of money—that is, if we had to rely upon primitive barter for our exchange activities. Thus money helps to make possible the efficient specialization of economic activities. The item used as money should ideally be valuable (in relation to bulk), divisible, durable, easily recognizable, and portable. All these properties were more or less satisfied by the cigarettes that were used as money in the prisoner-of-war camp described in the text.

Money is like oil that lubricates the social engine of production. As this analogy suggests, for many purposes the essential workings of the economic system can be studied without reference to money, just as the essential workings of a machine can be studied without considering lubriciation. For example, the essential role played by farmers in society is to provide food, in exchange for which they acquire other commodities from the rest of us; this role can be studied without worrying about how these exchanges take place. However, monetary problems become extremely important when something goes wrong with the monetary system. The example of the prisoner-of-war camp illustrated two common malfunctions. The first is the *debasing* of the currency. This occurs when someone reduces the currency's value by such maneuvers as clipping coins or thinning out cigarettes. This reduction in the currency's value means a rise in the price of goods in terms of money—that is, inflation. The other serious malfunction is a large fluctuation in the supply of money, such as occurred when the supply of Red Cross cigarettes was temporarily halted for several weeks or when the supply arrived in unexpectedly large batches. Such events produce large fluctuations in the value of money.

There are two reasons why specialization helps us to produce efficiently. The first is *comparative advantage*, and the second is *economies of scale*.

The notion of comparative advantage was illustrated in the text by the example of the gardener and the doctor. The doctor had an absolute advantage in both doctoring and gardening. In other words, she was both a better gardener and a better doctor than the gardener. By the same token, we say that the gardener had an absolute disadvantage at both gardening and doctoring. However, the gardener had a *comparative* advantage in gardening, and likewise the doctor in the practice of medicine. By this we mean that while the doctor was superior to the gardener in both the activities of gardening and doctoring, the doctor's superiority was greater in doctoring than in gardening. As the example in Box 3-3 demonstrates, it was efficient for the doctor to specialize in that activity for which she had the greatest superiority, that is, in which she had a comparative advantage. Likewise, while the gardener was inferior in both activities, it paid him to specialize in the activity in which his inferiority was the smallest, that is, the one in which he had a comparative advantage. To repeat, each agent has a comparative advantage in the activity in which that agent's superiority is the greatest or in which that agent's inferiority is the least.

If there are economies of scale, then the cost per unit of producing an item falls as production is increased, at least up to a point. For example, the cost per car of producing 10 cars during the year would be astronomical because of the heavy outlay for plant and equipment that would be involved for such a small output. However, if annual production were increased to 1 million cars, the cost per car would be significantly reduced. This clearly offers a basis for specialization, because if people had to produce their own cars, few of us would be able to afford one. But with the large auto manufacturers doing the production, the economies of scale allow most families to afford at least one car.

Thus, even if no one had a comparative advantage in anything, specialization would still occur because of these economies of scale.

IMPORTANT TERMS

Specialization Specialization occurs when each of us concentrates on performing a specific task, rather than choosing to be self-sufficient. It is sometimes referred to as the division of labor.

Exchange The process of trading what you have for what you would rather have. This is the basic form of social interaction studied by economists and is made necessary by specialization.

Barter A primitive method of exchange whereby different goods or services are exchanged directly for one another without the use of money.

Money Money performs three functions: it serves as (1) a medium of exchange (that is, the item which enters into most exchanges so as to avoid barter), (2) standard of value (that is, a unit in which we keep accounts, quote prices, and sign contracts), and (3) a store of value.

Gresham's law This is commonly expressed as the proposition that "bad money drives out good." In other words, if two different kinds of money are equally valuable as money, then the one which is the more valuable in other uses will tend to disappear from circulation as money.

Absolute advantage A has an absolute advantage over B in some activity if A performs the activity more productively than B.

Comparative advantage A has a comparative advantage over B in some activity I as compared to another activity J (1) if A has an absolute advantage over B in I and B has an absolute advantage over A in

J, (2) if A's absolute advantage over B is greater in I than in J, or (3) if B's absolute advantage over A is less in I than in J. Be sure to remember this, because comparative advantage is one of the most important concepts in economics.

Economies of scale These are said to exist if any increase in the scale of an activity can be accomplished with a reduction in the quantity of each input per unit of output.

True-False Questions

T F **1.** In order for specialization to work, we need to have a "coincidence of wants."

T F **2.** Economies tend to become more specialized over time because the more we specialize, the more we are able to exchange.

T F **3.** The widespread practice of the debasing of the currency is a result of Gresham's law.

T F **4.** Barter is inconvenient partly because many commodities cannot readily be divided into smaller parts.

T F **5.** One advantage of a money economy is that it makes possible multilateral transactions.

T F **6.** A commodity can be used as money without any government intervention to certify that commodity and regulate its supply.

T F **7.** Money is the only commodity that can be used as a store of value.

T F **8.** Specialization is efficient if everyone undertakes all those activities in which he or she has an absolute advantage.

T F **9.** Economies of scale provide a basis for specialization even when no one has a comparative advantage in producing anything.

T F **10.** The principle which makes Adam Smith's pin factory work so much more efficiently than if each person produced pins individually is the principle of comparative advantage.

T F **11.** Canada's Free Trade Agreement with the United States in automobiles allows Canada to take advantage of economies of scale in producing cars.

Multiple-Choice Questions

1. Cigarettes were used in the prisoner-of-war camp as money because
- **(a)** They were valuable in relation to bulk.
- **(b)** They were easily divided into small units.
- **(c)** They were durable.
- **(d)** **(a)** and **(b)**.
- **(e)** All of the above.

2. Not too long ago it was discovered that the price of silver had risen by so much that there was more than 10 cents' worth of silver in every dime. According to Gresham's law, you would expect that
- **(a)** Nickels and quarters would come to be withdrawn from circulation.
- **(b)** Dimes would come to be withdrawn from circulation.
- **(c)** People would start using silver itself instead of dimes.
- **(d)** People would begin melting down nickels and quarters in order to sell the metal itself.

3. Suppose that, in Canada, a person could produce one shirt in 1 hour of work while another could produce a chair in the same length of time. In the United States, on the other hand, it would take a person 1½ hours to produce a shirt and another person 2 hours to produce a chair. Then the United States has
- **(a)** An absolute advantage in producing shirts
- **(b)** An absolute advantage in producing chairs
- **(c)** A comparative advantage in producing shirts
- **(d)** A comparative advantage in producing chairs

4. Economies of scale
- **(a)** Are required in order for any comparative advantage to exist
- **(b)** Are simply a consequence of the principle of increasing opportunity cost
- **(c)** Are made easier to exploit by the widespread use of monetary exchange
- **(d)** Appear to be getting less important as technological progress is made toward alleviating the problem of scarcity

5. Suppose that the PPCs of countries A and B were as they are drawn in Figure 3-1. Then we could say that
- **(a)** Country A has a comparative advantage in producing food.
- **(b)** Country B has a comparative disadvantage in producing clothing.
- **(c)** Country A has an absolute advantage in producing clothing.
- **(d)** Nothing can be said on the basis of this diagram about comparative or absolute advantage.

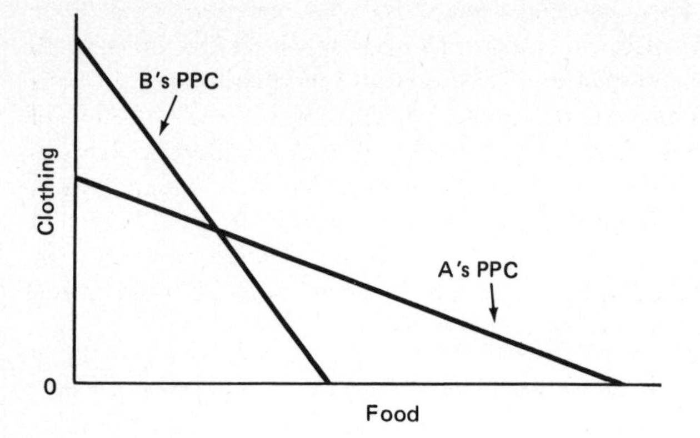

FIGURE 3-1

Exercises

1. Table 3-1 shows how many cars can be produced in a country with various amounts of inputs. (A unit of input is defined as a particular quantity of workers and capital.) Likewise, Table 3-2 gives the production possibilities for television sets. Suppose that the economy has 5 units of input in total with which to produce cars and television sets. Then in Figure 3-2, plot out the PPC for the country. How is the shape of this PPC different from that of the PPCs constructed in the previous chapter? ______________

____

In this example, are there economies of scale in the production of cars? ______ In the production of televisions sets? ______ Does the opportunity cost of producing cars increase or decrease as the quantity is increased? ____________ Does the opportunity cost of

FIGURE 3-2

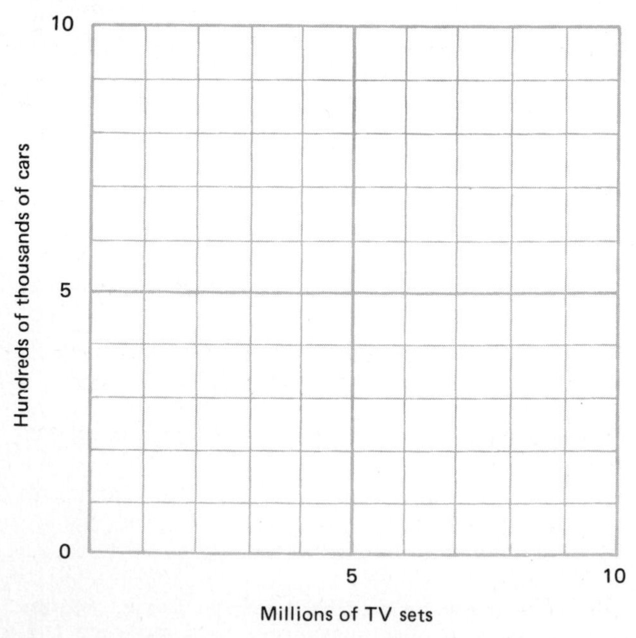

Table 3-1

PRODUCTION POSSIBILITIES FOR CARS	
Number of cars	Units of input
100,000	1
200,000	2
400,000	3
700,000	4
1,000,000	5

Table 3-2

PRODUCTION POSSIBILITIES FOR TELEVISION SETS	
Number of sets	Units of input
2,000,000	1
4,000,000	2
6,000,000	3
8,000,000	4
10,000,000	5

producing television sets increase or decrease as the quantity is increased? ____________

2a. Suppose that for county *A* each acre of land will produce 100 bushels of wheat or 30 bushels of corn, whereas for county *B* each acre of land will produce 40 bushels of wheat or 20 bushels of corn. Suppose that each county has 4,000 acres. Fill in Table 3-3, giving the production possibilities for *A* and *B*.

Table 3-3

A's production possibilities*		*B*'s production possibilities*	
Wheat	Corn	Wheat	Corn
0	______	0	______
100	______	40	______
200	______	80	______
300	______	120	______
400	______	160	______

*In thousands of bushels.

2b. Plot the PPCs for the two counties in Figure 3-3.

FIGURE 3-3

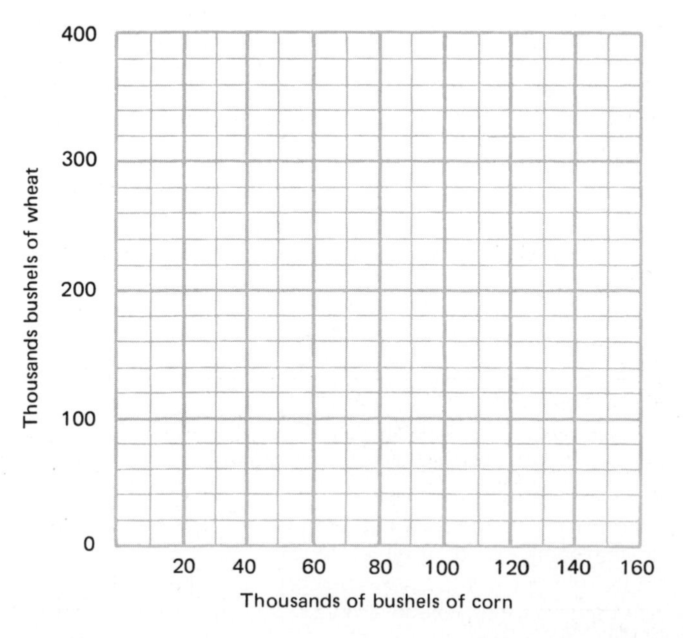

2c. County ______ has an absolute advantage in producing corn; county ______ has an absolute advantage in producing wheat; county ______ has a comparative advantage in producing corn; and county ______ has a comparative advantage in producing wheat.

Suppose that county *A* devoted all its land to producing corn and *B* devoted all its land to producing wheat. Then *A* would produce ______ thousand bushels of corn and *B* would produce ______ thousand bushels of wheat. Suppose, furthermore, that they were then to trade with each other at the price of 10 bushels of wheat for every 4 bushels of corn. Then if residents of *B* wanted to consume 120,000 bushels of wheat, they could sell 40,000 bushels of wheat (this is the excess of 160,000 production over 120,000 consumption). They could sell this for 16,000 bushels of corn (remember, every 10 bushels of wheat trades for 4 bushels of corn), which they could also consume. This is shown in Table 3-4.

Table 3-4

B's CONSUMPTION POSSIBILITIES*

Consumption of wheat	Production of wheat	Sales of wheat	Purchase of corn	Consumption of corn
160	160	______	______	______
120	160	40	16	16
80	160	______	______	______
40	160	______	______	______
0	160	______	______	______

*In thousands of bushels.

Under these assumptions, we have just seen that county *B* could possibly consume the combination of 120,000 bushels of wheat and 16,000 bushels of corn. This is illustrated as point *X* in Figure 3-4.

2d. Fill in the rest of Table 3-4. Plot the resulting consumption possibilities in Figure 3-4 and join them with a smooth curve labeled B_1.

2e. Under the same assumptions about specialization and prices, fill in *A*'s consumption possibilities in Table 3-5 and plot them in Figure 3-4, joining them with a smooth curve labeled A_1.

2f. Now, suppose that *A* were to devote all its land to the production of wheat and *B* to devote all its land to the production of corn. Then ______ bushels of wheat and ______ bushels of corn would be produced. Once again, suppose that the counties trade corn for wheat at the price of 4 bushels of corn for 10 bushels of wheat.

2g. Fill in the consumption possibilities of each county in Tables 3-6 and 3-7 and plot them in Figure 3-4, labeling the resulting curves A_2 and B_2 respectively.

FIGURE 3-4

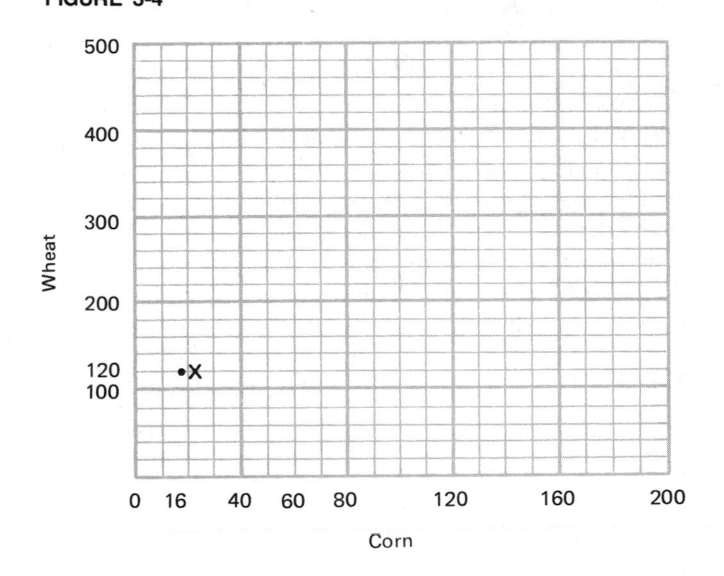

Table 3-5

A's CONSUMPTION POSSIBILITIES*

Consumption of corn	Production of corn	Sales of corn	Purchase of wheat	Consumption of wheat
120	120	______	______	______
80	120	40	100	100
40	120	______	______	______
0	120	______	______	______

*In thousands of bushels.

Table 3-6

A's CONSUMPTION POSSIBILITIES*

Consumption of wheat	Sale of wheat	Consumption of corn
400	____	____
200	____	____
0	____	____

*In thousands of bushels.

Table 3-7

B's CONSUMPTION POSSIBILITIES*

Consumption of corn	Sale of corn	Consumption of wheat
80	____	____
40	____	____
0	____	____

*In thousands of bushels.

2h. Why does A_2 lie to the northeast of A_1 and B_2 to the northeast of B_1? ____________________

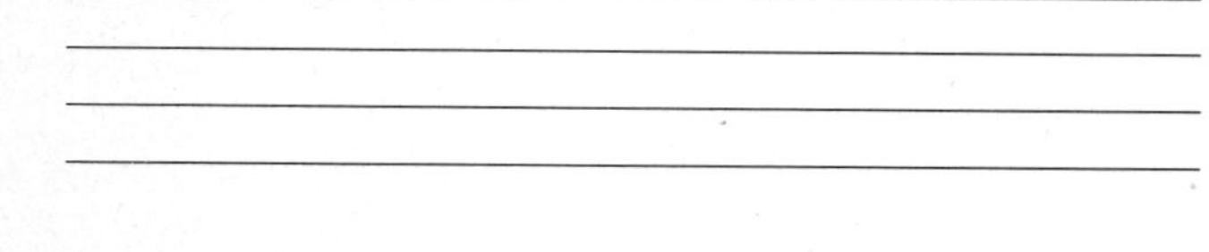

Essay Questions

1. Why do you think that gold, silver, and other precious metals have commonly been used as the medium of exchange throughout history?

2. Although most transactions involve money, there are still barter transactions. For example, some people will take in nonpaying boarders into their homes on the understanding that these boarders will do odd jobs around the house and take care of the garden. A less obvious but still valid example is the case of the business executive who is paid partly in the form of a salary but also partly in the form of stock options, a luxurious office, and other executive "perks." Why do you suppose that people still engage in barter when they could just as well use the system of monetary exchange? What sorts of transactions would you expect to be undertaken, nowadays, by barter rather than with money?

3. The example in Box 3-1 in the text pointed out one of the dangers of specialization—the feeling of alienation fostered by large organizations. What other dangers of specialization can you think of?

4. The textbook shows that comparative advantage is one explanation of specialization, but it does not explain why some countries, regions, or people might have a comparative advantage. How would you explain, for example, the apparent comparative advantage in corn production of the Midwestern states over the New England states? Why does Pennsylvania have a comparative advantage in steel output by comparison with most of the other 49 states? Why do Taiwan and Hong Kong have a comparative advantage over other countries in the manufacture of textiles and light electronics components?

5. On the basis of our discussion of specialization, why do you suppose that economists are usually in favor of reducing tariffs and other barriers to international trade?

***6.** We often talk about money as if it were a single uniform commodity, whereas in reality it consists of several different things, such as dimes, nickels, dollar bills, 50-dollar bills, and so forth. The list of things that can be used in exchange goes beyond this, of course; for example, your balance in a checking account can be used, as when you acquire goods by writing a check. Likewise, if you have a credit card or a bank charge card, that too can be used to purchase goods. If you were to try to count the amount of money in the United States economy, what items would you include in your definition of money, and how would you count them up?

***7.** Suppose that money as we know it were to be replaced by computer accounts, so that, every time you were paid, your employer would simply register a positive balance for you in your computer account. Also, every time you purchased something in a store, the cashier in the store would simply deduct the price of the item from your computer account by means of a remote terminal. Would you still expect to see the same problems in this kind of monetary system as in the system of the prisoner-of-war camps that used cigarette money?

***8.** Suppose that there are three people, *A*, *B*, and *C*, and three commodities, 1, 2, and 3. Suppose that *A* wants to sell one unit of 1 and buy one unit of 2, *B* wants to sell one unit of 2 and buy one unit of 3, and *C* wants to sell one unit of 3 and buy one unit of 1.

First, explain why it is impossible for *A*, *B*, and *C* to carry out their desired trade through the use of direct barter, in which every agent is only willing to trade what he has for what he ultimately wants. Show how the problems of direct barter could be overcome if indirect barter were used; that is, if each agent were willing to sell what he has in exchange for either of the two other commodities whether or not he wanted it.

What sorts of practical problems do you suppose would arise if the United States economy were to be conducted on the basis of indirect barter? Finally, suppose that a fourth commodity, money, were introduced. How would this help to eliminate some of the difficulties of barter?

Answers

True-False Questions: **1** F **2** F **3** F **4** T **5** T **6** T **7** F **8** F **9** T **10** F **11** T
Multiple-Choice Questions: **1** e **2** b **3** c **4** c **5** a
Exercises:
1. The PPC is bowed in to the origin instead of bowed out. Yes, no, decrease, decrease.

2a. Table 3-3

A		B	
Wheat	Corn	Wheat	Corn
0	120	0	80
100	90	40	60
200	60	80	40
300	30	120	20
400	0	160	0

2b. Figure 3-3 completed.

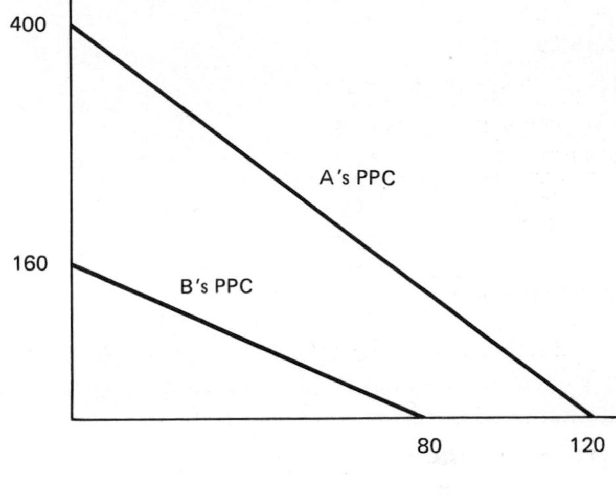

2c. *A*, *A*, *B*, *A*, 120, 160.

2d. Table 3-4

160	160	0	0	0
120	160	40	16	16
80	160	80	32	32
40	160	120	48	48
0	160	160	64	64

2e.

Table 3-5

120	120	0	0	0
80	120	40	100	100
40	120	80	200	200
0	120	120	300	300

2f. 400, 80

2g. Figure 3-4

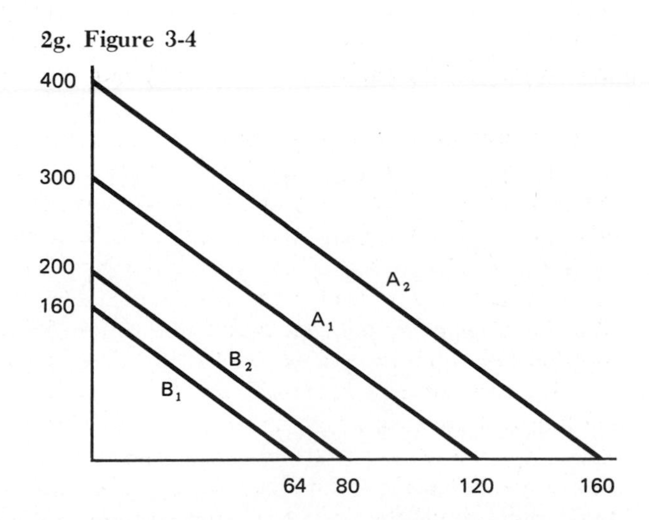

Table 3-6

400	0	0
200	200	80
0	400	160

Table 3-7

80	0	0
40	40	100
0	80	200

2h. Because in the case of A_2 and B_2, each county specializes in producing the commodity for which it has a comparative advantage, which is more efficient than the alternative of producing according to comparative *dis*advantage.

chapter 4
Demand and Supply: The Market Mechanism

Learning Objectives

After you have studied this chapter in the textbook and the study guide, you should be able to

Explain what the demand curve represents and why it slopes downward to the right

Explain what the supply curve represents and why it slopes upward to the right

Explain why the equilibrium price is the only one at which the plans of buyers and sellers are mutually consistent

Explain why the actual price will tend to converge upon the equilibrium price

List three "demand shifters" and three "supply shifters"

State the rule for determining in which directions the equilibrium price and quantity move when the demand curve shifts

State the rule for determining in which directions the equilibrium price and quantity move when the supply curve shifts

Give one example each of a pair of commodities that are (1) substitutes in demand, (2) complements in demand, (3) substitutes in supply, and (4) complements in supply, explaining in each case why they are so

Give an example illustrating why, to understand fully how the market mechanism decides what should be produced, we need to look not only at product markets but also at factor markets

Give an example illustrating why, to understand fully how the market mechanism decides "how" and "for whom," we need to look not only at factor markets but also at product markets

State one advantage and one disadvantage of the market mechanism as a means of answering the questions posed by scarcity

CHAPTER HIGHLIGHTS

In every economy some mechanism is needed to decide *what* should be produced, *how*, and *for whom*. Different economic societies solve these three interrelated problems in different ways, but—except for China and other socialist countries—most countries rely heavily upon the "market mechanism." This chapter is an account of the market mechanism, how it works, and how it answers the questions of what, how, and for whom.

This is a key chapter in the book and, indeed, in your study of economics, because it introduces you to the central concepts of supply and demand. These concepts are essential for understanding how the market mechanism works.

The demand curve describes the maximum amounts that demanders would willingly buy at various market prices. It has a downward slope, from left to right, because the lower the price, the more would demanders be willing to purchase. Next, the supply curve presents the maximum amounts that suppliers would be willing to sell at various prices. It slopes upward from left to right because the higher the price, the more suppliers are willing to sell.

Neither the demand curve nor the supply curve tell us what the market price will be or what quantity will be bought and sold on the market. In order to answer the question of what price and quantity will rule in the market, we must put the two curves together, as in Figure 4-3 in the text. Our theory predicts that the actual price and quantity that will prevail in this market will be given by the point at which the supply curve intersects the demand curve. This point is referred to as the *equilibrium point*; it determines the equilibrium price and equilibrium quantity. At any higher price, sellers would be willing to sell more than demanders would be willing to buy (there would be a surplus); at any lower price, demanders would be willing to buy more than sellers would be willing to sell (there would be a shortage). Only at the equilibrium point is there a harmony between the amounts that would be willingly bought and sold.

The way the market mechanism operates to establish the equilibrium price is as follows. If the price is above equilibrium, some sellers find themselves unable to sell all they want, because the sellers as a whole are trying to sell more than is being demanded. In order to attract business, the sellers will compete against each other by lowering their asking prices. Thus the price would be brought down to the equilibrium. On the other hand, if the price is below its equilibrium value, some buyers find themselves unable to buy all they want because the buyers as a whole are trying to buy more than is being supplied. In order to satisfy their frustrated demands, the buyers will compete against each other by offering to pay higher prices. Thus the price will rise to the equilibrium. Once the equilibrium has been reached, buyers and sellers can all trade just the amounts they want, so no one will be encouraged to bid the price up or down.

The value of the equilibrium price depends on the exact location and shape of the supply and demand curves. These, in turn, depend upon various outside factors. Factors affecting the demand curve (demand shifters) include (1) people's incomes, (2) their tastes, and (3) prices of other goods. Factors affecting the supply curve (supply shifters) include (1) technology, (2) the weather, and (3) costs of inputs.

Supply and demand curves often allow us to predict what would happen to the equilibrium price and quantity when these outside factors change. The important rule to remember is as follows: (1) If the demand curve shifts to the right, leaving the supply curve in the same position, then both price and quantity will rise; (2) if the supply curve shifts to the right, leaving the demand curve in the same position, then quantity will rise but price will fall. (Of course, if either curve shifts to the left, then exactly the opposite consequences follow.) In short, *a change in demand tends to make price and quantity move in the same direction, whereas a change in supply tends to make price and quantity move in opposite directions.* The analysis of what happens when both curves shift must be postponed until later chapters.

Supply and demand theory is usually used to analyze a single market in isolation. However, we must not forget there is often a strong interconnection between markets. When the price changes in one market, it may cause the demand or supply curve to shift in other markets. This brings us to the important distinction between *complementary* goods and *substitutable* goods. Two goods are substitutes in demand if a rise in the price of one good causes the demand curve for the other to shift to the right. For example, a rise in the price of Fords shifts the demand curve for Chevrolets to the right. At the same price of Chevrolets, more people will now buy Chevrolets instead of Fords. Two goods are complements in demand if an increase in the price of one shifts the demand for the other to the left. For example, stereo speakers and turntables are complements in demand, because people often buy them together in sets. If the price of a speaker increases, a stereo set will be more expensive; as a result, fewer sets will be demanded. Therefore the demand for turntables will also decline, even if their own price remains unchanged. Likewise, two goods are substitutes in supply if a rise in the price of one shifts the supply curve of the other to the left. For example, wheat and oats can both be produced using the same land, labor, and capital. When the price of oats rises, farmers will be encouraged to produce more oats. To do so, they will divert some resources away from producing wheat. Thus less wheat will be supplied. Finally, two goods are complements in supply if a rise in the price of one causes a rightward shift in the supply curve of the other. For example, consider corn and corn oil. Suppose the price of corn rises. Then more corn will be supplied. But you can't produce more corn without at the same time producing more corn oil. Thus more corn oil will be supplied.

Supply and demand theory apply only to perfectly competitive markets. A market is perfectly competitive if each buyer and seller takes the market price as given as "outside his or her control." If this does not hold, then the supply and demand curves as we have presented them cannot exist. That is, it makes no sense to talk about how much a seller would supply (or a buyer demand) at a given price if the buyer or seller does not in fact take the price as given. A market is most likely to be perfectly competitive if there are many buyers and sellers. For example, the single wheat farmer rightly sees himself as too small a part of the market to have any influence over the price of wheat. *Imperfectly* competitive markets will be studied in Chapters 21 and 22.

Figure 4-7 in the text illustrates how the market mechanism would decide "what," "how," and "for whom" if all markets were perfectly competitive. "What" is determined primarily in product markets. For example, as tennis becomes more popular, the demand curve for tennis racquets shifts to the right. As a result, the price of tennis racquets rises and more tennis racquets are produced. But supply and demand theory applies to markets for factors of production (land, labor, and capital). "How" and "for whom" are determined primarily in factor markets. For example, a sudden increase in immigration would shift the supply curve of labor to the right. As a result, the price of labor (that is, the wage rate) would fall. This would encourage producers to use more labor-intensive techniques. In other words, "how" production occurs would be affected. Likewise this immigration would reduce the incomes of the workers who were already here, because it would reduce their wages. And it would increase the profits going to manufacturing firms, who now pay less for their labor input. Thus more of the economy's output could now be purchased by the owners of manufacturing firms (capitalists) and less by the workers who were already here. In other words, "for whom" would be affected.

Figure 4-7 also illustrates the importance of links between markets. To understand how the market mechanism answers any of these questions, it is not enough to look at just one market. For example, the increased popularity of tennis may be a result of increases in people's incomes that enable them to afford such an expensive pastime. If so, we must understand why incomes have risen before we can truly understand why the production of tennis racquets has increased. But as we have seen, people's incomes are primarily determined in factor markets. Thus we need to look also at factor markets to understand how the market mechanism decides "what." Likewise, the increase in the popularity of tennis increases the profits of sports equipment manufacturers, who now receive a higher price for their output, and of professional tennis players, who now compete for larger prizes because people are now willing to pay more to watch tennis matches. In other words, we need to look also at product markets (in this case the market for tennis equipment) to understand fully how the market mechanism decides "for whom."

Finally, the textbook analyzes the strengths and weaknesses of the market mechanism as a means of answering these questions. Remember that what matters is the overall merit of the market system not in absolute terms but by comparison with the alternatives, such as central planning. It is possible, to paraphrase Winston Churchill's assessment of democracy, that the market mechanism is "the worst system imaginable, except for all the others."

IMPORTANT TERMS

Demand curve The schedule showing the maximum amounts that demanders are willing to buy at various prices.

Supply curve The schedule showing the maximum amounts that sellers are willing to sell at various prices.

Excess demand Also known as shortage. The amount by which the quantity demanded exceeds the quantity supplied at the given price. If this quantity is negative, it is called an excess supply, or surplus.

Equilibrium A situation in which the quantity demanded equals the quantity supplied. That is, the excess demand equals zero. In this situation, the equilibrium price and the equilibrium quantity prevail.

Market The organization through which suppliers and demanders interact. This is sometimes a very loose organization, as in the case of most labor markets.

Market mechanism The system that operates through markets to decide what will be produced, how it will be produced, and for whom. An important part of the market mechanism in perfectly competitive markets is the tendency of competition to drive prices toward their equilibrium values, thereby eliminating shortages and surpluses.

Perfect competition The situation in which no one has any perceptible influence over the market price. This is most likely to prevail where there are many buyers and sellers.

Oligopoly A situation in which there are few sellers.

Monopoly A situation in which there is only one seller. Both this and oligopoly are examples of *imperfect competition*, because individual sellers do have some control over the market price and do not act as price takers.

Ceteris paribus Literally, "other things being equal." Supply and demand curves are constructed *ceteris paribus*. That is, they are constructed under the assumption that all outside factors—such as income, technology, prices of other goods, etc.—are held constant.

Substitutes Two goods are substitutes in demand if an increase in the price of one causes an increase in the demand for the other. They are substitutes in supply if an increase in the price of one causes a decrease in the supply of the other.

Complements The opposite of substitutes. Two goods are complements in demand if an increase in the price of one causes a decrease in the demand for the other. They are complements in supply if an increase in the price of one causes an increase in the supply of the other.

Externality The economic activity of agent *A* (by "agent" we mean, for example, a consumer or a firm) produces an externality if the activity affects the well-being of other agents without agent *A* having to pay for it (in the case of an adverse effect on others) or receiving payment for it (in the case of a beneficial effect).

Normal product (Also called *superior* product.) A product for which the demand curve shifts to the right when there is a general increase in people's incomes. The opposite of this is an inferior product, whose demand declines with a rise in incomes.

True-False Questions

T (F) **1.** In the United States, the government exerts almost no influence over the solution to the problem of scarcity.

(T) F **2.** In a Marxist state, the government owns most of the capital equipment.

T (F) **3.** With the advent of telephones and other sophisticated communications systems, very few transactions now occur in markets.

(T) F **4.** The effectiveness of the market mechanism is largely due to the dual role of prices in creating incentives and disseminating information.

(T) F **5.** An oligopoly is defined as a situation where there are only a few sellers.

T (F) **6.** Under perfect competition, every buyer and seller takes the quantity as given and is left only with price decisions.

(T) F **7.** Imperfect competition can exist even when there are very many buyers.

(T) F **8.** A monopolist exploits market power by keeping prices up and quantity down.

(T) F **9.** The demand curve for coffee will probably shift to the right if the price of tea increases.

T (F) **10.** The demand curve will slope down because at a lower price producers are less willing to sell.

(T) F **11.** The supply curve for radios will probably not shift out as a result of a general rise in people's incomes.

(T) F **12.** A rise in incomes may actually cause a decline in demand for some good.

T (F) **13.** If the price of golf clubs were to rise, the demand for golf balls would probably rise.

T (F) ×**14.** If the price of golf clubs were to rise, the supply of tennis rackets would probably fall.

T (F) **15.** If the price of corn were to rise, the supply curve for corn would probably shift to the right.

(T) F **16.** If incomes were to rise, we would expect—at least in the case of a normal good—that both price and quantity would rise.

T (F) ×**17.** A rise in the overall quality of education received by members of the labor force would be likely to shift the demand curve for labor to the right.

T F 18. If the population of the United States were to decrease suddenly as a result of an epidemic, we would expect this to produce a decrease in both the wage rate and the quantity of employment.

T F 19. A fall in the price of tea results in a movement along the demand curve for tea rather than a shift in the demand curve for tea.

T F 20. One of the distinct advantages of the market mechanism is that it automatically results in a just distribution of incomes.

T F 21. Most economists agree that the unregulated market mechanism is less efficient if there are major externalities than if there aren't.

T F 22. The example of rent controls in New York City given in the textbook demonstrates not so much the perfection of the market mechanism as the unfortunate consequences that sometimes arise from well-intentioned plans for replacing it.

Multiple-Choice Questions

1. The market mechanism
- **(a)** Works only in a market for produced commodities, not in markets for factors of production
- **(b)** Operates so as to harmonize the plans of buyers and sellers
- **(c)** Works best in a situation of perfect competition
- **(d)** **(a)** and **(c)**
- **(e)** **(b)** and **(c)**

2. A market
- **(a)** Is always limited to a small geographical location
- **(b)** Can be limited geographically in commodities with large transportation costs
- **(c)** Is likely to be unlimited even across international boundaries in the presence of high protective tariffs
- **(d)** Is never international in scope even without protective tariffs or transportation costs

3. A high price for a commodity provides an incentive
- **(a)** For demanders to economize in their use of that good
- **(b)** For demanders to seek alternatives to using that good
- **(c)** For producers to expand production
- **(d)** **(a)** and **(c)**
- **(e)** All of the above

4. A market with one buyer and only a few sellers is an example of
- **(a)** Perfect competition
- **(b)** Oligopoly
- **(c)** Monopoly
- **(d)** **(a)** and **(b)**
- **(e)** **(a)** and **(c)**

5. In perfect competition, prices are determined only by
- **(a)** Impersonal market forces
- **(b)** The buyers
- **(c)** The sellers
- **(d)** The costs of producing the good
- **(e)** The government

6. The demand curve
- **(a)** Alone determines the equilibrium price and quantity in the market
- **(b)** Does not always shift out when the price of some other good rises
- **(c)** Usually shifts when there is a technological change in producing the good
- **(d)** **(a)** and **(b)**
- **(e)** **(b)** and **(c)**

7. An excess supply
- **(a)** Is the same thing as a shortage
- **(b)** Is the same thing as a negative excess demand
- **(c)** Usually occurs when the price is below the equilibrium price
- **(d)** **(a)** and **(b)**
- **(e)** **(a)** and **(c)**

8. A rise in the price of tea would probably be accompanied by
- **(a)** An increase in the equilibrium quantity of tea
- **(b)** A decrease in the equilibrium quantity of tea
- **(c)** An increase in the equilibrium quantity if the rise in price were caused by a shift in the demand curve with no shift in the supply curve
- **(d)** No change in the equilibrium quantity

9. If the price of houses is observed to rise at the same time as there is a reduction in the quantity of houses produced, then we can infer that this may have been caused by
- **(a)** An increase in demand with no change in supply
- **(b)** A reduction in demand with no change in supply
- **(c)** An increase in supply with no change in demand
- **(d)** A reduction in supply with no change in demand

10. An increase in the cost of producing tennis rackets (but not of producing tennis balls) should cause
- **(a)** An increase in the price of rackets and a decrease in the price of balls
- **(b)** An increase in the price of balls and an increase in the quantity of rackets
- **(c)** An increase in the price of rackets and an increase in the quantity of balls
- **(d)** A decrease in the quantity of rackets and an increase in the quantity of balls

11. Suppose that, because of a change in tastes, households become less inclined to purchase large cars and more inclined to purchase small cars. Then, assuming that small-car drivers use less gas than large-car drivers, this change in taste should result in
- **(a)** An increase in the quantity of small cars and an increase in the price of gas
- **(b)** An increase in the quantity of large cars and a decrease in the price of small cars
- **(c)** An increase in the price of small cars and a decrease in the price of gas

(d) An increase in the quantity of gas and a decrease in the quantity of large cars

12. Suppose that the price of umbrellas were to rise and the quantity of umbrellas to fall at the same time as there is a rise in the price of insulation and a rise in the quantity of insulation. With just this amount of information, you are asked to make a guess about what happened to the weather and to the costs of production of umbrellas and insulation. Which of the following possibilities is consistent with the above observations?

(a) The amount of rainfall rose, the weather became warmer, and there was no change in any cost of production.
(b) The weather got colder and the cost of producing umbrellas rose.
(c) The weather stayed the same, and the costs of production rose for both umbrellas and insulation.
(d) The cost of producing insulation rose but not the cost of producing umbrellas.

13. Suppose the price of high-fidelity turntables were to rise. Then this would produce

(a) A movement along the demand curve for turntables
(b) A shift to the right in the demand curve for tape decks
(c) A movement along (and up) the demand curve for tape decks
(d) **(a)** and **(b)**
(e) **(a)** and **(c)**

14. A tariff on imports of clothing from Hong Kong would probably

(a) Raise the price of clothing in the United States
(b) Lower the quantity of clothing demanded in the United States
(c) Increase the amount of production in the United States clothing industry
(d) **(b)** and **(c)**
(e) All of the above

15. An example of an externality is

(a) The increased danger of fire damage to farmers whose fields lie near the right-of-way of a railroad, from which sparks fly whenever a train passes
(b) The increase in your heating bill if you try to keep your house warmer in the winter
(c) The rise in property value that a homeowner receives when the neighbors decide to beautify their properties
(d) **(a)** and **(b)**
(e) **(a)** and **(c)**

16. A major problem with any alternative to the market mechanism for solving the basic problem of scarcity is that

(a) It is difficult to think of an alternative that solves the problem of income distribution as fairly as does the market mechanism.
(b) Externalities can be dealt with only through the market mechanism.
(c) Any alternative is faced with the difficulty of finding a device as efficient as prices for creating incentives and disseminating information.
(d) Without the artificially stimulated demand that comes about through advertising in a free market economy, firms would be unable to sell all their output.

Exercises

1. In Figure 4-1 is plotted the supply curve, which is a straight line with the equation $Q = -30 + 4P$. The way to go about plotting a curve like this is as follows: First, choose some convenient value for P, such as 10, then put this into the equation of the supply curve to get $Q = -30 + 4 \times 10 = 10$. This tells us that when $P = 10$, $Q = 10$, so that the point A is on the supply curve. Then choose some other value of P, say $P = 15$, and put it into the equation of the supply curve, which produces $Q = -30 + 4 \times 15 = 30$. Thus the point $P = 15$ and $Q = 30$; that is, point B is on the supply curve. Once we have determined these two points, we can plot the whole supply curve by drawing the straight line that passes through A and B. **(a)** Suppose that the demand curve is also a straight line, with the equation $Q = 20 - P$. Then if $P = 15$, the quantity demanded is ______. If $P = 5$, then the quantity demand equals ______. Plot the demand curve in Figure 4-1. The equilibrium price is ______ and the equilibrium quantity is ______. **(b)** Suppose now that there were an increase in demand because of

FIGURE 4-1

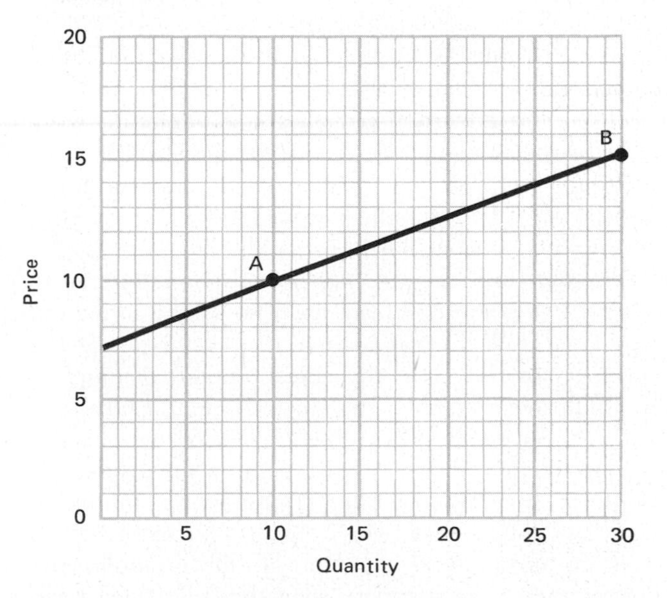

an increase in income, such that the quantity demanded at any price rose by 15 units; thus the new demand curve has the equation $Q = 35 - P$. Then, with $P = 15$, the quantity demanded would be ______; with $P = 5$, the quantity demanded would be ______. Plot the new demand curve in Figure 4-1. The new equilibrium price is ______ and the new equilibrium quantity is ______. Why have both the equilibrium price and the equilibrium quantity risen? __________

____

(c) Now suppose that we are back with the original demand curve but that the supply curve is the straight line whose equation is $Q = -10 + 2P$. In this situation, when $P = 10$ the quantity supplied is ______; when $P = 15$, the quantity supplied is ______. Plot in this new supply curve. With the new supply curve but the old demand curve, the equilibrium price is ______ and the equilibrium quantity is ______. **(d)** With this new supply curve, suppose once again that the demand curve shifts because of an increase in income such that the quantity demanded rises by 15 at each price. Then the new equilibrium price is ______ and the new equilibrium quantity is ______. Why is it that, when the demand curve shifted this time, the price rose by more and the quantity by less than in the previous case? ______________________

____

2. The textbook discusses what happens when the government prevents the price from rising to its equilibrium value, as in the case of rent controls. In some cases, the government prevents the price from falling to its equilibrium value, as in the case of minimum wage laws. Suppose that the supply curve for labor looks like the curve labeled S in Figure 4-2 and that the demand curve is the one labeled D_1. (For the time being, you may ignore the curves D_2 and D_3.) In the absence of any minimum wage laws, the equilibrium would be established at point J, with a wage rate equal to OM and a quantity of employment OC. Suppose now that the government imposes a minimum wage equal to the amount OA. Then the quantity of labor demanded at that wage would be ______ and the quantity of labor supplied would be ______. Thus there would be a surplus equal to the amount ______. In this situation, the wage rate would normally tend to fall, but it is prevented from doing so by the minimum wage law. Thus we may assume that it remains at the level OA. In this case, the actual amount of employment will most likely be the amount ______. One way for the government to raise the amount of employment back up to where it would have been in the absence of minimum wage laws, without giving up the minimum wage laws themselves, would be to offer a subsidy to firms for hiring workers. Thus if, for example, the subsidy were \$1 per worker, then the "effective" wage

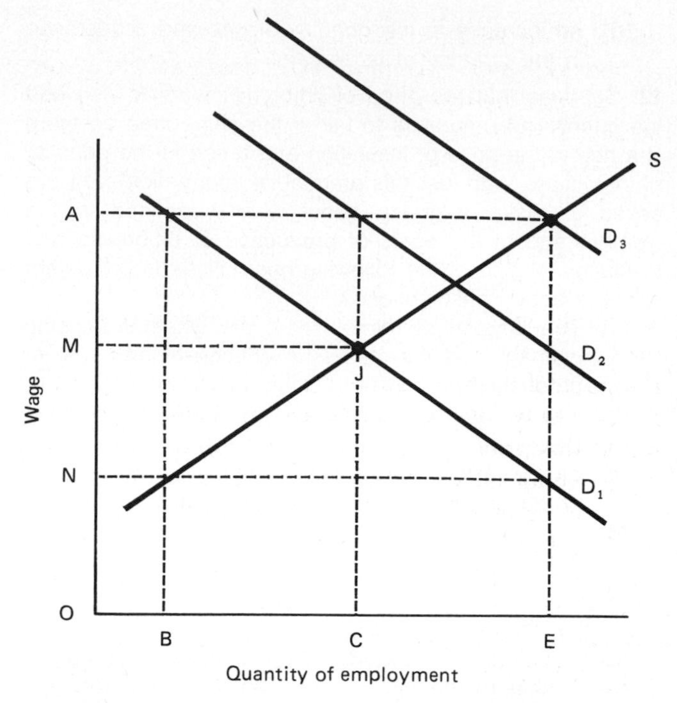

FIGURE 4-2

that the firms would have to pay would be the wage received by the workers minus \$1. This would have the effect of shifting the demand-for-labor curve up by an amount exactly equal to \$1. Thus, in order for the government to restore the level of employment to its value before the minimum wage legislation, it would have to offer a subsidy equal to the amount AM, shifting the demand curve to D_2. In this situation, firms would be paying an effective wage equal to ______ and workers would be receiving a wage equal to ______. The surplus of labor would still exist, but it would now be equal to the amount ______. In order to eliminate this surplus, the government would have to increase its subsidy to the amount ______, shifting the demand curve to D_3. In this case the workers would be receiving the wage ______, the employers would be paying the effective wage ______, the amount of employment would be ______, and the total amount of subsidy paid out by the government would be __________.

Essay Questions

1. Sometimes economists distinguish between goods in different locations, even if they are the same good. Consider "milk in Washington, D.C." as one good and "milk in Baltimore, Maryland" as another. Would you expect the price of milk in these two cities to be similar? Precisely the same? Explain.

2. Suppose that, as a result of an increase in the number of children in Baltimore, there were an increase in demand for milk in that city. If you were an all-powerful social planner, you would probably want to persuade the people in Washington to give up some of their milk so that the children of Baltimore would not have to do without. What sort of rationing scheme might you devise to accomplish this goal? How would you know how much to allocate to each family? How large a staff do you think you would need to carry out your plan? (There are over 2 million families living in Baltimore and Washington.) Suppose that you allowed market forces to work freely. What would happen to the price of milk in Baltimore? What would happen to the quantity of milk supplied in Baltimore? How would this price change affect the position of the supply curve for milk in Washington? What would happen to the price of milk in Washington? To the quantity of milk supplied in Washington? Draw supply and demand diagrams for these two commodities to illustrate what is happening. In what sense would your intentions as a social planner be carried out by these market forces? When the market forces are allowed to work, who decides how much to allocate to each family, and how many extra people are required to carry out this allocation? Which policy—the rationing scheme or the market solution—works more efficiently? Are there any disadvantages to the more efficient scheme?

3. Try to sort out the following bit of confused logic: "If supply *increases*, the price will fall. But if the price falls, supply will *decrease*. Therefore supply cannot increase." Rewrite the passage, clearing up the ambiguities and correcting the errors.

4. The prices printed on a restaurant menu apply regardless of whether the restaurant is crowded or half-empty on any particular evening. **(a)** If you ran a restaurant, would you try to adjust prices, raising them on evenings when the restaurant was crowded (demand was high) and lowering them on evenings when demand was slack? Explain. **(b)** Would you charge a different price for an evening meal than for the same luncheon meal? Why or why not?

***5.** People who speculate in commodity markets are often regarded as social parasites who make a living from others' misfortunes without contributing to society. Speculators buy whenever they think that the price is going to rise and sell when they think that it is going to fall. Can you think of any useful social contribution that is made by speculators? To be more specific, consider the speculators in agricultural societies who used to hoard grain whenever a crop failure had just occurred. If no one had hoarded grain but everyone had just gone on selling it at the old price, what would have happened to consumption of the grain? How long would the grain have lasted? When the grain had almost run out, what would have happened to the price of grain? With this in mind, who had the better foresight, the speculators or those who would rather have seen them eliminated? Would you expect prices to fluctuate more over time if speculators were allowed to operate or if they were eliminated? Why? See whether you can illustrate this with supply-and-demand diagrams for the two commodities "grain now" and "grain in the future." Can you make an analogy between the milk suppliers in the previous question who had to decide whether to sell their milk in Baltimore or Washington and the speculators in the present question who have to decide whether to sell their grain now or in the future?

Answers

True-False Questions: **1** F **2** T **3** F **4** T **5** T **6** F **7** T **8** T **9** T **10** F **11** T **12** T **13** F **14** T **15** F **16** T **17** T **18** F **19** T **20** F **21** T **22** T

Multiple-Choice Questions: **1 e 2 b 3 e 4 b 5 a 6 b 7 b 8 c 9 d 10 a 11 c 12 b 13 d 14 e 15 e 16 c**

Exercises:

1. **(a)** 5, 15, 10, 10; **(b)** 20, 30, 13, 22, because the demand curve has shifted to the right; **(c)** 10, 20, 10, 10; **(d)** 15, 20, because the second supply curve is steeper.

2. *OB, OE, BE, OB, OM, OA, CE, AN, OA, ON, OE, AN × OE.*

chapter **5**

The Economic Role of the Government

Learning Objectives

After you have studied this chapter in the textbook and the study guide, you should be able to

Identify three levels of government and three economic roles of government
State the four primary motives of government spending
Explain the free-rider problem
Explain the difference between a progressive tax and a regressive tax, giving an example of each
State seven different objectives of the tax system
Identify at least five different federal regulatory agencies
State two reasons why government regulation is sometimes justified
Identify the two main problems with regulatory agencies

CHAPTER HIGHLIGHTS

The proper economic role of the government is the issue that Smith, Keynes, and other great economists have wrestled with over the generations and which future generations of economists will undoubtedly be wrestling with also. Meanwhile, as the economists argue, the role of government expands. The purpose of this chapter is to introduce you to the details of the expanding government sector.

In the United States there are three levels of government: federal, state, and local. Their economic role takes three forms: spending, taxation, and regulation.

Spending

Government spending takes the form of (1) purchases of goods and services and (2) transfer payments. As Figures 5-2 and 5-3 point out, total government purchases have not grown over the past decade (as a fraction of national output), but government transfer payments have. Until 1974, national defense was the largest single item of federal government spending, but defense has now been overtaken by income security expenditures designed to augment and stabilize people's incomes.

There are four primary motives for government spending:

1. Governments attempt to provide goods and services which the private sector would otherwise fail to provide or would provide at a much higher cost. This is especially true of *public goods* such as national defense, which—because of the free-rider problem—no private person would find it in his or her interest to organize and finance. (If I buy equipment for the Army, others get as much protection from it as I do. Defense cannot be left to voluntary private decisions like this, because then everyone would leave it up to others. That is, everyone would try to "ride free" rather than pitching in.)

2. The government attempts to work toward an equitable distribution of income (see Chapter 1) mainly through its transfer payments, which are designed to boost the incomes of specific recipients such as the aged, the sick, the unemployed, and dependent children.

3. The government often assumes the paternalistic role of encouraging the consumption of "merit goods" such as education, which is heavily suported by the government, and food for children, which is provided through the food-stamp program.

4. The government often increases or decreases its expenditures in pursuit of the goal of economic stability (see Chapter 1), trying to stimulate economic activity when a recession threatens and to restrain it when inflation threatens.

Taxation

The biggest source of federal revenue is the personal income tax, which is a progressive tax. (That is, it takes a larger fraction of a taxpayer's income the larger that income is.) The next biggest sources are social security contributions and the corporate income tax. For state governments, the biggest source is the sales tax. This tends to be regressive (to take a *smaller* fraction of a taxpayer's income the larger that income is) because the rich tend to spend a larger fraction on nontaxable services than do the poor. The biggest source for local governments is the property tax, which also tends to be regressive, because the poor generally spend a larger fraction of their income on housing than do the rich. Because of these and other regressive elements in the tax structure and because of various loopholes, the overall tax burden at all levels appears to be more or less proportional. (That is, everyone, regardless of income, appears to pay about the same fraction of income in taxes.)

The tax system has several objectives, some of which conflict with others:

1. One objective is to aim for *neutrality*. That is, to raise funds for government spending in a way that interferes as little as possible with the free market.

2. Another is to aim for *simplicity*. That is, to minimize the burden of bureaucratic red tape on the citizenry.

3. Some people believe that taxation policy should follow the *benefit principle*. That is, the principle that—on the whole—those who receive government services are the ones who pay for them.

4. The government sometimes tries to discourage activities that involve external costs (costs not paid for by those who generate them) by imposing extra taxes on such activities. Pollution penalties are an example. Likewise, the government sometimes tries to encourage activities that create external benefits by subsidizing them, as when it provides flu shots at no charge.

5. The government can also try to use taxes to achieve the goal of equity, as when it imposes higher tax rates on those with higher incomes.

6. By raising taxes during inflationary times (to reduce private spending) and lowering them during recessions (to stimulate private spending), the government can pursue the goal of economic stability.

7. The government can also attempt to impose its paternalistic preferences by raising specific taxes so as to discourage such "demerit" activities as smoking, drinking, and living in rental accommodations.

Regulation

Government regulations run all the way from local bylaws and zoning restrictions up through the activities of the large federal regulatory bodies such as the Federal Trade Commission (FTC), the Food and Drug Administration (FDA), the Environmental Protection Agency (EPA), and many others. The main purpose of these agencies is to oversee private affairs in areas where it is believed that the market mechanism will not attain an ideal outcome because (1) private individuals and business firms are not concerned enough about such things as product safety and environmental hazard or (2) the unregulated market might end up as a monopoly. The main problems with these regulatory agencies are (1) that they have a tendency to stifle productive efforts with red tape and (2) that they tend to be biased toward producers because producers in an industry find it in their own interest to put pressure on the agency that regulates the industry, whereas the consumers who buy the products of the industry usually have too many other concerns to bother organizing that sort of pressure on the other side.

IMPORTANT TERMS

Government transfers Expenditures by the government other than those on goods or services. These expenditures merely transfer income to the recipients from the taxpayers. Examples are social security and welfare payments.

Progressive A tax is *progressive* if it takes a larger proportion of your income the larger your income is. The opposite to progressive is *regressive*. The intermediate case, in which the tax takes a constant proportion of all incomes, is called a *proportional* tax.

Average tax rate The total tax, as a fraction or percentage of income.

Marginal tax rate The additional tax, as a fraction or percentage of *additional* income.

Revenue sharing The transfer of revenue by the federal government to state and local governments. This is called *general* revenue sharing if there are no strings attached to the transfers.

Selected government regulatory agencies
ICC: Interstate Commerce Commission
FTC: Federal Trade Commission
FDA: Food and Drug Administration
EPA: Environmental Protection Agency
SEC: Securities and Exchange Commission
FPC: Federal Power Commission
FCC: Federal Communications Commission
FAA: Federal Aviation Administration
CAB: Civil Aeronautics Board
EEOC: Equal Employment Opportunity Commission
CFTC: Commodity Futures Trading Commission
OSHA: Occupational Safety and Health Administration

Public good One from which free riders cannot (easily) be excluded.

Merit goods Goods that the government deems to be particularly desirable.

Tax neutrality The degree to which the tax system leaves unaffected the allocation of goods and services achieved by the market mechanism.

Subsidy A negative tax. The payment by the government to anyone undertaking some specified activity. For example, the government subsidizes agricultural output by guaranteeing minimum payments to farmers who grow certain crops.

The benefit principle The principle that those who use government services are the ones who should pay for them.

Tax loophole Any provision that allows someone legally to escape paying taxes. The existence of loopholes is the source of much of the support for tax reform.

True-False Questions

T F **1.** Taxes are used to discourage certain activities that the government deems undesirable.

T F **2.** To an economist, social security contributions are indistinguishable from private insurance premium payments.

T F **3.** The periods of greatest percentage growth in government spending during the twentieth century have been wartimes.

T F **4.** The fraction of national output going to national defense in the United States is less now than it was in the 1950s.

T F **5.** In the past decade, the federal government's transfer payments have not risen by as much as its purchases of goods and services.

T F **6.** Unemployment compensation is a form of transfer payment.

T F **7.** In the United States, taxes are a smaller proportion of total output than they are in Japan.

T F **8.** The corporate income tax raises more revenue for the federal government than do social security contributions.

T F **9.** Employee contributions to social security constitute a progressive tax.

T F **10.** Under the 1972 general revenue sharing program, more than half of all money transferred to states must be passed on to local governments.

T F **11.** Increases in the price level (inflation) tend to increase the fraction of people's income collected through the income tax.

T F **12.** Maintaining regulatory agencies is one of the two or three largest items in the federal government's budget.

T F **13.** The main purpose of the FDA is to prevent the development of monopolies in United States industry.

T F **14.** The FTC is mainly concerned with preserving the country's natural energy resources.

T F **15.** A clean environment is an example of a public good.

T F **16.** One of the difficulties of using the tax system to attain the goal of an equitable distribution of income is that it is hard to give income to people without creating a disincentive to work.

T F **17.** Neutrality is always the principal objective of tax policy.

T F **18.** The benefit principle is the principle that free riders cannot be excluded from the benefits of public goods.

T F **19.** According to recent estimates, the United States tax system is highly progressive no matter how you look at it.

T F **20.** Capital gains are not taxed as heavily as interest income.

T F **21.** To judge from the personal income tax provisions, marriage is one of the "merit goods" being encouraged by the federal government.

Multiple-Choice Questions

1. In the late 1970s, defense spending was approximately what percent of national output in the United States?
- **(a)** 6%
- **(b)** 10%
- **(c)** 14%
- **(d)** 20%

2. Over the past decade, the fastest growing item of government spending has been
- **(a)** Foreign aid
- **(b)** National defense
- **(c)** Government transfers
- **(d)** Government purchases other than national defense

3. Which of the following countries has the largest taxes as a proportion of total output?
- **(a)** The United States
- **(b)** India
- **(c)** West Germany
- **(d)** Sweden

4. The personal income tax
- **(a)** Is the largest single source of federal government revenue
- **(b)** Is a regressive tax
- **(c)** Collects a larger fraction of people's incomes as inflation proceeds
- **(d)** **(a)** and **(b)**
- **(e)** **(a)** and **(c)**

5. National defense is
- **(a)** The largest single item of federal government spending
- **(b)** A pure public good
- **(c)** A merit good
- **(d)** **(a)** and **(b)**
- **(e)** **(a)** and **(c)**

6. In the presence of externalities,
- **(a)** There is a presumption that the government should not intervene.
- **(b)** Governments should only intervene with a view to stabilizing the economy during recession.
- **(c)** The government should only intervene with a view to achieving an equitable distribution of income.
- **(d)** The government should intervene for reasons that have little to do with stability or equity.

7. Government support of higher education is
- **(a)** Mainly undertaken by state governments
- **(b)** Sometimes justified by regarding education as a merit good
- **(c)** Sometimes justified as a way of helping poor people
- **(d)** **(a)** and **(b)**
- **(e)** All of the above

8. The provision in the personal income tax for deducting mortgage interest payments.
- **(a)** Is neutral in its effects on the economy
- **(b)** Is usually justified as a means of pursuing the goal of economic stability
- **(c)** Discourages people from living in rental housing
- **(d)** None of the above

9. If the taxes that finance the education of medical students were mainly collected from families of medical students, this would be an example of
- **(a)** Tax neutrality
- **(b)** An externality
- **(c)** The benefit principle
- **(d)** A tax loophole

10. Tax loopholes have the effect of
- **(a)** Making the United States tax system more progressive than it would otherwise be
- **(b)** Creating incentives and disincentives in the economy
- **(c)** Making the United States tax system more neutral
- **(d)** Giving fuller scope to the benefit principle

Essay Questions

1. What would be the advantages and disadvantages of living in a country like Sweden, where the proportion of national output going to the government is larger than in the United States?

2. What do you suppose the United States would be like to live in if there were no federal government regulatory agencies? Try to imagine what would happen if specific agencies—such as the FAA, the EPA, etc.—were absent.

3. Why are local police services in most communities not provided by private security firms?

4. Explain what sort of externality is created by

the following activities: someone smoking a cigarette in a movie theater, a car traveling on a highway, someone mowing a lawn, a jet plane taking off from an airport. In each case, try carefully to identify all the external costs and benefits.

5. The big spurts of growth in government spending have been during wartime, and the recent growth has been mainly in the form of transfer payments aimed at achieving a more equitable distribution of income. Using these two facts and any others you think may be relevant, can you suggest an explanation of why the government has grown so rapidly in the twentieth century? According to your explanation, will the growth of government continue for the next 50 years?

***6.** When the government increases its expenditures, it may increase taxes in order to finance those expenditures or it may borrow the money, thereby increasing the size of the public debt. If it borrows the money, does this mean that you do not have to pay for these government expenditures? Who must eventually pay the interest on the government debt?

Answers

True-False Questions: 1 T 2 F 3 T 4 T 5 F 6 T 7 F 8 F 9 F 10 T 11 T 12 F 13 F 14 F 15 T 16 T 17 F 18 F 19 F 20 T 21 F

Multiple-Choice Questions: 1 a 2 c 3 d 4 e 5 b 6 d 7 e 8 c 9 c 10 b

chapter 6
Business Organization and Finance

Learning Objectives

After you have studied this chapter in the textbook and the study guide, you should be able to

Describe the three main types of business firm and give one example of each
List three advantages of the proprietorship or partnership as a form of enterprise
List four advantages of the corporate form of enterprise
Describe five different ways for a corporation to raise funds
Explain the advantages and disadvantages of investing your money in (*a*) bonds or (*b*) shares
Describe the main function of financial markets
Explain the difference between a balance sheet and an income statement
State the fundamental identity of the balance sheet

CHAPTER HIGHLIGHTS

This chapter is intended to acquaint you with the various ways in which business firms are organized and financed. There are three basic types of firm:

1. The *single proprietorship*, owned and operated by an individual as part of his or her private affairs. An example is the typical corner store or gas station.

2. The *partnership*, which is like the proprietorship except that it is owned and operated jointly by several individuals. Examples include most law firms and many small businesses.

3. The *corporation*, the form of most of the familiar giant firms like General Motors and the IBM Corporation. Corporations are owned by their shareholders, who have limited liability. That is, the shareholders are not personally responsible for the company's debts.

Small business firms often choose to be proprietorships or partnerships because (1) this form offers the greatest flexibility and freedom from legal complications, (2) it avoids the double taxation on dividend income (the profits of the corporation are taxed as part of the corporation's income and the dividends are taxed again as part of the shareholder's personal income), and (3) it may help the business to raise funds because lenders know that the owner or owners are personally responsible for repaying the company's debts.

On the other hand, the corporate form has advantages because (1) it offers continuity of the enterprise—that is, if a shareholder passes away or wants to sell out, the company can continue smoothly under new ownership without having to be legally reconstituted; (2) the sale of new shares in the corporation is often an effective source of funds for expansion that is unavailable to the unincorporated firm; (3) the limited liability of the shareholders makes their investment in the enterprise less risky than if the company's debts were considered by law as their own personal debts; and (4) the corporate form offers tax advantages that can more than offset the double taxation of dividend income.

The corporation can raise funds by (1) issuing new *common shares*, each of which represents a fraction of the ownership of the company; (2) selling *bonds*—that is, borrowing money over a long period from the bond purchasers; (3) borrowing from a bank or other financial intermediary just as you or I might do; (4) issuing *preferred shares*, which are like common shares but whose dividends are more certain; or (5) issuing *convertible bonds*, which are like ordinary bonds except that the holder may choose to convert them, at a fixed ratio, into common or preferred shares.

All these securities can normally be bought and sold in the market. For example, if General Electric issues 20-year bonds and you buy one of them, you may decide after a year that you want to sell it. If you do, then General Electric owes the principal and the remaining interest to the new bondholder instead of to you. Financial markets are important and are mostly organized by *brokers*, who match up buyers and sellers (in return for which they charge a commission); by *investment bankers*, who arrange for the marketing of newly issued securities; and by various other *financial intermediaries*, such as banks, savings and loan associations, and insurance companies.

Because of this possibility of resale, any security has a market price that can go up or down from day to day and year to year. One source of financial return to holders of securities (indeed the main source for holders of most common shares) is the rise in market value (*capital gain*) that will occur if the company prospers. The other source consists of the *dividends* or *interest* paid by the security. The semiannual interest payment is fixed on most bonds. Dividends are fairly certain on preferred shares and can be highly variable on common shares. Because of the uncertainty of dividends and because the price of a share can fall, buying common shares is a *risky* venture. Buying preferred shares is less risky, and buying bonds is usually safer still (although buying "junk bonds" of corporations on the brink of bankruptcy can be a great gamble). However, common shares probably offer the greatest prospect of gain over the very long run. That is, they give the highest *return* on average—it's just that there is a high risk that you won't get that "average." Investors also care about the *liquidity* of securities; that is, their ability to be sold for a stable or predictable value on short notice. Claims on financial intermediaries (for example, bank deposits) are usually the most liquid of all securities.

Just as the buyer of securities must make a complex decision regarding risk, return, and liquidity, so the issuer of the security faces a difficult choice. If a corporation raises funds by issuing new shares, it will be further diluting control in the company and—if the stock market is temporarily depressed—may end up selling off a part of the corporation to the new shareholders at an unreasonably low price. On the other hand, if it borrows (either directly from a financial intermediary or by issuing new bonds), it puts itself in a risky position because the interest payments must be made. In contrast, dividends on shares can be made at the option of the corporation. But by borrowing, the firm is able to acquire *leverage*, which gives it a potential for large gains at the expense of a greater risk of failure. Leverage is just what you or I would acquire if we were to invest borrowed money in the stock market. If the stock goes up, we can make a large gain; but if it goes down, we can get wiped out.

The major function of financial markets is to allocate the accumulated savings of the millions of United States households into the millions of business investment projects that are undertaken every year. The investment bankers and others who organize these markets are basically deciding who shall have a claim upon the resources that are temporarily released when you or I decide to save part of our income rather than spend it. They do this by deciding which borrowers are credit-worthy and which projects are economically feasible. This is one way in which we rely upon the market to cope with the problem of scarcity. In the Soviet economy, by way of contrast, the government owns these resources and decides to which investment projects they will be devoted.

While there are reasons for thinking that the market solution to this allocation problem is generally a good one (although it does perhaps leave excessive room for charlatans and swindlers to harm the ignorant and unsuspecting), there is a major economic problem associated with financial markets—the problem of instability of the economy. When the economy moves into recession, many firms reduce their spending on new projects because of declining sales. This reduced spending makes the recession worse. This problem is one of the major concerns of macroeconomics, the subject of Parts 2 and 3 of the text.

Another major purpose of this chapter is to introduce the principles of business accounting. The two basic forms of account are the *balance sheet*, which gives a picture of the firm's stocks of assets and liabilities at a single *point* in time; and the *income statement* which describes the flow of expenditures and receipts by the firm over an *interval* of time (usually a year). The fundamental identity of the balance sheet is that assets ≡ liabilities + net worth. (The three bars denote an identity—something that must be true simply because the terms are defined that way, not because of any hypothesis about the way people behave.) In other words, net worth is defined as the difference between the firm's assets (what it owns) and its liabilities (what it owes). A similar role is played by *profit* in the income statement. Gross (pretax) profit is defined as being the firm's sales receipts minus its expenses. Part of the after-tax profit (net income) is paid to shareholders in the form of dividends; the rest is retained earnings. One component of costs worth studying is *depreciation*, or the allowance for wear and obsolescence of capital equipment. Firms try to make this item as large as possible (on paper!) in order to minimize their taxes. As a result, capital that has been completely depreciated on a company's books may actually still be in operating condition.

IMPORTANT TERMS

Single proprietorship, partnership, corporation The three forms of business organization. These are described in the Chapter Highlights.

Bonds, convertible bonds, common shares, preferred shares The four most common forms of corporate securities. These too are described in the Chapter Highlights.

Balance sheet, income statement The two basic forms of business accounts. Once again, see the Chapter Highlights.

Asset What is owned.

Liability What is owed.

Net worth The difference between the firm's assets and its liabilities. This measures the value of ownership or *equity* in the company.

Capital gain The return to an investor as a result of a rise in the market value of securities. In the case of a fall in the market value, there is a *capital loss*.

Dividend The income paid to shareholders out of a corporation's after-tax profits.

Interest The income paid regularly to the owner of a bond.

Book value of stock A firm's net worth divided by the number of shares outstanding. This represents the book value of a single share in the firm.

Depreciation The allowance made for wear on and obsolescence of the firm's capital.

Financial intermediary Any institution such as a bank or a savings and loan association that borrows from small savers by issuing liquid assets to them and that lends to ultimate borrowers. Financial intermediaries exist because they can specialize in gathering financial information and in pooling risk for small savers.

Investment banker A banker that deals mainly in corporate securities. See "underwrite," below.

Broker The representative of a buyer or seller in financial markets.

Underwrite An investment banker often underwrites the new issues of a company's securities by guaranteeing to the company that all the securities will be sold. If the investment banker fails to sell them all, then it must buy the unsold securities itself.

Leverage This is usually measured by the ratio of a company's debt to its net worth. A company with high leverage is one that has borrowed a great deal in relation to the scale of its operations.

Line of credit A commitment by a banker or other lender to lend up to a predetermined amount—at the borrower's option—to a corporation or other borrower.

Liquidity This is a property that investors value in a security, namely the property of being salable at a stable and predictable price upon short notice.

Risk premium The extra return, or yield, that must be paid on securities whose return is risky (such as most common shares).

Profit The difference between receipts and expenditures of the business firm. After-tax profits are usually referred to as *net income*. The net income that is not paid out in the form of dividends is retained profit (or retained earnings).

True-False Questions

(T) F 1. The vast majority of business firms are single proprietorships.

T (F) 2. Partnerships can issue preferred shares but not common shares.

(T) F 3. Every corporation must have issued shares at some time, although it need never issue any bonds.

T (F) 4. A shareholder has unlimited liability.

(T) F 5. One reason for using the corporate business form is that it often allows for the financing of expansion far beyond what the single proprietor could manage.

T F 6. A corporation's income that is used to make a dividend payment is actually taxed twice: once by the corporate income tax and once by the personal income tax.

T F 7. Common shares do not permit the holder to vote upon who will direct the company.

T F 8. Preferred shares offer a higher yield but are considered riskier investments than common shares.

T F 9. A corporation must make interest payments to its bondholders even if its preferred shareholders receive no dividend that year.

T F 10. One of the services that are provided by financial intermediaries is liquidity.

T F 11. The buyer of a convertible bond profits if the market price of the shares falls.

T F 12. The balance sheet indicates how a business fared during some particular interval of time, usually a year.

T F 13. The income statement is sometimes called the profit-and-loss statement.

T F 14. A firm's net worth is the amount of money that shareholders initially paid for their shares when they were first issued.

T F 15. Accounts payable constitute one item of a firm's liabilities.

T F 16. Straight-line depreciation is a method by which equal amounts of depreciation are counted each year until the total value of the item has been accounted for.

T F 17. Warrants are liquid claims on financial intermediaries.

T F 18. Investment bankers may join together in the form of a syndicate in order to underwrite a large issue of some corporation's securities.

T F 19. A house is usually a more liquid asset than a government bond.

T F 20. Business firms that try to achieve a high degree of leverage generally do so to minimize the riskiness of their operations.

T F 21. Business firms that establish a line of credit with a bank usually do so to obtain a more certain availability of finance.

T F 22. Municipal government bonds offer a lower yield than federal government bonds, mainly because of the risk premium on the federal bonds.

T F 23. High rates of inflation are generally associated with high rates of interest.

T F 24. Corporate bonds are generally regarded as a "hedge against inflation."

T F 25. The Securities and Exchange Commission has no power to make publicly owned corporations disclose information concerning their operations.

T F 26. One of the advantages of direct government control of the country's capital stock in a socialist country is that the government is in a better position to increase physical investment expenditures during a recession than are private business firms.

Multiple-Choice Questions

1. The partnership as a form of business firm
   - (a) Is used by most large law firms
   - (b) Is a means of limiting the liability of any single owner
   - (c) Is the most common of all in the United States
   - (d) Provides the simplest way for any single owner to sell his or her share of the company on the open market

2. The profits earned by a partnership
   - (a) Are taxed twice under the United States tax laws
   - (b) Are often retained by the firm, in which case the owners don't count them as part of their taxable income
   - (c) Are counted as capital gains for the partners
   - (d) Are treated as part of the partners' taxable incomes and therefore subject to the personal income tax

3. The corporate form of business enterprise
   - (a) Is typical of small businesses
   - (b) Suffers from a lack of continuity when one of the owners dies
   - (c) Is a social device that has been in common use ever since the industrial revolution occurred
   - (d) Can possibly make it hard for the firm to raise funds because it limits the amount that lenders can collect from the firm if it goes bankrupt
   - (e) None of the above

4. Normally the riskiest type of security to buy is a
   - (a) Bond
   - (b) Common share
   - (c) Convertible bond
   - (d) Preferred share

5. Corporate income taxes amount to approximately what percent of the corporation's before-tax profits?
   - (a) 40
   - (b) 56
   - (c) 68
   - (d) 70

6. Whenever a corporation issues bonds rather than raising funds by issuing new shares, it
   - (a) Decreases its leverage
   - (b) Decreases its risk
   - (c) Decreases the flexibility of its financial obligations
   - (d) None of the above

7. Preferred shares are so called because
   - **(a)** At the same price, shareholders would prefer them to common shares.
   - **(b)** Their holders must receive preferred treatment when the corporation is deciding whether to pay dividends on some (but not all) shares.
   - **(c)** They can be converted into bonds if the holder so prefers.
   - **(d)** Dividends on preferred shares receive preferential tax treatment compared with those on common shares.

8. The return realized by a bondholder
   - **(a)** Consists mainly in a guaranteed interest payment
   - **(b)** Never takes the form of a capital gain
   - **(c)** Is only paid each year if there is enough profit to pay a dividend on the preferred shares
   - **(d)** **(a)** and **(b)**
   - **(e)** **(b)** and **(c)**

9. Retained earnings
   - **(a)** Appear only on the balance sheet of the firm
   - **(b)** Appear only on the income statement of the firm
   - **(c)** Are always retained in the form of cash or some other liquid asset
   - **(d)** None of the above

10. The total amount of depreciation reported during any particular year by firm XYZ, Inc., will be
   - **(a)** Higher if XYZ leases its trucks than if it owns them
   - **(b)** The same as in any other year if a straight-line depreciation method is used, even if XYZ's capital stock is expanding
   - **(c)** Relatively low if XYZ's capital equipment is relatively new
   - **(d)** Not much affected by the amount of actual wear suffered by XYZ's capital equipment during the year

11. Financial intermediaries
   - **(a)** Offer liquidity to their creditors
   - **(b)** Buy only common shares
   - **(c)** Are able to reduce risk to the small saver by means of "risk pooling"
   - **(d)** **(a)** and **(b)**
   - **(e)** **(a)** and **(c)**

12. A high degree of leverage
   - **(a)** Can be a source of economic instability if possessed by a large number of firms and individuals
   - **(b)** Puts a firm in a risky position
   - **(c)** Increases the liquidity of the levered firm's bonds
   - **(d)** **(a)** and **(b)**
   - **(e)** **(a)** and **(c)**

13. Considering the tax provisions on interest income from different kinds of bonds,
   - **(a)** It is better to buy corporate bonds than federal government bonds because the interest from the former is not subject to state income taxes.
   - **(b)** You will profit more from buying U.S. government bonds rather than state or local government bonds if you are in a high tax bracket (i.e., pay a high marginal tax rate) than if you are in a low tax bracket.
   - **(c)** It is probably better to buy federal government securities than local government securities if you are in a very low tax bracket, because the yield on locals is so low that it probably won't give you as much after-tax return as the federals.
   - **(d)** It is always better to buy local government bonds than any other kind.

Exercises

1. From the following data, prepare a balance sheet in Table 6-1 below as of December 31, 1980, for the ABC Corporation. All figures refer to December 31, 1980, unless otherwise stated. You may assume that there are no assets or liabilities other than those explicitly listed. If in doubt, refer to the example of Table 6-1 in the textbook.

Accounts payable	$800
Accounts receivable	900
Long-term bonds issued	1,800
Plant and equipment	3,000
Inventory on hand December 31, 1979	800
Cash on hand	400
Accrued liabilities	600
Increase in inventory during 1980	200
Common stock	1,200
Holdings of marketable securities	50
Preferred stock	700

Table 6-1

BALANCE SHEET OF ABC CORPORATION

Assets		Liabilities and net worth	
A/R	$900	A/P	$800
Cash	400	Long Term Bonds	1,800
Inventory	1,000	Accrued Liab.	600
Market. Sec	50		
Plant & equip	3,000	Common Stock	1,200
	$5,350	Preferred "	700
			5,100
		Retained Earnings	250
			$5,350

2. The balance sheet for Chrematistics Incorporated (CI) on December 31, 1977, included the following information:

Cash	$ 65,000
Long-term debt	700,000
Plant and equipment	500,000
Accounts receivable	35,000
Retained earnings	100,000
Accounts payable	15,000
All other assets	250,000
Short-term debt	55,000
All other liabilities	30,000

Therefore, at this date CI's total assets were $__________, its total liabilities were $__________, and its net worth was $__________. If the firm had 3,000 shares outstanding at this date, the book value of its stock was $__________ per share.

For the calendar year 1978, CI's income statement showed that its sales were $480,000 and its costs were $380,000. Therefore, its before-tax profits were $__________. If it paid an average tax rate of 20 percent, its net income was $__________. It paid $22,000 in the form of dividends, so its retained earnings for the year were $__________.

CI's capital equipment in 1978 consisted of one minicomputer, bought (new) for $140,000 three years ago; an office building bought for $200,000, six years old, and other office equipment—all over 5 years old—bought for $160,000. Suppose that CI has been using a straight-line method of depreciation on its capital equipment, assuming a lifetime of 40 years on its building and 5 years on everything else. Then its total depreciation cost for 1978 was $__________. In its balance sheet of December 31, 1978, CI would report retained earnings of $__________.

Essay Questions

1. Why is it that very large companies tend to be corporations rather than partnerships or single proprietorships? Why has the twentieth century seen such a large growth in the corporate form of business enterprise? Do you think that the rise of the corporation has helped or hindered the development of the American economy in the twentieth century? Explain your answers.

2. Would it be possible for a firm's net worth to be negative? If so, what would this mean? Would it ever pay you to buy shares in a firm with negative net worth?

3. Suppose that all firms were charged by the government for the external costs resulting from their operations and were paid by the government for the external benefits that they rendered to others. How do you suppose this would affect the income statement and balance sheet of the typical firm engaged in strip-mining? Of the typical firm that sells lawn-care services?

4. Suppose that, for purposes of calculating depreciation, a firm estimates the lifetime of a machine as 3 years rather than as 5 years. What difference will this make to the total amount of depreciation cost that the firm will claim over a 5-year period following the purchase of the machine? What difference will it make to the timing of these depreciation costs (that is, to how the depreciation costs are spread out over the 5-year period)? Explain carefully why it would generally be in the best interest of the firm to estimate the lifetime as 3 years rather than 5 years. Hint: Remember that a dollar this year is worth more to the firm than a dollar 4 years from now, because a dollar this year can be put into the bank, where it will gather interest so as to yield much more than a dollar in 4 years' time.

5. Explain carefully what is meant by the Gilbert and Sullivan lines quoted in Box 6-1 of the text: "If you succeed, your profits are stupendous, and if you fail, pop goes your eighteen pence." What basic concept explained in the text do these lines illustrate?

6. Why do you suppose that corporations publish their income statements and their balance sheets? Who is interested in reading these? Would corporations publish this information if they were not forced to by government regulations? Suppose that they did publish this information but that there were no laws regulating the way these numbers could be calculated. What difference do you suppose this would make in the accounts published by the firms?

7. Suppose that you are in charge of finance for a large corporation. How would you go about raising funds for *(a)* the construction of a large plant, expected to remain in operation for at least 25 years; *(b)* the acquisition of larger inventories of raw materials; and *(c)* a temporary cash deficit resulting from the decision of many of your customers not to pay their bills until next month?

***8.** In 1975 there was a threat that New York City might go bankrupt (indeed, it did default on some of its debt). Many felt that if it did go bankrupt, there would be serious consequences for economic stability in the United States. Explain the chain of events that such a bankruptcy might have touched off.

Answers

True-False Questions: **1** T **2** F **3** T **4** F **5** T **6** T **7** F **8** F **9** T **10** T **11** F **12** F **13** T **14** F **15** T **16** T **17** F **18** T **19** F **20** F **21** T **22** F **23** T **24** F **25** F **26** T

Multiple-Choice Questions: **1** a **2** d **3** d **4** b **5** a **6** c **7** b **8** a **9** d **10** d **11** e **12** d **13** c

Exercises:

1. Table 6-1

BALANCE SHEET OF ABC CORPORATION

Assets			Liabilities and net worth			
Cash	$ 400		Accounts payable	$ 800		
Marketable securities	50		Accrued liabilities	600		
Receivables	900		Long-term debt	1,800		3,200
Inventories	1,000	2,350				
Land, plant, and equipment		3,000	Net worth			2,150
			Capital stock		1,900	
			Retained earnings		$ 250	
Total assets		$5,350				

2. 950, 800, 150, 50, 100, 80, 58, 33, 158

PART TWO
HIGH EMPLOYMENT AND A STABLE PRICE LEVEL

chapter 7
Measuring National Product and National Income

Learning Objectives

After you have studied this chapter in the textbook and the study guide, you should be able to

Explain what the twin concepts of national product and national income attempt to measure

State the difference between the "upper-loop" and "lower-loop" approaches to measuring national product

Explain the main reason why using dollar values to add up goods and services is less than ideal

State why the concept of "value added" is important for national income accounting

Explain the exact relationship between net investment and changes in the country's capital stock

State and explain the accounting identity GNP $\equiv C + I_g + G + X - M$

CHAPTER HIGHLIGHTS

The purpose of this chapter is to introduce some of the principles that economists and statisticians use and some of the problems that they encounter when trying to measure national product—the economy's total output of goods and services.

When we calculate national product, we must somehow add apples and oranges, tons of steel and bushels of wheat. The only practical way to do this is the one actually used—namely, to add up the monetary value of all these goods and services at their going market prices. There are many reasons why this method is less than ideal, but the most important one is that the value of money is not the same from one year to the next. If national product has risen from one year to the next, it might be because all prices rose, not because of an increase in the quantity produced of any good or service. To deal with this problem, we compute an index of prices each year. When the *current-dollar* or *nominal* national product is divided by this index (then multiplied by 100), the resulting figure is a measure of *constant-dollar* or *real* national product. Study Box 7-1 and Table 7-2 in the text until you understand how a price index is constructed and how it is used to compute *real* national product.

In measuring national product, care must be taken to avoid double counting. In other words, we want to count the golf clubs that were produced, but we don't also want to count the steel, leather, wood, aluminum, glue, and so forth that were produced to make the clubs. The golf clubs we call *final* products, and the various ingredients are called *intermediate products*. We want to count only the total final product. As shown in Box 7-2 in the text, this is the same as computing all the *value added* at each stage of production. Value added is the difference between the value of output that emerges from a given stage of production and the value of the raw materials that entered that stage of production.

The most common measure of national product is *gross national product* (GNP). This measures the total production of goods and services in the economy over a particular year. It equals the sum of personal consumption expenditures (C), gross private domestic investment expenditures (I_g), government purchases of goods and services (G), and exports of goods and services (X) minus imports of goods and services (M). In symbols: $GNP \equiv C + I_g + G + X - M$. This important identity states that all the country's output except that which is sold abroad is bought in the country for use as a consumption good, for use as a private investment good, or for the government's use. Imports are subtracted off because some of the expenditures included in C, I_g, and G are expenditures on goods produced in other countries, whereas we want to measure production in this country only.

Gross investment includes all current production of plant and equipment for private use as well as the net increase in business inventories. Even if a good is an intermediate good like steel, it is counted as a final investment good if it is added to inventories. Government purchases do not include all government expenditures because many of these expenditures are just *transfer payments*, such as unemployment insurance benefits.

Producing this output results in wear and tear on the nation's capital goods; that is, *depreciation*. Gross investment represents the annual addition to the country's capital stock, but depreciation represents an annual subtraction from that stock. Thus the *net* addition to the country's capital stock, which we call *net* investment (I_n), is just gross investment minus depreciation; $I_n \equiv I_g -$ depreciation. Net national product (NNP) is the same as GNP except that it counts net investment rather than gross investment; in symbols, $NNP \equiv C + I_n + G + X - M$. Thus $NNP \equiv GNP -$ depreciation.

"National product" and "national income" (NI) mean almost the same thing. The reason can best be understood by referring to the circular flow of spending, which is represented in the text by Figure 7-2. The basic idea is simple—one person's expenditure is another person's receipt. If I buy a dollar's worth of output, this creates a dollar's worth of income for the seller of that product. There is one complication: Some of the money that people spend on output goes directly to the government in the form of sales tax, so it doesn't count as anyone's income. Thus $NI = NNP -$ sales taxes (this is not exactly correct as it ignores several other minor taxes). National income measures the total income (wages and salaries, rent and interest, proprietors' income, and corporate profits) in the economy resulting from current productive activity. It does not include such items as transfer payments that are not a reward for productive activity. Thus it is not the same as *personal disposable income*, which measures all the income available for households to spend regardless of its source. The exact relationships between all these measures of product and income are set out in Figure 7-4 in the text.

The appendix to this chapter explains the MEW (measure of economic welfare), an ambitious attempt by two Yale economists to calculate a better measure of economic well-being. This measure includes an estimate of the value of our leisure as well as of the goods and services that we produce, and it makes adjustments for the quality of life that take into account environmental pollution and urban congestion.

IMPORTANT TERMS

National product The dollar value of all final goods and services produced in the country during the year.

Nominal national product National product for a particular year, computed using the market prices prevailing in the same year. Also called current-dollar national product.

Real national product National product for a particular year, computed using the market prices that prevailed in a *base* year that may not be the current year. Also called *constant-dollar* national product.

Index of prices A weighted average of prices in some year, expressed as a percentage of the same weighted average in a *base* year. To compute real national product, divide nominal national product by the price index for that year, then multiply by 100.

Final product A good or service that was produced during the year and not used up as an input into the production of some other good or service.

Intermediate product A good used as an input in producing some other good or service. These are not counted separately when national product is calculated. To avoid double counting, we include only final products.

Value added The value of a firm's output minus the value of intermediate products acquired by the firm. National income can be computed as the sum of all value added in the economy.

Personal consumption expenditures (C) The total value of expenditures by residents of the country on consumer goods during the year.

Government purchases of goods and services (G) All government expenditures during the year except for transfer payments.

Gross private domestic investment expenditures (I_g) The total amount spent in the country on capital goods that were produced during the year. It includes expenditures on plant and equipment and net additions to inventories. (It also includes, under the heading "residential construction," expenditures on currently produced houses.)

Depreciation The dollar value of the annual wear on and obsolescence of the country's capital stock.

Net private domestic investment expenditures (I_n) The annual net addition to the country's capital stock. It is defined as $I_n = I_g -$ depreciation.

Exports of goods and services (X) The total value of all goods and services produced by residents of the country but sold to residents of other countries during the year.

Imports of goods and services (M) The total expenditures by residents of the country on foreign-produced goods and services during the year.

Gross national product (GNP) Defined as GNP $\equiv C + I_g + G + X - M$.

Net national product (NNP) Defined as NNP $\equiv C + I_n + G + X - M$ or equivalently as NNP $\equiv$ GNP $-$ depreciation.

National income (NI) The total value of all income received during the year by residents of the country in return for current productive activity. It includes the sum of wages and salaries, rent and interest, proprietors' income, and corporate profits. It equals NNP minus sales taxes and other minor taxes.

Personal income Equals NI + transfer payments $-$ corporate profit taxes $-$ undistributed corporate profits $-$ social security taxes paid by employers.

Personal disposable income Equals personal income minus personal taxes.

Personal saving Equals personal disposable income $- C -$ interest paid by consumers.

Measure of economic welfare (MEW) A measure, computed by two Yale economists, which is like NNP except that it includes the value of leisure and adjusts for environmental pollution and for urban congestion.

True-False Questions

T F **1.** Nominal GNP is measured in dollars.
T F **2.** Real GNP is measured in dollars.
T F **3.** Nominal GNP is computed by dividing real GNP by a price index.
T F **4.** If nominal GNP goes up, so must real GNP.
T F **5.** If real GNP goes up, then either nominal GNP must go up or the price index must go down, or both.
T F **6.** A price index is the sum of all prices in the economy.
T F **7.** If the price index rises, the value of money falls.
T F **8.** National income is defined in such a way that it must always be equal to net national product.
T F **9.** In measuring GNP, we try to avoid counting the production of any intermediate products except those that are added to inventories.
T F **10.** Personal consumption expenditures include expenditures on consumer durables.
T F **11.** Government purchases of goods and services do not include all government expenditures.
T F **12.** National income can be greater than gross national product.
T F **13.** Some of the items included in C are sold directly to foreigners.
T F **14.** GNP $= C + I_n + G + X - M$.
T F **15.** Gross investment is greater than the net annual addition to the country's stock of capital.
T F **16.** Personal income is the same thing as personal disposable income.
T F **17.** Personal income includes some profit income.

Multiple-Choice Questions

1. This year's real GNP measures the dollar value of
(a) Current output at current prices
(b) Current output at base-year prices
(c) Base-year output at current prices
(d) Base-year output at base-year prices

2. Suppose that national product consisted simply of

guns and butter. During 1980, suppose that 100 guns and 1,500 pounds of butter are produced. Suppose that prices were $10 per gun and $1 per pound of butter in the base year 1972 and $15 per gun and $2 per pound of butter in 1980. Then nominal national product for 1980 is

(a) $2,500 **(c)** $4,500
(b) $3,000 **(d)** $6,000

3. Using the same data as in the previous question, we may conclude that real national product for 1980 is

(a) $1,000 **(c)** $2,000
(b) $1,500 **(d)** $2,500

4. From the answers to the previous two questions, we may conclude that in 1978 the 1980 price index is

(a) 180 **(c)** 240
(b) 200 **(d)** 300

5. If the price index goes up and real GNP goes down, then

(a) Nominal GNP must rise.
(b) Nominal GNP must fall.
(c) Nominal GNP will rise if the percentage fall in real GNP is greater than the percentage rise in the price index.
(d) Nominal GNP will rise if the percentage rise in the price index is greater than the percentage fall in real GNP.

6. The difference between GNP and NI equals

(a) Sales taxes
(b) The price index
(c) Transfer payments
(d) Sales taxes plus depreciation
(e) Transfer payments plus depreciation

7. The sum of wages and salaries plus rents, interest, and profits (where proprietors' incomes are included in these categories) equals

(a) Net national product
(b) National income
(c) Personal income
(d) Personal disposable income

8. Suppose a firm incurs economic costs of $100 in wages and salaries, $50 in rent and interest, and $160 for inputs purchased from other firms. If it produces an output worth $400, then its value added is

(a) $350 **(c)** $250
(b) $300 **(d)** $240

9. Suppose that the firm described in the previous question allowed $40 for depreciation, then its profit was

(a) $150 **(c)** $100
(b) $140 **(d)** $ 50

10. If during the year I paid $1,000 in social security taxes and collected $800 in unemployment insurance benefits, then the combined effect of these two items was to

(a) Reduce national income by $200
(b) Reduce personal income by $1,000
(c) Increase national income by $800
(d) Reduce personal disposable income by $200

11. If I buy $20,000 worth of common stock in the Xerox Corporation, then this will contribute $20,000 to

(a) gross investment
(b) Net investment
(c) **(a)** and **(b)**
(d) None of the above

12. If during a year I_g equaled 150 and I_n equaled 30, then the country's capital stock rose by

(a) 150 **(c)** 30
(b) 120 **(d)** Minus 120

Exercises

1. You are given the following (incomplete) data for country *A* during a particular year:

C	$900
I_g	400
Wages and salaries	800
Interest and rent	100
Corporate profits (after taxes)	250
Personal taxes	350
Depreciation	50
G	450
Corporate income taxes	150
Contributions to social security	0
Sales taxes	200
Transfer payments	200
Undistributed corporate profits	150
Proprietors' income	400

Compute the following:

NI $1,700
NNP ______
GNP ______
$X - M$ ______
Personal income ______
Personal disposable income ______
I_n ______

2. Suppose that country *Y* produces two goods, a consumption good and an investment good. The first two rows of Table 7-1 give the current-dollar value of the total production of the two goods. Fill in the next row indicating nominal GNP each year in country *Y*. The next two rows indicate the market prices of the two goods each year. Fill in the next two rows giving the number of units of each good produced each year. Then fill in the next two rows giving the value of production of each good in constant dollars (i.e., at 1976 prices). Fill in the next row giving real GNP and the next row giving the value of the price index, using 1976 as the base year.

Table 7-1

	1976	1977	1978
Current-dollar value of *C* production	400	450	600
Current-dollar value of *I* production	100	150	200
Nominal GNP	___	___	___
Price of *C*	5	9	10
Price of *I*	20	25	40
Quantity of *C* production	___	___	___
Quantity of *I* production	___	___	___
Constant-dollar value of *C* production	___	___	___
Constant-dollar value of *I* production	___	___	___
Real GNP	___	___	___
Index of prices	___	___	___

Essay Questions

1. In what sense does the gross national product tend to overstate the level of economic well-being in a country in a particular year? In what sense does it tend to understate it?

2. Explain step by step how you would go about computing the Net National Product of a country by measuring the flows in the upper loop of the circular flow. How would you do it by measuring the flows in the lower loop? Explain why you should arrive at the same answer using either approach.

3. Why do you suppose that the statistics on depreciation are unreliable? How is this connected to the tax system?

4. Consider a man who has been spending his time as a homemaker, without being paid by anyone. Suppose he were to take a job in a factory, and that the factory worker whom he replaced went to work for him as a domestic servant doing all the things he used to do as a homemaker. Suppose that the former homemaker is just as good a factory worker as the former factory worker and that the former factory worker is just as good a homemaker as the former homemaker. What has been the effect on economic well-being? When the government statistician computes GNP, how will this role-switching affect the value that is obtained? Will the resulting change in GNP overstate or understate the change in economic welfare?

5. Suppose that the house which you bought at the beginning of the year increases in value by $15,000 by the end of the year. Should you consider this as part of your income? Is it part of your disposable income? Should the national income accountant count it as part of national income? As part of personal disposable income?

***6.** What do you suppose is the purpose of distinguishing government expenditures from transfer payments? If you wanted to measure the total size of the government sector, which do you think would be a better measure, the total level of spending by the government or the amount of purchases of goods and services by the government?

***7.** Suppose that there are no undistributed corporate profits, no depreciation, and no interest payments by households. Define TR as the size of government transfer payments and T is the total amount of taxes collected by the government. Prove that the following relationship holds: $\text{GNP} \equiv C + S + T - TR$. Next, prove that $I_g + G + TR + X \equiv S + T + M$.

Answers

True-False Questions: 1 T 2 T 3 F 4 F 5 T 6 F 7 T 8 F 9 T 10 T 11 T 12 F 13 F 14 F 15 T 16 F 17 T

Multiple Choice Questions: 1 b 2 c 3 d 4 a 5 d 6 d 7 b 8 d 9 d 10 d 11 d 12 c

Exercises:

1.	
NI	1,700
NNP	1,900
GNP	1,950
$X-M$	200
Personal income	1,600
Personal disposable income	1,250
I_n	350

2. Table 7-1

	1976	1977	1978
Nominal GNP	500	600	800
Quantity of *C* production	80	50	60
Quantity of *I* production	5	6	5
Constant-dollar value of *C* production	400	250	300
Constant-dollar value of *I* production	100	120	100
Real GNP	500	370	400
Index of prices	100	162	200

chapter 8
Equilibrium with Unemployment: *An Introduction to Keynesian Economics*

Learning Objectives

After you have studied this chapter in the textbook and the study guide, you should be able to

Show how national output and the price level react to increases in aggregate demand (*a*) when the aggregate supply schedule is horizontal and (*b*) when it is vertical

State the difference between the aggregate supply curves assumed by classical economics and Keynesian economics

List the four components of aggregate demand

State the three main characteristics of the consumption function and illustrate them in a diagram

Derive the saving function from the consumption function

State the three main characteristics of the saving function and illustrate them in a diagram

Explain why the level of national product at which the aggregate demand schedule intersects the 45-degree line is an equilibrium

State and derive the formula for "the" multiplier

Explain the distinction between leakages and injections

Express the equilibrium condition for national product in three different ways

CHAPTER HIGHLIGHTS

The purpose of this chapter is to introduce the basic principles of macroeconomics. These principles derive from the British economist Lord Keynes, so much so that our present-day macroeconomic theory is often called Keynesian economics. Keynes revolutionized the subject in 1936 with the book commonly referred to as *The General Theory*. In this work, Keynes attacked "classical" theory on the grounds that it was unable to explain large-scale unemployment or to suggest policies to deal with it. The purpose of learning about Keynes and his attack on "the classics" is to get some perspective on the nature and origin of modern-day macroeconomic theory. But the main objective of this chapter is to understand the theory; the history is just a means to this end.

The first element of this theory is *aggregate supply*. As illustrated in Figure 8-1 in the text, when the economy is at less than full employment, firms can supply more output with little or no increase in price; but even large price increases may not induce them to produce beyond the point of full employment. The theory of this chapter assumes that the economy is on the horizontal range of the aggregate supply function, where prices don't have to change in order for output to rise. This simplifying assumption may be justified when there is large-scale unemployment, but that is not always the case. The "classical" economics that Keynes attacked dealt with the vertical segment of the aggregate supply function. This too is a simplifying assumption, which might be justified in a situation of high employment.

The next element of the theory is *aggregate demand*. This consists of (1) consumption demand, (2) investment demand, (3) government expenditures on goods and services, and (4) net export demand (exports minus imports). As you can see by drawing your own diagram, if the supply curve is horizontal, then the *price* of output will be determined by the position of the supply curve but the *quantity* of output will be determined by aggregate demand. Since we are interested in the quantity of aggregate output (national product), aggregate demand is the key concept for Keynesian economics.

The determination of aggregate demand can be quite complex. In order to illustrate the basic principles, this chapter considers what would happen in a very simplified economy with no government sector, no foreign trade, no depreciation, and no undistributed corporate profits. In such an economy, GNP = NNP = NI = personal disposable income. (Make sure you know why, using the definitions in the last chapter.) The only components of aggregate demand are consumption and investment. To make things even simpler, we suppose that the demand for investment is fixed at some constant value, and we focus upon consumption.

Consumption expenditures (C) depend upon personal disposable income (DI). The relationship between C and DI is called *the consumption function*. This is one of the most important concepts of macroeconomic theory. The consumption function has three main characteristics: (1) as DI increases, C increases; (2) when this happens, the change in C (ΔC) is less than the change in DI (ΔDI)—the fraction $\Delta C/\Delta$DI is called the marginal propensity to consume (MPC); (3) below some level of DI (called the "break-even" point), C will actually be larger than DI (this is possible because people can spend more than their disposable incomes by running down their assets or going into debt). These characteristics are all illustrated by Figure 8-4 in the text. As an exercise, try drawing consumption functions that do *not* have each of these three characteristics.

Saving (S) equals DI minus C. (For those of you who remember the last chapter's definition, we are assuming that no interest is being paid by consumers.) Thus a saving function can be derived directly from the consumption function, and it has three main characteristics:

1. If DI increases, then so will S.

2. The change in S (ΔS) is less than the change in DI (ΔDI); the fraction $\Delta S/\Delta$DI is the marginal propensity to save (MPS). Also, what is not consumed is saved. Therefore, $\Delta C + \Delta S = \Delta$DI. Dividing both sides by ΔDI, we find that MPS + MPC = 1.

3. Below some level (the break-even point again), people will dissave (that is, S is negative).

Figure 8-7 in the text shows how the equilibrium quantity of output is determined. The aggregate demand schedule is constructed by adding the given level of investment demand on top of the consumption function. The "45-degree line" is just a visual aid for translating the quantity of output to the vertical axis. Point A represents an equilibrium quantity of output because at that output firms are producing a quantity that is just equal to what is being demanded. At higher quantities of NP, aggregate demand is less than NP; and at lower quantities of NP, aggregate demand is greater than NP. Business firms will want to be able to meet the demand for their product, but they will not want to produce more than they can sell. Thus they will be led to produce the equilibrium level of NP.

A key concept is *the multiplier*. If investment demand increases, the resulting rise in output will be greater than the increase in investment demand; that is, it will be some *multiple* of the increase in investment demand, which we call "the" multiplier. (We put "the" in quotes because there are other multipliers in economics.) The increase in output caused by the initial increase in investment demand will create extra income. That is, households with higher income will increase their consumption expenditures. This generates more output, more income, and so forth as the effects of the initial increase in demand ripple through the economy. The exact size of "the" multiplier is $1/(1-\text{MPC})$.

The equilibrium quantity of NP is described by three different conditions, all of which amount to the same thing: (1) NP equals aggregate demand. This is the condition that we have been using so far. (2) Actual investment equals the demand for investment. When NP exceeds aggregate demand, the unsold goods that pile up in firms' inventories are actually part of investment, but this investment was *not* demanded. When aggregate demand exceeds NP, the inventories of business firms will be running down faster than firms had planned; this reduction of inventories is actually negative investment that was not demanded. Only when aggregate demand equals NP is actual investment just equal to the demand for investment, because only then is there no unintended investment (or disinvestment) in inventories. (3) Planned investment and savings are equal. One way to see this is as follows. By the definition of DI:

$$(a) \qquad \text{DI} = C + S$$

But, as we have already mentioned, in this simplified economy

$$(b) \qquad \text{DI} = \text{NP}$$

It follows from Equations (*a*) and (*b*) that

$$(c) \qquad \text{NP} = C + S$$

Let I^* represent the demand for investment. Then the level of aggregate demand is:

$$(d) \qquad \text{AD} = C + I^*$$

Now subtract Equation (*d*) from Equation (*c*):

$$(e) \qquad \text{NP} - \text{AD} = S - I^*$$

Equation (*e*) states that if NP = AD (the first equilibrium condition), then $S = I^*$ (the third equilibrium condition).

IMPORTANT TERMS

Aggregate supply The relationship between the average level of prices and the amount of output that firms are willing to produce. Aggregate supply shows how the average level of prices and output respond to changes in aggregate demand.

Aggregate demand Total spending on goods and services. That is, aggregate demand = consumption demand + investment demand + government purchases of goods and services + net exports.

Fallacy of composition The mistake of supposing that what is true for a given individual is true for all individuals collectively.

Consumption function The relationship between personal disposable income and personal consumption expenditures.

Break-even point The amount of disposable income at which saving equals zero.

Marginal propensity to consume (MPC) $\Delta C/\Delta \text{DI}$. That is, the slope of the consumption function.

45-degree line The line through the origin with slope equal to unity. Since this line is equidistant from each axis, it serves as a visual aid to translate what is on the horizontal axis to the vertical axis.

Saving function The relationship between personal disposable income and personal saving. This is simply disposable income minus the consumption function.

Marginal propensity to save (MPS) $\Delta S/\Delta \text{DI}$. That is, the slope of the saving function. (Remember that MPS + MPC = 1.)

The demand for investment The amount of investment demand that firms would like to undertake. Also called *desired investment* or *planned investment*.

Undesired inventory investment The investment in inventories that occurs not because firms wanted the investment but because they incorrectly estimated demand when making their production decisions. This can be positive or negative.

Actual investment The amount of investment that actually occurs. It equals the sum of desired investment plus undesired inventory investment.

Equilibrium national product The quantity of national product at which aggregate demand just equals national product. Also (1) the quantity at which undesired inventory investment is zero and (2) the quantity at which desired investment and saving are equal.

Full-employment national product The quantity of national product that the economy is capable of producing with its existing quantities of land, labor, and capital.

"The" multiplier The ratio of the change in national product to an initial change in aggregate demand. In the simple model studied in this chapter, it equals 1/(1−MPC), or 1/MPS.

Leakage Any withdrawal from the circular flow of spending. In the simple model of this chapter, the only leakage is saving.

Injection Any outside addition to the circular flow of spending. In the simple model of this chapter, the only injection is investment.

Paradox of thrift The paradoxical conclusion, derived from the simple model of this chapter, that if people become thriftier (that is if they decide to save more), the result will be to reduce or leave unaffected the amount saved. This result depends critically upon the simplifying assumptions used in this chapter and, in particular, the assumption of a horizontal aggregate supply curve.

True-False Questions

T F 1. Keynes' *General Theory* was written during the Great Depression.

T F 2. Keynes believed that a market economy, if left alone, would never generate massive unemployment except for short periods of time.

T F 3. Unemployment, according to Keynesian economics, is caused by insufficient aggregate supply.

T F 4. Keynesian economics is most useful when the aggregate supply curve is horizontal.

T F 5. If the aggregate supply curve is horizontal, then the level of prices does not depend upon aggregate demand.

T F 6. If the aggregate supply curve is vertical, then the quantity of national product is independent of aggregate demand.

T F 7. According to classical economics, the aggregate supply curve is horizontal.

T F 8. The multiplier measures the change in investment that would be caused by a shift in the consumption function.

T F 9. The slope of the consumption function is usually greater than unity.

T F 10. The slope of the consumption function is also the MPC.

T F 11. One minus the slope of the saving function is the MPS.

T F 12. The slope of the 45-degree line depends upon the MPC.

T F 13. At the break-even point, saving is zero.

T F 14. At the break-even point, the demand for investment is zero.

T F 15. The horizontal difference between the consumption function and the 45-degree line equals saving.

T F 16. If the MPC is positive, then the MPS is negative.

T F 17. The consumption function and the saving function are two alternative ways of illustrating precisely the same information.

T F 18. If NP exceeds its equilibrium value, then saving is greater than desired investment.

T F 19. If NP is less than its equilibrium value, then actual investment is greater than desired investment.

T F 20. If output equals aggregate demand, then actual inventory investment is zero.

T F 21. Actual investment is the sum of desired investment and undesired inventory investment.

T F 22. The equilibrium NP is always the full-employment NP.

T. F 23. The size of "the" multiplier is always greater than unity as long as the MPC is a positive fraction.

T F 24. The slope of the aggregate demand schedule equals the MPS.

T F 25. "The" multiplier equals the ratio of additional consumption to additional investment.

T F 26. The larger the MPS, the smaller the multiplier.

T F 27. Saving is an injection into the circular flow of spending.

T F 28. Investment is an injection into the circular flow of spending.

T F 29. According to the paradox of thrift, if the desire to save increases, that will only result in an increase in the production of capital goods.

T F 30. When desired investment increases, NP must continue to rise until the resulting increase in saving equals the increase in desired investment.

T F 31. If DI is above the break-even point, then saving must be greater than desired investment.

Multiple-Choice Questions

1. In Keynesian economics, the aggregate supply curve is
- **(a)** Assumed to be horizontal for levels of output below full employment
- **(b)** Assumed to be horizontal for all levels of output
- **(c)** The same as in "classical" economics
- **(d)** The 45-degree line

2. If the aggregate supply curve is horizontal, then
- **(a)** No more output will be produced unless the price level increases.
- **(b)** The price level is determined by aggregate demand.
- **(c)** The quantity of NP is determined by aggregate demand.
- **(d)** **(a)** and **(b)**
- **(e)** **(a)** and **(c)**.

3. The MPC is the ratio of
   (a) Additional *C* to additional DI
   (b) Additional *C* to total DI
   (c) Total *C* to additional DI
   (d) Total *C* to total DI
4. If the MPC were negative, then
   (a) The MPS would be greater than 1.
   (b) The aggregate demand schedule would slope downward to the right.
   (c) The multiplier would be negative.
   (d) (a) and (b).
   (e) (a) and (c).
5. At levels of DI above the break-even point,
   (a) Saving is negative.
   (b) Intended investment is negative.
   (c) Output exceeds aggregate demand.
   (d) None of the above.
6. If the MPS equals 1/3, then "the" multiplier equals
   (a) 1/3
   (b) 1-1/2.
   (c) 3.
   (d) "The" multiplier depends upon the MPC, not upon the MPS.
7. In the simple economy studied in this chapter, actual investment always equals
   (a) The demand for investment
   (b) NP minus *C*
   (c) Saving
   (d) (a) and (b)
   (e) (b) and (c)
8. Undesired inventory accumulation is negative if
   (a) NP exceeds aggregate demand
   (b) *C* is less than DI
   (c) Desired investment exceeds saving
   (d) (a) and (b)
   (e) (b) and (c)
9. If NP is below its full-employment level, then
   (a) Aggregate demand exceeds NP.
   (b) The aggregate supply curve must be vertical.
   (c) NP will increase if aggregate demand increases.
   (d) (a) and (c).
   (e) (b) and (c).
10. The paradox of thrift is valid only if
   (a) The aggregate supply curve is vertical.
   (b) There is no mechanism by which an increase in saving will create an increase in the demand for investment.
   (c) The demand for investment is fixed and does not depend upon the level of NP.
   (d) The level of prices adjusts so as to maintain continuous full employment.
11. According to Keynesian theory, which of the following would *not* produce an increase in the equilibrium NP?
   (a) An increase in intended investment
   (b) An upward shift in the consumption function
   (c) An upward shift in the saving function
   (d) (a) and (b)
   (e) (a) and (c)

Exercises

1. Table 8-1 represents the same sort of simple economy as the one studied in this chapter. Suppose that the MPC = 0.8. Fill in the second column, giving the level of consumption demand at each level of DI. Suppose that the demand for investment is 40. Then fill in the third column, giving the level of aggregate demand at each level of NP. Now fill in the fourth and fifth columns, giving (respectively) the amount of saving and the amount of undesired inventory investment that would occur at each level of NP. Then fill in the sixth column, giving S minus investment demand. The equilibrium level of NP equals ______. The break-even level of DI equals ______.

Table 8-1

(1) DI(=NP)	(2) *C*	(3) Aggregate demand	(4) Saving	(5) Undesired inventory investment	(6) *S* minus investment demand
0	20	______	______	______	______
100	______	______	______	______	______
200	______	______	______	______	______
300	______	______	______	______	______
400	______	______	______	______	______
500	______	______	______	______	______

2. Suppose that the equation of the consumption function is $C = 25 + (0.75)$ DI. In other words if DI equals, say, 100, then $C = 25 + (0.75 \times 100) = 100$. Plot out the consumption function in Figure 8-1. Plot the saving function in Figure 8-2. Suppose that the demand for investment equals 25. Plot the demand for investment in Figure 8-2. Plot the aggregate demand schedule and the 45-degree line in Figure 8-1. The MPC equals ______, the MPS equals ______, "the" multiplier equals ______, and the equilibrium level of NP equals ______. Now suppose that the demand for investment increases by 25; it now equals 50. Plot the new aggregate demand schedule in Figure 8-1 and the

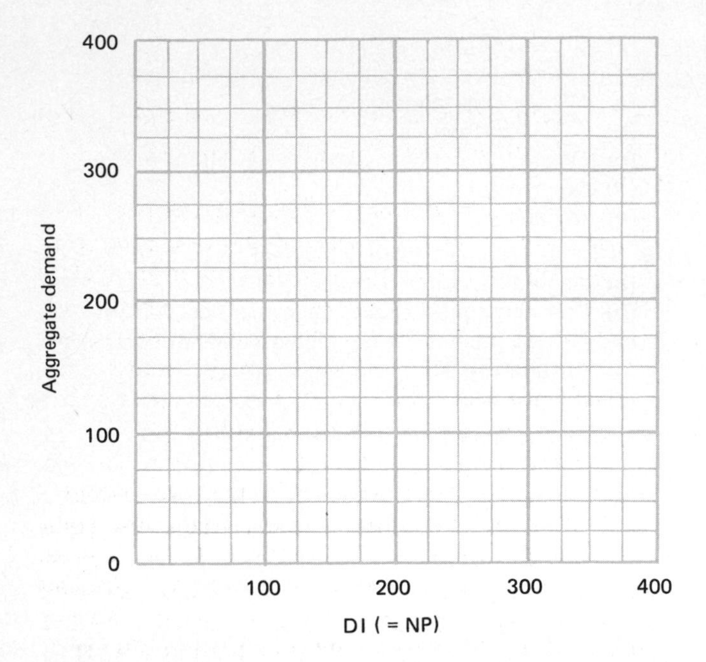

FIGURE 8-1

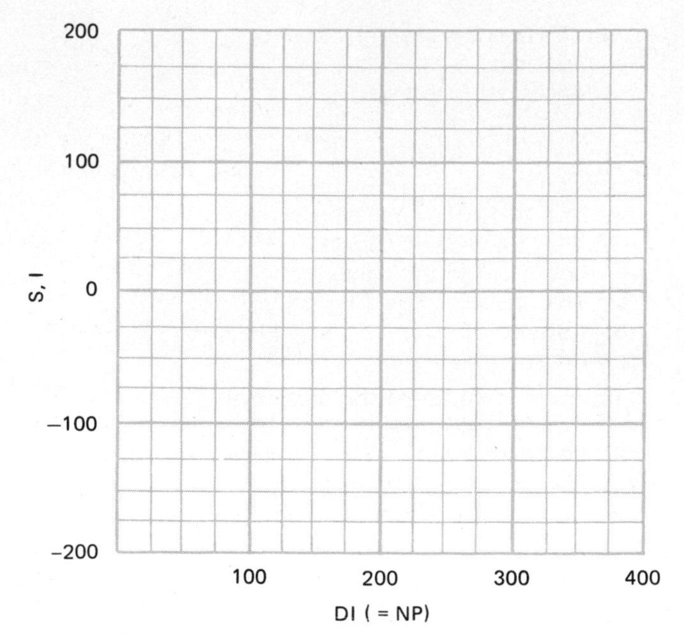

FIGURE 8-2

new investment demand schedule in Figure 8-2. The new equilibrium NP equals ______. At the value of NP that used to be the equilibrium, aggregate demand is now (more, less) than NP by the amount ______, saving is now (more, less) than the demand for investment by the amount ______, and the level of undesired inventory investment equals ______.

3. In Figure 8-3, the equilibrium quantity of NP equals ______. At that quantity of NP, *C* equals ______, *S* equals ______, investment demand equals ______, actual investment equals ______, and undesired inventory investment equals ______. When NP equals OB, then *C* equals ______, *S* equals ______, investment demand equals ______, actual investment equals ______, undesired inventory investment equals ______, *S* minus investment demand equals ______, and actual investment minus desired investment equals ______. When NP equals OX, then undesired inventory investment equals ______, *S* minus investment demand equals ______, and actual investment minus planned investment equals ______.

4. Suppose that the MPC equals 0.5 and that investment demand rises by 400. In the first column of Table 8-2, fill in the increase in demand at each round of spending, as in Table 8-3 in the text. In the second column, fill in the total increase in demand (investment plus consumption) that has occurred up to that round. The total increase in demand in *all* the rounds will be ______.

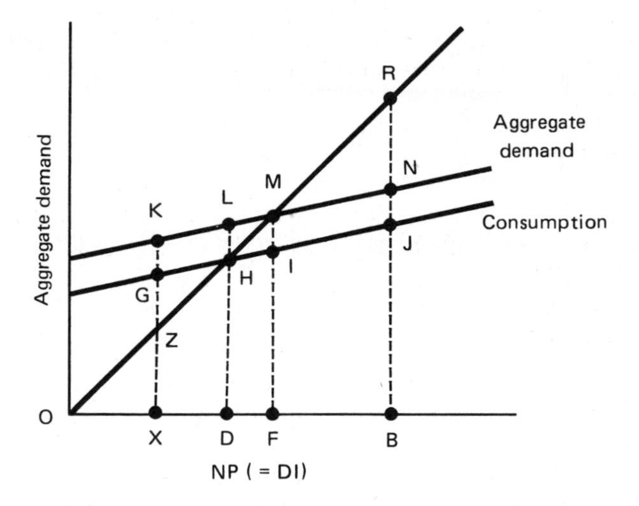

FIGURE 8-3

Table 8-2

		(1) Change in aggregate demand	(2) Cumulative total
First round	Investment of	______	______
Second round	Consumption of	______	______
Third round	Consumption of	______	______
Fourth round	Consumption of	______	______
Fifth round	Consumption of	______	______
Sixth round	Consumption of	______	______
Seventh round	Consumption of	______	______

Essay Questions

1. "If aggregate supply is horizontal, then—in order to achieve full employment—the government may have to step in so as to increase aggregate demand." Do you agree? Explain.

2. In the text, personal disposable income was stated as the main determinant of consumption expenditures. What variables other than personal disposable income do you think would be important in determining consumption expenditures?

3. In the text, the level of investment demand was assumed to be constant. What variables do you think would be important in determining investment demand?

4. In the simple model of this chapter, the only component of aggregate demand that depended upon national income in any way was consumption. What other components would you think would depend upon national income in a more realistic model? Why?

5. Draw a diagram illustrating the situation that would exist if the MPC were greater than unity. In such a situation, is there an equilibrium level of national product? If so, what would happen if the actual level of national product were greater than the equilibrium level? In this case, what would the size of "the" multiplier be?

6. "If the demand for investment goods rises, that will just divert some of our resources from producing consumption goods and put them to work in producing investment goods. The economy can't produce both more investment goods and more consumption goods unless the production possibilities frontier shifts out." Do you agree with this statement? Do you think a Keynesian economist would agree with it?

7. Explain why saving is a leakage. Try to identify two other leakages and explain why they are leakages.

***8.** One of the conditions characterizing the equilibrium level of national product is that desired investment and saving are equal. Show that it is always true that actual investment and saving are equal, whether national product is at its equilibrium level or not. How would this result have to be altered if saving were not the only leakage? (Hint: Refer back to essay question 7 in the previous chapter.)

Answers

True-False Questions: 1 T 2 F 3 F 4 T 5 T 6 T 7 F 8 F 9 F 10 T 11 F 12 F 13 T 14 F 15 F 16 F 17 T 18 T 19 F 20 F 21 T 22 F 23 T 24 F 25 F 26 T 27 F 28 T 29 F 30 T 31 F

Multiple-Choice Questions: 1 a 2 c 3 a 4 d 5 d 6 c 7 e 8 c 9 c 10 b 11 c

Exercises:

1. 300, 100.

Table 8-1

DI(=NP)	C	Aggregate demand	Saving	Undesired inventory investment	*S* minus investment demand
0	20	60	−20	−60	−60
100	100	140	0	−40	−40
200	180	220	20	−20	−20
300	260	300	40	0	0
400	340	380	60	20	20
500	420	460	80	40	40

2. 0.75, 0.25, 4, 200, 300, more, 25, less, 25, -25.
3. *OF*, *FI*, *IM*, *IM*, *IM*, O, *BJ*, *JR*, *JN*, *JR*, *NR*, *NR*, *NR*, −*ZK*, −*ZK*, −*ZK*.
4. 800.

Table 8-2

	1	2
First	400	400
Second	200	600
Third	100	700
Fourth	50	750
Fifth	25	775
Sixth	12½	787½
Seventh	6¼	793¾

chapter 9
Fiscal Policy

Learning Objectives

After you have studied this chapter in the textbook and the study guide, you should be able to

Explain why government expenditures are regarded as injections and taxes as leakages

Show how the introduction of a government affects the nature of equilibrium in the model economy studied in the last chapter

Show how the consumption function is affected by lump-sum taxes

Show how the consumption function is affected by proportional taxes

Explain why an increase in government spending has a greater effect upon aggregate demand than does a decrease in taxes of the same amount

Explain how automatic stabilizers work and give an example

Describe how the full-employment budget is measured

Explain why the full-employment budget is a better indicator of the effects of fiscal policy than is the actual budget

State the connection between fiscal drag and automatic stabilizers

Explain why balancing the actual budget every year can be a policy trap

Outline three different strategies for restraining government spending

State three reasons why the burden of the national debt may be serious

CHAPTER HIGHLIGHTS

The government can influence the level of aggregate demand through its monetary and fiscal policies. This chapter deals with fiscal policy—that is, the government's policy regarding expenditures and taxes.

When aggregate demand is too low to provide full employment, a recessionary gap exists. An increase in government spending or a decrease in taxes may close this gap by raising aggregate demand and bringing national income up to its full-employment level. When aggregate demand is higher than needed to provide full employment, an inflationary gap exists, which may be closed by a decrease in government spending or an increase in taxes.

Government spending, like investment, is an injection into the circular flow of spending; and taxes, like saving, are a leakage. As in the last chapter, planned injections and leakages must be equal for national income to be at its equilibrium level. In other words, G plus planned I must equal T plus S.

Government spending, like investment spending, contributes directly to aggregate demand. Changes in government spending have the same multiplied effects on national income as do changes in investment spending. Changes in taxes also affect national income, but not to the same extent, because they only affect aggregate demand indirectly. Any increase in taxes immediately produces a dollar-for-dollar decrease in disposable income. This, in turn, causes households to reduce consumption spending, which is one component of aggregate demand. Because the marginal propensity to consume is less than one, a $1 increase in taxes causes the consumption function to shift down by less than $1. This means that if government spending and taxes are increased by equal amounts, the effects do not cancel out. Rather, national income will rise.

Not all changes in the amount of taxes and government spending are a result of changes in fiscal policy. For example, when national income rises, more income tax must be paid; this produces an *automatic* rise in the amount of taxes collected without any change in tax rates.

Any tax that rises automatically when national income rises is an *automatic stabilizer*. So is any item of government spending that falls whenever national income rises. Automatic stabilizers are like shock absorbers that prevent national income from "bouncing around" too much.

Automatic stabilizers are not always beneficial. When there is less than full employment, we may want national income to increase. But any increase will be dampened by automatic stabilizers. This side effect of automatic stabilizers is called *fiscal drag*.

Automatic stabilizers tend to produce government deficits when the economy is in recession by making taxes low and government spending high. Likewise, they tend to produce surpluses during prosperity. Most economists regard this as a small price to pay for the benefits of stabilization. However, many would argue that the budget should act as a restraint on government spending and tax policy. Restraint may be provided by a guideline of balancing the full-employment budget every year. However, such a strategy would rule out countercyclical fiscal policy except for the effects of automatic stabilizers. A bolder strategy is to aim for a full-employment deficit during recession and full-employment surplus during prosperity. However, this may mean that the actual budget is in deficit on average; thus some economists argue that the government should aim for a *cyclically balanced* budget.

Restraint on government spending can also be accomplished by placing direct limits on the size of government spending or on the amount of taxes that the government is allowed to collect. A more direct attack on this problem may be accomplished by the application of zero-base budgeting, by which the Carter administration has hoped to eliminate some of the more wasteful government spending programs.

The full-employment budget is often used as an indicator of whether the government's fiscal policy is working to increase aggregate demand or to reduce it. It is a better indicator than the actual budget, which includes effects of automatic stabilizers as well as those of deliberate policy. For example, an actual budget deficit does not necessarily indicate an expansionary fiscal policy. The deficit may simply be the result of the currently low level of national income.

One long-run problem of government deficits is that they add to the national debt. Some regard this debt as a burden upon future generations of taxpayers. However, for the most part, repayment of the debt is just a transfer from one group of citizens (the general taxpayers) to another (the holders of government bonds).

Nevertheless, the national debt may be a burden if (1) the transfer to bondholders creates an "undesirable" distribution of income, (2) the taxes required to pay the interest generate an "excess burden," or (3) to avoid raising taxes the government creates new money to pay the interest, thus fueling inflation.

IMPORTANT TERMS

Fiscal policy The use of deliberate changes in government spending programs or tax rates to affect the level of aggregate demand.

Recessionary gap The amount by which the aggregate demand schedule would have to shift upward from a situation of less than full employment to produce full employment. Sometimes called the *deflationary gap*.

Inflationary gap The amount by which the aggregate demand schedule would have to shift downward to remove excess demand at the full-employment national product.

Lump sum tax Any tax whose amount does not depend upon the level of national income.

Marginal tax rate When more taxes are paid because of an increase in national income, the marginal tax rate is the change in taxes as a fraction of the change in income. (That is, $\Delta T/\Delta \text{NI}$.)

Government budget surplus Taxes minus transfer payments minus government purchases of goods and services. A *negative* surplus is called a budget *deficit*.

Full-employment surplus The budget surplus that would exist if the economy were at full employment, with the existing tax rates and government spending programs.

Automatic stabilizer Any tax or government spending program that makes the government surplus increase automatically (without any change in government policy) when national income rises and fall automatically when national income falls.

Fiscal drag The retarding effect on aggregate demand produced by automatic stabilizers when an increase in aggregate demand is desired.

Fiscal dividend The increase in the budget surplus enjoyed by the government due to automatic stabilizers when national income rises.

Cyclically balanced budget A government budget designed so that the surpluses received during the expansion phase of the business cycle are just equal to the deficits incurred during the contraction phase. In other words, a budget that is balanced "on average" over the business cycle.

Excess burden The decrease in efficiency of the economy which results when people change their behavior to avoid paying taxes. The primary burden of taxes is measured by the amount of taxes collected.

Zero-base budgeting The principle of evaluating every spending program from the ground up every year or so. It contrasts with *incremental* budgeting, whereby existing programs are normally continued and decisions are focused on additions to the budget of the previous year.

True-False Questions

T F **1.** The effect of a discretionary increase in government spending is to increase the equilibrium quantity of national income.

T F **2.** If there exists an inflationary gap, then the equilibrium quantity of national product is below the full-employment quantity.

T F **3.** Lump-sum taxes constitute an automatic stabilizer.

T F **4.** With a proportional income tax, the consumption function becomes flatter when the marginal tax rate rises.

T F **5.** If unemployment insurance benefits were increased, the consumption function would become steeper.

T F **6.** The problem of fiscal drag can arise only if automatic stabilizers are not strong enough.

T F **7.** If the full-employment budget is balanced and national income is below its full-employment level, then the actual budget must be in surplus.

T F **8.** In the absence of discretionary fiscal policy, the full-employment surplus would tend to rise when national income rose.

T F **9.** Automatic stabilizers do not tend to stabilize the actual budget deficit.

T F **10.** The net burden of the national debt upon future generations is greater if the spending that was financed by this debt was at the expense of investment spending rather than consumption.

T F **11.** The national debt is more burdensome if the spending which it financed occurred at a time when national income was above its full-employment level as opposed to a period of recession.

Multiple-Choice Questions

1. Suppose that the MPC equals 2/3 and that all taxes are lump-sum taxes. Then, if taxes increase by 75, the consumption function will shift

(a) Down by 75 **(c)** Down by 50
(b) Up by 75 **(d)** Up by 50

2. Suppose that the MPC equals 0.75 and that all taxes are lump-sum taxes. If the equilibrium value of national income is $140 billion and the full employment value is $200 billion, then the size of the recessionary gap is

(a) $15 billion **(c)** $60 billion
(b) $45 billion **(d)** $160 billion

3. Pick the best example of an automatic stabilizer:

(a) Local property taxes
(b) Temporary tax increases legislated by Congress to reduce inflationary pressures
(c) The corporate income tax
(d) Inheritance taxes

4. A proportional income tax

(a) Makes the consumption function flatter than it would be with only lump-sum taxes
(b) Makes the multiplier larger than it would be with only lump-sum taxes

(c) Acts as an automatic stabilizer
(d) (a) and (c)
(e) (b) and (c)

5. The full-employment budget surplus:
(a) Is made larger by a discretionary increase in taxes
(b) Is increased when taxes rise due to the presence of some automatic stabilizer
(c) Must be in surplus if the actual budget is in surplus and the economy is at full employment
(d) (a) and (c)
(e) (b) and (c)

6. In the absence of discretionary fiscal policy
(a) The full-employment surplus would rise when national income rose.
(b) The actual surplus would rise when national income rose.
(c) The full-employment surplus would fall when national income rose.
(d) The actual surplus would fall when national income rose.

7. The policy of achieving a balanced budget on the average over each business cycle
(a) Requires a full-employment surplus on average if there is less than full employment (on average) throughout the business cycle
(b) Requires the actual budget to fall when national income rises
(c) Cannot be achieved if the actual budget is always in balance
(d) None of the above

8. In 1977, the public debt was approximately what percent of GNP?
(a) 30 (c) 80
(b) 50 (d) 125

9. The federal government cannot go broke because
(a) With the power to tax, they can always raise the revenue to pay their debt.
(b) They can print more bonds if they are in financial difficulties.
(c) They can print more money to pay their debts.
(d) None of the above.

10. The size of the recessionary gap is equal to
(a) The multiplier times (actual income minus full employment income)
(b) The multiplier times (full employment income minus actual income)
(c) (Actual income minus full employment income) divided by the multiplier
(d) (Full employment income minus actual income) divided by the multiplier

Exercises

1. The equation of the consumption function which is plotted in Figure 9-1 is $C = 200 + 0.5Y$. where C denotes consumption and Y national income. The variable on the horizontal axis is national income, and the consumption function is plotted under the assumption that no taxes are collected ($T = 0$). The MPC = ______. Suppose now that a lump-sum tax of 200 is collected. When $Y = 400$, disposable income will be ______ and consumption will be ______. When $Y = 600$, disposable income will be ______ and consumption will be ______. Plot this consumption function in the same figure. As a result of the lump-sum tax, the consumption function has shifted down by ______. Suppose now that, instead of a lump-sum tax, a proportional income tax is collected, where $T = \frac{1}{3}Y$. The marginal tax rate is ______. When $Y = 300$, $T =$ ______, disposable income = ______, and $C =$ ______. When $Y = 600$, $T =$ ______, disposable income = ______, and $C =$ ______. Plot this new consumption function in the same figure.

2. In Figure 9-2, the full-employment amount of national income is equal to the distance OM. The size of the deflationary gap is ______. The equilibrium amount of national income is ______. If a line were drawn indicating the total amount of leakages (saving plus taxes), then that line would pass through the injections line at point ______. At the full-employment level of national income, would the leakages line lie

FIGURE 9-1

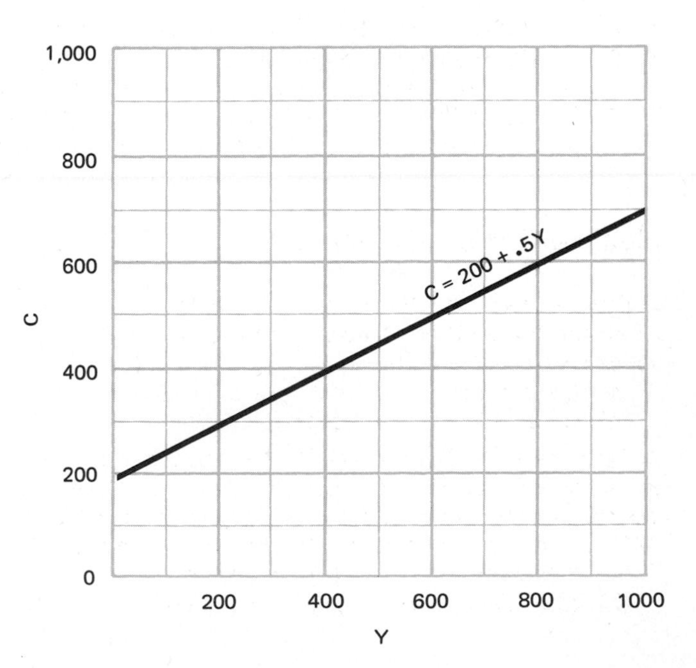

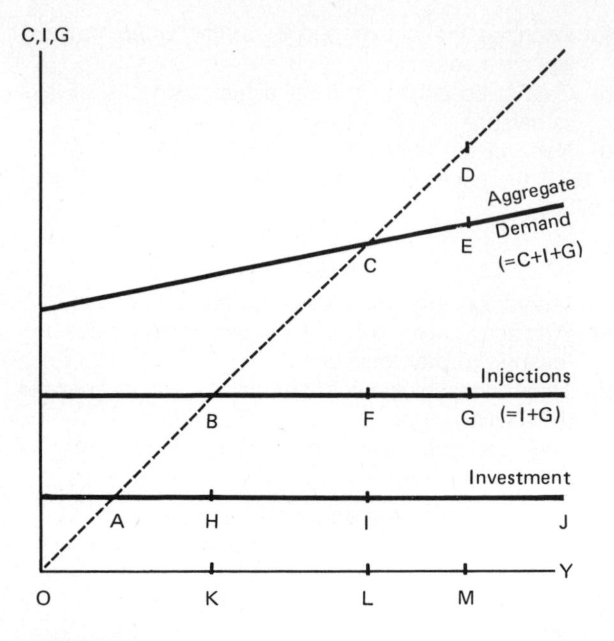

FIGURE 9-2

above or below the injections line? ______ The vertical distance between these two lines at full employment would be ______.

Essay Questions

1. If the government increases transfer payments, how does this affect aggregate demand? Will it have the same dollar-for-dollar effect as an increase in government purchases?

2. Critically evaluate the following statement: "Any system of unemployment insurance is inherently self-defeating as a measure to combat cyclical unemployment, because even though the payment of benefits to the unemployed will help to raise aggregate demand, the contributions (taxes) from employed workers will lower aggregate demand."

3. Suppose that the Mexican peso were devalued (it became worth fewer United States dollars). What would happen to the value of bonds held by Americans who had lent pesos to the Mexican government? With this in mind, why do you suppose that much of the national debt of some countries is denominated in units of foreign currency rather than their own currency? What sorts of countries would you expect to have most of their debt denominated in terms of their own currency? If a country denominates its debt in foreign currency, how should it decide which foreign currency to use?

4. The government can finance its expenditures through taxes, debt financing, or the printing of money. Contrast and compare the advantages and disadvantages of each of these three forms of finance.

***5.** Several economists have argued that the income tax should be indexed to the cost of living. That is, the basic exemptions and all tax brackets should go up, say, by 10 percent whenever the cost of living rises by 10 percent. How would indexation affect the role of the income tax as an automatic stabilizer? (Hint: Whenever national income rises, the cost of living usually rises too. That is, the aggregate supply curve is not perfectly horizontal.)

***6.** According to the theory of fiscal policy outlined in this chapter, when taxes rise, national income falls. On the other hand, when automatic stabilizers were discussed in the text, it was pointed out that when national income falls, taxes fall. Putting these two together, we are led to the nonsensical result that when taxes rise, taxes fall. How can this be true?

Answers

True-False Questions: 1 T 2 F 3 F 4 T 5 F 6 F 7 F 8 F 9 T 10 T 11 T
Multiple-Choice Questions: 1 c 2 a 3 c 4 d 5 d 6 b 7 a 8 a 9 c 10 d
Exercises: 1. 0.5, 200, 300, 400, 400, 100, 1/3, 100, 200, 300, 200, 400, 400; 2. *DE*, *OL*, *F*, above, *DE*.

chapter 10 Money and the Banking System

Learning Objectives

After you have studied this chapter in the textbook and the study guide, you should be able to

State the three basic functions of money
Explain the difference between demand deposits and time and savings deposits
Define M_1 and M_2
Explain the difference between a commercial bank and a central bank
List five functions of the Fed
Explain the distinction between member banks and nonmember banks
Explain the distinction between national banks and state banks
Describe how the process of deposit expansion works
State the formula for the deposit multiplier
Give two reasons why this formula sets only an upper limit on the expansion of bank deposits

CHAPTER HIGHLIGHTS

The purpose of this chapter is to introduce some of the basic concepts of money and banking as a preliminary to studying the workings of monetary policy.

Money performs three basic functions:

1. It is a *medium of exchange;* that is, it is the item that you give up when you buy something and that you acquire when you sell something.

2. It is a *standard of value;* that is, we keep accounts, quote prices, and sign contracts in units of money.

3. It is a *store of value;* that is, by saving money, you can defer buying goods until later.

Banks evolved from medieval goldsmiths. These goldsmiths issued warehouse receipts as "claim checks" on gold that was deposited with them for safekeeping. These warehouse receipts were the forerunners of modern bank deposits. The goldsmiths also found that they could lend out some of the gold that had been deposited with them. Thus they held in the warehouse only a fraction of the gold that had been deposited with them. This worked as long as not too many depositors came in at once to withdraw their gold, as long as the loans were repaid, and as long as the goldsmith kept enough gold in reserve (not lent out). This practice was the forerunner of the modern fractional reserve banking system.

There are two standard definitions of the money supply: (1) M_1 is the sum of currency in the hands of the public plus demand deposits in banks; (2) M_2 is the sum of M_1 plus the public's time and savings deposits with banks.

The banks that you use are known as *commercial banks*. There are about 14,000 of these in the United States. Like the goldsmiths, their major roles are to accept money on deposit for saving and for writing checks and to lend money to businesses and to individuals (and also to governments).

Above the commercial banks stands the Federal Reserve, which is the *central bank* of the United States. The roles of the "Fed" are to (1) regulate the money supply; (2) issue paper currency; (3) act as the banker of the commercial banks, lending to them and accepting deposits from them; (4) supervise and inspect the commercial banks; and (5) act as the federal government's bank.

Less than half the commercial banks in the United States are members of the Federal Reserve System, but these member banks account for almost three-quarters of all bank deposits. Banks are required by law to hold reserves equal to a fraction of their deposits. The Fed can set this fraction, known as the *required reserve ratio*, between 7 and 22 percent on demand deposits and between 3 and 10 percent on time deposits. Reserves can be held in the form of currency or deposits with the Fed.

The purpose of the required reserve ratio is to limit the amount of money that can be created by the banking system. As the lengthy example in the text illustrates, the volume of bank deposits, D, can potentially expand up to the level $D = A/R$, where R is the required reserve ratio and A is the amount of reserves that the banks have acquired. This expansion of deposits takes place following a deposit of currency by the public. As one bank lends out its excess reserves to a customer, this customer may deposit the proceeds of the loan in another bank. This second bank can lend out its excess reserves, and so on, until deposits have expanded to the point where no more excess reserves remain. However, the potential limit A/R may not be reached if (1) bankers hold excess reserves or (2) in the expansionary process some people hold their new money in the form of currency rather than depositing it.

IMPORTANT TERMS

Monetary policy The practice, pursued by the central bank, of trying to regulate aggregate demand by changing the money supply.

Purchasing power of money The value of money in terms of goods and services. During an inflation, the purchasing power of money falls.

Currency That part of the money supply which is in the form of Federal Reserve notes (paper currency) and coins.

Demand deposits Deposits with commercial banks, against which checks can be written. Demand deposits do not yield interest.

Savings and time deposits Deposits with commercial banks which are not checkable but which do yield interest. Savings deposits are mainly held by individuals and time deposits by business firms.

M_1 Currency plus demand deposits held by the general public.

M_2 Currency plus demand deposits plus savings and time deposits held by the general public.

Liquid assets Assets that are readily convertible into cash at low cost and a predictable dollar value.

Near-money Any asset, like shares with a savings and loan association, which has many of the same characteristics as savings and time deposits. Near-moneys are liquid assets.

Federal Reserve The central bank of the United States.

Commercial banks The banks that you are familiar with, that deal directly with the public.

Bank reserves Commercial banks' holdings of currency and deposits with the Federal Reserve.

Required reserve ratio The fraction of their deposit liabilities that commercial banks are required to hold in the form of reserves.

Required reserves The total amount of reserves that banks must hold as a consequence of the required reserve ratio.

Excess reserves Any reserves that the banks hold over and above their required reserves. The sum of required reserves plus excess reserves equals total reserves.

Secondary reserves The commercial banks' holdings of liquid assets.

Federal funds market The market in which banks with excess reserves lend to banks with inadequate reserves.

Demand deposit multiplier The maximum amount by which demand deposits may expand as a result of someone depositing \$1 in a commercial bank. This multiplier is the reciprocal of the required reserve ratio.

True-False Questions

T F 1. Money is a store of value.
T F 2. Money is the only store of value.
T F 3. Fractional-reserve banking is a twentieth-century invention.
T F 4. Bank panics would not occur if banks held reserves equal to 100 percent of deposits.
T F 5. The Federal Reserve sets the reserve requirements for all the banks in the United States.
T F 6. All national banks are members of the Federal Reserve System.
T F 7. Only national banks are members of the Federal Reserve System.
T F 8. Demand deposits pay no interest.
T F 9. M_2 is never smaller than M_1.
T F 10. Money is a liquid asset.
T F 11. Banks never hold excess reserves.
T F 12. The required reserve ratio applies only to secondary reserves.
T F 13. The federal funds market is the market in which the federal government borrows from banks.

Multiple-Choice Questions

1. The study of money is important for economics because
- **(a)** Making money is the object of all economic activity.
- **(b)** Monetary policy is important for regulating aggregate demand.
- **(c)** Money is a source of potential instability in the economic system.
- **(d)** **(a)** and **(c)**.
- **(e)** **(b)** and **(c)**.

2. Which of the following is *not* a role of money?
- **(a)** Store of value
- **(b)** Instrument of barter
- **(c)** Medium of exchange
- **(d)** Standard of value

3. Which of the following events could possibly start a bank panic?
- **(a)** A sudden decision by a lot of people to deposit their currency in commercial banks
- **(b)** A sudden increase in defaults on bank loans
- **(c)** A sudden decision by a lot of people to switch their funds from demand deposits to savings deposits
- **(d)** **(a)** and **(b)**
- **(e)** **(a)** and **(c)**

4. If the required reserve ratio is 0.125, then the demand deposit multiplier equals
- **(a)** 1.25 **(c)** 8.0
- **(b)** 8/7 **(d)** 12.5

5. If I deposit $20,000 in a commercial bank and the required reserve ratio is 0.1, then the potential expansion of demand deposits resulting from this act is
- **(a)** $2,000 **(c)** $22,000
- **(b)** $20,000 **(d)** $200,000

6. Which of the following is *not* one of the roles of the Federal Reserve?
- **(a)** To regulate commercial banks
- **(b)** To act as a bankers' bank
- **(c)** To act as the federal government's bank
- **(d)** To conduct fiscal policy
- **(e)** None of the above

7. State banks constitute what percent of the total number of banks?
- **(a)** 0–24 **(c)** 50–74
- **(b)** 24–49 **(d)** 75–100

8. Deposits with state banks constitute what percent of total deposits?
- **(a)** 0–24 **(c)** 50–74
- **(b)** 24–49 **(d)** 75–100

9. Which of the following is largest?
- **(a)** Currency in the hands of the public
- **(b)** M_1
- **(c)** M_2
- **(d)** Time and savings deposits

10. Which of the following was largest in the United States in 1978?
- **(a)** Demand deposits
- **(b)** Time and savings deposits
- **(c)** Currency in the hands of the public
- **(d)** Total bank reserves

Exercises

1a. If I deposit $100,000 in a demand deposit account with Bank A and the required reserve ratio is 0.2, then the immediate increase in bank A's total reserves is ____________ and the immediate increase in bank A's required reserves is ____________. Thus the immediate increase in bank A's excess reserves is ____________. As a result of this transaction, the total amount of currency in the hands of the public has gone (up, down) by the amount ____________, the total amount of demand deposits has gone (up, down) by the amount ____________, the total amount of M_1 has (increased, decreased, not changed), and the total amount of M_2 has (increased, decreased, not changed).

b. If bank A now lends its new excess reserves to

someone who immediately puts the proceeds of the loan into a demand deposit in bank B, then the immediate effect is to make bank A's total reserves go (up, down) by __________, to make bank A's required reserves (increase, decrease, stay unchanged), to make bank A's excess reserves go (up, down) by _______, to make bank B's total reserves go (up, down) by __________, to make bank B's required reserves go (up, down) by __________, and to make bank B's excess reserves go (up, down) by __________. As a result of this loan, the total amount of currency in the hands of the public has (increased, decreased, stayed the same), the total amount of demand deposits has (increased by __________, decreased by _______, stayed the same), the total amount of M_1 has gone (up, down) by __________, and the total amount of M_2 has (increased by __________, decreased by _____, stayed the same).

c. If the process continues like this until all excess reserves have been eliminated, then the result of the whole process, starting from my initial deposit, will have been to make the total supply of currency in the hands of the public go (up, down) by _______, to make the total amount of bank deposits go (up, down) by __________, to make M_1 go (up, down) by __________, to make M_1 go (up, down) by __________, and to make M_2 (go up by ______, go down by __________, stay the same).

2. Show what happens as a result of each of the following transactions by filling in the appropriate number for that transaction in the balance sheet. Each balance sheet should represent the *change* in total assets and total liabilities of all the commercial banks. In each case, suppose that the required reserve ratio is 0.2 on demand deposits and 0.1 on savings deposits.

Each transaction should be considered separately from all of the others.

A. Someone puts $25,000 of currency into a demand deposit account.

B. Someone makes a cash withdrawal of $100,000 from a savings account in order to hold the money in the form of currency.

C. Someone switches $200,000 from a demand deposit account to a savings deposit account.

D. A bank lends $40,000 to someone who holds that money in the form of cash.

E. A bank lends $100,000 to someone who uses that $100,000 to pay off a loan to someone who puts the $100,000 into a savings deposit.

Balance Sheet A

Change in assets			Change in liabilities	
Loans		______		
Total reserves		______		
			Demand deposits	______
Required reserves	______			
			Savings deposits	______
Excess reserves	______			

Balance Sheet B

Change in assets			Change in liabilities	
Loans		______		
Total reserves		______		
			Demand deposits	______
Required reserves	______			
			Savings deposits	______
Excess reserves	______			

Balance Sheet C

Change in assets			Change in liabilities	
Loans		______		
Total reserves		______		
			Demand deposits	______
Required reserves	______			
			Savings deposits	______
Excess reserves	______			

Balance Sheet D

Change in assets			Change in liabilities	
Loans		________		
Total reserves		________		
			Demand deposits	________
Required reserves	________			
			Savings deposits	________
Excess reserves	________			

Balance Sheet E

Change in assets			Change in liabilities	
Loans		________		
Total reserves		________		
			Demand deposits	________
Required reserves	________			
			Savings deposits	________
Excess reserves	________			

Essay Questions

1. What do you suppose would happen if the Federal Reserve abolished all reserve requirements on member banks?

2. Most deposits with commercial banks are now covered by Federal Deposit Insurance. Thus, if there is a banking panic and your bank finds itself unable to meet your request to withdraw the money that you have deposited with it, you can collect your deposit from the Federal Deposit Insurance Corporation. Since the institution of the FDIC, there has not been a major bank panic in the United States. Why do you suppose this has been the case?

3. It has been argued that the existence of near-moneys makes it more difficult for banks to predict their deposits and withdrawals than if these near-moneys did not exist. Why do you suppose this is the case? (Hint: Consider what happens to banks deposits and withdrawals when savings and loan associations begin offering higher interest rates on their deposits.)

4. It has also been argued that the existence of a federal funds market helps to make the monetary system less prone to instability. See whether you can fill in some of the details of this argument. (Hint: Over any given week, do you think it is easier to predict the deposits and withdrawals of a particular bank or of the banking system as a whole?)

5. Suppose that the required reserve ratio on all deposits is 0.2 and that banks always hold excess reserves equal in amount to 5 percent of their total deposits. Suppose, furthermore, that everyone holds all his or her money in the form of bank deposits rather than currency. By how much would bank deposits increase in this situation if I were to discover $10,000 in my attic and to deposit this in my bank account?

6. In what sense do bankers "create money"? How can this be reconciled with the view, often expressed by individual bankers, that they don't create money—they just lend out the money that is deposited with them?

***7.** Suppose that the required reserve ratio on deposits is 0.2 and that banks hold no excess reserves. Suppose, furthermore, that everyone holds half his or her money in the form of bank deposits and half in the form of currency. In this case, how much would total bank deposits increase if someone were to discover $20,000 and to deposit half of it in a bank account?

***8.** Many people think that, in the future, most payments will be made through an electronic transfer system. That is, when you buy something from a store, instead of paying with cash or a check, the store will use a remote computer terminal to transfer money instantaneously from your account to theirs. How would the institution of such an electronic transfer system affect the amount of money that people wish to hold in the form of currency? How would it affect the total amount by which bank deposits would be expanded following the deposit of some new currency into a bank account?

***9.** Recall the three different roles of money. For each role, can you think of another item, other than money, that also plays this role in specific cases?

***10.** Banks often find it difficult to predict how much money is going to be deposited or withdrawn from their accounts on any given day or during any given week. Which do you think they find it easier to predict: deposits and withdrawals of demand deposits or deposits and withdrawals of savings deposits? Why? How is this connected to the fact that banks historically have tended to hold more reserves against demand deposits than against the same amount of savings deposits?

Answers

True-False Questions: **1 T 2 F 3 F 4 T 5 F 6 T 7 F 8 T 9 T 10 T 11 F 12 F 13 F**
Multiple-Choice Questions: **1 e 2 b 3 b 4 c 5 d 6 d 7 c 8 b 9 c 10 b**
Exercises:

1. (a) 100,000; 20,000; 80,000; down; 100,000; up; 100,000; not changed; not changed; (b) down; 80,000; stay unchanged; down; 80,000; up; 80,000; up; 16,000; up; 64,000; stayed the same; increased by 80,000; up; 80,000; increased by 80,000; (c) down; 100,000; up; 500,000; up; 400,000; go up by 400,000.

2. Balance Sheet A

Change in assets			Change in liabilities	
Loans		0		
Total reserves		25,000	Demand deposits	25,000
Required reserves	5,000		Savings deposits	0
Excess reserves	20,000			

Balance Sheet B

Change in assets			Change in liabilities	
Loans		0		
Total reserves		−100,000	Demand deposits	0
Required reserves	−10,000		Savings deposits	−100,000
Excess reserves	−90,000			

Balance Sheet C

Change in assets			Change in liabilities	
Loans		0		
Total reserves		0	Demand deposits	−200,000
Required reserves	−20,000		Savings deposits	+200,000
Excess reserves	+20,000			

Balance Sheet D

Change in assets			Change in liabilities	
Loans		40,000		
Total reserves		−40,000	Demand deposits	0
Required reserves	0		Savings deposits	0
Excess reserves	−40,000			

Balance Sheet E

Change in assets			Change in liabilities	
Loans		100,000		
Total reserves		0	Demand deposits	0
Required reserves	+10,000		Savings deposits	100,000
Excess reserves	−10,000			

chapter 11
The Federal Reserve and the Tools of Monetary Policy

Learning Objectives

After you have studied this chapter in the textbook and the study guide, you should be able to

Identify the three major tools of monetary policy
Describe how each of these tools works
Explain how the Federal Reserve System is organized
List the three major effects of open market purchases of government securities by the Fed
State two major problems with the discounting procedure of the Federal Reserve System
Explain why the discounting procedure may promote economic stability
Explain why only small changes in reserve requirements are made
Show why a rise in interest rates means the same thing as a fall in bond prices
Identify two minor tools of monetary policy
Explain what "backs up" our money supply

CHAPTER HIGHLIGHTS

This chapter describes how monetary policy is conducted. The three major tools of monetary policy used by the Federal Reserve System—commonly known as the Fed—are: (1) open market operations, (2) changes in the discount rate, and (3) changes in required reserve ratios.

The United States is divided into 12 Federal Reserve Districts, each with its own Federal Reserve Bank. Each of these banks has a president and nine directors. Coordinating this system of banks is the Board of Governors of the Federal Reserve System (known as the Federal Reserve Board) in Washington, whose seven members are appointed to 14-year terms by the President (subject to congressional confirmation). The Chairman of the Federal Reserve Board, who has a 4-year term, is also appointed by the President.

Changes in reserve requirements are decided by the Board, within limits set by Congress. Discount rates, which may vary from district to district, are changed by the Board, but only at the suggestion of the regional Federal Reserve Bank. Open market operations are conducted by the New York Federal Reserve Bank under the direction of the Federal Open Market Committee, which consists of the members of the Board and the presidents of five of the district banks, one of which is always the New York Federal Reserve Bank.

Open market operations involve purchases or sales by the Fed of government securities in the open market. The Fed operates in the market for these securities in the same way as a private firm, with one exception: When the Fed buys securities, it creates the money to pay for them, and when it sells securities, it destroys the money that is received in the sale. An open market purchase of securities by the Fed has three main effects: (1) it increases the money supply, (2) it increases the reserves that commercial banks are able to lend out, and (3) it lowers interest rates on securities. All three effects operate in reverse following an open market sale.

Increases in the discount rate can be used to make commercial banks less willing to make loans. The commercial banks usually borrow from the Fed only when their reserves are temporarily low. When the cost of this borrowing is raised, they can protect themselves against having to borrow so often by lending out fewer of their excess reserves. The problems with the discounting procedure (the procedure whereby the member banks borrow from the Fed) are (1) that it introduces "slippage" into open market operations by allowing member banks to maintain reserves through borrowing even when open market sales are taking place and (2) that it can provide a "hidden subsidy" to banks that are sometimes able to borrow from the Fed at a rate substantially lower than that at which they could borrow elsewhere. However, the discounting procedure can also make the banking system more stable, because it provides member banks with a "lender of last resort" in the event of difficulties.

Changes in reserve requirements are very potent. They operate directly on the deposit multiplier discussed in the previous chapter. When the required reserve ratio is increased, banks are forced to curtail their loans. This can have drastic consequences, as in the 1930s, when large increases in reserve requirements were responsible for prolonging the Great Depression. The Fed now tries to avoid such errors. Recent changes in reserve requirements have been small.

There are two minor tools of monetary policy:

1. Selective credit controls have been implemented. An example is margin requirements on stock-market transactions. The purpose of margin requirements is to prevent excessive speculation from causing a financial crisis as in the stock-market crash of 1929.

2. Moral suasion is sometimes exercised. An example is the "voluntary" restraint on banks' foreign lending in the mid 1960s, which was encouraged by the Fed.

When the Fed purchases securities on the open market, it creates money "out of thin air." Our money is not backed by gold. Dollar bills retain their value because they are scarce and are generally accepted by sellers of goods and services. The acceptability of demand deposits is reinforced by the FDIC, which ensures that bank deposits can be converted into cash. Ultimately, the only thing that backs our money is the Fed's determination not to create it so fast that it becomes worthless.

IMPORTANT TERMS

Open market operation The purchase or sale by the Fed of government securities in the open market.

Discount rate The interest rate at which the Fed lends to member banks.

Federal Reserve Banks The operating arms of the Fed. There is one in each of the 12 Federal Reserve Districts.

Federal Reserve Board The coordinating agency of the Federal Reserve System, consisting of seven members appointed by the President.

Federal Open Market Committee (FOMC) A committee consisting of the seven members of the Federal Reserve Board and the presidents of five of the Federal Reserve Banks, which meets monthly to decide how the Fed's open market operations are to be conducted. (All twelve presidents of the regional Federal Reserve Banks attend the FOMC, but only five are voting members at one time.)

Treasury bill A short-term government security, often bought or sold in open market operations. It usually matures (the loan is repaid) 90 days after it is issued.

Prime rate The lowest interest rate at which anyone can borrow from a commercial bank.

Perpetuity A bond with an infinite term to maturity. In other words, a perpetuity is a promise to pay a certain sum of money every year forever.

Coupon A coupon payment on a bond is the annual (or semiannual or quarterly) payment of interest.

Present value The present value of a stream of

future returns is the amount that the ownership of that stream of returns is worth on the market today. (See Box 11-1.)

Selective credit controls Restrictions imposed by the Fed upon transactions in particular credit markets.

Margin requirement A requirement limiting the amount that can be borrowed to buy shares on the market. It stipulates the maximum percentage of a stock purchase that can be financed with borrowed money.

Legal tender An item (such as a dollar bill) is legal tender if it must be accepted by a creditor in the settling of a debt.

Federal Deposit Insurance Corporation (FDIC) An agency of the federal government that insures deposits in a national bank or other member of the FDIC up to $40,000 per deposit.

Gold standard The historical system under which paper currency was convertible at a fixed price into gold.

True-False Questions

T F **1.** Changes in reserve requirements are the most commonly used tool of monetary policy.
T F **2.** The Federal Reserve System was established in the twentieth century.
T F **3.** There are eight Federal Reserve districts.
T F **4.** Open market operations are conducted only at the suggestion of the district banks.
T F **5.** The discount rate may vary from one Federal Reserve district to another.
T F **6.** An open market sale by the Fed causes bank reserves to rise.
T F **7.** An open market purchase by the Fed causes security prices to rise.
T F **8.** An increase in interest rates means the same thing as an increase in security prices.
T F **9.** A treasury bill is a particular kind of perpetuity.
T F **10.** Under the discounting procedures of the Federal Reserve System, the Federal Reserve Banks must lend whatever amounts the member banks want to borrow at the existing discount rate.
T F **11.** The discounting procedure involves a hidden subsidy whenever the treasury bill rate is less than the discount rate.

Multiple-Choice Questions

1. In carrying out monetary policy, the Fed relies mainly upon
- **(a)** Open-market operations
- **(b)** Changes in reserve requirements
- **(c)** Moral suasion
- **(d)** Selective credit controls

2. The voting membership of the Federal Open Market Committee consists of
- **(a)** All Federal Reserve Board members and all Federal Reserve Bank presidents
- **(b)** All Federal Reserve Board members and some Federal Reserve Bank presidents
- **(c)** Some Federal Reserve Board members and all Federal Reserve Bank presidents
- **(d)** Some Federal Reserve Board members and some Federal Reserve Bank presidents

3. An open market sale by the Fed of $800 million will cause
- **(a)** Bank reserves to increase by at most $800 million
- **(b)** Bank reserves to decrease by at most $800 million
- **(c)** Excess bank reserves to decrease by at most $800 million
- **(d)** **(a)** and **(c)**
- **(e)** **(b)** and **(c)**

4. If the Fed undertakes an open-market purchase and the seller of the security is a commercial bank, then
- **(a)** Bank reserves will increase by as much as if the seller had been a private corporation that holds no currency.
- **(b)** Bank reserves will increase by less than if the seller had been a private corporation that holds no currency.
- **(c)** Excess reserves will change by less than if the seller had been a private corporation that holds no currency.
- **(d)** **(a)** and **(c)**.
- **(e)** **(b)** and **(c)**.

5. If a 90-day $100,000 treasury bill sells for $99,000, then the annual interest rate is approximately
- **(a)** 1 percent
- **(b)** 4 percent
- **(c)** 10 percent
- **(d)** 12 percent

6. If the annual interest rate on a 90-day $100,000 treasury bill is 12 percent, then its price is about
- **(a)** $88,000
- **(b)** $92,000
- **(c)** $97,000
- **(d)** $98,800

7. If a perpetuity pays $100 every 6 months and the annual rate of interest is 5 percent, then the market price of the perpetuity is
- **(a)** $400
- **(b)** $1,000
- **(c)** $2,000
- **(d)** $4,000

8. If a $100 bond which reaches maturity in 2 years pays an annual coupon of $10, then its market price is
- **(a)** More than $100 if the rate of interest exceeds 10 percent
- **(b)** Less than $100 if the rate of interest exceeds 10 percent
- **(c)** Equal to $50 if the rate of interest equals 20 percent

(d) (a) and (c)
(e) (b) and (c)

9. Of the following, the biggest asset in the Federal Reserve System's balance sheet is
- **(a)** U.S. government securities
- **(b)** Member-bank borrowing
- **(c)** Gold
- **(d)** Federal Reserve notes

10. The biggest item on the right-hand side of the Federal Reserve System balance sheet is
- **(a)** Deposits of member banks
- **(b)** Deposits of the United States treasury
- **(c)** Federal Reserve notes
- **(d)** Net worth

11. The gold standard
- **(a)** Exercises discipline upon central banks
- **(b)** Has been strengthened considerably in recent years
- **(c)** Was never used by the United States
- **(d)** **(a)** and **(c)**
- **(e)** **(b)** and **(c)**

Exercises

1. Suppose the required reserve ratio on all deposits is 0.2.

A. In balance sheets A, show the initial effects of an open market purchase of $10 million of securities by the Fed where the seller is a corporation that deposits the proceeds of the sale immediately with its bank, which keeps the funds in the form of a deposit with the Fed.

B. In balance sheets B, show the ultimate effects of the above transaction, assuming that the deposit expansion process continues up to its maximum limit given by the deposit multiplier. Assume that each bank in the process holds all its extra reserves in the form of deposits with the Fed.

C. In balance sheets C, show the initial effects of a decrease in the required reserve ratio from 0.2 to 0.1, assuming that the banks originally had $100 billion in reserves and no excess reserves.

D. In balance sheets D, show the ultimate effects of the change in C, assuming that the deposit creation process continues up to the limit determined by the deposit multiplier and assuming that all reserves continue to be held in the same form as before.

Balance Sheets A

Federal Reserve System		All commercial banks	
	Federal Reserve notes ________	Loans ________	Deposits ________
		Total reserves ________	
Federal government securities ________			
	Deposits of member banks ________	Required reserves ________	
	Net worth ________	Excess reserves ________	

Balance Sheets B

Federal Reserve System		All commercial banks	
	Federal Reserve notes ________	Loans ________	Deposits ________
		Total reserves ________	
Federal government securities ________			
	Deposits of member banks ________	Required reserves ________	
	Net worth ________	Excess reserves ________	

Balance Sheets C

Federal Reserve System		All commercial banks	
	Federal Reserve notes ________	Loans ________	Deposits ________
		Total reserves ________	
Federal government securities ________			
	Deposits of member banks ________	Required reserves ________	
	Net worth ________	Excess reserves ________	

Balance Sheets D

Federal Reserve System		All commercial banks	
	Federal Reserve notes ________	Loans ________	Deposits ________
		Total reserves ________	
Federal government securities ________			
	Deposits of member banks ________	Required reserves ________	
	Net worth ________	Excess reserves ________	

2. (This exercise is only for those who have studied Box 11-1.) Consider a $100 bond with an annual coupon of $10. In Table 11-1, fill in the price of the bond under the different assumptions concerning the term to maturity and the rate of interest.

TERM TO MATURITY

Rate of interest	1 year	2 years	Perpetuity
8%	________	________	________
10%	________	________	________
12%	________	________	________

What general proposition is suggested by this example concerning the relationship between (*a*) the term to maturity of the bond and (*b*) the size of the effect upon the price of the bond of a change in the rate of interest?

____

____

____

Essay Questions

1. Suppose that a bank has invested most of its assets in long-term securities that yield a rate of interest just slightly above the rate of interest that the bank is paying on its savings and time deposits. What sort of trouble will the bank run into if other banks now begin offering higher interest rates on their savings and time deposits? Explain how the discounting procedure of the Federal Reserve System would come in handy in this event.

2. The discounting procedure was referred to in the text as a source of "slippage" in open market operations. Name two other potential sources of such slippage, explaining in each case why slippage might occur.

3. Show by means of an example how, if you buy shares on a 50 percent margin, both your losses and gains will be increased by 100 percent.

4. What are the pros and cons of having a discount rate that fluctuates automatically with the rate of interest on treasury bills, as is the case in some countries?

5. What would the pros and cons be of having the chairman of the Fed appointed for a 14-year rather than a 4-year term?

6. One of the drawbacks of using fiscal policy to affect aggregate demand is that a change in taxes or in government spending usually requires congressional approval, which may take a long time to obtain. Are the three major instruments of monetary policy also subject to this drawback?

***7.** Consider the three effects, mentioned in the text, of an open market purchase of government securities by the Fed. Explain how each of them individually would affect the level of aggregate demand in the economy.

***8.** It has been suggested by some people that the Fed should pay interest on member bank reserves. How would this affect the profits of the member banks? The profits of the Federal Reserve System? How do you think this might affect the overall size of the money supply? Explain why, if the rate of interest on reserves were set equal to the discount rate, member banks would be unlikely to hold any treasury bills.

***9.** "Holding money is not as risky as holding bonds, because interest rates may change." Do you agree? Explain.

Answers

True-False Questions: 1 F 2 T 3 F 4 F 5 T 6 F 7 T 8 F 9 F 10 F 11 F
Multiple-Choice Questions: 1 a 2 b 3 e 4 a 5 b 6 c 7 d 8 b 9 a 10 c 11 a
Exercises:
1.

Balance Sheets A

Federal Reserve System		All commercial banks	
	Federal Reserve notes 0	Loans 0	Deposits $10 million
		Total reserves $10 million	
Federal government securities $10 million			
	Deposits of member banks $10 million	Required reserves $ 2 million	
	Net worth 0	Excess reserves $ 8 million	

Balance Sheets B

Federal Reserve System		All commercial banks	
	Federal Reserve notes 0	Loans $40 million	Deposits $50 million
		Total reserves $10 million	
Federal government securities $10 million			
	Deposits of member banks $10 million	Required reserves $10 million	
	Net worth 0	Excess reserves 0	

Balance Sheets C

Federal Reserve System		All commercial banks	
Federal government securities 0	Federal Reserve notes 0 Deposits of member banks 0 Net worth 0	Loans 0 Total reserves 0 Required reserves −$50 billion Excess reserves +$50 billion	Deposits 0

Balance Sheets D

Federal Reserve System		All commercial banks	
Federal government securities 0	Federal Reserve notes 0 Deposits of member banks 0 Net worth 0	Loans $500 billion Total reserves 0 Required reserves 0 Excess reserves 0	Deposits $500 billion

2. Table 11-1

Rate of interest	1 year	2 years	Perpetuity
8%	$101.85	$103.57	$125.00
10%	$100.00	$100.00	$100.00
12%	$ 98.21	$ 96.62	$ 83.33

The longer the term to maturity, the greater the change in the price of the bond for any change in the interest rate.

PART THREE
FIVE GREAT MACROECONOMIC QUESTIONS OF OUR TIME

chapter 12

Monetary and Fiscal Policy:

Which Is the Key to Aggregate Demand?

Learning Objectives

After you have studied this chapter in the textbook and the study guide, you should be able to

Identify three links in the chain of events connecting changes in the money supply to changes in aggregate demand (according to the Keynesian view of monetary policy)

List the four bits of information required to calculate the rate of return on an investment project

State two major reasons why, according to the Keynesian view, monetary policy may be ineffective

State three reasons why, according to the Keynesian view, monetary policy may be more effective in reducing aggregate demand than in increasing it

Explain the chain of events that occurs, according to the monetarist view, when the supply of money exceeds the demand for money (and when the demand for money exceeds the supply of money)

List five key propositions of monetarism

Describe the quantity theory of money and its connection to monetarism

Explain how *crowding out* may occur

Explain why it is difficult to settle the Keynesian-monetarist controversy by looking at the facts

State four advantages of the "eclectic" policy of using both monetary and fiscal policy

Explain how the wrong mix of monetary and fiscal policy may reduce the rate of economic growth

CHAPTER HIGHLIGHTS

Macroeconomics is full of controversy. The controversy studied in this chapter involves the relative power of monetary and fiscal policy. On this issue, there are two extreme schools of thought (although most economists take an intermediate position between these extremes). One school—consisting of strong Keynesians—believes that fiscal policy is very important in determining aggregate demand, while monetary policy has little or no effect. The other school—consisting of strong monetarists—believes just the opposite. This chapter is organized around five issues concerning this controversy: (1) The Keynesian view of how monetary policy works (or doesn't work), (2) the monetarist view of how monetary policy works, (3) the monetarist argument that fiscal policy has little effect on aggregate demand, (4) the statistical evidence on the controversy, and (5) the "eclectic" case for using both fiscal and monetary policies.

The Keynesian View of Monetary Policy

According to the Keynesian view, there are three links in the chain of events whereby an open market purchase of securities by the Fed affects aggregate demand. First, the purchase causes interest rates to fall, as discussed in Chapter 11. Second, the lower interest rates induce business firms to plan more investment projects. Third, this increase in investment demand has multiplied effects on the level of aggregate demand, as explained in Chapter 8. An open market sale sets off the same chain of events, but with all effects going in the opposite direction.

The second link is examined in this chapter. Business firms will undertake investment projects as long as the rate of return on such projects is at least as great as the rate of interest. The rate of return may be calculated provided that you know (1) the initial cost of the project, (2) the lifetime of the project, (3) the contribution of the project to annual sales during its lifetime, and (4) the annual operating costs of the project. Given this information on all the potential investment projects in the economy, an economist can construct the schedule showing the demand for investment—that is, the *marginal efficiency of investment* (MEI) schedule.

According to the Keynesian view, there may be two major reasons why monetary policy is ineffective: (1) The rate of interest may not fall much in the first link, especially if it is already low. (Box 12-1 explains the extreme situation of the liquidity trap, where the rate of interest doesn't fall at all.) (2) If the MEI schedule is steep in the second step, then a change in the rate of interest will have only a weak effect on desired investment. This is illustrated by Figure 12-5 in the text. This second reason is subject to two criticisms: (*a*) It is difficult to measure the degree of responsiveness of investment demand to the rate of interest. (*b*) When interest rates rise, there may be a large effect on investment demand even with a steep MEI schedule. This is because bankers may ration credit in order to limit loans, thus forcing firms to curtail their investment plans for lack of finance (that is, forcing firms off the MEI schedule in Figure 12-6 in the text).

There are three reasons why the effects of monetary policy may be asymmetrical—that is, why restrictive policy may work more strongly than expansive policy:

1. The rate of interest cannot be driven below zero, but there is no limit to how high it can be forced.

2. Banks are forced to reduce their lending when their reserves fall below the required amount; but no matter how many excess reserves they have, they cannot be forced to expand their lending if they are not inclined to do so.

3. Through credit rationing, banks can force business firms to borrow less than they want; but no one can force them to borrow more than they want.

The Monetarist View of Monetary Policy

The monetarist or classical view centers around the *equation of exchange*: $MV = PQ$. (See Important Terms, below.) This equation must hold true because of the way V is defined. But monetarists then add the proposition that V is stable, thus moving from the equation of exchange to the *quantity theory of money*. Underlying this theory is a proposition involving the demand for money. Suppose that people always wish to hold the fraction $(1/V)$ of their annual income (PQ) in the form of money. If they all find themselves holding more than this, everyone will try to run down excess cash holdings by buying other assets, goods, and services. But one person's expenditure is another's receipts. The excess cash is a "hot potato" that gets passed around. However, the attempt to get rid of this excess cash stimulates aggregate demand, which will raise P and/or Q. This will continue until people's nominal incomes have risen to the point where they no longer regard their cash holdings as excessive—in other words, until $M = (1/V)PQ$, which is just a rewritten version of the equation of exchange. (Study Figure 12-7 in the text and the surrounding discussion. Then, as an exercise, restate the argument, starting from the situation in which people find themselves holding less money than they wish.)

The five key propositions of monetarism are as follows:

1. The money supply is the most important variable in determining the level of aggregate demand.

2. In the long run, the *real* level of national output, Q, tends toward its full-employment level independently of monetary factors, so that the only long-run effect of a change in M is a change in P.

3. The short-run effect of a change in M is a change in *both* P and Q.

4. If M is stable, then aggregate demand will also be reasonably stable.

5. Therefore, the Fed should aim at keeping a steady rate of growth of M (say 4 percent) rather than try to vary M in an effort to smooth out the business cycle.

The Monetarist View of Fiscal Policy

Monetarists' reservations concerning fiscal policy are expressed in the notion of "crowding out." When the government spends more or cuts taxes, it normally finances the resulting deficit by borrowing from the public. (If it borrows from the Fed, then the money stock will rise, and a monetarist would consider this monetary policy, not fiscal policy.) The increase in the demand for borrowing tends to raise interest rates, which—as in the Keynesian view of monetary policy—tends to reduce investment demand.

How much crowding out occurs depends upon the responsiveness of investment demand to changes in interest rates—the same factor that Keynesians refer to in denying the importance of monetary policy.

The Evidence

The main statistical evidence consists of studies that measure how closely aggregate demand moves together with monetary or fiscal variables. These studies have tended to show that aggregate demand and the money supply were much more closely related than were aggregate demand and various measures of fiscal policy. However, as Keynesians are quick to point out, when A (the quantity of money) and B (aggregate demand) move together, this does not prove that A *causes* B. Increases in aggregate demand may induce business firms to take out more bank loans, thus causing the money supply to expand. In other words, changes in aggregate demand may be causing changes in the money supply, rather than the reverse. Indeed, there are two more possibilities: (1) that the relationship is purely coincidental (not likely, given the frequency with which it has been observed) or (2) both aggregate demand and the money supply may be influenced by some third variable.

The other kind of evidence involves specific historical episodes. A case in point is the 1968 temporary tax surcharge, which failed to have the restrictive effect predicted by Keynesians at the time. Historical episodes may be cited which undercut either extreme position, whether Keynesian or monetarist.

The Case for Both Monetary and Fiscal Policy

The "eclectic" case can be built around four major points:

1. When we know as little as we do about how the economic system operates, it makes sense to diversify—to use some of each kind of policy—rather than putting all our eggs into one policy basket.

2. When any particular policy is relied upon exclusively to restrain aggregate demand, some groups inevitably will be hurt more than others by the necessary cutbacks. Using a combination of restrictive policies is one way of "spreading the pain."

3. Relying exclusively upon fiscal policy to promote expansion may be unwise because government programs that are initially seen as "temporary" have a way of becoming permanent.

4. On the other hand, some economists think that relying exclusively upon monetary policy to promote expansion may be ineffective because of the asymmetry mentioned previously.

A major problem arises because of the mix of monetary and fiscal policies which may be adopted. The Fed may be biased toward restrictive monetary policies that reduce investment demand, while the government may be biased toward expansive fiscal policies, which further reduce investment demand. As a result of these two biases, there may be a low rate of investment and consequently a low rate of growth.

IMPORTANT TERMS

Keynesian The label attached to economists whose analytic framework is based on Keynes' *General Theory*. These economists generally stress the importance of fiscal policy.

Monetarist The label attached to economists who base their analysis of inflation and business cycles on the quantity theory of money. (These economists are also sometimes referred to as classicists.) The monetarist school stresses the importance of monetary rather than fiscal policy as a determinant of aggregate demand.

Marginal efficiency of investment (MEI) The schedule or curve that shows the amounts of investment which are expected to yield various rate of return. This represents a demand schedule (or curve) for investment.

Liquidity preference Another expression for the demand for money. (Box 12-1 explains that liquidity preference is the stock of money that people wish to hold at any point in time, expressed as a function of the rate of interest on bonds.)

Credit rationing A situation in which bankers restrict the amount that they will lend to their customers, even when these customers are credit-worthy and would like to borrow more at the going rates of interest.

Income velocity of money The number of times that the average dollar is used during the year to purchase final output.

Equation of exchange The equation $MV = PQ$, where M denotes the supply of money, V denotes the imcome velocity of money, P denotes the price level, and Q denotes the level of real output in the economy during the year. V is defined as being equal to PQ/M; therefore, the equation of exchange is a tautology.

Tautology A statement that is true by definition, such as the statement that older people are not so young as younger people.

Quantity theory of money The proposition that V is stable and that, therefore, a change in M will cause an approximately proportional change in PQ. (Most quantity theorists believed that, in the long run, Q would move to the full-employment level. Thus, in the long run, the effect of a change in M would be a change in P.)

Crowding out The effect of expansive fiscal policy in reducing the level of investment demand by causing interest rates to rise.

Pure fiscal policy A fiscal policy that leaves the supply of money unaffected. (In other words, changes in taxes or government spending are reflected in changes in the publicly held government debt—not in changes in the quantity of money.)

True-False Questions

T F **1.** Keynesians tend to advocate the use of monetary policy rather than fiscal policy.

T F **2.** Milton Friedman is usually identified as one of the leading monetarists.

T F **3.** According to the Keynesian view of monetary policy, an open market purchase of securities by the Fed will usually cause an increase in investment demand.

T F **4.** According to the Keynesian view of monetary policy, an open market sale of securities by the Fed is likely to increase the level of consumption demand.

T F **5.** If the demand for investment goods is relatively unresponsive to changes in the rate of interest, then the MEI schedule is steep.

T F **6.** The rule that says "undertake an investment project if and only if its rate of return (appropriately adjusted for risk) is at least as great as the rate of interest" is likely to be followed by business firms, even if they do not have to borrow to undertake their investment projects.

T F **7.** According to the monetarist view of fiscal policy, fiscal policy is less effective the less responsive is the demand for investment goods to changes in the rate of interest.

T F **8.** If credit is rationed, business firms may be forced off the MEI schedule.

T F **9.** Keynesians think that expansive monetary policy may be less effective than restrictive monetary policy.

T F **10.** The equation of exchange may be regarded as a tautology because of the way the price level is defined.

T F **11.** On the whole, monetarists are more inclined than Keynesians to believe that the free market system is inherently stable.

T F **12.** Monetarists believe that velocity is stable because the demand for money is stable.

T F **13.** If the supply of money exceeds the demand for money, then nominal income is likely to fall.

T F **14.** "Crowding out" refers to the effects of monetary policy on the level of investment demand.

T F **15.** The case for using both fiscal and monetary policy might be weakened if we knew a great deal more about how the economic system functions.

Multiple-Choice Questions

1. Which of the following is not one of the three major links in the chain of events connecting changes in the money supply to changes in aggregate demand according to the Keynesian view?

(a) Changes in the quantity of money cause changes in the rate of interest.

(b) Changes in the demand for investment cause changes in the demand for consumption goods.

(c) Changes in the rate of interest cause changes in the degree of credit rationing.

(d) Changes in the rate of interest cause changes in the demand for investment goods.

2. Which of the following circumstances tends to weaken the effectiveness of fiscal policy?

(a) A steep MEI schedule
(b) A flat MEI schedule
(c) A policy of financing the government's deficit by borrowing from the public rather than by printing money
(d) **(a)** and **(c)**
(e) **(b)** and **(c)**

3. Which of the following views do you think is *least* likely to be held by a monetarist?

(a) In the long run, the level of real output tends toward its full-employment value.
(b) The Federal Reserve should vary the rate of growth of the money supply frequently so as to stabilize aggregate demand.
(c) In the long run, changes in the money supply cause proportional changes in prices.
(d) In the short run, the money supply is the most important single variable in determining aggregate demand.

4. The income velocity of money

(a) Is defined by the equation of exchange in such a way that it must always be constant.
(b) Is believed by Keynesians to be approximately constant.
(c) Will be stable if the demand for investment goods is stable.
(d) Will, according to Keynesian thought, decrease when the Fed undertakes open market purchases of securities.

5. The effects of the 1968 tax surcharge in the United States

(a) Were generally regarded as having confirmed the strong Keynesian view of macroeconomics
(b) Did not produce any decisive evidence because both monetary and fiscal policy were restrictive at the same time
(c) Were inconsistent with the predictions of strong Keynesians
(d) Involved a smaller decline in aggregate demand than expected by monetarists

6. Which of the following is *not* a point in favor of an "eclectic" policy of using both monetary and fiscal policy?

(a) There tends to be an expansionary bias to fiscal policy and a contractionary bias to monetary policy.
(b) In reality, there is much we don't know about the detailed workings of the economic system.
(c) Temporary government programs tend to become permanent.
(d) When restrictive policies are called for, the government should try to "spread the pain."

7. If the government simultaneously undertakes an expansive monetary policy and a restrictive fiscal policy, then we can be fairly sure that

(a) The rate of interest will rise.
(b) The rate of interest will fall.
(c) The level of real output will rise.
(d) The level of real output will fall.

8. If the government wants to increase the level of real output but to leave the rate of interest unaffected, this can be accomplished by only one of the following combinations, namely

(a) Expansionary monetary policy and expansionary fiscal policy
(b) Expansionary monetary policy and restrictive fiscal policy
(c) Restrictive monetary policy and expansionary fiscal policy
(d) Restrictive monetary policy and restrictive fiscal policy

Exercises

1a. In Figure 12-1, the curves labeled *A* and *B* denote two different MEI schedules. Of the two, curve (*A*, *B*) is the one in which the demand for investment is least responsive to the rate of interest. According to curve *A*, when the rate of interest is 0.10, the demand for investment is ______, and when the rate of interest is 0.05, the demand for investment is ______. According to curve *B*, when the rate of interest is 0.10, the demand for investment is ______, and when the rate of interest is 0.05, the demand for investment is ______. If two economies, *A* and *B*, are identical in every respect except that the MEI schedule is given by curve *A* in economy *A* and by curve *B* in economy *B*, then monetary policy is stronger in economy (*A*, *B*) and fiscal policy is stronger in economy (*A*, *B*).

FIGURE 12-1

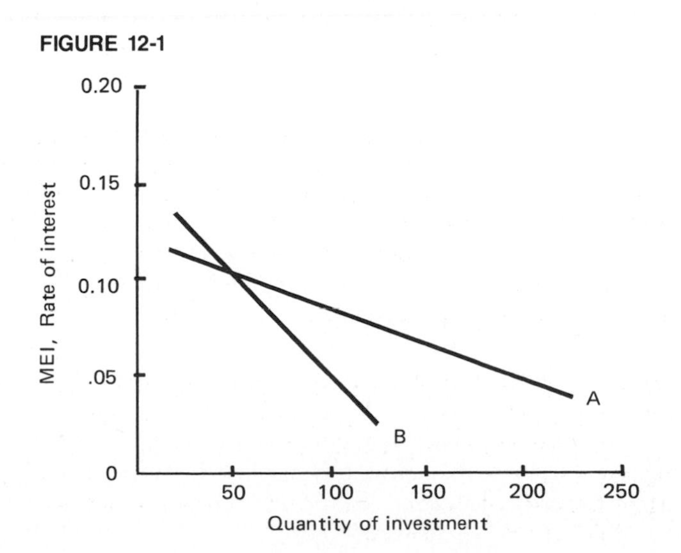

1b. Figure 12-2 shows the 45-degree line and the

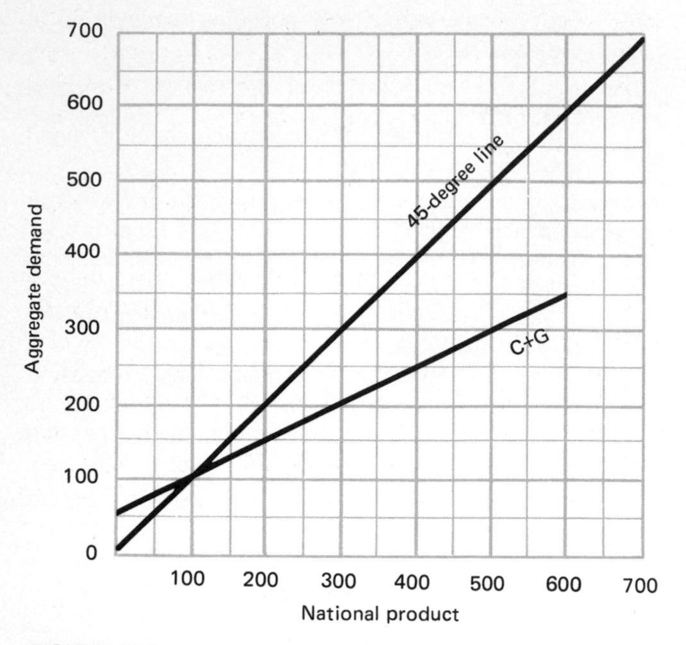

FIGURE 12-2

line indicating consumption demand plus government demand for goods and services. In this economy, "the" multiplier has a value of ______. (Refer back to Chapter 9 if you have trouble.) Draw a line indicating total aggregate demand ($C + I + G$) in economy A, assuming a rate of interest of 0.10. Do the same assuming a rate of interest of 0.05. Do the same for economy B, first assuming 0.10 then 0.05.

1c. If open market purchases by the central bank caused the rate of interest to fall from 0.10 to 0.05, then the increase in national product in economy A would be ______; in economy B, it would be ______. If government demand for goods and services rose by 150 and the rate of interest remained unaffected by this change, then national product would rise in economy A by ______ and in economy B by ______. But if that increase in government demand caused the rate of interest to rise from 0.05 to 0.10, then the overall effect of the fiscal policy measure would be to make national product rise by ______ in economy A and by ______ in economy B.

2. Table 12-1 lists the pertinent data on different investment projects, starting with the most profitable project, A, and going down to the least profitable project, D. Calculate the MEI schedule in Table 12-2. (Study footnote 1 in Chapter 12 of the text before attempting this question.)

Table 12-1

	Initial cost*	Lifetime of project	Annual* additions to sales	Annual* operating cost	Scrap* value
Project *A*	50	Infinite	20	5	—
Project *B*	25	17 years	6	1	25
Project *C*	15	2 years	7	1	5.55
Project *D*	10	1 year	8	4.5	7

*These data are all expressed as millions of dollars.

Table 12-2

Marginal efficiency of investment (percent per annum)	Quantity of investment (millions of dollars)
______	50
______	75
______	90
______	100

Essay Questions

1. Recall the reasons given in the text why monetary policy may have asymmetrical effects. Can you think of a reason why the policy of changing income taxes to affect aggregate demand may also have asymmetrical effects?

2. Evaluate the following statement: "The equation of exchange is completely useless because it is a mere tautology."

3. In the text, it was argued that the existence of credit rationing might make monetary policy more powerful than it would be without credit rationing. Can you think of any reasons why the existence of credit rationing might similarly alter the effectiveness of fiscal policy?

4. See how many different groups you can identify that would gain more than the average when the government undertakes an expansive fiscal policy. Which groups would gain the least or perhaps even lose? Do the same thing for an expansive monetary policy.

5. Most economists try to keep their political beliefs out of scientific discussions. But this is often difficult when it comes to policy questions. In fact, it is often easy to predict an economist's political beliefs by reading his or her analysis of economic policy. If you were to read two articles on economic policy, one advocating Keynesian policies and the other advocating monetarist policies, which author would you think the more likely to hold the view that the government is interfering too much in private economic affairs? Why?

6. Recall the difficulties standing in the way of getting a precise measure of the responsiveness of the demand for investment goods to changes in the rate of interest. Can you think of similar reasons why it might be difficult to measure the responsiveness of the demand for money to changes in the rate of interest? How would you go about trying to identify this degree of responsiveness?

7. Why might a monetarist be more likely than a Keynesian to believe that the MEI schedule is relatively flat?

8. Why might a monetarist be more likely than a Keynesian to believe that the marginal propensity to consume was relatively small?

***9.** The opposite of a liquidity trap (Box 12-1) would be a situation in which the rate of interest had no effect at all upon the demand for money. Would such a situation be more compatible with monetarist or Keynesian theory? Why?

Answers

True-False Questions: 1 F 2 T 3 T 4 F 5 T 6 T 7 F 8 T 9 T 10 F 11 T 12 T 13 F 14 F 15 T
Multiple-Choice Questions: 1 c 2 e 3 b 4 d 5 c 6 a 7 b 8 a
Exercises:
1a. *B*, 50, 200, 50, 100, *A*, *B*.
1b. 2.
1c. 300, 100, 300, 300, 0, 200.

FIGURE 12-2 completed:

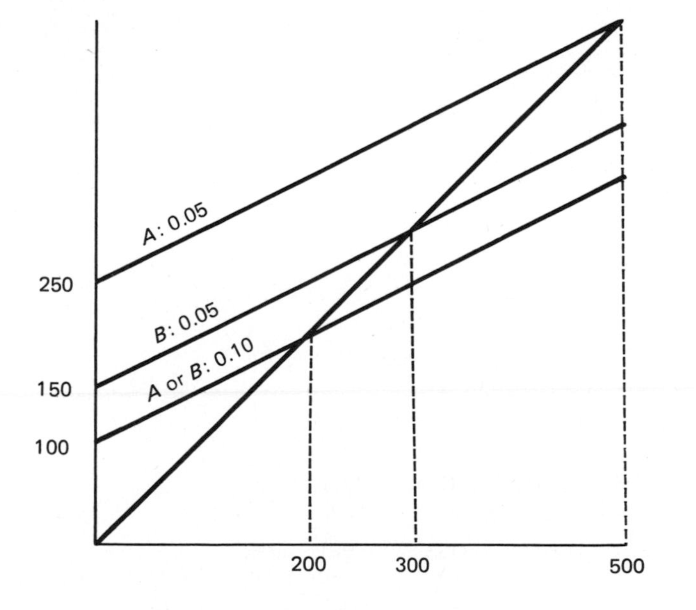

2. Table 12-2

Marginal efficiency of investment (percent per annum)	Quantity of investment (millions of dollars)
30%	50
20%	75
10%	90
5%	100

chapter 13
Aggregate Supply: *How Can Inflation and Unemployment Coexist?*

Learning Objectives

After you have studied this chapter in the textbook and the study guide, you should be able to

State two reasons why the Kennedy-Johnson wage-price guideposts broke down

Explain three arguments against the use of guideposts and other forms of wage-price control

Explain why, according to cost-push theories, the Phillips curve has shifted up since the late '60s.

Explain why, according to the accelerationist theory, the Phillips curve has shifted up since the '60s

List two reasons why cost-push theories are similar to the Phelps-Friedman theory and two reasons why they are different

State the essential difference between the Phelps-Friedman theory and the theory of Eckstein and Brinner

Show in a Phillips-curve diagram (like Figure 13-12 in the text) how a stable growth of aggregate demand promotes a low average rate of unemployment

Explain the arguments both for and against two popular proposals to ease the transition to a lower rate of inflation

List three kinds of proposals that have been suggested to reduce the natural rate of unemployment

CHAPTER HIGHLIGHTS

This chapter deals with the problems of inflation and unemployment. It covers the following topics: (1) the Phillips curve, (2) wage-price guideposts, (3) cost-push theories of inflation, (4) accelerationist theories of inflation, and (5) major problems confronting economic policy in the 1980s.

The Phillips Curve

The Keynesian macroeconomics of Part II of the text assumed an L-shaped aggregate supply curve (recall Figure 8-1). According to this view, there can be large-scale unemployment (when aggregate demand is low) or inflation (when aggregate demand is high), but not both. However, the facts do not fit this simple L-shaped function. Indeed, the observations for the past three decades don't seem to fit any simple pattern (Figure 13-3). They do, however, suggest two questions: (1) What is the nature of the "Phillips curve" traced out by the data for the 1960s? and (2) Why for periods during the 1970s, did high unemployment exist together with a rapid rate of inflation?

Wage-Price Guideposts

The Phillips curve suggested that an expansive aggregate demand policy aimed at reducing the rate of unemployment would also cause inflation. In order to prevent premature inflation as the economy was expanded toward full employment, the Kennedy-Johnson administration introduced wage-price guideposts. Specifically, they proposed that (1) prices should not be raised and (2) money wages should not rise by more than the increase in labor productivity in the economy as a whole, estimated in the early '60s to be 3.2 percent per annum.

These guideposts eventually broke down for at least two reasons: First, exceptions had to be made. In particular, not all prices could be kept constant because productivity lagged in some industries. Thus the guideposts were not firmly enforced. Second, after inflation started growing, it was difficult to persuade workers to accept wage increases within the guideposts when that would result in little or no increase in their real wages.

Many argue that guideposts and wage-price controls should not be used, for the following reasons:

1. The effectiveness of guideposts may be questioned. In particular, they may put a floor rather than a ceiling to wage increases, because any self-respecting union will aim to get at least as much as the guideposts allow. Similarly, it is tempting for governments to adopt expansive policies in the false hope that the controls will prevent inflation.

2. If the guideposts are effective, they will create excess demands (shortages) of particular goods, thus reducing the efficiency of the economy.

3. Guideposts infringe upon personal freedom.

Cost-Push Theories

The easiest way to distinguish between demand-pull and cost-push inflation is that an increase in demand-pull inflation is a movement upward to the left along a given Phillips curve, whereas cost-push inflation involves an upward shift of the Phillips curve. As Figure 13-4 in the text illustrates, the Phillips curve has shifted upward since the late '60s. This has given support to cost-push theories, most of which emphasize the dramatic increase in world oil prices in 1973–74. According to these theories, the increase in oil prices raised costs of manufacturing, which firms passed on to consumers in the form of higher prices. Faced with a higher cost of living, labor unions bargained for higher wages, which pushed prices up further.

Accelerationist Theories

The accelerationist theory of Friedman and Phelps offers a different explanation for this upward shift. It makes the bold claim that the Phillips curve is not even a stable relationship in the long run. There are two key assumptions to this theory. The first is that workers do not suffer from money illusion. That is, they bargain for real wages, not money wages. At "equilibrium" (that is, at the "natural rate" of unemployment), workers will bargain for real wage increases equal to the increase in labor productivity. At lower rates of unemployment, they will insist on higher increases. And at higher rates of unemployment, they will settle for smaller increases. This means that—in the short run—the actual rate of unemployment can be reduced below the "natural" rate, but only if workers underestimate the rate of inflation. For example, suppose the rate of growth of productivity is 3 percent and workers expect no inflation. Then, if unemployment is below the natural rate, workers will insist on more than 3 percent increases in money wages. They will bargain, say, for 4 percent increases, expecting also to get a 4 percent increase in *real* wage (since they expect no inflation). But if wages rise by 4 percent while productivity rises by only 3 percent, then prices will in fact rise at 1 percent (4 percent money wage increase minus 3 percent productivity growth). This means that the workers' expectations were *mistaken*. They expected no inflation but actually experienced 1 percent inflation. Thus, as long as unemployment is below its natural rate, inflation will be higher than expected.

This brings us to the second key assumption of the Phelps-Friedman theory, which is that workers' expectations may be mistaken in the short run but not in the long run. Once workers realize that prices are rising at 1 percent, they will insist on 5 percent increases in money wages, still hoping for 4 percent increases in real wages. Thus the rate of inflation will rise even if the rate of unemployment remains unchanged. Why? Because as workers adjust their expectations to the experience of higher inflation, the Phillips curve is caused to shift upward.

The most important implication of the Phelps-Friedman theory is that the long-run Phillips curve is vertical at the natural rate of unemployment, for, as we have seen, inflation will continue to increase at any rate of unemployment below the natural rate. Likewise, any rate above the natural rate will generate ever-accelerating *de*flation. But *at* the natural rate of unemployment, the rate of inflation will be constant. Workers' expectations will be confirmed and inflation will neither accelerate nor decelerate.

The accelerationist theory is similar to the cost-push theory because both attempt to explain the upward shift in the Phillips curve and both involve a similar wage-price spiral. However, they are different because (1) the cost-push theory stresses the role of the market power of big unions and corporations, whereas the accelerationist theory stresses the lagged response of workers' expectations, and (2) incomes policies help to control inflation by restraining market power according to cost-push theory but, according to accelerationist theory, they attack the symptoms rather than the causes of inflation.

The theory of Eckstein and Brinner is similar in some respects to the Phelps-Friedman theory. The Eckstein-Brinner theory maintains that the long-run Phillips curve is vertical for rates of inflation above 2 or 3 percent but negatively sloped for lower rates. The key to this theory is the assumption of downward wage rigidity. At any one time, some workers' wages will be falling behind those of others. Such changes in relative wages are an important part of the market mechanism in an ever-changing economy. At a high rate of inflation (2 or 3 percent or more), this can happen without anyone's money wage having to fall. Workers in industry *A* may find their wages rising at 8 percent, while wages in industry *B* are rising at 3 percent. The *B* workers are falling behind, but their money wages are still rising. At a low rate of inflation, however, this change in relative wages might require, for example, that the wages of *A* workers rise at 2 percent and the wages of B workers *fall* by 3 percent. If the *B* workers resist any decline in their nominal wages, then unemployment will result in their industry.

Major Policy Problems of the 1980s

The first major problem is how to maintain a stable aggregate demand. Fluctuations in aggregate demand increase the average rate of unemployment. This is because when inflation rises, the resulting decrease in unemployment is less than the increase in unemployment that results from an equal-sized fall in the rate of inflation (Figure 13-12). Thus, maintaining a *stable* aggregate demand is important for maintaining a low average rate of unemployment.

The second problem is how to ease the transition to a lower rate of inflation. If tight aggregate demand policies are used to combat inflation, the economy will move downward to the right along the short-run Phillips curve, thus causing an increase in unemployment. Thus the problem is how to combat inflation without causing unemployment. Two proposals have been suggested to deal with this problem. (1) Some advocate wage-price controls and guidelines. For example, Okun, Wallich, and Weintraub have put forth tax-based incomes policy (*TIP*) proposals. These programs would use the tax system to reward firms that successfully resist wage increases by their employees or to punish those that don't. Such proposals have rekindled the controversy of the 1960s—in particular the debate over the effectiveness of controls. (2) Indexation of wages and other contracts has been proposed. If wages were indexed, then, as inflation was reduced, wages would come down automatically rather than having to wait for contracts to expire. Against indexation, it has been argued that if inflation got going again, it would be reinforced by the automatic upward increase in indexed wages.

The third major policy problem is how to reduce the natural rate of unemployment. Since the early '60s, the natural rate seems to have increased from about 4 percent to perhaps as much as 6 percent because of the increased proportion of teenagers (who have higher-than-average unemployment rates) in the labor force and the increased generosity of unemployment insurance benefits, which reduce the pressures on the unemployed to take a job. Three kinds of proposals have been suggested: (1) reduced discrimination against blacks and others in order to reduce their unemployment rates, (2) training programs to reduce structural unemployment, and (3) using the government as employer of last resort, as suggested in the 1976 version of the Humphrey-Hawkins bill. Opponents of the employment-of-last-resort idea argue, first, that the cost may be extremely high and, second, that it is difficult to design incentives for people to move out of last-resort employment and into the private sector.

IMPORTANT TERMS

Full Employment A situation in which the only unemployment that exists is the kind that cannot be permanently eliminated by an increase in aggregate demand. Full employment was estimated to occur at about 4 percent unemployment in the 1960s, but the corresponding figure may be as high as 6 percent today.

Natural rate of unemployment The "equilibrium" rate of unemployment. The term "natural rate" is used by those who believe that the long-run Phillips curve is vertical.

Frictional unemployment Unemployment caused by workers changing jobs and by normal delays in finding jobs.

Structural unemployment Unemployment resulting from such things as changes in the location of industry or in the composition of output.

Phillips curve A downward-sloping relationship between the rate of unemployment and the rate of inflation.

Stagflation A situation of high unemployment and rapid inflation.

Trade-off A choice between two conflicting goals, such as high employment and low inflation.

Premature inflation The inflation that occurs before the economy reaches the rate of unemployment desired by the government.

MDTA The Manpower Development and Training Act of 1962, which provided on-the-job and other training for the unemployed, for young people, and for older workers with inadequate or obsolete skills.

Labor productivity The average amount produced by a worker. It is calculated by dividing real output by the number of workers employed.

Real wage The quantity of goods and services which the wage will buy. It is measured by adjusting the money wage for inflation. For example, if the money wage rises by 5 percent while prices rise by 2 percent, then the real wage has increased by 3 percent.

Wage-price guideposts Rules set up by the government to limit increases in wages and prices.

Jawboning The attempt to enforce wage-price guideposts (or other proposals) by official persuasion or pressure.

Incomes policy A policy aimed at limiting inflation by limiting increases in money wages and in other types of income.

Demand-pull inflation The inflation that occurs when demand is high and eager buyers bid up the prices of goods and services.

Cost-push inflation The inflation that occurs when wages and other costs rise and these costs are passed along to consumers in the form of higher prices. Also known sometimes as *market power* inflation.

Wage-price spiral The "vicious circle" in which higher wages are justified on the grounds that prices have risen and higher prices are justified on the grounds that higher wages are being paid.

Money illusion People have money illusion if their behavior changes in the event of a proportionate change in prices and in money income (and in the money value of assets).

Long-run Phillips curve The curve (or line) traced out by the possible points of long-run equilibrium; that is, the points where people have adjusted completely to the prevailing rate of inflation.

TIP Tax-based incomes policy. An incomes policy backed up by tax credits to firms that are successful in holding the line on wages and/or by tax penalties on those who exceed the guidelines.

Wage indexation The practice of building automatic cost-of-living adjustments into labor market contracts. Thus, an indexed contract would include an *escalator clause* that might say, for example, that—in addition to a basic agreed-upon increase in wages—the wage rate will increase by an extra amount every month equal to the rate of increase in the consumer price index.

Employer of last resort A government is an employer of last resort if it offers jobs to all those who are unable to find work in the private sector of the economy.

True-False Questions

T F **1.** The Keynesian aggregate supply curve implies an L-shaped Phillips curve.

T F **2.** There is structural unemployment even when the rate of unemployment is at its natural level.

T F **3.** During the 1960s, the government estimated the natural rate of unemployment to be about 6 percent.

T F **4.** In the decade between 1966 and 1975, the Phillips curve appears to have shifted down.

T F **5.** The phenomenon of stagflation can be explained only by cost-push theories of inflation.

T F **6.** There is general agreement among economists that the short-run Phillips curve is less steep than the long-run Phillips curve.

T F **7.** Training programs (like the MDTA and CETA) are aimed at moving to a different point on the Phillips curve.

T F **8.** The wage-price guideposts of the Kennedy-Johnson administration stated that the rate of change of money wages should be equal to that of labor productivity in the economy as a whole.

T F **9.** One of the problems with price controls is that they tend to produce surpluses in markets where the controls are effective.

T F **10.** If money wages rise by 5 percent while prices rise by 2 percent, then the real wage has increased by 3 percent.

T F **11.** The TIP proposal of Okun is meant to work by stimulating aggregate demand.

T F **12.** Wage-price controls are intended to eliminate black markets.

T F 13. Cost-push inflation tends to shift the Phillips curve up rather than to cause a movement upward along a given Phillips curve.

T F 14. Advocates of cost-push theories are more likely than advocates of the accelerationist theory to believe that market power is important in the inflationary process.

T F 15. Accelerationists believe that there is only one rate of inflation consistent with equilibrium in the long run.

T F 16. The theory of Eckstein and Brinner implies the same long-run Phillips curve as does that of Phelps and Friedman.

T F 17. If people have money illusion, then the Phelps-Friedman argument does not apply.

T F 18. According to the accelerationist theory, we cannot eliminate inflation and have unemployment at its natural rate until the expectations of inflation have been eliminated.

T F 19. For a given average rate of inflation, the higher the variability in inflation, the lower the average rate of unemployment.

T F 20. Wage indexation makes the Phillips curve steeper in the short run.

T F 21. One of the reasons commonly proposed for explaining the rightward shift in the natural rate of unemployment in recent years is the increasing proportion of teenagers in the work force.

Multiple-Choice Questions

1. The Phillips curve is
- **(a)** L-shaped according to the accelerationist theory
- **(b)** Vertical in the long run according to cost-push theory
- **(c)** Vertical in the short run according to accelerationist theory
- **(d)** None of the above

2. Which of the following kinds of unemployment does not exist when the rate of unemployment equals its natural rate?
- **(a)** Frictional
- **(b)** Aggregate demand
- **(c)** Structural
- **(d)** All of the above

3. Since the 1960s
- **(a)** The short-run Phillips curve appears to have shifted up.
- **(b)** The long-run Phillips curve appears to have shifted to the left.
- **(c)** The long-run Phillips curve appears to have shifted to the right.
- **(d)** **(a)** and **(b)**.
- **(e)** **(a)** and **(c)**.

4. Which of the following events is least likely to shift the short-run Phillips curve?
- **(a)** An increase in aggregate demand which did not affect workers' expectations of inflation
- **(b)** A shift in workers' expectations of inflation
- **(c)** A decision by big unions to take a harder bargaining position
- **(d)** A successful labor-force retraining program

5. Which of the following was a policy objective throughout most of the Kennedy-Johnson administration?
- **(a)** To move to the right of the Phillips curve by using wage-price guideposts
- **(b)** To use monetary policy in order to reduce inflation
- **(c)** To stimulate aggregate demand through monetary and fiscal policies
- **(d)** **(a)** and **(b)**
- **(e)** **(a)** and **(c)**

6. Which of the following is an assumption of the accelerationist theory?
- **(a)** People do not suffer from money illusion.
- **(b)** In the long run, people's expectations will adapt to experience.
- **(c)** There is downward rigidity of nominal wages.
- **(d)** **(a)** and **(b)**.
- **(e)** All of the above.

7. Which of the following most accurately describes the Eckstein-Brinner theory of inflation?
- **(a)** The long-run Phillips curve is vertical.
- **(b)** The short-run Phillips curve is vertical.
- **(c)** The long-run Phillips curve is vertical above an inflation rate of 2 or 3 percent.
- **(d)** The short-run Phillips curve is vertical above a rate of inflation of 2 or 3 percent.

8. One of the problems that has been pointed out with the proposal for wage indexation is that it would cause wages to
- **(a)** Fall too rapidly when inflation was being eliminated
- **(b)** Rise too rapidly when inflation got started
- **(c)** Rise too slowly when inflation got started
- **(d)** Fall too slowly when inflation was being eliminated

9. Which of the following would be least likely to reduce the natural rate of unemployment?
- **(a)** Policies that reduce the amount of discrimination against black workers
- **(b)** Policies that would increase the level of aggregate demand
- **(c)** A reduction in the generosity of unemployment insurance benefits
- **(d)** A reduction in the proportion of teenagers in the labor force

Exercises

1. Figure 13-1 represents the Phillips curve for a year (year one) when the expected rate of inflation was zero. The natural rate of unemployment is ______ percent, at which rate, according to this Phillips curve, the rate of inflation would be ______ percent. When the rate of unemployment is 3 percent, the rate of inflation would be (more, less) than the expected rate of inflation by ______ percent. Suppose that during year two the expected rate of inflation was 2 percent. Draw the Phillips curve for year two in the same diagram. In year two, if the rate of unemployment is still 3 percent, then the rate of inflation will be ______ percent.

If, on the other hand, inflation is kept constant at 3 percent, the rate of unemployment will be ____ percent. If the rate of inflation is kept at 3 percent, then, according to the accelerationist theory, the expected rate of inflation will eventually be ______ percent and the rate of unemployment will eventually be ______ percent. According to the accelerationist theory, if aggregate demand policies are aimed at keeping the rate of unemployment at 3 percent, the rate of inflation will ______________________________.

2. Figure 13-2 depicts a market for wheat. Suppose that the market is perfectly competitive and that, because of expansionary fiscal and monetary policies, the demand for wheat shifts up from D to D'.

Suppose that a rise in the prices of all other commodities and factors of production increases costs and therefore shifts the supply curve up from S to S'. If the price of wheat is allowed to rise, it will go from

FIGURE 13-1

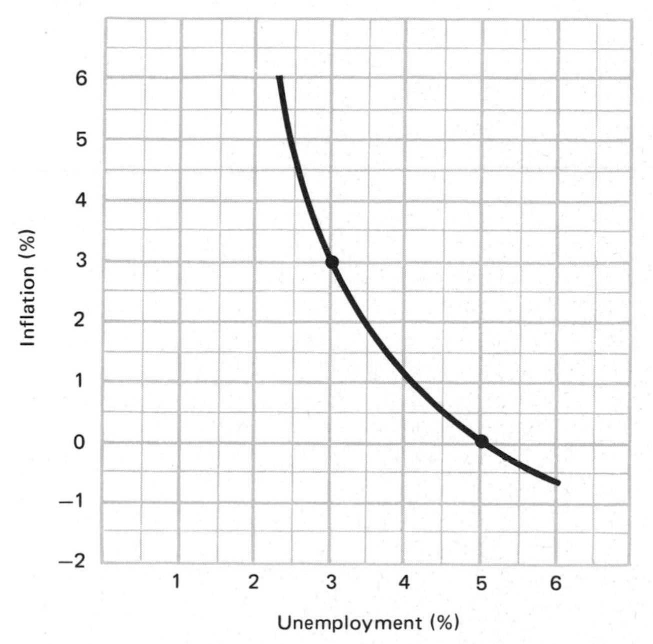

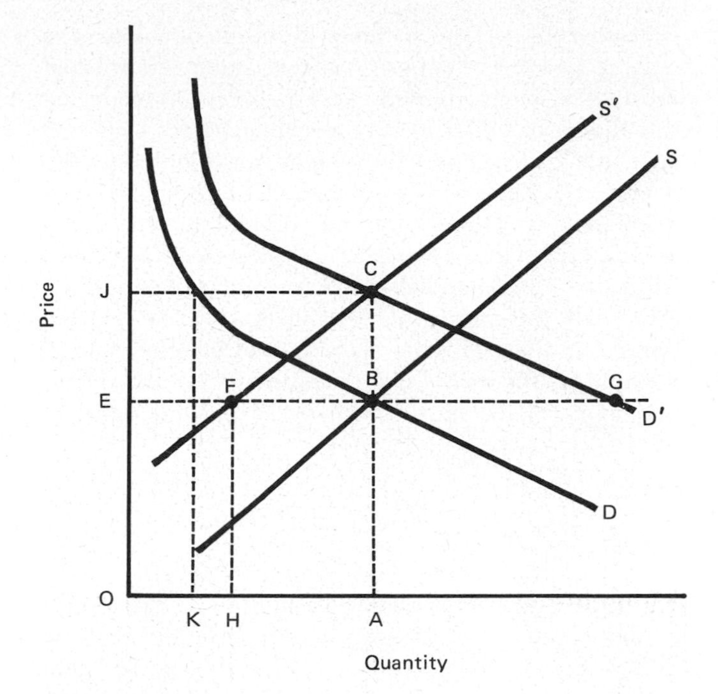

FIGURE 13-2

______ to ______, and the quantity of output will be ______. Now suppose that the government imposes price controls to prevent the price from rising in this market (but not in others), so that the supply and demand curves shift but the price stays the same. There will be an excess (supply, demand) equal to ______, and the actual quantity of output will (increase, decrease) until it equals ______.

3. In Figure 13-3 below, the curve labeled P_1 is a short-run Phillips curve of the usual shape, based on an expected rate of inflation of 5 percent. According to this curve, if inflation equals 5 percent every year, then the rate of unemployment will equal ______ per-

FIGURE 13-3

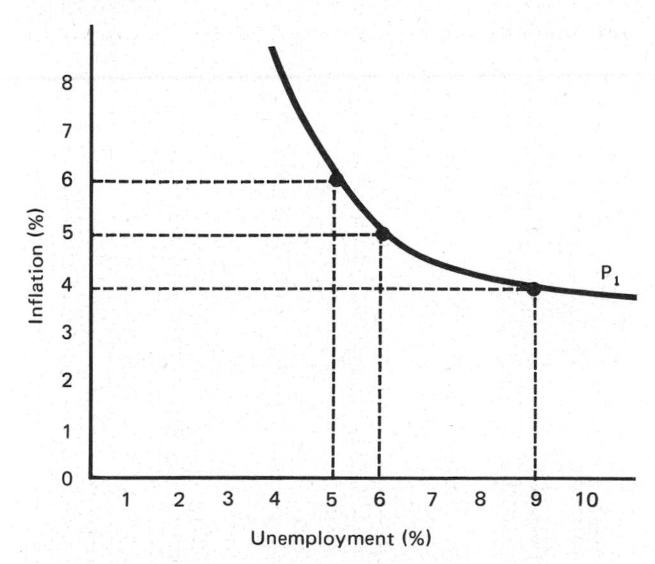

cent every year. The natural rate of unemployment is ______ percent. Suppose that the rate of expected inflation remains constant at 5 percent. Then if the actual rate of inflation increases temporarily to 6 percent, the rate of unemployment will (increase, decrease) to ______ percent; if the actual rate of inflation decreases to 4 percent, the rate of unemployment will (increase, decrease) to ______. Therefore if actual inflation is 6 percent half the time and 4 percent the other half, the average rate of inflation will be (higher, lower, no different) than if the rate of inflation were 5 percent all the time, but the average rate of unemployment will be (more, less) by an amount equal to ______ percent.

Essay Questions

1. Explain why, according to the accelerationist argument, the rate of unemployment cannot be maintained permanently *above* its natural rate by tight aggregate demand policies.

2. Most economists agree that the long-run Phillips curve is steeper than the short-run Phillips curve. It is also commonly accepted that politicians, when deciding upon aggregate demand policies, care more about what will happen between now and the next election than in the more distant future. Putting these two ideas together, show why politicians may adopt expansive policies (aimed at moving to the left, up the Phillips curve) even when they realize that voters dislike inflation.

3. If you study Figure 13-4 in the text, you will notice that there appear to be loops in the Phillips curve. That is, the time path traced out in this diagram from the early '50s to the present time seems to be following a clockwise spiral upward and to the right. The text describes why an upward shift in the Phillips curve may occur. Can you think of any reason why these loops might exist? (Hint: This question is related to question 2.)

4. According to the short-run Phillips curve, if unemployment rises, inflation should fall. But in many years unemployment and inflation *both* rise. How would an accelerationist explain this? How would a cost-push theorist explain it?

5. The accelerationist argument stresses the distinction between the long-run Phillips curve and the short-run Phillips curve. Explain how wage indexation might make these two curves more similar.

Answers

True-False Questions: 1 T 2 T 3 F 4 F 5 F 6 T 7 F 8 T 9 F 10 T 11 F 12 F 13 T 14 T 15 F 16 F 17 T 18 T 19 F 20 T 21 T

Multiple-Choice Questions: 1 d 2 b 3 e 4 a 5 c 6 d 7 c 8 b 9 b

Exercises:

1. 5, zero, more, 3, 5, 4, 3, 5, become more and more rapid.

FIGURE 13-1 completed.

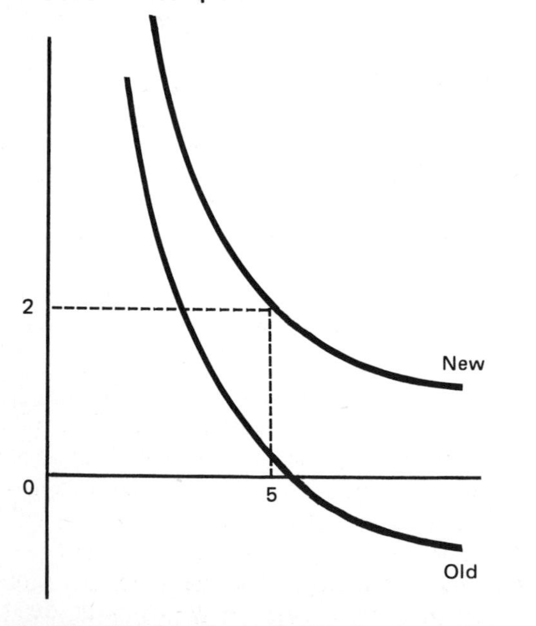

2. *OE*, *OJ*, *OA*, demand, *FG*, decrease, *OH*.
3. 6, 6, decrease, 5, increase, 9, no different, more, 1.

chapter 14
Why is the Economy Unstable

Learning Objectives

After you have studied this chapter in the textbook and the study guide, you should be able to

Identify the four phases of the business cycle
Explain why investment demand tends to fluctuate more than consumption demand
Explain how a decline in sales affects a firm's investment, describing the three steps involved
State the reason why a decline in investment demand contains the seeds of a recovery
Explain how the size of the MPC affects economic stability
State two reasons why international developments may cause instability in the domestic economy
Explain how the leakage of demand into imports may help to stabilize the economy
Explain why state and local governments have neither the incentive nor the ability of the federal government to engage in countercyclical fiscal policies
State three reasons why the federal government's monetary and fiscal policies may be procyclical

CHAPTER HIGHLIGHTS

This chapter addresses the question of why business fluctuations continue to occur in spite of the management of aggregate demand with fiscal and monetary policies. As you might guess, there is no single answer to this question; there are a number of reasons for instability.

The business cycle is divided into four phases: recession, trough, expansion, and peak. This cycle is not regular. No two cycles are of exactly the same length, nature, or severity; often it is hard to tell, for example, exactly when a recession has ended.

This chapter discusses the cause of the cycle in terms of the four components of aggregate demand: (1) investment, (2) consumption, (3) net exports, and (4) government spending. It also addresses the question of why fiscal and monetary policies have not been more successful in combating instability.

Investment

The percentage changes in investment over the cycle are usually much larger than in any other component. Thus, much of business cycle theory has been aimed at explaining the fluctuations in investment. The basic principle involved is the accelerator principle. There are five major implications that follow from this principle:

1. The percentage changes in investment tend to be much larger than the percentage changes in consumption. (We already know this as a fact; the accelerator principle offers an explanation of it.)

2. Net investment depends upon the rate of change of consumption, not upon the level of consumption.

3. A reduction in the *rate of growth* of consumption can cause a *decline* in investment. As a consequence, an unsustainably rapid expansion may lead to a recession.

4. The level of investment can collapse following even a small reduction in consumption.

5. In order for investment to recover from a decline, the level of consumption does not have to stop falling; it only has to fall at a slower rate than before. (Thus, a decline in economic activity contains the seeds of a recovery.)

All these five points are illustrated by Table 14-1 in the text. (It may help to work through the other examples in Problem 14-3 in the text and in Exercise 1 below.)

The accelerator principle applies not only to machinery investment but also to investment in buildings and inventories. However, the rigid relationship between capital and sales shown in the basic accelerator (Table 14-1 in the text) is an oversimplification. In fact, there is no rigid relationship between sales and capital in the form of buildings, equipment, and inventories. This is because firms want their capital to vary with their *long-run* sales, not with every little rise or fall in their weekly or monthly sales. As a consequence, a decline in sales affects a firm's investment in three steps:

1. At first, there is little or no effect on production. For a period, the firm is likely to absorb a decline in sales by building up inventories (unsold goods) rather than by changing its production plans for what may turn out to be a temporary sales decline.

2. If the decline persists for some weeks, the firm will begin cutting back production to reduce its inventories, and eventually it will also reduce its new orders for machinery.

3. Finally, as the decline in sales slows down, the firm will increase its new orders for machinery.

Three general conclusions may be drawn from this discussion:

1. The accelerator principle will probably not turn a temporary drop in consumption into a recession.

2. If a drop in consumption is more than temporary, the accelerator principle will add momentum to the downward movement in aggregate demand.

3. This downward movement cannot persist forever, because the rate of decline of consumption will eventually slow down. (After all, consumption does not fall continuously toward zero.)

Consumption

Three points are to be noted about consumption:

1. The demand for consumer durables may be similar to the demand for investment goods. (After all, both are long-lived assets that are bought with a view to the long-term benefits that they provide.)

2. The higher the marginal propensity to consume, the larger will be the multiplier, and therefore the less stable will the economy tend to be.

3. However, the fact that the MPC is less than one contributes to stability, in the sense that a rise in income will generate extra leakages (saving) that dampen the rise.

Net Exports

International transactions can be a source of instability for two reasons: (1) Big changes in international prices (such as the quadrupling of oil prices in 1973–1974) can have effects on the United States economy that are large and difficult to predict. (2) Also, recessions or expansions in other countries can cause recessions and expansions in the United States. For example, as Western Europe goes into an expansion, its demand for our exports will increase, encouraging production to the United States.

But foreign trade can also contribute to stability. As our income rises, we tend to import more, and imports constitute a leakage from the circular flow of spending. In other words, the relationship between income and import demand acts as an automatic stabilizer, reducing the size of the multiplier.

Government Expenditures

State and local governments have neither the incentive nor the ability to carry out significant countercyclical fiscal policies. If they try to spend more to stimulate the economy during a recession, much of the additional spending will leak out into the rest of the national economy. (That is, additional goods will be bought from other states or localities.) Also, state and local governments may have trouble borrowing funds to finance expansive policies during a recession. Indeed, spending by state and local governments may exert a *de*stabilizing influence on the economy, because their financial problems may cause them to cut their spending during recessions.

At the federal level, we should distinguish between automatic and discretionary stabilization. As noted in Chapter 9, automatic stabilizers may be quite powerful. In addition, our discussion in Chapter 9 suggested that discretionary policy should ideally be stabilizing (that is, countercyclical). But fiscal and monetary policies have sometimes been procyclical. Three broad reasons have been suggested for this:

1. There are lags in the operation of policy—a recognition lag, an action lag, and an impact lag—and these lags make it difficult to design policies for the conditions which will exist when they have their effects. Thus, expansive policies aimed at combating a recession may not take hold until the recovery is well advanced, when further stimulus is no longer appropriate.

2. The policy makers' other objectives may conflict with the objective of stabilizing the economy. Those who support the theory of the political business cycle believe that expansions may be deliberately engineered by politicians just before elections in hopes that the electorate will vote for the incumbents.

3. The Fed may have contributed to instability by trying to stabilize the rate of interest. If the economy moves into a recession because of a drop in business investment demand, the demand for loans will decrease and the rate of interest will begin to fall. If the Fed is trying to stabilize interest rates, it will react by undertaking open market sales to keep interest rates up. But this means a decline in the rate of monetary growth, which will contribute even further to the developing recession. Some economists believe that the unwillingness of the Fed to adjust its interest-rate targets rapidly enough in 1974 contributed to the recession. If the Fed had allowed interest rates to fall more rapidly and had paid more attention to the rate of growth of the money supply, this recession would probably have been less severe.

IMPORTANT TERMS

Business cycle The alternating rise and fall in economic activity.

National Bureau of Economic Research (NBER) A private research organization which has measured and studied the business cycle.

Recession The downward phase of the business cycle. A recession has occurred if the seasonally adjusted real gross national product has declined for two successive quarters.

Trough The low point of a business cycle, occurring at the end of the recession phase.

Expansion The upward phase of the business cycle, occurring after the trough.

Peak The high point of the business cycle, occurring after an expansion and before the succeeding recession.

Seasonal adjustment Some economic variables have regular seasonal fluctuations. The data on such a variable are seasonally adjusted when these regular seasonal fluctuations have been removed from the data. Thus, seasonally adjusted data reflect the effects of all influences other than the regular seasonal effects. (See Box 14-1 in the text.)

Accelerator principle The principle that the *level* of net investment demand depends upon the *rate of change* of consumption demand.

Inventory recession A recession is an inventory recession if it is caused largely by a decline in inventory investment.

Capital-output ratio The value of a firm's capital divided by its output during a given period.

Consumer durable Any consumption good that can normally be expected to last for over a year.

Marginal propensity to import The change in imports as a fraction of a change in national product.

Countercyclical policy Government policy that has tended to stabilize economic activity. The opposite to this is procyclical policy.

Recognition lag The interval between the time when economic conditions change and the time when the need to take corrective action is recognized.

Action lag The interval between the time when the need for policy action is recognized and the time when such action is actually taken.

Impact lag The interval between the time when a policy action is taken and the time when the major effects of the policy actually occur.

Political business cycle A business cycle that is caused by changes in policies aimed at increasing the chances of politicians being reelected.

Treasury–Federal Reserve Accord of 1951 The agreement whereby the Fed was released from its commitment to hold down the rate of interest on government bonds.

True-False Questions

T F 1. Business cycles occur regularly every 7 years.

T F 2. A recession is said to have occurred if the seasonally adjusted real gross national product declines for two consecutive quarters.

T F 3. The accelerator principle involves the effect of net exports on economic stability.

T F 4. According to the accelerator principle, even if the rate of decline of sales slows up, the level of investment will continue to fall.

T F 5. Because of the lags involved in investment decisions, even brief declines in aggregate demand are amplified by the accelerator principle.

T F 6. A large marginal propensity to import tends to promote economic stability.

T F 7. State and local governments have neither the incentive nor the ability of the federal government to engage in countercyclical fiscal policies.

T F 8. The automatic stabilizers discussed in Chapter 9 reduce the magnitude of economic fluctuations.

T F 9. The "action lag" refers to the delay in the effect of the accelerator principle.

T F 10. The lags in the effect of policy would probably create less of a problem for economic stability if we knew more about how the economic system works.

T F 11. One reason why the Fed ran into criticism in connection with the 1974–1975 recession is that it was attempting to stabilize the rate of growth of the money supply rather than the rate of interest.

Multiple-Choice Questions

1. Which of the following is not one of the four phases of the business cycle?

(a) Expansion
(b) Recession
(c) Peak
(d) Inflation

2. Which of the following years is commonly regarded as a peak associated with the most violent business cycle in United States History?

(a) 1921
(b) 1929
(c) 1933
(d) 1975

3. According to accelerator principle,

(a) The rate of change of investment depends upon the rate of change of consumption.
(b) The rate of change of investment depends upon the level of consumption.
(c) The level of investment depends upon the rate of change of consumption.
(d) The level of investment depends upon the level of consumption.

4. Suppose that a firm's sales go from 100 to 120 in the first year and from 120 to 130 in the second year. Then, according to the accelerator principle, the firm's net investment will

(a) Increase in both years
(b) Increase in year two but not necessarily in year one
(c) Increase in year one but not necessarily in year two
(d) Decrease in year two

5. Which of the following is true about the historical record in the United States?

(a) Investment is almost always the largest component of aggregate demand.
(b) Consumption is almost always the largest component of aggregate demand.
(c) Of all components of aggregate demand, consumption usually has the largest percentage fluctuations.
(d) **(a)** and **(c)**.
(e) **(b)** and **(c)**.

6. Which statement does *not* follow from our discussion of the accelerator principle?

(a) The accelerator principle offers a reason why downward movements in aggregate demand are eventually reversed.
(b) Firms are more likely to reduce investment demand if they believe the decline in demand for their output is permanent than if they believe it is temporary.
(c) Long-lived declines in aggregate demand tend to be amplified because of the accelerator principle.
(d) The accelerator principle shows that even when a firm's sales start falling faster, its investment demand may increase.

7. The lag that occurs in the operation of fiscal policy because Congress takes time to approve changes in tax laws is

(a) An action lag
(b) A recognition lag
(c) An impact lag
(d) All of the above

8. "The political business cycle" refers to

(a) The cycle in economic activity resulting from policies aimed at getting politicians reelected
(b) The shifting trend of opinion for or against big business
(c) The cycle in the fortunes of political parties that is due to economic events beyond anyone's control
(d) The cycle in the fortunes of political parties that is deliberately engineered by big-business interests

Exercises

1. Suppose that a manufacturer of tennis balls wants 5 machines for every 100,000 balls sold in a year. Suppose that the manufacturer starts off at the beginning of year one with 50 machines and that it replaces 10 machines every year no matter how many machines it has that year. Suppose that its annual sales behave as indicated in Table 14-1 in this exercise. Fill in the rest of the table. (If you have trouble, refer back to Table 14-1 in the text.)

Table 14-1

Year	Annual sales (hundreds of thousands)	Desired no. of machines	Net invest-ment	Gross invest-ment
1	10	50	0	_____
2	10	_____	_____	_____
3	12	_____	_____	_____
4	16	_____	_____	_____
5	14	_____	_____	_____
6	14	_____	_____	_____
7	12	_____	_____	_____
8	10	_____	_____	_____
9	9	_____	_____	_____
10	10	_____	_____	_____
11	10	_____	_____	_____

Table 14-2*

National income	Saving	Taxes	Imports	Invest-ment	Govern-ment spending	Exports	Total leakages	Total injections
$100	$10	$20	$10	$15	$26	$15	$_____	$_____
120	12	24	12	15	26	15	_____	_____
140	14	28	14	15	26	15	_____	_____
160	16	32	16	15	26	15	_____	_____
180	18	36	18	15	26	15	_____	_____
200	20	40	20	15	26	15	_____	_____

*All figures represent billions of dollars.

2a. In an open economy (one with exports and imports), there are three kinds of leakages (recall this concept from Chapters 8 and 9)—saving, taxes, and imports—and three kinds of injections (recall this also from Chapters 8 and 9)—investment, government spending, and exports. Suppose that the values of planned injections and leakages at different levels of national income are given by Table 14-2. Fill in the last two columns showing the total values of planned leakages and injections. The equilibrium level of national income is $_____ billion, at which level total injections are $_____ billion. The marginal propensity to import is _____. Suppose that investment spending were to rise to $31 billion regardless of the level of national income. Then the equilibrium national income would be $_____ billion, at which level total injections would be $_____ billion. The size of the investment multiplier in this economy is _____.

2b. Now suppose that there is a change in the demand for imports. Suppose that when national income equals 140, imports still equal 14, but now the marginal propensity to import is 0.2. Fill in Table 14-3.

Table 14-3*

National income	Imports	Total leakages
$100	$_____	$_____
120	_____	_____
140	14	_____
160	_____	_____
180	_____	_____
200	_____	_____

*All figures represent billions of dollars.

The equilibrium level of national income (assuming investment demand of $15 billion) equals $______ billion. Now suppose that investment spending rises to $35 billion. Then the new equilibrium level of national income is ______. The size of the investment multiplier is now ______.

2c. Therefore we may conclude that the larger the marginal propensity to import, the (larger, smaller) the investment multiplier. This implies that a high marginal propensity to import exerts a (stabilizing, destabilizing) influence on the economy.

Essay Questions

1. Why are recessions defined in terms of the movement of seasonally adjusted real gross national product rather than seasonally unadjusted?

2. If seasonally adjusted real gross national product were constant for several quarters in a row, we would not say that a recession had occurred. Under such circumstances, what is likely to happen to the average person's real income? What do you think would happen to the rate of unemployment? In the light of this, can you suggest another way of telling when a recession has occurred?

3. Some people have argued that the United States economy could never undergo another great depression because the FDIC would prevent another bank panic like the one in the early thirties and the Fed's margin requirements prevent speculative indulgence of the sort that preceded the 1929 crash. Do you agree or disagree?

4. Consider your own expenditures on consumption. Did they vary from year to year by more or less than your income? Do they vary from month to month by more or less than your income? From week to week? From day to day? In the light of this, why do you suppose that the percentage changes in consumption demand over the business cycle are generally much smaller than the percentage changes in investment demand?

5. "The accelerator principle shows how business cycles could be caused by even small fluctuations in the demand for investment goods." Do you agree or disagree? Explain.

6. Why do you think a business firm might not want its production or investment decisions to respond to temporary fluctuations in demand? How can a business firm decide when a fluctuation in demand is temporary and when it is permanent?

7. Suppose that the President were to ask Congress for a reduction in tax rates during each month when the unemployment rate was above 4 percent and for an increase in tax rates whenever the rate of unemployment was below 4 percent. Do you suppose that this would accomplish the goal of stabilizing the rate of unemployment at 4 percent? Why or why not?

8. The business cycle in Canada follows very closely that of the United States. Periods of recession in the United States are usually periods of recession in Canada, and periods of expansion in the United States are usually periods of expansion in Canada. Why do you suppose the business cycles of these two countries are so closely related?

***9.** According to monetarists, the business cycle is primarily monetary in origin; that is, recessions and expansions are caused principally by decreases and increases in the rate of growth of the money supply. Others think that it is "real" in origin—that is, that recessions and expansions are caused by decreases and increases in the level of investment demand or some other component of aggregate demand independently of monetary causes. Also, it has been observed that the rate of interest tends to rise during the expansion phase of the business cycle and to fall during recession. Does this fact tend to support the case of the monetarists or that of their opponents? Why?

***10.** It has also been observed that the money supply is generally procyclical. Can you think of a way in which an opponent of monetarism could explain this observation without having to give up his or her "real" explanation of the business cycle? (Hint: Refer back to the section on the statistical evidence in Chapter 12.)

Answers

True-False Questions: 1 F 2 T 3 F 4 F 5 F 6 T 7 T 8 T 9 F 10 T 11 F
Multiple-Choice Questions: 1 d 2 b 3 c 4 d 5 b 6 d 7 a 8 a

Exercises:

1. Table 14-1

Year	Desired no. of machines	Net invest-ment	Gross invest-ment
1	50	0	10
2	50	0	10
3	60	10	20
4	80	20	30
5	70	−10	0
6	70	0	10
7	60	−10	0
8	50	−10	0
9	45	−5	5
10	50	5	15
11	50	0	10

2a. Table 14-2

National income	Leakages	Injections
100	40	56
120	48	56
140	56	56
160	64	56
180	72	56
200	80	56

140, 56, 0.1, 180, 72, 2.5.

b. Table 14-3

National income	Imports	Total leakages
100	6	36
120	10	46
140	14	56
160	18	66
180	22	76
200	26	86

140, 180, 2.

c. smaller, stabilizing.

chapter 15
Fine Tuning or Stable Policy Settings?

Learning Objectives

After you have studied this chapter in the textbook and the study guide, you should be able to

Describe the three steps that were involved in formulating the activist policies of the 1960s

State four arguments against activism

Describe two commonly advocated policy rules

State four arguments against the use of policy rules

Explain how the nature of the long-run Phillips curve affects the case for policy rules

CHAPTER HIGHLIGHTS

This chapter deals with the controversy over rules versus discretion. The aim is to acquaint you with the arguments and counterarguments put forth by each side in the controversy and with the general points of agreement that have so far resulted.

The case for discretionary (or activist) policy has origins in Keynes' *General Theory*. The advocates of discretion argue that aggregate demand will tend to be inadequate and unstable unless activist fiscal and monetary policies are undertaken. This view was influential in the early 1960s. During that era, government policy was aimed at (1) estimating potential GNP for the next several years, (2) forecasting where the economy will actually go (and therefore the size of the GNP gap) with different alternative policy settings, and then (3) selecting fiscal and monetary policies which, according to these forecasts, will close the GNP gap in a reasonably short period. In preparing these forecasts, economists use a number of techniques, including econometric models, survey data, and leading indicators.

The case against discretion consists of the following four arguments:

1. Economists' forecasting ability is so weak, especially in forecasting the lags in government policy, that discretionary policy makers—like the panicky helmsman—may overreact to current events.

2. Government policy affects real national output

with a lag, but it affects the price level with an even longer lag. Because of this, there is an inflationary bias to activist policy. Political decision-makers may choose expansionary policies for the short-run benefits of increasing real output, planning to worry later about the inflationary consequences.

3. Activists may tend to overestimate potential GNP. This can add another inflationary bias because an activist may strive to attain an unrealistically high level of aggregate demand. (On this point, see Figures 15-5 and 15-6 in the text.)

4. The use of discretion by government officials reduces individual freedom; we should be as free as possible from government meddling.

Advocates of rules argue that the best policy is one that follows rules designed to permit the system to function smoothly in the long run rather than to offset short-run fluctuations in aggregate demand. Two commonly advocated rules are (1) that the Fed be required to make the money supply grow by some fixed amount, say 4 or 5 percent, each year, and (2) that the federal government be required each year to achieve a balanced full-employment budget. (Recall this concept from Chapter 9.)

Neither of these rules has ever been adopted in the United States. Opponents of rules have made the four following arguments:

1. The policy maker is foolish to adopt rigid rules that may become outdated as circumstances change in unforeseen ways.

2. The benefits of stable policy are questionable. There is no guarantee that stable monetary and fiscal policies will lead to stable aggregate demand. Indeed, stable monetary policy according to one definition of money will probably lead to *un*stable monetary policy according to other definitions because, for example, M_1 and M_2 follow quite different time paths.

3. The rules that have been advocated may have a bias toward slow growth and high unemployment. For example, the adoption of a rule aimed at producing no inflation may generate too much unemployment in the short run. It may also cause high unemployment in the long run unless the long-run Phillips curve is really vertical.

4. Since no rule is ever really fixed, the attempt to stick to a rigid rule and let the chips fall where they may can actually produce violent swings in policy when the government's resolve finally gives and the rule is broken. An example sometimes referred to is the sudden introduction of wage-price controls by President Nixon in 1971, after 2½ years of trying to stick to a stable policy.

Advocates of rules make their case by referring to the chaotic economic events of the first half of the 1970s, especially the rising inflation, which they attribute to overexpansive activist policies in the '60s. Activists point to the continuous expansion from 1961 to 1969, which they attribute to the same activist policies.

General agreement has emerged on the following three points: (1) Policy makers should be more aware of lags in the economic system than they were in the 1960s. (2) Sharp changes of direction in economic policy (as took place in the 1960s and early '70s) are to be avoided. (3) More attention should be paid to the long-term effects of policy, especially the effects on inflation, than was paid in the 1960s.

The appendix describes the forecasting errors that economists made following World War II, when most of them predicted a severe recession but were proved wrong by the postwar recovery. The forecasters' biggest mistake was in underestimating consumption demand. This prompted economists to develop theories of the consumption function, such as Duesenberry's, which were more sophisticated than the simple one of Chapter 8. These more advanced theories explain why the MPC can be much larger at some times (after World War II) than others (1929–1944).

IMPORTANT TERMS

Discretionary policy Monetary or fiscal policy that is changed from time to time according to the judgment of the policy maker. Also called activist policy.

Policy rules Formulas that prevent policy makers from using their discretion.

Fine-tuning The extreme case of discretionary policy, in which policy is adjusted with the aim of smoothing out even minor fluctuations in aggregate demand.

Secular stagnation The situation in which the economy settles down to a permanent situation of very high unemployment (rates of over 10 percent). Many economists predicted secular stagnation for the United States economy following World War II, but very few now regard it as a real danger.

Potential GNP The amount of GNP that could be produced with full employment.

GNP gap Potential GNP minus actual GNP.

Leading indicator Any variable that tends regularly to reach a turning point before turning points in the general level of economic activity.

True-False Questions

T F 1. Advocates of discretionary policy tend to be more in the Keynesian tradition than are advocates of rules.

T F 2. One rule commonly advocated by monetarists is for the Fed to maintain the same interest rate from month to month.

T F 3. Fine-tuning is not a policy advocated by those in favor of rules.

T F 4. Advocates of discretionary policy often refer to the long expansion of the 1960s as evidence in support of their case.

T F 5. Activists are more inclined than proponents of rules to support restrictive policies.

T F 6. If economists could forecast better, the activist case would be strengthened.

T F 7. Forecasts by the Council of Economic Advisers of annual rates of growth of GNP tend to be accurate within 1 percent most of the time.

T F 8. Changes in aggregate demand generally have a shorter lag in affecting prices than in affecting quantities.

T F 9. According to the advocates of rules, activists tend systematically to underestimate potential GNP.

T F 10. The fact of rising inflation over the past decade is often pointed to by critics of discretionary policy as evidence of the bias of activists.

T F 11. The issue of economic freedom is involved in the controversy over rules versus discretion because the more rules we have to obey, the less freedom we have.

T F 12. Advocates of rules are more inclined than activists to believe that the long-run Phillips curve is vertical.

T F 13. The wage-price controls instituted in 1971 do not constitute an example of a policy rule commonly advocated by monetarists.

T F 14. Activists do *not* agree that if policy rules are followed, aggregate demand will be stabilized.

T F *15. (For those who have studied the Appendix.) The major mistake of the forecasters after World War II was that the rise in consumption was overestimated.

T F *16. (For those who have studied the Appendix.) If the MPC is measured using data taken over a long period of time, the estimate tends to be higher than when the data cover a shorter period of time.

Multiple-Choice Questions

1. Discretionary policies are
- **(a)** Advocated mainly by those following the classical tradition
- **(b)** Advocated mainly by those following the Keynesian tradition
- **(c)** Partly dependent for their success upon the accuracy of forecasts
- **(d)** **(a)** and **(b)**
- **(e)** **(b)** and **(c)**

2. A common example of a policy rule advocated by monetarists is to
- **(a)** Make the money supply grow by 4 percent each year
- **(b)** Let the rate of growth of the money supply during any year equal 4 percent of the GNP gap of the previous year
- **(c)** Fix the rate of unemployment at its natural level
- **(d)** Always balance the government budget

3. Suppose the Council of Economic Advisers forecasts a GNP gap of $50 billion for the coming year under the assumption of no change in government policy (that is, actual GNP *below* potential GNP by $50 billion). Then an
- **(a)** Advocate of rules would prescribe an increase in government spending
- **(b)** Advocate of rules would prescribe a decrease in government spending
- **(c)** Activist would prescribe an increase in government spending
- **(d)** Activist would prescribe a decrease in government spending

4. Which of the following is a commonly used tool of forecasting?
- **(a)** Survey data
- **(b)** Econometric models
- **(c)** Leading indicators
- **(d)** All of the above

5. Which of the following was a period of continuous expansion in the United States economy?
- **(a)** 1929–1944
- **(b)** 1951–1959
- **(c)** 1961–1969
- **(d)** 1973–1975

6. Which of the following is *not* a major point in the case against activist policy?
- **(a)** Activists tend to overestimate potential GNP.
- **(b)** Activists tend to advocate policies with an expansionary bias.
- **(c)** Activists tend to underreact to changes in aggregate demand.
- **(d)** Activist policies are contrary to individual freedom.

7. Which of the following is *not* a major point in the case against policy rules?

(a) No rule is ever really fixed anyway.
(b) There is a long historical experience of following monetary and fiscal rules which suggests that they don't work.
(c) Rules introduce too much rigidity into policy making.
(d) The benefits of following rules are nebulous, as illustrated by the difficulty of choosing the appropriate definition of money.

8. There is now substantial agreement that
(a) Sharp changes in policy should be avoided.
(b) Policy during the 1960s on the whole was not expansionary enough.
(c) During the 1970s, governments should be less concerned with lags in the economic system than they were in the 1960s.
(d) **(a)** and **(b)**.
(e) **(a)** and **(c)**.

9. Fear of secular stagnation
(a) Was common immediately after World War II
(b) Was increased by the postwar forecasting errors
(c) Is not common among advocates of rules
(d) **(a)** and **(b)**
(e) **(a)** and **(c)**

***10.** (For those who have studied the Appendix.) According to Duesenberry's theory of the consumption function, if national income rises but is still below its previous peak, then the rise in consumption
(a) Will be less than if national income were above its previous peak
(b) Will be greater than if national income were above its previous peak
(c) Will be the same as if national income were above its previous peak
(d) May or may not be greater than if national income were above its previous peak, depending upon whether or not national income rose during the previous year

Exercise

In this exercise, you must choose a fiscal policy. See if you can learn from this what kind of problems beset policy makers attempting discretionary policy in the presence of imperfectly understood economic lags.

a. Suppose your advisers tell you that potential GNP is now $990 billion and that it will grow by $60 billion per year for each of the next 4 years. (All figures are in constant dollars.) Last year (year zero) and the year before, actual GNP was $810 billion and *G* (the level of government spending on goods and services) was $250 billion. Next, suppose that your advisers tell you that the government spending multiplier is 3, that they do not foresee any lags in the economic system, and that aggregate demand will not change unless *G* changes. In Table 15-1, chart the behavior of potential GNP and actual GNP as well as the GNP gap under different assumptions about *G*.

Table 15-1

	Year I	Year 2	Year 3	Year 4
Potential GNP	990	____	____	____
A: G	250	250	250	250
Actual GNP	810	810	810	810
GNP gap	180	____	____	____
B: G	310	330	350	370
Actual GNP	____	____	____	____
GNP gap	____	____	____	____
C: G	280	310	340	370
Actual GNP	____	____	____	____
GNP gap	____	____	____	____

In this example, policy (*A*, *B*, *C*) is the neutral policy of keeping the same level of government spending, policy (*A*, *B*, *C*) is the activist policy of trying to eliminate the GNP gap immediately, and policy (*A*, *B*, *C*) is the "gradualist" policy of eliminating the GNP in stages over 4 years.

b. Now suppose that your advisers were mistaken. Instead of no lag, the multiplier operates with a 1-year lag, so that any change by one unit in *G* this year would cause a three-unit change in GNP *next* year but no change in GNP *this* year. Then show the results of the three policies in Table 15-2.

c. Next suppose that as well as the lag there are shifts in aggregate demand that were unforeseen by your advisers. Suppose that the changes in investment from one year to the next were as indicated in Table 15-2 and that these changes, just like changes in *G*, affected GNP with a multiplier of 3 and with a 1-year delay. Show the outcomes of the three policies in Table 15-4.

Table 15-2

	Year 1	Year 2	Year 3	Year 4
A: Actual GNP	810	810	810	810
GNP gap	180	____	____	____
B: Actual GNP	810	____	____	____
GNP gap	____	____	____	____
C: Actual GNP	____	____	____	____
GNP gap	____	____	____	____

Table 15-3

	Year 0	Year 1	Year 2	Year 3
Change in investment	0	+50	+40	+20

Table 15-4

	Year 1	Year 2	Year 3	Year 4
A: Actual GNP	____	____	____	____
GNP gap	____	____	____	____
B: Actual GNP	____	____	____	____
GNP gap	____	____	____	____
C: Actual GNP	____	____	____	____
GNP gap	____	____	____	____

Table 15-4 shows a potential hazard of activist policies. The activist policy *B*, instead of just closing the GNP gap in years two, three, and four, would result in a sizable (recessionary, inflationary) gap. The less active, "gradualist" policy *C* would result in a (smaller, larger) gap. And the best policy in terms of producing the smallest average gap over the years two through four would be the (neutral, activist, gradualist) policy.

Essay Questions

1. Why can't the government always eliminate the GNP gap by continuing to change government spending as long as the gap persists?

2. Suppose that a 4 percent monetary rule was adopted. Then suppose that, because of the introduction of an electronic transfer system for making payments, there was a large increase in the income velocity of money. What would happen to the price level? Could this have been avoided if the rule hadn't been adopted? Can you think of a way to set up a rule that would allow for such contingencies?

3. What is meant by the statement that leading indicators have predicted seven of the last five recessions?

4. Explain why activist policies have more inflationary bias than those advocated by the proponents of rules.

5. Policy makers have objectives in addition to the major goals of economic policy. They are concerned, for example, about national defense and human rights. How does the presence of these other objectives affect the cases for and against adopting policy rules?

6. Explain why economists who attach a great deal of importance to the long-run consequences of economic policy are more likely to be advocates of policy rules than are those who are more concerned with the short-run consequences.

***7.** Some government policy makers tend to be skeptical of the forecasts produced by their economic advisers. Discuss, with reference to the experience after World War II in the United States, whether or not such skepticism is justified.

Answers

True-False Questions: **1** T **2** F **3** T **4** T **5** F **6** T **7** T **8** F **9** F **10** T **11** F **12** T **13** T **14** T **15** F **16** T

Multiple-Choice Questions: **1** e **2** a **3** c **4** d **5** c **6** c **7** b **8** a **9** e **10** a

Exercise:

a. Table 15-1

Year 1	Year 2	Year 3	Year 4
990	1,050	1,110	1,170
810	810	810	810
180	240	300	360
990	1,050	1,110	1,170
0	0	0	0
900	990	1,080	1,170
90	60	30	0

A, B, C

b. Table 15-2

Year 1	Year 2	Year 3	Year 4
810	810	810	810
180	240	300	360
810	990	1,050	1,110
180	60	60	60
810	900	990	1,080
180	150	120	90

c. Table 15-4

Year 1	Year 2	Year 3	Year 4
810	960	1,080	1,140
180	90	30	30
810	1,140	1,320	1,440
180	−90	−210	−270
810	1,050	1,260	1,410
180	0	−150	−240

inflationary, smaller, neutral

chapter 16
Fixed or Flexible Exchange Rates?

Learning Objectives

After you have studied this chapter in the textbook and the study guide, you should be able to

Identify three sources of demand for a country's currency in the foreign exchange market and three sources of supply

List four options available to a government when the demand for its currency shifts to the left (or supply shifts to the right) in the foreign exchange market

Explain why exchange market intervention does not provide a permanent solution to a disequilibrium in the foreign exchange market

Describe how governments are supposed to operate under the gold standard

Explain why exchange rates could not move beyond the gold points under the gold standard

Describe the automatic adjustment mechanism of the gold standard

List four shortcomings of the gold standard

Describe how the "adjustable peg" worked

State three major differences between the gold standard and the gold exchange standard

List four major problems with the adjustable peg

Describe two proposals that were suggested to improve the adjustable peg

State two principal disadvantages of a flexible exchange rate

CHAPTER HIGHLIGHTS

This chapter deals with the issue of whether a government ought to regulate its country's exchange rate, and if so, how. The main topics covered under this general issue are (1) the mechanics of the foreign exchange market, (2) the gold standard, (3) the adjustable peg system that most countries used from 1945 to the early 1970s, and (4) the floating exchange-rate system that many countries have used since 1973.

The Foreign Exchange Market

International trade differs from domestic trade because it, unlike domestic trade, involves (1) tariffs and other barriers and (2) different moneys (currencies). The exchange rates between the different currencies are determined in the foreign exchange market. In this market the demand for, say, the Canadian dollar is the amount of Canadian dollars that people wish to acquire in exchange for foreign currencies. It arises from the demands by foreigners for (1) Canada's exports of goods (like automobiles and newsprint), (2) Canadian services (like hotel accommodation), and (3) Canadian assets (like ownership of Canadian factories and natural resources). Likewise, the supply of Canadian dollars in the market is the amount that people wish to give up in order to acquire foreign currencies. It arises from (1) Canada's imports of goods, (2) Canadian demand for foreign services, and (3) Canadian demand for foreign assets.

An exchange rate is the price of one currency in terms of another. It may be quoted either way; for example, $1 Canadian = $0.90 U.S. means the same as $1 U.S. = $1.11 Canadian. An equilibrium exchange rate is one at which the amount of currency supplied is equal to the amount demanded.

When demand decreases (shifts to the left), the equilibrium price of a currency falls. In response to this, the government has four options: It can (1) let the rate fall, (2) purchase the surplus to prevent the price from falling, (3) try to decrease the supply by direct actions like higher tariffs or exchange controls limiting the amounts of foreign currencies that people can buy, or (4) try to decrease the supply and increase the demand by restrictive monetary and fiscal policies that reduce domestic incomes and prices, thus stimulating exports and reducing imports. If option 2 is chosen and the shift in demand is permanent, then some combination of options 3 and 4 must also be used or eventually the government will run out of foreign exchange reserves with which to buy up the surplus amounts of its own currency.

The Gold Standard

The gold standard of the nineteenth and early twentieth centuries is an example of a fixed exchange-rate system (that is, a system which fixes the exchange rate within limits). Under the gold standard, the government (1) promises to buy or sell gold freely in exchange for the domestic currency at a fixed *official price*, (2) allows its citizens freely to export and import gold, and (3) allows the country's money supply to rise when there is an inflow of gold into the country and to fall when there is an outflow. (This is called obeying the "rule of the game.")

Under this system, a country's exchange rate will be fixed within limits (the *gold points*) around the mint parity that is calculated from the official prices of different currencies. For example, if the United States and Canada each have an official price of $35 per ounce of gold, the mint parity is $1 Canadian = $1 U.S. If the exchange rates went, say, to $1 Canadian = $0.90 U.S., then an arbitrager could sell Canadian dollars to the Canadian government for gold, ship the gold to the United States, and sell it to the United States government for the same number of United States dollars, then use the United States dollars to buy even more Canadian dollars in the foreign exchange market (paying $0.90 in United States currency for each Canadian dollar), thus making large profits. (Study this example and the one on pages 351 to 352 of the text to see how arbitrage works.) In fact, the Canadian dollar would never fall this low. As soon as it reached the gold point (at which such arbitrage became profitable in view of the cost of transporting the gold), the demand created by arbitragers would prevent the rate from falling any further.

Under the gold standard, there was an automatic mechanism ensuring that no country would "run out" of gold. If a country had a large deficit in international payments, then the demand for its currency would be less than the supply (as in Figure 16-3 in the text), the exchange rate would move to the gold point, and gold would leave the country. If the government obeyed the "rule of the game," this would cause the country's money supply to contract, leading to a reduction in prices and incomes in the economy. And this, in turn, would correct the deficit automatically by increasing demand and reducing supply for the country's currency in the foreign exchange market. (That is, option 4 in the discussion of the foreign exchange market, above, automatically comes into play.)

There were four problems with the gold standard:

1. The automatic adjustment could be quite costly for a country with a payments deficit because the monetary contraction could cause severe unemployment.

2. The burden of adjustment was unevenly divided between deficit and surplus countries. The latter found it easy not to follow the "rule of the game," instead allowing their gold reserves to accumulate without increasing their money supplies. This forced much or all of the adjustment onto deficit countries.

3. With gold acting as the ultimate monetary reserve, a large superstructure of money was built upon a small base of gold. This meant that any disturbance that caused a "crisis of confidence" could lead to a large outflow of gold, thus causing a drop in the money supply and starting a recession.

The Adjustable Peg

The adjustable peg operated as follows:

1. The United States fixed its dollar in terms of gold (at $35 per ounce of gold).

2. Other countries intervened in their foreign exchange markets to fix their exchange rate in terms of the United States dollar within 1 percent of the official "par value."

3. Countries with a temporary balance-of-payments disequilibrium were expected to maintain their fixed exchange rates by running down their reserves (in case of deficit) or allowing their reserves to increase (in case of surplus).

4. These reserves were held in the form of *(a)* gold, *(b)* United States dollars, *(c)* a reserve position in the IMF, or *(d)* after 1970, Special Drawing Rights or SDRs.

5. Countries faced with a "fundamental" disequilibrium were permitted to change their official par value.

6. Countries were expected not to intervene with trade barriers and exchange controls except under extreme circumstances.

This system was also called the *gold exchange standard*. The major differences between it and the gold standard are twofold: (1) Free private ownership of gold was crucial for the gold standard, whereas United States citizens were not allowed by law to own gold under the adjustable peg (except for artistic or other special purposes), and (2) the official rates were expected to be "permanently" fixed under the gold standard but not under the adjustable peg.

There were four major problems with the adjustable peg system:

1. It was never clear how to distinguish between a "fundamental" and a "temporary" disequilibrium.

2. If a government attempted to peg its exchange rate when speculators felt there was a fundamental disequilibrium that was not being adequately dealt with by the government, the speculators often made large profits at the government's expense. For example, when a country had a large balance of payments deficit, speculators would sell its currency in such large quantities that the government was unable to maintain the peg, and was forced to devalue. Thus the speculators were able to sell high (before the devaluation) and buy low (after the devaluation).

3. Surplus countries were reluctant to revalue or to take expansionary measures that might cause inflation. As a consequence, deficit countries believed that they had to bear an unfair share of the adjustment burden.

4. The key position of the United States dollar was somewhat precarious. If the United States government maintained a strong payments position (with a surplus or a small deficit), then other countries found it difficult to acquire foreign exchange reserves (most of which were held in the form of United States dollars). But if it ran large deficits (thereby providing the other countries with dollars), the holders of the United States dollars might fear that the United States would be unable to maintain the convertibility of dollars into gold. This could induce them to sell their dollars for gold, which would deplete the United States government's gold reserves, making it even more difficult for the United States to maintain the dollar's convertibility. Thus a "run" on the United States gold reserves could start, similar in nature to the banking panics of the nineteenth and early twentieth centuries.

Two proposals were suggested to improve this system: (1) the crawling peg, which would permit gradual changes in the official rate (par value) every month to add more flexibility to the system, and (2) wider bands which would allow the rate to deviate by more than 1 percent from its official value. The crawling peg was never introduced, but wider bands were adopted in the Smithsonian agreement of December 1971.

Floating Rates

Under the flexible or floating rate system that has been in effect since 1973, a government need not intervene in its foreign exchange market (that is, it may adopt a "clean float"). If so, the exchange rate will assume its equilibrium value. But most countries have adopted a "dirty float," by buying and selling in the market to influence exchange rates.

The advantage of a flexible rate is that it avoids the problems of the other two systems. The two principal disadvantages are: (1) Frequent changes in exchange rates may be the source of disruptive uncertainty for those dealing in international markets. (2) Flexible exchange rates can increase the danger of inflation. A country whose expansionary monetary and fiscal policies are generating inflation is relieved of having to deal with the deficits that would result under fixed rates. It can instead allow its currency to depreciate. Depreciation in turn causes a further increase in the country's price level by making imported goods cost more.

The appendix describes the balance-of-payments accounts of the United States.

IMPORTANT TERMS

Foreign exchange The money of another country. Also called foreign currency.

Foreign exchange market A market in which one country's currency is bought or sold in exchange for another country's.

Exchange rate The price of one country's currency in terms of another's. A country's exchange rate can be expressed either as the price of foreign currency in terms of the domestic currency, or as the price of the domestic currency in terms of foreign currency.

Tariff A tax imposed upon a foreign good that is imported. Also called a duty.

Quota A limit on the quantity of a good that can be imported.

Mint parity The exchange rate between two currencies under the Gold Standard, calculated from the two countries' official gold prices.

Arbitrage A set of transactions aimed at making a profit because of an inconsistent set of prices.

Gold point An exchange rate at which an arbitrager can just break even by buying gold in one country, shipping it to another country, and selling it in that country. There is one gold point on each side of the mint parity.

International adjustment mechanism Forces that work to reduce surpluses or deficits in international payments.

International payment deficit A country has an international payments deficit when its foreign expenditures exceed its receipts from abroad. In other words, the supply of its currency exceeds the demand for it in the foreign exchange market. The opposite of a deficit is a surplus.

Sterilization Steps by a central bank to cancel out the automatic effects of a deficit or surplus on the country's money supply.

Adjustable peg The system involving most countries in the world from 1945 to 1973.

IMF The International Monetary Fund, set up in 1944 to operate the adjustable peg system.

Par value The official exchange rate (or price of gold) chosen by a country under the adjustable peg system.

Fundamental disequilibrium This term was introduced but not defined by the IMF. It might be defined as an international payments deficit or surplus that is not just temporary.

Foreign exchange reserves Holdings by a central bank or government of foreign exchange.

Devaluation The reduction by a country of its currency's par value. An increase is called a *re*valuation.

Speculator Anyone who buys a foreign currency (or any other asset) in the hope of making a profit when its price rises.

SDR Special Drawing Right. A new form of international money first issued by the IMF in 1970 to provide more international reserves for its members.

Floating exchange rate The system under which governments do not maintain any particular value for their exchange rates. Also called *flexible* exchange rate.

Clean float The central bank and treasury of a country with a clean float refrain from intervening in the foreign exchange market.

Dirty float Under a dirty float, the central bank or treasury *does* intervene in the foreign exchange market, with the objective of affecting the exchange rate.

Depreciation A decrease, under a floating exchange rate, in the value of a currency in foreign exchange markets. An increase is called an appreciation.

The following definitions are from the Appendix:

****Merchandise account*** The record of a country's exports and imports of goods.

****Goods and services account*** The record of a country's exports and imports of goods and services.

****Current account*** The record of all international transactions of the residents of a country not involving the acquisition or sale of an asset.

****Capital account*** The record of all acquisitions or sales of foreign assets by domestic residents or of domestic assets by foreign residents.

****Official settlements balance*** The net total of all international transactions except for those involving official reserves.

True-False Questions

T F **1.** The only important difference between domestic trade and international trade is that tariffs often interfere with international trade but not with domestic trade.

T F **2.** The demand for British exports is one source of the demand for British pounds in the foreign exchange market.

T F 3. Foreign purchases of a country's assets constitute one source of demand for the country's currency.

T F 4. The gold standard was an example of a fixed exchange-rate system.

T F 5. A gold point is the official price of gold.

T F 6. If an exchange rate is always within the two gold points, then no arbitrage causing gold to be exported or imported will take place.

T F 7. A restrictive monetary policy in a country will shift the supply curve for domestic currency to the right in the foreign exchange market.

T F 8. Surplus countries had an easier time avoiding adjustment problems than did deficit countries under both the gold standard and the adjustable peg.

T F 9. If a country on the gold standard made arbitrage illegal, then its exchange rate could go beyond the gold points.

T F 10. If a country on the gold standard increased its money supply when it had a net inflow of gold, then it was not obeying the "rule of the game."

T F 11. Under the adjustable peg, a country was expected not to change its exchange rate even in the presence of "fundamental" disequilibrium.

T F 12. One of the problems of the adjustable peg was that if the United States restricted the supply of dollars, it would experience a balance-of-payments deficit.

T F 13. Under the adjustable peg until 1971, countries were expected normally to maintain an exchange rate within 1 percent of par.

T F 14. The Smithsonian Agreement of 1971 replaced the adjustable peg with a crawling peg.

T F 15. The Smithsonian Agreement widened the bands around the official exchange rate beyond the 1 percent specified in the original IMF articles.

T F 16. SDRs were first issued in 1960.

T F 17. Under a clean float, a government intervenes to reduce fluctuations in the exchange rate.

Multiple-Choice Questions

1. Which of the following is *not* a source of demand for a country's currency in the foreign exchange market?
- **(a)** The exports of that country
- **(b)** That country's sales of services to foreigners
- **(c)** That country's demand for official reserves
- **(d)** Purchases by foreigners of that country's assets

2. Which of the following events would be likely to shift the demand for a country's currency to the right in the foreign exchange market?
- **(a)** A restrictive monetary policy in that country
- **(b)** A restrictive monetary policy in other countries
- **(c)** An increase in the price level in other countries
- **(d)** **(a)** and **(b)**
- **(e)** **(a)** and **(c)**

3. An increase in the demand by foreigners for British assets will cause
- **(a)** The demand for pounds to shift to the right in the foreign exchange market
- **(b)** The pound to appreciate under a flexible exchange rate
- **(c)** The pound to depreciate under a flexible exchange rate
- **(d)** **(a)** and **(b)**
- **(e)** **(a)** and **(c)**

4. Under the gold standard, an increase in the American demand for imports could possibly cause
- **(a)** A reduction in the inflow of gold to the United States
- **(b)** An increase in the outflow of gold from the United States
- **(c)** The price of United States dollars to rise to the gold point
- **(d)** **(a)** and **(b)**
- **(e)** All of the above

5. Which of the following was *not* a part of the gold standard?
- **(a)** Governments had to intervene in foreign exchange markets to peg their exchange rates.
- **(b)** Governments had to ensure convertibility between their currencies and gold at the official price.
- **(c)** The money supply was supposed to vary in the same direction as the stock of gold in each country.
- **(d)** Private citizens were free to import or export gold.

6. Under the gold standard, if the official price of gold was \$20 per ounce in the United States and £4 per ounce in the United Kingdom, then mint parity was
- **(a)** \$5 per pound
- **(b)** £5 per dollar
- **(c)** \$5 per pound plus some amount depending upon the cost of shipping gold between the United States and the United Kingdom
- **(d)** None of the above

7. Suppose that England and Germany are on the gold standard, that the official price of gold is £4 per ounce in England and 82 marks per ounce in Germany, and that the exchange rate on the market is 20 marks per pound.

Suppose I bought 100 ounces of gold in the United Kingdom with pounds, shipped the gold to Germany, sold it to the German government for German marks, and converted those German marks into pounds in the foreign exchange market. Then, assuming no cost of shipping and transacting, I would make a profit of

(a) 10 marks **(c)** − 10 marks
(b) £10 **(d)** − £10

8. Which of the following was *not* a problem with the gold standard?

(a) The burden of adjustment was placed more heavily upon the deficit than on the surplus countries.
(b) The adjustment mechanism could be costly in the short run, especially for deficit countries.
(c) It was a potential source of monetary instability in the member countries.
(d) Exchange rates were, in fact, changed quite regularly.

9. Which of the following was a difference between the gold standard and the gold exchange standard?

(a) It was illegal for United States citizens to own gold under the gold standard.
(b) Exchange rates were adjustable under the gold exchange standard.
(c) Governments had to intervene in foreign exchange markets under the gold exchange standard.
(d) **(a)** and **(b)**.
(e) **(b)** and **(c)**.

10. Which of the following statements about the workings of the adjustable peg is *not* correct?

(a) A country could adjust its exchange rate in the presence of a fundamental disequilibrium.
(b) The IMF was set up to provide funds to countries facing temporary payments deficits.
(c) Countries were expected to impose exchange controls when faced with fundamental disequilibrium.
(d) The IMF could make a loan to a deficit country contingent upon that country taking restrictive monetary and fiscal policy measures.

11. If, under the adjustable peg, a country (other than the United States) increased the official domestic price of its currency in terms of the dollar, this was called

(a) Devaluation **(c)** Depreciation
(b) Revaluation **(d)** Appreciation

12. Under a clean float, the depreciation of a currency is likely to cause

(a) A decrease in that country's exports
(b) An increase in the domestic price level
(c) An increase in that country's balance-of-payments deficit
(d) None of the above

Exercise

The data in Table 16-1 describe the demand and supply for pounds in the foreign exchange market.

Table 16-1

Exchange rate ($ per £)	Amount demanded (millions of £)	Amount supplied (millions of £)
1.25	100	40
1.50	90	50
1.75	80	60
2.00	70	70
2.25	60	80
2.50	50	90
2.75	40	100

a. The equilibrium exchange rate is $______ per pound, or £______ per dollar. The equilibrium quantity of pounds transacted in the market is £__________. The equilibrium quantity of dollars transacted in the market is $______. Plot the supply and demand curves in Figure 16-1 and label the demand curve D_1.

b. If the demand for pounds decreased by £20 million at each exchange rate, the equilibrium exchange rate would be $______ per pound. Plot the new demand curve in Figure 16-1 and label it D_2. The equilibrium quantity of pounds transacted would be £______ and the equilibrium quantity of dollars transacted would be $______. If the rate was held fixed by the government at its *previous* equilibrium value, Britain would as a consequence have a balance-of-payments (surplus, deficit) of £__________ or $__________.

c. Suppose that Britain and the United States are on a gold standard, with an official price of gold of $22.50 per ounce in the United States and £10 per ounce in Britain. Then mint parity is $______ per pound. Suppose that the cost of shipping gold from England to the United States is $2.50 per ounce and that there is no

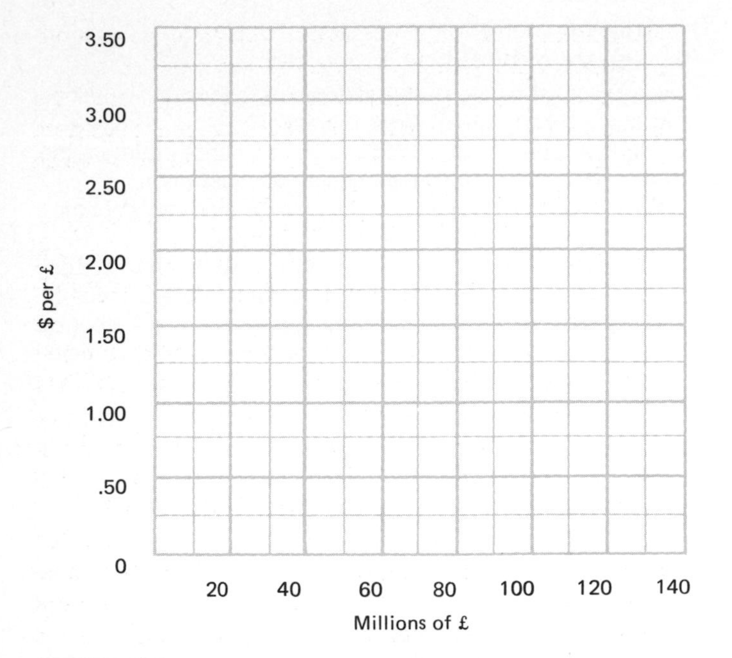

FIGURE 16-1

other cost to arbitraging. Then, if an arbitrager took £100, she could buy ______ ounces of gold in the United Kingdom. If she shipped this gold to the United States and sold it to the United States government, she would receive $______ from the United States government and have to pay $______ for shipping, so that she would receive $______ net of the shipping cost. If she sold these dollars (the net proceeds of the sale) on the foreign exchange market, she would receive her original £100 if the exchange rate were $______ per pound. Thus the gold export point is $______ per pound.

d. Likewise, if this arbitrager took $225, she could buy ______ ounces of gold in the United States. If she shipped the gold to Britain (at the same shipping cost), she would have to pay $______ for shipping, so that her total outlay would be $______ for buying and shipping the gold. The government of the United Kingdom would pay her £______ for this gold. If she sold these pounds on the foreign exchange market, the exchange rate would have to be $______ per pound for her just to receive enough to cover her total outlay. Thus the other gold point is $______ per pound.

e. In Figure 16-1, draw horizontal lines across the diagram at the two gold points. If demand and supply are as indicated in Table 16-1, then under this gold standard the exchange rate will be $______ per pound, the demand for pounds will be £__________, the supply of pounds will be £__________, ______ ounces of gold will be exported by arbitragers, and Britain will have a balance-of-payments (deficit, surplus, equilibrium). If demand now falls by £20 million, as discussed earlier, while arbitrage is allowed to take place, the exchange rate will be ______ per dollar, the demand for pounds (excluding arbitrage) will be £__________, and the supply of pounds (excluding arbitrage) will be £__________. The difference between these will be purchased by arbitragers, who will export __________ ounces of gold to the United States. Britain will have a balance-of-payments (deficit, surplus) of £__________.

f. Finally, suppose that demand is increased from the schedule in Table 16-1 by £20 million at each exchange rate. Plot the new demand curve in Figure 16-1 and label it D_3. Then the equilibrium exchange rate would be $______ per pound and the equilibrium quantity of pounds transacted would be £__________. Under the gold standard as discussed above, the exchange rate would now be $______ per pound, arbitragers would export ______ ounces of gold from Britain, and Britain would have a balance-of-payments (deficit of £__________, surplus of £__________, equilibrium).

Essay Questions

1. Suppose that, under the adjustable peg, the government of Britain announced that it was going to devalue the pound by 10 percent in 3 days. How would this affect the demand and supply for pounds sterling today? What would happen to the official reserve holdings of the British government? Would there be much risk in speculating today in the market for pounds? Why would the British government probably not be able to wait for 3 days?

2. In early 1969, there was a public controversy between the German central bank (which wanted a revaluation of the mark) and the German government (which didn't). What effect do you think this controversy had on exchange markets? On the operation of German monetary policy? Why do you think the central bank took the public position which it did?

3. Under the adjustable peg system, some countries felt that it was unfair for the United States to be able to benefit from being (virtually) the only country whose currency was held as reserve by other countries. This benefit is commonly referred to as *seignorage*. In what sense does seignorage actually benefit the United States? (Hint: Suppose that your friends were all willing to lend you money on the basis of your

IOUs, which they would then pass back and forth among each other to settle their debts from time to time. How would you benefit?)

4. Suppose you are a United States importer of British cloth. You have just succeeded in selling $2 million worth of cloth to a United States customer for delivery in 6 months, and you do not want to buy that cloth from your supplier in England until just before your promised delivery date; otherwise, you would have to store the cloth at great cost. Your supplier in England has promised to sell you the cloth at that time at a cost of £900,000 including shipping, handling, and insurance. The exchange rate right now is $2 per pound, so that if it stays the same for 6 months, you will realize a profit on this deal of $200,000. What will happen to your profit if the pound appreciates between now and then? What if the pound depreciates? How could you eliminate the risk of suffering a loss if there was a forward market in pounds? (In a forward market, you can contract now to buy or sell pounds at a future date at a price determined now.)

5. In what sense is it true that a country under a floating exchange rate always has an automatic way of eliminating balance-of-payments deficits or surpluses? Why, then, do some countries still have balance-of-payments deficits under a floating exchange rate?

6. "Any event which would tend to increase the deficit of a country under a fixed exchange-rate system would tend to depreciate its currency under a clean float." Do you agree? Why or why not?

7. Explain why it is easier for a country to sterilize the reserve changes resulting from a balance-of-payments surplus than from a balance-of-payments deficit.

8. How does the gold standard impose a discipline upon central banks and governments that are inclined to pursue inflationary policies?

9. Suppose that all banks were required to keep 100 percent reserves of gold. Would this remove any of the problems with the gold standard? Explain.

10. "Under the adjustable peg, when the United States pursued inflationary policies, it exported inflation to the rest of the world. But under the present floating rate, the other countries can choose not to import inflation from the United States. Instead, they can allow their currencies to appreciate with respect to the United States dollar." Do you agree? Why or why not?

Answers

True-False Questions: 1 F 2 T 3 T 4 T 5 F 6 T 7 F 8 T 9 T 10 F 11 F 12 F 13 T 14 F 15 T 16 F 17 F

Multiple-Choice Questions: 1 c 2 e 3 d 4 d 5 a 6 a 7 b 8 d 9 e 10 c 11 b 12 b

Exercise: **a.** 2, 0.50, 70 million, 140 million.
b. 1.75, 60, 105, deficit, 20 million, 40 million.
c. 2.25, 10, 225, 25, 200, 2, 2.
d. 10, 25, 250, 100, 2.50, 2.50.
e. 2, 70 million, 70 million, 0, equilibrium, ½, 50 million, 70 million, 2 million, deficit, 20 million.
f. 2.25, 80 million, 2.25, 0, equilibrium.

FIGURE 16-1 completed.

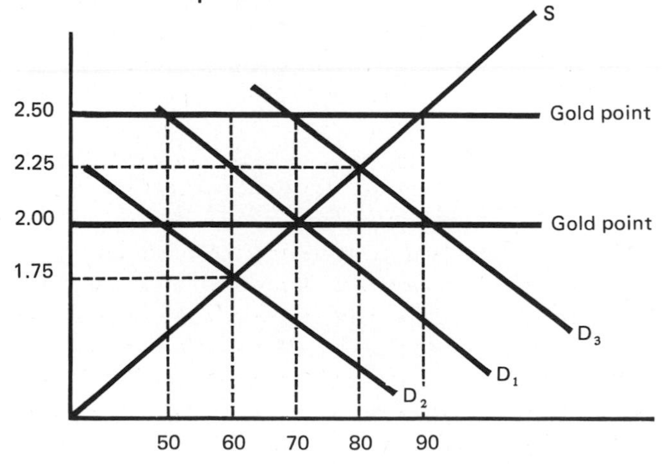

PART FOUR
MICROECONOMICS: IS OUR OUTPUT PRODUCED EFFICIENTLY?

chapter 17
Demand and Supply: The Concept of Elasticity

Learning Objectives

After you have studied this chapter in the text and the study guide, you should be able to

Define elasticity of demand and elasticity of supply

Explain the connection between the elasticity of a demand or supply curve and the flatness of the curve

Explain how the elasticity of demand affects the degree to which a shift in the supply curve alters the total expenditure on a good

List four factors that increase the elasticity of demand for a good

List three factors that increase the elasticity of supply for a good

Explain why the burden of a commodity tax falls most heavily on the side of the market (i.e., demanders *or* suppliers) with the lowest elasticity

Describe the special economic problems of agriculture

Show how the causes of these special problems are illuminated by the concept of elasticity

CHAPTER HIGHLIGHTS

In this chapter we begin a detailed study of microeconomics. It carries on from the supply and demand analysis of Chapter 3. In that chapter, it was argued that demand curves generally slope down and supply curves generally slope up, but nothing was said about how steep or flat those slopes might be. For many important applications of supply and demand theory, we need to know something about the steepness or flatness of the curves. This information is summarized in the concept of *elasticity*.

When the supply curve of a good shifts to the right, *(a)* demanders buy more of the good, but *(b)* they pay a lower price per unit. Whether they end up paying more or less for the good than before depends upon which effect is larger, *(a)* or *(b)*. This, in turn, depends upon the shape of the demand curve. For example, if the demand curve is almost vertical, then—as you can see by drawing your own diagram—

there will be a drop in price but almost no increase in quantity, with the likely effect that demanders end up paying less for the good. Likewise, if the demand curve is horizontal, the price will not fall but the quantity demanded will increase, so that the amount paid will increase.

We say that the demand curve is *elastic* if, in the above example, total expenditure on the good rises. It is *inelastic* if total expenditure falls. The *elasticity of demand* is defined as the ratio of the percentage change in quantity to the percentage change in price. It can be shown mathematically that demand is elastic if the elasticity is greater than one (in absolute value) and inelastic if the elasticity is less than one. As an exercise, what is the elasticity of demand if the demand curve is vertical?____________. If it is horizontal?____________.

Thus, elasticity measures the responsiveness—or flexibility—of demanders when confronted with a price change. If demand is elastic, then a 10 percent decrease in price causes them to respond by increasing the amount demanded by more than 10 pecent. This is why they end up spending more on the good. If demand is inelastic, they may increase their purchases, but not by 10 percent. In this case, they end up spending less on the good. In the borderline case where the elasticity of demand equals one, they increase the amount demanded by exactly 10 percent, with the result that they spend the same amount of money on the good, buying 10 percent more goods at a price per good of 10 percent less.

There is an important fallacy to avoid. The concept of elasticity was introduced with a reference to the steepness or flatness of a demand curve. However, elasticity and flatness *are not the same thing*. In particular, one curve may be flatter than another without having a greater elasticity. An example of this is given in Figure 17-3 in the text. However, there is one important case where elasticity does reflect flatness. When two demand curves pass through the same point, the flatter demand curve is more elastic than the steeper one at that point.

The elasticity of supply is similarly defined, in moving up the supply curve, as the ratio of the percentage change in quantity supplied to the percentage change in price. Once again, this is a measure of the responsiveness or flexibility of suppliers when confronted with a price change. The supply curve is *elastic* if the elasticity of supply is greater than one or *inelastic* if the elasticity of supply is less than one. As in the case of the elasticity of demand, the elasticity of supply is only a rough measure of flatness. If two supply curves pass through the same point, the flatter one is also the more elastic at that point. But when the two curves do not intersect, the flatter one is not necessarily the more elastic one.

The elasticity of demand tends to be greater (1) if a commodity is a luxury rather than a necessity, (2) if the commodity is a large item in demanders' budgets rather than a small one, (3) if there exist close substitutes for the commodity—that is, if it is not irreplaceable, (4) if we are considering the long-run demand curve rather than that for the short run. The elasticity of supply tends to be greater (1) if the commodity has a low cost of storage than if it is highly perishable, (2) if there exist goods which are close substitutes in production than if that commodity is about the only thing that can be produced by the given input resources, (3) if we are considering the long-run supply curve rather than that for the short run. Perhaps the most important of all these items are those referring to the short run versus the long run. It stands to reason that if people are given a longer time to adjust to a change in price, they will do more adjusting than if they are given only a short time in which to adjust. Try to provide a similar explanation for each of the other items mentioned in this paragraph.

The text discusses two important applications of the concept of elasticity. The first of these is the question of who bears the burden of a commodity tax. If demand is very elastic relative to supply, suppliers will pay most of the tax. But if supply is very elastic relative to demand, demanders will pay most of the tax. Once again, there is a commonsense explanation. The more flexible side of the market is in the less vulnerable position and therefore is less damaged by the burden of taxation in that market. Study Figure 17-5, which analyzes this question, until you can reproduce it on your own.

The other important application deals with the special problems of agriculture. In agriculture we find (1) a highly inelastic demand curve; (2) a highly inelastic supply curve (at least in the short run); (3) large year-to-year fluctuations in the short-run supply curve, depending upon the state of the harvest from one year to the next; (4) a great deal of technological change in recent decades, which has produced large rightward shifts in the supply curve; and (5) relatively little rightward shift over the same period of time in the demand curve because as incomes increase over time, people don't spend much of the increase on food. Items 1 to 3 have given rise to large fluctuations in prices and incomes. You can see why this should happen by drawing very steep demand and supply curves and shifting the supply curve back and forth. Notice how the equilibrium price responds very sharply to the shifts in the supply curve. Since the demand curve is inelastic and is staying put while the supply curve shifts, rises in the price are accompanied by rises in farm incomes (amounts spent by demanders on agricultural products) and reductions in price are accompanied by reductions in farm incomes. Items 4 and 5 have contributed to a downward trend in agricultural prices. This, too, can be seen by constructing demand and supply curves. When the supply curve is shifted to the right by more than the rightward shift in the demand curve, the price obviously declines.

The concept of elasticity can be put to many different uses. To keep it simple, just remember this rule: Whenever a change occurs that produces a shift in the demand or supply curve, the resulting change in price will be greater *(a)* the smaller the elasticity of demand and *(b)* the smaller the elasticity of supply.

IMPORTANT TERMS

Total revenue The amount of money received by the sellers of a product. This also equals the amount of money spent by demanders on the product (except for sales taxes and other minor items).

Elasticity of demand The ratio of the percentage change in quantity demanded to the percentage change in price, which is obtained by comparing two points on a demand curve. If the elasticity is greater than one, we say that the demand curve is elastic; if it is less than one, we say that it is inelastic.

Elasticity of supply The ratio of the percentage change in quantity supplied to the percentage change in price, obtained by comparing two different points on the same supply curve. If this elasticity is greater than one, we say that the supply curve is elastic; if it is less than one, we say that the supply curve is inelastic.

True-False Questions

T F **1.** The elasticity of demand is the same thing as the flatness of the demand curve.

T F **2.** If demand is inelastic, a change in price does not change the quantity demanded.

T F **3.** The concept of elasticity applies only to the demand curve, not to the supply curve.

T F **4.** If the elasticity of demand is less than one, total revenue and price always move in the same direction as we go from one point to another on a demand curve.

T F **5.** If the elasticity of demand equals one, then total revenue does not change when a price change moves us to another point on the demand curve.

T F **6.** The elasticity of supply is greater in the short run than in the long run.

T F **7.** If the supply curve is a straight line and if the elasticity of supply is equal to one all along the supply curve, the supply curve passes through the origin.

T F **8.** If the elasticity of demand equals zero, 100 percent of a commodity tax will be paid by demanders.

T F **9.** If both the elasticity of demand and the elasticity of supply are greater than 1, both suppliers and demanders pay a small fraction of the total tax on a commodity.

T F **10.** If a sales tax is imposed on a commodity, the resulting increase in the equilibrium price of that commodity will be higher the smaller is the elasticity of demand.

T F **11.** The problems of agriculture discussed in the text are aggravated by the inelasticity of the demand for agricultural products.

T F **12.** These same problems of agriculture are aggravated by the fact that fluctuations in national income over the business cycle cause large fluctuations in the demand for agricultural products.

T F **13.** When a technological change shifts the supply curve to the right (with the demand curve remaining unchanged), the equilibrium price must fall.

T F **14.** Under the same circumstances (as in question 13), the total revenue received by suppliers must fall if the demand curve is inelastic.

Multiple-Choice Questions

1. When there is a rightward shift in the demand curve, total revenue

- **(a)** Must rise
- **(b)** Must fall
- **(c)** Will rise only if the demand curve is inelastic
- **(d)** Will rise only if the supply curve is inelastic

2. When the demand curve shifts to the right, the rise in price is greatest if

- **(a)** Demand is elastic and supply is elastic.
- **(b)** Demand is elastic and supply is inelastic.
- **(c)** Demand is inelastic and supply is elastic.
- **(d)** Demand is inelastic and supply is inelastic.

3. A shift in the demand curve will not change the price if
- **(a)** The elasticity of demand equals zero.
- **(b)** The elasticity of supply equals zero.
- **(c)** The elasticity of demand equals infinity.
- **(d)** The elasticity of supply equals infinity.

4. If a 1 percent change in price produces a 10 percent change in the quantity demanded, the elasticity of demand is
- **(a)** 10
- **(b)** 1
- **(c)** 0.1
- **(d)** 0.01

5. Suppose that the minimum wage is above the market-clearing wage. Suppose it is increased further by Congress. Then the total income earned by workers
- **(a)** Must fall
- **(b)** Must rise
- **(c)** Will fall only if the demand for labor is elastic
- **(d)** Will fall only if the demand for labor is inelastic

6. If the supply curve for apples shifts to the left,
- **(a)** The rise in price will be greater in the short run than in the long run.
- **(b)** The rise in price will be less in the short run than in the long run.
- **(c)** The rise in price will be the same in the long and short runs.
- **(d)** The price will rise in the short run but fall in the long run.

7. If the demand for tennis rackets rises due to an increase in the popularity of tennis,
- **(a)** The resulting rise in price will be greater the greater the elasticity of supply.
- **(b)** The resulting increase in the quantity purchased will be greater the greater the elasticity of the supply.
- **(c)** The rise in price will be greater in the short run than in the long run.
- **(d)** **(a)** and **(c)**.
- **(e)** **(b)** and **(c)**.

8. The demand for a commodity will tend to be less elastic when
- **(a)** The commodity is a luxury.
- **(b)** The commodity has several close substitutes.
- **(c)** We are considering the long-run demand curve, not the short-run curve.
- **(d)** The commodity is a small item in most buyers' budgets.

9. The problem of instability in food prices would be alleviated if
- **(a)** The demand for food were not so elastic
- **(b)** Food products were more easily storable
- **(c)** Farmers were better able to predict next year's prices in advance
- **(d)** **(a)** and **(c)**
- **(e)** **(b)** and **(c)**

10. The long-term decline in agricultural prices in the United States might be reversed if
- **(a)** There were a decline in the rate of technological progress in agriculture
- **(b)** There were a decline in the rate of population growth throughout the world
- **(c)** There were a decline in the price of fertilizers
- **(d)** There were several years of good weather and therefore of bountiful crops throughout the world

Exercises[1]

1a. The data in Table 17-1 describe hypothetical demand and supply curves for apples. Plot these curves in Figure 17-1.

The equilibrium price of apples is $______ per bushel, and the equilibrium quantity is ______ million bushels. When the price rises from $10 to $20, the percentage change in price is[1]______; the percentage change in quantity demanded is[1]______; the elasticity of demand is ______; the percentage change in quantity supplied is[1]______; the elasticity of supply is ______________________.

1b. Suppose now that the government imposes a sales tax of $10 per bushel of apples (you may assume that initially there were no sales taxes at all). Then fill in Table 17-2.

Plot the new demand and supply curves in Figure

Table 17-1

Price per bushel paid by demanders	Millions of bushels demanded	Millions of bushels supplied
$ 5	25	5
10	20	10
15	15	15
20	10	20
25	5	25

[1]*Note on computing elasticities* (see footnote 4, page 382 in the text): When one is measuring the percentage change in a variable (price, quantity, or income) in order to compute an elasticity, a small problem always arises. Should the change in the variable be expressed as a percentage of its original value or as a percentage of its new value? It turns out that you get a different measure of elasticity depending upon which of these you choose. Since there does not seem to be any obvious reason for choosing one rather than the other, economists use an average of the two. This is how you should compute the elasticities in Exercise 1.

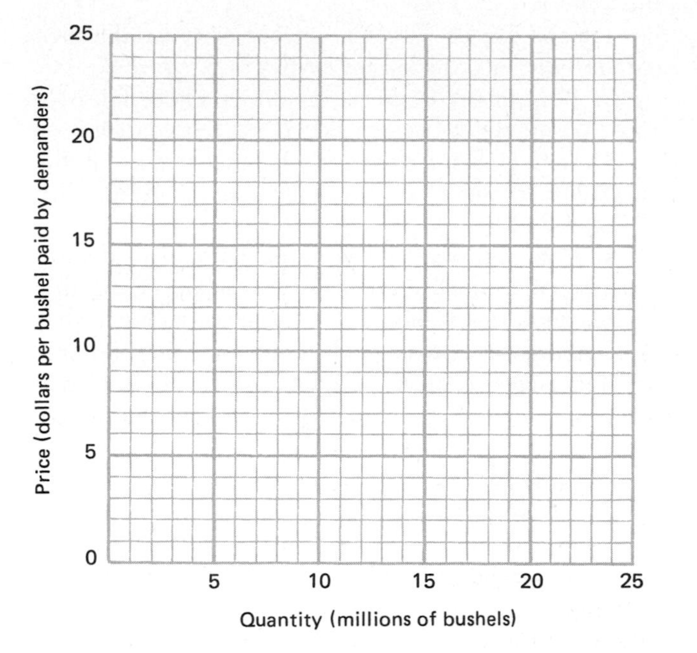

FIGURE 17-1

17-1. The new equilibrium price (paid by demanders) is $______, and the new equilibrium quantity is ______. Of the $10 per bushel paid in sales tax, the sellers are paying $______ and the demanders are paying $______.

1c. Draw a straight-line demand curve passing through the point (P = 15, Q = 15), which is less elastic than the one already drawn. If this new demand curve were to replace the old one, the equilibrium price before the imposition of the tax would be[2] __________, the equilibrium quantity before the tax would be __________, the equilibrium price after the tax would be __________, and the equilibrium quantity after the tax would be __________ than with the old demand curve. With the new demand curve, the amount of tax paid by the demanders would be __________ and the amount paid by suppliers would be __________ than with the old demand curve.

***2a.** In Figure 17-2, the elasticity of the supply curve S_1 is (smaller, larger) than that of S_2 at A.

Table 17-2

(1) Price per bushel paid by demanders (including tax)	(2) Price per bushel received by sellers (after tax)	(3) Millions of bushels demanded	(4) Millions of bushels supplied
$10	$______	______	______
15	______	______	______
20	______	______	______
25	______	______	______

Suppose that in either case the supply curve shifts to the right by the amount AB (to S_1' and S_2', respectively). Then if the demand curve is D_1, the fall in price with S_1' is (smaller, larger) than with S_2' and the rise in quantity is (smaller, larger) with S_1' than with S_2'.

FIGURE 17-2

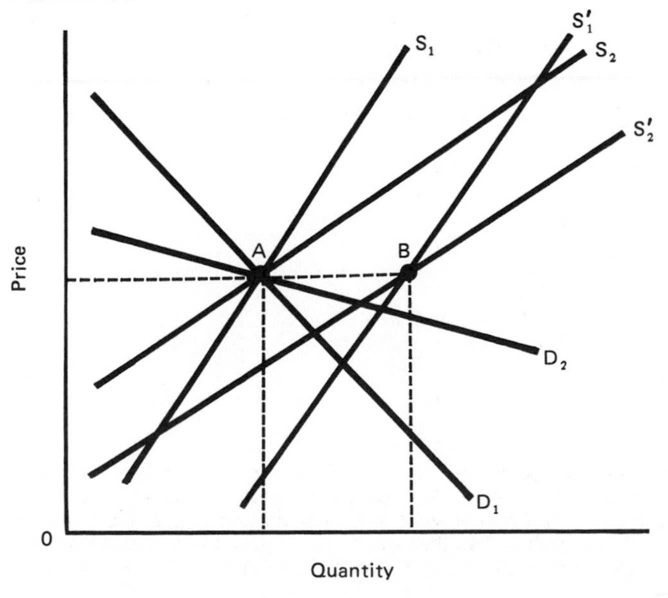

2b. Still referring to Figure 17-2, the demand curve D_1 is (less, more) elastic than D_2 at A. When S_1 shifts to S_1', the fall in price with demand curve D_1 is (smaller, larger) and the rise in quantity is (smaller, larger) than with D_2.

2c. In Figure 17-3, the elasticity of the demand curve D_1 is (smaller, larger) than that of D_2 at A. Suppose that in either case the demand curve shifts to the right by the amount AB (to D'_1 and D'_2, respectively). Then, if the supply curve is S_1, the rise in the price with D'_1 is (smaller, larger) than with D_2', and the rise in quantity is (smaller, larger) with D_1' than with D_2'.

2d. Still referring to Figure 17-3, the supply curve S_1 is (less, more) elastic than S_2 at A. When D_1 shifts to D_1', the rise in price with supply curve S_1 is (smaller, larger) and the rise in quantity is (smaller, larger) than with S_2.

[2]For this and all subsequent questions in this exercise, answer "higher," "lower," or "no different."

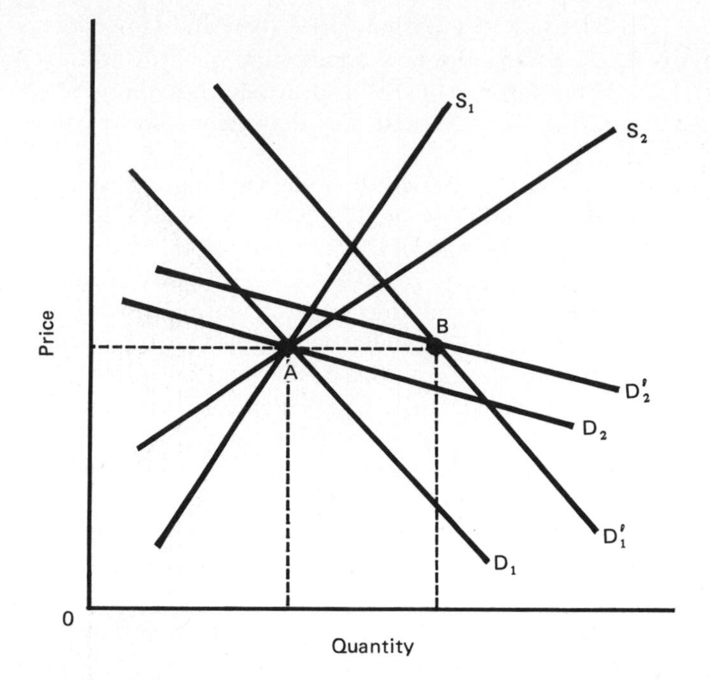

FIGURE 17-3

Essay Questions

1. Toward the end of the Chapter Highlights, the following general rule is given: The smaller the elasticities of supply and demand, the larger the changes in equilibrium prices resulting from shifts in supply and demand. Is it possible to state a similar rule with respect to equilibrium quantities? (Hint: See Exercise 2 above.)

2. Suppose that General Motors discovered that the demand for its cars was inelastic. It would then undoubtedly raise its prices. Why?

3. Why might farmers sometimes cheer for poor crops? (Hint: Refer back to Box 17-3.) Do you suppose that United States farmers would cheer more if the crop failure occurred in the United States rather than in Canada? Why?

4. Over the past 50 years, the number of domestic servants in the United States has fallen drastically. Do you think this is because of the price and availability of labor-saving household appliances? Or is it due to rising wages in other occupations? Or do both factors play a role? Explain how each affects the supply and demand for domestic help.

***5.** It has been argued that stores issue trading stamps to discriminate against people who cannot be bothered collecting, licking, and redeeming the stamps. These people end up paying a higher price for their purchases than those who use the stamps, because only the users receive a "discount" in the form of the items purchased with stamps. Suppose you were the owner of a large chain of stores and you wanted to engage in this kind of price discrimination. Suppose that, if you did institute trading stamps, the rise in price to the nonusers would just equal the fall in price to the users. What would happen to your total revenue if the demand by users were elastic and the demand by nonusers inelastic? What would happen to your total revenue if the demand by users were inelastic and the demand by nonusers elastic? Would you find this kind of price discrimination profitable if the nonusers' elasticity were higher than the users' elasticity? Would you find it profitable if the users' elasticity were higher than the nonusers' elasticity?

Answers

Chapter Highlights: zero, infinite.
True-False Questions: 1 F 2 F 3 F 4 T 5 T 6 F 7 T 8 T 9 F 10 T 11 T 12 F 13 T 14 T
Multiple-Choice Questions: 1 a 2 d 3 d 4 a 5 c 6 a 7 e 8 d 9 e 10 a
Exercises: **1a.** $15, 15, 66⅔, 66⅔, 1, 66⅔, 1.

Table 17-2

(1)	(2)	(3)	(4)
$10	$ 0	20	0
15	5	15	5
20	10	10	10
25	15	5	15

1b. 20, 10, 5, 5.
1c. no different, no different, higher, higher, higher, lower.
2a. smaller, larger, larger.
2b. less, larger, smaller.
2c. smaller, larger, larger.
2d. less, larger, smaller.

chapter 18
Demand and Utility

Learning Objectives

After you have studied this chapter in the text and the study guide, you should be able to

Show how the market demand curve is constructed by adding up the individual demand curves

Define marginal utility

Explain the principle of diminishing marginal utility

Show why the condition "price = marginal utility" must be satisfied by the rational demander

Prove that the demand curve is the same thing as the marginal utility curve

Explain why consumer surplus exists

Show why consumer surplus is measured by the area inside the shaded triangle, as in Figures 18-4 and 18-5 in the text

Explain how the concept of consumer surplus can be applied, as in the case of the Florida freeze

CHAPTER HIGHLIGHTS

We have seen that in many cases a successful application of supply and demand theory requires detailed information concerning the elasticities of supply and demand as well as knowledge about what factors are likely to produce shifts in the curves and how large those shifts will be. In the absence of precise information of this sort, we can often proceed on the basis of informed guesses. For example, even if we do not have precise statistical information, we can be confident that a rise in the price of margarine will produce a significant rightward shift in the demand curve for butter. Our ability to make such informed guesses depends on our understanding of the factors underlying the supply and demand curves. The present chapter takes a first look at the factors underlying the demand curve.

The first and most obvious point to note concerning the demand curve is that it is simply the sum of all the individual demand curves, as illustrated in Figure 18-1 in the text.

Underlying the individual demand curves are the two basic concepts introduced in Chapter 2—scarcity and choice. In particular, each individual demander must decide how much of one scarce item (money) to give up for the purpose of acquiring another scarce item (the particular good in question). How do buyers make this choice? Experience has shown that our best working hypothesis is to assume that they make the choice *rationally*, in the light of their own self-interest.

This brings us to the important concept of *marginal utility*, which is the increase in material well-being (utility) that the individual would derive from being able to consume just one more unit of the good in question. In order to make this concept objectively meaningful, we often measure the utility gain in terms of money.

The principle of diminishing marginal utility states that as a consumer buys more and more of a good, the utility acquired from one more unit will eventually fall. This implies that the individual will purchase just that amount of the good that makes marginal utility equal to price. If the consumer were to buy less than this amount, marginal utility would be greater than price. For example, in Figure 18-4 in the text, if the consumer buys only 2 units, marginal utility is 15 and price is 10. In this situation, it would clearly be in the consumer's interest to purchase more because the cost of buying another unit (the price) is less than the gain (marginal utility). As an exercise, go through the same logic to show why, if more than this optimal amount were purchased, the consumer would be better off purchasing less.

It follows that the demand schedule *is the same thing* as the marginal utility schedule. For example, suppose that, according to the marginal utility schedule, the marginal utility is 3 if the quantity purchased is 50. Then—obviously—if the price equals 3, the individual will want to purchase 50.

An important idea introduced in this chapter is that of *consumer surplus*. Consumer surplus is the extra benefit received by demanders by virtue of the fact that they are purchasing in a free market at a single price. Suppose that the price of some good is $3 and that your demand for that good is 50 units. Then you are paying $150 in order to consume 50 units. Now suppose that the market is taken over by some "exploiter" who will not let you freely choose the quantity that you wish to purchase. Instead, you are given an all-or-nothing choice. Either you pay $200 for that 50 units or you'll get nothing. When faced with this choice, you may actually decide to pay the extra $50 in order to keep consuming the good. Why? Because of diminishing marginal utility. The fiftieth unit of the good is worth just $3 to you, but the first unit was worth a lot more than that. Therefore the utility you get from the entire purchase exceeds what you have to pay for it; the difference is consumer surplus. As you can see in Figures 18-4 and 18-5 in the text, consumer surplus is measured diagrammatically by the total area inside the "triangle" formed by the demand curve, the price axis, and the horizontal line indicating the price of the good.

The concept of consumer surplus is applied in the text to the case of the 1977 Florida freeze. This example illustrates the important technique of cost-benefit analysis, which is often used in applied economics. Notice how the technique allows us to compare the gains to producers with the losses to consumers in order to arrive at the overall effect for the well-being of the society as a whole. This example also illustrates an important *fallacy of composition* (that is, arguing that what applies to an individual also applies to all individuals taken together). Any individual farmer whose crops were damaged was worse off than if those crops had survived; but, taken together, all farmers were *better* off, because of the inelasticity of demand, than if the crops had all survived.

IMPORTANT TERMS

Utility The benefit or satisfaction ultimately derived from goods.

Marginal utility The *additional* utility derived from one more unit of a good. This can be measured in dollar terms.

Diminishing marginal utility The hypothesis that —beyond some point—the more of a good that is consumed, the less is the marginal utility.

Consumer equilibrium A situation in which price equals marginal utility. A consumer who is not in such an equilibrium is not acting rationally to maximize utility.

Consumer surplus The difference between the total utility derived from a good and the amount paid for it.

True-False Questions

T F **1.** The height of the individual demand curve measures the total utility derived from that good.

T F **2.** When the price of a good falls, the consumer surplus that an individual receives from that good will rise.

T F 3. In the special case where the individual's demand curve is perfectly horizontal, that individual receives no consumer surplus from the good in question.

T F 4. Marginal utility cannot increase with a rise in the amount of a good purchased.

T F 5. The Florida freeze discussed in the text would not have affected the amount of income received by Florida farmers if the elasticity of demand for their crops had been equal to one.

T F 6. The Florida freeze would not have resulted in any overall loss to the nation if the elasticity of demand had been equal to one.

Multiple-Choice Questions

1. If the elasticity of an individual's demand curve is relatively large,

- **(a)** That individual's consumer surplus is relatively small.
- **(b)** That individual's marginal utility diminishes very rapidly.
- **(c)** That individual's total utility is diminishing.
- **(d)** **(a)** and **(b)**.
- **(e)** **(b)** and **(c)**.

2. "Diminishing marginal utility" means that as more of a good is purchased, eventually

- **(a)** The benefit from an extra unit decreases.
- **(b)** The benefit from an extra unit increases.
- **(c)** The total benefit derived from the good decreases.
- **(d)** **(a)** and **(c)**.

3. If the marginal utility of a good is 5 and its price is 6, then utility is not maximized because

- **(a)** The consumer is buying too much of the good and its marginal utility is higher than it ought to be.
- **(b)** The consumer is buying too much of the good and its marginal utility is lower than it ought to be.
- **(c)** The consumer is buying too little of the good and its marginal utility is higher than it ought to be.
- **(d)** The consumer is buying too little of the good and its marginal utility is lower than it ought to be.

4. Suppose that Table 18-1 indicates the total utility received by a consumer from consuming various amounts of clothing. Then

Table 18-1

Units of clothing consumed	Total utility
0	0
1	1
2	4
3	6
4	7

- **(a)** The marginal utility is diminishing no matter how much clothing is consumed.
- **(b)** The increase in total utility from consuming another unit is greater when consumption equals 1 than when consumption equals 3.
- **(c)** Marginal utility is highest with the second unit of consumption.
- **(d)** **(a)** and **(b)**.
- **(e)** **(b)** and **(c)**.

5. The marginal utility of a particular good depends not only upon the amount of that good consumed but also on the amount of other goods consumed. For example, suppose the amount of butter consumed increases while the amount of margarine remains constant. Then

- **(a)** Marginal utility of butter rises and marginal utility of margarine rises.
- **(b)** Marginal utility of butter rises and marginal utility of margarine falls.
- **(c)** Marginal utility of butter falls and marginal utility of margarine rises.
- **(d)** Marginal utility of butter falls and marginal utility of margarine falls.

6. Suppose that the amount of bread consumed increases but the amount of butter remains constant. Then

- **(a)** Marginal utility of bread rises and marginal utility of butter rises.
- **(b)** Marginal utility of bread rises and marginal utility of butter falls.
- **(c)** Marginal utility of bread falls and marginal utility of butter rises.
- **(d)** Marginal utility of bread falls and marginal utility of butter falls.

Exercises

1. Suppose that a consumer's total utility from haircuts is given by Table 18-2. Fill in the column giving the marginal utility of each additional haircut.

Suppose that the price of a haircut is $2. Then fill in the column giving the total yearly cost of haircuts. Next, fill in the column giving the difference between total utility and total cost. This difference is maximized when the consumer buys ______ haircuts per year. Therefore the consumer will demand ______ haircuts per year at $2 per haircut. At this quantity, the marginal utility of the last haircut during the year is (more, less) than the price, and the marginal utility of one more haircut would be (more, less) than the price.

If the price is $1 per haircut, the equilibrium condition ("marginal utility equals price") is satisfied when ______ haircuts are demanded and also when ______ haircuts are demanded. What possible reason could there be for the fact that the marginal utility of

Table 18-2

Number of haircuts per year	Total utility of haircuts (in dollars)	Marginal utility of haircuts	Total cost per year of haircuts at $2 each	Total utility minus total cost at $2 each
0	$ 0.00	0.00	________	________
1	1.00	________	________	________
2	6.00	________	________	________
3	10.00	________	________	________
4	13.00	________	________	________
5	15.50	________	________	________
6	16.50	________	________	________
7	16.25	________	________	________

the seventh haircut is negative? Can you think of any way in which the consumer could be induced to buy seven haircuts per year?

2a. In Figure 18-1, suppose that the relevant supply curve is the one labeled S_1 and ignore for now the one labeled S_2 Then the equilibrium price will be *OB* and the equilibrium quantity will be ________. The total revenue received by producers will be equal to the area ________. The total amount paid by demanders will be equal to the area ________. The total utility enjoyed by demanders of this good will be equal to the area ________, and the consumer surplus will be equal to the area ________.

2b. Now, suppose that, as a result of some technological improvement, the supply curve shifts out to the one labeled S_2. After this shift, the equilibrium price will be ________, the equilibrium quantity will be ________, the revenue received by producers will be ________, the amount paid by demanders will be ________, the total utility enjoyed by consumers will be ________, and the consumer's surplus will be ________.

FIGURE 18-1

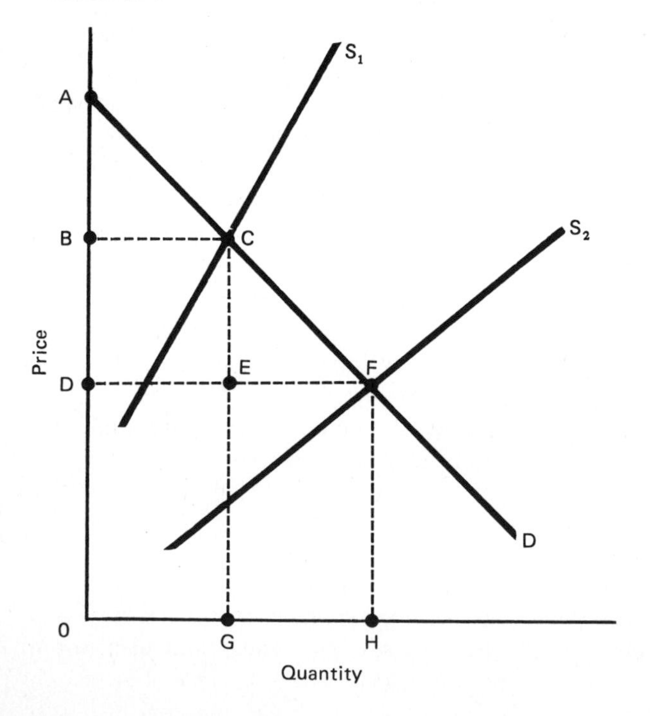

2c. As a result of this change in supply, the net gain to consumers is measured by the area ________, while the producers lose the area ________ but gain the area ________. Therefore the overall gain to the nation is measured by ________.

Essay Questions

1. No matter how you look at it, it's obvious that people derive more utility from the water in the world than they do from all the diamonds in the world. Yet diamonds cost far more than water. Adam Smith tried to explain this apparent paradox simply by noting that value in exchange did not always reflect value in use. Can you give an explanation by noting that the price of water reflects its *marginal* utility but that its value to us depends on the *total* utility that it provides? Do you suppose that diamonds would be more expensive than water if water were as scarce as diamonds? What role does diminishing marginal utility play in the explanation of this paradox?

2. To judge by the amount of time spent, most people seem to derive more utility from watching television than from going to movies. Yet they will pay $3 or $4 to go to a movie when they could stay home and watch television for nothing. Is this consistent with utility theory?

3. When Henry Ford invented the mass production of automobiles, what effect do you suppose this had on the typical American marginal utility schedule for horse-drawn carriages? What do you suppose it did to the price of horse-drawn carriages? To the elasticity of demand for carriages?

4. In Chapter 17, it was pointed out that when a tax is put on a commodity, the largest portion of that tax would be paid by people in the least flexible (most inelastic) situation. Do you suppose that people who derive relatively large consumer surpluses from the good would pay a large or a small portion of the tax? Why?

5. Heroin addicts find that the more they consume, the more they want. But eventually their desire tails off; if they get enough, they can poison themselves. Does this contradict or illustrate diminishing marginal utility?

Answers

True-False Questions: **1 F 2 T 3 T 4 F 5 T 6 F**
Multiple-Choice Questions: **1 a 2 a 3 b 4 e 5 d 6 c**
Exercises: **1.** Table 18-2

Marginal utility	Total cost	Total utility minus total cost
$0.00	$ 0.00	$0.00
1.00	2.00	−1.00
5.00	4.00	2.00
4.00	6.00	4.00
3.00	8.00	5.00
2.50	10.00	5.50
1.00	12.00	4.50
−0.25	14.00	2.25

5, 5, more, less, 1, 6.

2a. *OG, OBCG, OBCG, OACG, ABC.*
2b. *OD, OH, ODFH, ODFH, OAFH, ADF.*
2c. *DBCF, DBCE, GEFH, GCFH.*

chapter 19
Costs and Supply

Learning Objectives

After you have studied this chapter in the text and the study guide, you should be able to

Explain the distinction between fixed and variable costs, showing why there are no fixed costs in the long run

Define marginal cost

Show why the condition "price = marginal cost" must be satisfied by the profit-maximizing competitive firm

Demonstrate why the supply curve is the same thing as the portion of the marginal cost curve lying above the average variable cost curve

Show in a diagram how long-run and short-run average cost curves are related to each other by an envelope relationship

Define producer surplus and explain why it exists

Explain why producer surplus is measured the way it is in Figure 19-9 in the text

State the distinction between accounting costs and economic costs

CHAPTER HIGHLIGHTS

Just as the previous chapter took a look at what underlies the demand curve, so this chapter looks at what underlies the supply curve. Once again, the assumption of rational self-interest is involved. In this case, we assume that producers supply whatever amount will give them the greatest possible profit.

In order to understand a firm's profit-maximizing behavior, we must investigate the nature of the firm's costs. That is the main purpose of this chapter. We begin with the short-run case in which the amount of capital equipment employed by the firm cannot be varied. In this case, its outlays on capital may be regarded as *fixed costs* (or overhead costs). In the short run, fixed costs cannot be avoided, even if the firm stops producing altogether. All other costs are regarded as *variable costs*. That is, they are outlays for such things as labor and materials that vary with the amount produced. In the long run, the firm may also vary the amount of capital equipment being used; therefore, in the long run, all costs are variable and none are fixed.

Just as marginal utility was crucial in determining demand, so *marginal cost*—the additional cost of producing one more unit—is crucial in determining supply. Just as marginal utility must eventually fall as the amount consumed rises, so marginal cost (MC) must eventually rise with the amount produced. Moreover, just as the marginal utility schedule is the same thing as an individual's demand schedule, so the MC schedule is the same thing as the firm's supply schedule. For the equilibrium condition, Price = MC must hold if the firm is maximizing its profit. If price exceeds MC, the firm could increase profits by raising output. The extra revenue from producing another unit (marginal revenue) is the price, and the extra cost is MC; since in this case the extra revenue exceeds the extra cost, profits will rise if output increases. Likewise, if MC exceeds price, profits can be increased by reducing output (make sure that you can explain this carefully).

There is an important complication. Even if price equals marginal cost, the firm's profits might be too low to warrant staying in business. In the short run, this will happen if price is less than average variable cost (AVC); as long as the price is at least as large as AVC, the firm will be earning something to help cover its fixed cost. Better to do this than to shut down and pay *all* the fixed cost. In the long run, since all costs are variable, the firm will shut down whenever the price is less than average cost (AC).

Thus the firm's short-run supply curve is that part of its short-run MC schedule lying above the AVC schedule (see Figure 19-3 in the text), and its long-run supply schedule is that part of its long-run MC schedule lying above its long-run AC schedule (see Figure 19-7 in the text).

The position of the short-run MC schedule depends upon the (fixed) amount of capital. In fact, there is a whole set of short-run MC schedules, each corresponding to a different capital stock. The long-run MC schedule represents the marginal cost of producing when the capital stock can be varied with the amount produced. Likewise, the short-run AC and AVC schedules depend upon the stock of capital, whereas the long-run AC curve assumes a variable capital stock. As explained in Figure 19-5 and in Box 19-2 in the text, this means that the long-run AC is the "envelope" curve that just touches underneath each of the short-run AC curves. One feature worth remembering is that the long-run MC schedule tends to be flatter than the short-run MC schedule. This implies that (as we already noted in Chapter 17) long-run supply curves are more elastic than short-run supply curves.

An important concept introduced in this chapter is that of "producer surplus." This is really the same thing as excess profit, and it is analogous to the concept of consumer surplus studied in the last chapter. The firm sells all its goods at a price equal to the cost of the *last* unit produced. It makes a profit because the cost of producing *earlier* units is less than this (that is, MC increases as output increases). As explained in Figure 19-9 in the text, the increase in producer surplus when the price increases is the area between the two prices to the left of the MC schedule. Study this explanation until you can reproduce it on your own.

Another important concept is that of economic cost as opposed to accounting cost. The difference is that the economist considers many implicit costs that are ignored by the accountant, such as the wages that the owner of a firm could have made if he or she had taken a job elsewhere instead and the interest income that the owner could have earned by investing the same capital elsewhere. The interest income that could have been earned is called the firm's *normal profit*. The general principle is that the economist tries to take into account all *opportunity costs* (that is, what factors of production could be earning elsewhere). Thus normal profits are a *cost*. When economists speak of "profit" they are referring to excess or supernormal profits above and beyond this. Supernormal profits are important for the operation of the market system because they act as a signal to attract resources into profitable uses and out of unprofitable ones.

Finally, the chapter shows how the industry's supply curve can be obtained from adding up the individual firms' supply curves, just as we added up the individual demand curves to obtain the market demand curve. Complications can arise because (1) as the price rises, more firms will enter the industry and (2) as the industry expands (that is, as the output of the industry increases), this expansion may itself cause the firms' MC schedules to shift. (On this last point, see Appendix 19-B of the text.)

IMPORTANT TERMS

Fixed costs Costs that do not vary as output increases. Also called "overhead" or "sunk costs."

Variable costs All costs that aren't fixed but which vary with the amount produced. In the long run, all costs are variable costs.

Total cost The sum of both fixed and variable costs.

Average cost The amount of total cost per unit produced.

Average variable cost The amount of variable cost

per unit produced. In the long run, since all costs are variable, average cost equals average variable cost; but in the short run, average cost exceeds average variable cost by an amount equal to average fixed cost.

Marginal Cost The increase in total cost resulting from an increased output of one unit.

Short run The time horizon over which the firm cannot vary its capital stock.

Long run The time horizon over which the capital stock is variable.

Marginal productivity The marginal productivity of a factor of production is the extra output that the firm can produce by hiring an extra unit of that factor. Generally speaking, a factor's marginal productivity must eventually decline; that is, if more of the factor is employed while other factors are held constant, the marginal productivity of that factor must eventually fall.

Marginal revenue The increase in total revenue from the sale of one more unit. In the present chapter, where we assume that the firm is a price taker, marginal revenue equals the market price.

Break-even point The point at which the marginal cost schedule intersects the average cost schedule. This is the point at which the firm would just make a zero profit.

Shut-down point The point at which the marginal cost schedule intersects the average variable cost schedule. If the price falls below this, the firm will shut down its operations even in the short run.

The law of diminishing returns As output increases beyond some point, the short-run marginal cost curve will rise; this follows from diminishing marginal productivity (see "marginal productivity," above).

Economies of scale Economies of scale exist if doubling *all* inputs more than doubles the firm's output. With economies of scale, the long-run average cost will be falling. (As explained in Figure 19-6 in the text, the firm can face both economies of scale and diminishing returns at the same time.)

Economic cost This equals explicit accounting cost plus the implicit costs that are not considered by accountants. (See Table 19-2 in the text.)

Opportunity cost The opportunity cost of an input is the return that it could earn in its best alternative use. Compare this definition with the one given in Chapter 2.

Normal profits The income that the firm could expect to receive if it were to invest its capital elsewhere. Normal profits are actually considered to be part of economic cost because they represent the opportunity cost of the firm's capital.

Producer surplus This is the same as economic profit and analogous to consumer surplus. It arises because the firm is able to sell all its output at the same price, whereas every unit of output except the last is produced at a cost below that price.

True-False Questions

T F **1.** Fixed costs are usually less than overhead costs.

T F **2.** Short-run marginal cost rises because of economies of scale.

T F **3.** The law of diminishing returns applies to a situation in which only one group of factors is varied, the others remaining constant.

T F **4.** The law of diminishing returns explains why the long-run supply curve slopes up.

T F **5.** The firm will produce something in the short run as long as the market price is above the minimum average variable cost.

T F **6.** If price is less than marginal cost, the firm is producing more than the profit-maximizing amount.

T F **7.** If average cost exceeds marginal cost, average cost must be falling.

T F **8.** The marginal cost schedule intersects the average cost schedule at the minimum point on the marginal cost schedule.

T F **9.** The firm's short-run supply schedule is that part of its short-run marginal cost schedule that lies above its average fixed cost schedule.

T F **10.** For every amount of capital stock, there is a different short-run supply schedule.

T F **11.** In the long run, there are no variable costs.

T F **12.** The long-run average cost schedule does not pass through the minimum point of any short-run average cost schedule.

T F **13.** The law of diminishing returns is a result of economies of scale.

T F **14.** The long-run shutdown point and break-even point are the same.

T F **15.** Accounting profit generally exceeds economic profit.

T F **16.** Economic profit generally exceeds normal profit.

T F 17. The role of supernormal profits in the economic system is to attract economic resources toward their most worthwhile employment.

T F 18. Producer surplus would exist even if the firm's marginal cost schedule were vertical.

T F 19. Producer surplus would exist even if the firm's marginal cost schedule were horizontal.

T F 20. An increase in price can never reduce producer surplus in the short run.

Multiple-Choice Questions

1. Fixed costs are
(a) Fixed only in the short run
(b) All costs that are not variable
(c) Part of normal profits
(d) **(a)** and **(b)**
(e) All the above

2. If total costs are rising, then marginal cost must be
(a) Rising
(b) Falling
(c) Positive
(d) Above average cost

3. The short-run supply curve slopes upward because of
(a) The hypothesis of diminishing marginal productivity
(b) Economies of scale
(c) The hypothesis of rising marginal cost
(d) **(a)** and **(b)**
(e) **(a)** and **(c)**

4. If average cost exceeds marginal cost, then
(a) Average cost must be rising.
(b) Average cost must be falling.
(c) Marginal cost must be rising.
(d) Marginal cost must be falling.

5. Long-run average cost
(a) Is falling if there are economies of scale
(b) Always exceeds average revenue
(c) Is drawn under the assumption that the firm's capital stock is fixed
(d) Is rising if there is diminishing marginal productivity

6. If the current market price falls short of the minimum point on all firms' long-run average cost schedules, then
(a) Firms will be dropping out of the industry.
(b) No firm will be producing, even in the short run.
(c) There must be economies of scale in the industry.
(d) Most firms will be expanding their capital stock.

7. Michael Merchant left his job, which paid $18,000 per year, and invested $300,000, which he could otherwise have invested at 10 percent per annum, to start a hardware store. His accounting profits for the first year of operation were $52,000; therefore his economic profits were
(a) 0
(b) $4,000
(c) $22,000
(d) $30,000
(e) $34,000

8. (See Appendix 19-C of the text.) When the market price equals OP in Figure 19-1, the firm's economic profit equals the area
(a) PUXY
(b) PUTQ
(c) PUSR
(d) **(a)** and **(b)**
(e) **(a)** and **(c)**

FIGURE 19-1

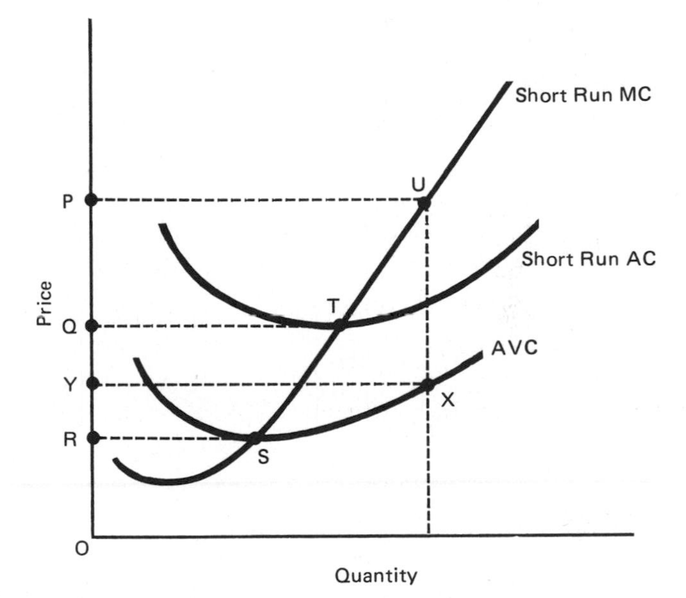

Exercises

1. In Figure 19-2, the curve labeled SMC denotes the firm's short-run marginal cost schedule, the one labeled SAC its short-run average cost schedule, and the one labeled AVC its short-run average variable cost schedule where all of these short-run schedules are drawn under the assumption that the firm has 10 units of capital. In Figure 19-3, the curve labeled LMC is the firm's long-run marginal cost schedule and the one labeled LAC is its long-run average cost schedule.

a. If the price equals OP_1, then in the short run the quantity supplied will be __________, total revenue will be __________, average cost will be __________, total cost will be __________, and economic profit will be __________.

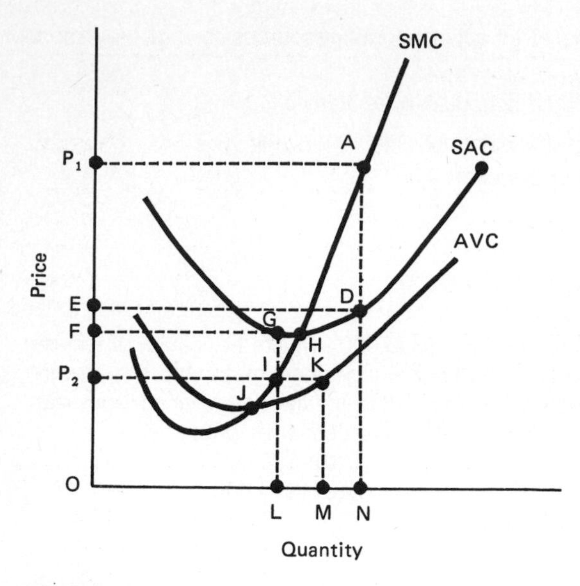

FIGURE 19-2

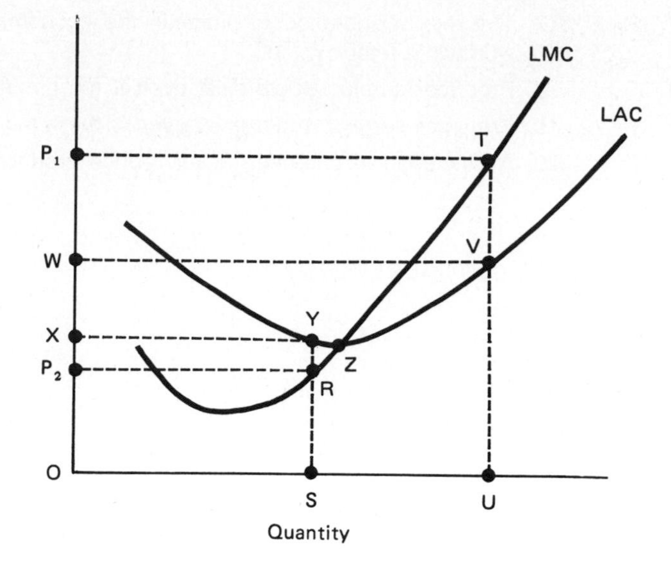

FIGURE 19-3

b. In the long run, if the price equals OP_1, the firm will supply ____________, total revenue will be ____________, average cost will be ____________, total cost will be ____________, and economic profit will be ____________.

c. If the price equals OP_2, then in the short run the firm will supply the quantity ____________, total revenue will be ____________, average cost will be ____________, total cost will be ____________, and economic profit will be ____________.

d. In the long run, if the price equals OP_2, the firm will supply ______, total revenue will be ______, total cost will be ______, and the economic profit will be ______.

e. In the short run, the break-even point is ______ and the shutdown point is ______. In the long run, the break-even point is ______ and the shutdown point is ______.

2. Table 19-1 describes the amounts of factor input that a firm would need to produce various amounts of output *(a)* assuming that the firm has 5 units of capital and *(b)* assuming that the firm has 10 units of capital.

The firm uses only two factors: labor and capital.

Table 19-1

5 units of capital			10 units of capital		
Output	Capital	Labor required	Output	Capital	Labor required
0	5	0	0	10	0
1	5	40	1	10	35
2	5	70	2	10	60
3	5	140	3	10	100
4	5	225	4	10	150
5	5	325	5	10	230
6	5	450	6	10	330

The cost of labor is \$100 per unit and the cost of capital is \$1,000 per unit. Then to produce, say, three units of output with five units of capital costs a total of \$19,000; that is, \$5,000 in fixed costs (five units of capital at \$1,000 per unit) plus \$14,000 in variable costs (140 units of labor at \$100 per unit). This is indicated in Table 19-2. Fill in the rest of this table.

3. Table 19-3 describes a firm's short-run costs. Fill in the missing parts of the table.

When the price equals \$55, the firm's profit maximizing output is ______ and its producer surplus is ______. When the price equals \$75, the firm's profit maximizing output is ______ and its producer surplus is ______. Of all possible prices, the lowest that would induce this firm to produce a positive amount of output in the short run is ______, and the lowest that would enable the firm to avoid suffering a loss in the short run is ______.

Table 19-2

	5 units of capital						10 units of capital					
Output	Total cost	Fixed cost	Variable cost	Average cost	Average variable cost	Marginal cost	Total cost	Fixed cost	Variable cost	Average cost	Average variable cost	Marginal cost
0				—	—	$0				—	—	$0
1												
2												
3	$19,000	$5,000	$14,000	$6,333	$4,667							
4												
5												
6												

Table 19-3

Output	Fixed cost	Variable cost	Average cost	Average variable cost	Marginal cost	Total revenue if price equals $55	Economic profit if price equals $55	Total revenue if price equals $75	Economic profit if price equals $75
0	$30	$ 0			$0				
1	30	90							
2	30	120							
3	30	170							
4	30	240							
5	30	320							

Essay Questions

1. Economists usually draw average cost curves as being U-shaped. What would it mean if the short-run average cost curve always sloped up (that is, did not initially slope down)? What would it mean if the long-run average cost curve always sloped up? Would it be possible for the long-run average cost curve always to slope down? If so, how would this be possible?

2. In the text, it is stated that the implicit costs that the economist considers—but the accountant doesn't—are opportunity costs. It can be argued that even those costs which the accountant does consider are opportunity costs. Defend this position.

3. Explain: If a firm is on its long-run supply curve, then the combination of capital and labor that it is using to produce this amount of output costs less than any other combination which could alternatively be used to produce the same amount of output.

4. Recall the definition of "externality" from Chapter 4. Do the various measures of cost that have been discussed in this chapter include those costs which are external to the firm? Why or why not? If you think not, then how would the cost curves of a company selling nuclear energy shift if these external costs *were* taken into account?

5. Consider the cost curves for a firm with a fixed amount of capital. Is it possible for price to equal marginal cost at more than one level of output? How? In such circumstances, which of these different output levels will be chosen by the profit-maximizing firm? Why? Following this line of reasoning, prove that the short-run supply curve can never be downward sloping.

Answers

True-False Questions: 1 F 2 F 3 T 4 F 5 T 6 T 7 T 8 F 9 F 10 T 11 F 12 F 13 F 14 T 15 T 16 F 17 T 18 T 19 F 20 T

Multiple-Choice Questions: 1 d 2 c 3 e 4 b 5 a 6 a 7 b 8 b

Exercises: **1a.** ON, OP_1AN, OE, $OEDN$, EP_1AD; **b.** OU, OP_1TU, OW, $OWVU$, WP_1TV; **c.** OL, OP_2IL, OF, $OFGL$, $-P_2FGI$; **d.** 0, 0, 0, 0; **e.** H, J, Z, Z.

2.

Table 19-2

Output	5 units of capital: Total cost	Fixed cost	Variable cost	Average cost	Average variable cost	Marginal cost	10 units of capital: Total cost	Fixed cost	Variable cost	Average cost	Average variable cost	Marginal cost
0	$ 5,000	$5,000	$ 0	$ —	$ —	$ 0	$10,000	$10,000	$ 0	$ —	$ —	$ 0
1	9,000	5,000	4,000	9,000	4,000	4,000	13,500	10,000	3,500	13,500	3,500	3,500
2	12,000	5,000	7,000	6,000	3,500	3,000	16,000	10,000	6,000	8,000	3,000	2,500
3	19,000	5,000	14,000	6,333	4,667	7,000	20,000	10,000	10,000	6,667	3,333	4,000
4	27,500	5,000	22,500	6,875	5,625	8,500	25,000	10,000	15,000	6,125	3,750	5,000
5	37,500	5,000	32,500	7,500	6,500	10,000	33,000	10,000	23,000	6,600	4,600	8,000
6	50,000	5,000	45,000	8,333	7,500	12,500	43,000	10,000	33,000	7,167	5,500	10,000

3.

Table 19-3

Output	Fixed cost	Variable cost	Average cost	Average variable cost	Marginal cost	Total revenue if price equals $55	Economic profit if price equals $55	Total revenue if price equals $75	Economic profit if price equals $75
0	$30	$ 0	$—	$—	$ 0	$ 0	$−30	$ 0	$−30
1	30	90	120	90	90	55	−65	75	−45
2	30	120	75	60	30	110	−40	150	0
3	30	170	66⅔	56⅔	50	165	−35	225	25
4	30	240	67½	60	70	220	−50	300	30
5	30	320	70	64	80	275	−75	375	25

0, −30, 4, 30, 56⅔, 66⅔.

chapter **20**

The Perfectly Competitive Market

Learning Objectives

After you have studied this chapter in the textbook and the study guide, you should be able to

Explain why the condition "marginal cost = marginal benefit" is necessary for economic efficiency

Explain why perfect competition results in an efficient outcome when there are no externalities

Give two examples illustrating the inefficiency that may result from perfect competition if there are externalities

State two possible shortcomings of the competitive system that may exist even without externalities

Explain how speculators may produce the same kind of effect as a government price-stabilization scheme

Demonstrate why the area of the "triangle" illustrated in Figure 20-4 in the text is an appropriate measure of the efficiency loss of a departure from perfect competition

CHAPTER HIGHLIGHTS

One sometimes hears it said that people should learn to cooperate more with each other rather than competing. But the economist will say that, on the contrary, competition is often the best method of ensuring cooperation. This is the message of Adam Smith's "invisible hand" (recall our discussion of this in Chapter 1). Each of us, in pursuing our own self-interest, is led by market forces (as if by an invisible hand) to promote the interests of others as well. The purpose of this chapter is to show how this can happen through the operation of perfectly competitive markets as well as to point out some of the possible shortcomings of such markets.

The basic idea is that, under ideal conditions, perfectly competitive markets will produce an *efficient* outcome. The explanation goes as follows: Efficiency requires the marginal cost of any activity to equal its marginal benefit; otherwise there would be a net social gain from changing the level of the activity. For example, if the marginal cost of producing wheat is less than the marginal benefit, then increasing the production of wheat will provide a net gain. How can this equality of marginal cost and marginal benefit be achieved? One way is by allowing the level of the activity to be determined in a perfectly competitive market. As we saw in Chapter 18, consumers in pursuing their self-interest will consume an amount such that their marginal benefit (marginal utility) equals the market price. As we saw in Chapter 19, firms in pursuing their self-interest will produce an amount such that marginal cost equals the market price. Therefore marginal benefit equals marginal cost, because they both equal the market price; the perfectly competitive outcome is therefore an efficient outcome. This result depends upon perfect competition, because the argument in Chapters 18 and 19 assumed that firms and consumers took the market price as given, and this is true only under perfect competition (recall the definition of perfect competition from Chapter 4).

This is the bare bones of the argument. But it involves two crucial assumptions that may or may not be true in any actual situation. The first is that the marginal utilities that consumers take into account equal the socially relevant marginal benefits. In many cases, this may be true. I'm the only one who benefits from my magazine subscription. But there may be external benefits. For example, my home improvements may benefit the entire neighborhood. I will improve my house only up to the point where my own marginal utility equals marginal cost. But the marginal social benefit of my improvements includes not just my own marginal utility. It also includes my neighbors' marginal utilities. Thus it will exceed marginal cost. If I were to increase my home improvements beyond this point, the extra benefit would exceed the extra cost. Why won't I do it? Because my neighbors enjoy much of the benefit but I have to pay all the cost.

The second crucial assumption is that the marginal cost to the firm reflects the marginal cost to society. This will not be the case if there are any external costs. Producers who pollute the environment ignore the costs created by this pollution because they aren't required to pay such costs (unless, of course, the Environmental Protection Agency enters the picture).

In short, the argument that the perfectly competitive market is efficient is valid only if there are no external costs or benefits. What happens if there are such externalities is the subject of Chapters 23 and 24.

Moreover, efficiency isn't everything. Even without externalities, there may be reasons for thinking that the perfectly competitive outcome can be improved upon. For one thing, it may involve an undesirable distribution of income. There are many possible ways of distributing income among different people, and each of these ways may result in a different equilibrium under perfect competition. They are all efficient. But the economist has no objective way of comparing these different efficient outcomes. In order to change from one to another, you would have to take income away from some people and give it to others. (If you could increase *everyone's* income, then the situation couldn't have been efficient to begin with.) But how do you compare one person's gain in utility with another's loss?

Another possible drawback of the competitive system is that it may aggravate the problem of economic instability, especially when production decisions must be made in the light of expectations concerning future prices. These expectations may be unstable, as in the case of the cobweb cycle discussed in Box 20-3. The starred sections of the chapter discuss how these problems might be reduced by private speculators or by government price-stabilization schemes. If private speculators make accurate forecasts, they will tend to iron out fluctuations in the market by selling off their holdings when the price is high (thereby keeping the price from rising even higher) and by buying more when the price is low (thereby keeping the price from falling even lower). Furthermore, speculators who make poor forecasts tend to go out of business. Government price-stabilization schemes in agricultural products work in a similar way by buying from farmers when the price is low and selling on the open market when the price is high.

If efficiency is promoted by the automatic forces of a perfectly competitive market, then an efficiency loss will generally result whenever those forces are interfered with. How big is this loss? Figure 20-4 in the text shows how it can be measured by the area of the "triangle" formed by the supply and demand curves between the actual (inefficient) output level and the perfectly competitive (efficient) output level. This triangle will appear again in many of the following chapters. Be sure you understand why it is an appropriate measure of this efficiency loss.

IMPORTANT TERMS

The paradox of value The paradox that many things which provide a great deal of total utility, such as water, have a smaller market value than other commodities that provide very little total utility, such as diamonds. To resolve this paradox, you have to understand that the market value (price) reflects marginal utility, not total utility.

Economic efficiency An activity is economically efficient if it is run at a level where marginal cost equals marginal benefit. In terms of our definitions in

Chapter 1, this refers to allocative efficiency rather than technical efficiency.

Efficiency loss The loss, measured in dollars, of producing at a level that isn't efficient.

****Pareto optimum*** This is a term used to describe an outcome that is economically efficient. A situation is Pareto-optimal if it is impossible to make anyone better off without making someone else worse off. Clearly, if someone *could* be made better off without hurting someone else, there is a dead-weight loss in the system; in other words, the outcome isn't efficient.

****Cobweb cycle*** The fluctuation of prices that results when a high price this year encourages producers to bring more to the market next year, which causes a low price next year, which encourages producers to bring less to the market the following year, which produces a high price the following year, and so on. This is also sometimes called the "hog cycle."

****Speculation*** The activity of buying and selling commodities with a view to profiting from future price changes. This tends to help stabilize movements in prices as long as speculators make reasonably good forecasts.

True-False Questions

T F **1.** Perfect competition prevails in most markets in the United States economy except for agricultural markets.

T F **2.** According to the paradox of value, demanders get more consumer surplus from high-price goods than they do from low-price goods.

T F **3.** The marginal social benefit of producing a good will exceed the typical buyer's marginal utility if there are external benefits.

T F **4.** Producers disregard external costs because they are not required to pay for them.

T F **5.** Suppose that the government imposes a maximum price that can be charged for some good with no externalities that is sold in a perfectly competitive market. Then, if the maximum price is below the equilibrium price, the marginal benefit from producing that good will exceed the marginal cost.

T F **6.** An economically efficient outcome is one with the best distribution of income.

T F **7.** Smith's invisible hand tends to guide everyone toward the amount of income that he or she deserves.

T F **8.** The perfectly competitive outcome yields the maximum possible sum of utilities of all the individuals in the economy.

T F * **9.** One of the drawbacks of the perfectly competitive system is that it yields unearned profits to speculators.

T F ***10.** Economists generally agree that government price-stabilization schemes are effective in relieving farm poverty.

Multiple-Choice Questions

1. One reason why water sells for less than diamonds is that

- **(a)** Not many people can afford diamonds.
- **(b)** Diamonds are not in high enough demand to warrant mass production.
- **(c)** The market mechanism fails to deal adequately with the paradox of value.
- **(d)** Diamonds have a higher cost of production than water.

2. In Figure 20-1 in the text,

- **(a)** There is a larger consumer surplus for water than for champagne.
- **(b)** The price of champagne would be lower than that of water if they both had the same supply curve.
- **(c)** The price of champagne would be lower than that of water if they both had had the same demand curve.
- **(d)** **(a)** and **(b)**.
- **(e)** **(a)** and **(c)**.

3. If more than the efficient amount of output of some good is produced, then

- **(a)** Both marginal benefit and marginal cost will be higher than in the efficient situation.
- **(b)** Both marginal benefit and marginal cost will be lower than in the efficient situation.
- **(c)** Marginal benefit will be higher and marginal cost lower than in the efficient situation.
- **(d)** Marginal benefit will be lower and marginal cost higher than in the efficient situation.

4. A technological breakthrough that reduces the cost of producing more fertilizer will

- **(a)** Increase the efficient level of fertilizer production
- **(b)** Decrease the efficient level of fertilizer production
- **(c)** Leave the efficient level of fertilizer production unchanged
- **(d)** Change the efficient level of fertilizer production, but not in a predictable direction

5. This same technological breakthrough in fertilizer production will

- **(a)** Increase the efficient level of corn production

(b) Decrease the efficient level of corn production
(c) Leave the efficient level of corn production unchanged
(d) Change the efficient level of corn production, but not in a predictable direction

6. A shift in people's tastes that makes them prefer corn flakes more and oatmeal less will
(a) Increase the efficient level of oat production
(b) Decrease the efficient level of oat production
(c) Leave the efficient level of oat production unchanged
(d) Change the efficient level of oat production, but not in a predictable direction

7. Prices in the market system
(a) Serve as a "rationing device" to decide who gets to consume how much of a scarce good
(b) Serve as a device to decide which producers will survive in the market
(c) Act as a signal to direct resources toward the production of goods in increasing demand
(d) (a) and (b)
(e) All of the above

***8.** According to the cobweb theory analyzed in Box 20-3,
(a) If this year's price is higher than the equilibrium price (the price at *E*), then next year's price will be too.
(b) If this year's price is higher, then next year's price will be lower.
(c) If this year's price is higher, then next year's quantity will be lower than the equilibrium quantity.
(d) (a) and (b).
(e) (a) and (c).

***9.** Private speculators
(a) Will likely profit if they reduce the fluctuations in price arising from the hog cycle
(b) Thrive best when their actions cause prices to fluctuate by even more than they would in the absence of speculation
(c) Are usually buying at the same time as the government price-stabilization program is selling
(d) Are more likely to be active in markets for highly perishable commodities than in markets for goods that can be stored for long periods of time at little cost

***10.** Government programs aimed at keeping farm prices up
(a) Do so at the expense of price stability
(b) Are successful only if the demand for farm goods is elastic
(c) Tend to benefit poor farmers at the expense of rich ones
(d) Raise farm incomes at the expense of economic efficiency

Exercises

All these exercises involve computing consumer and producer surpluses. You should review these concepts and their graphical measurement in Chapters 18 and 19 before proceeding. Also, you may assume for the sake of simplicity that all firms' *AC* curves pass through the origin. Thus the relevant area for measuring producer surplus is the whole area to the left of the supply curve between the origin and the equilibrium price.

1. Suppose that there are no externalities involving the manufactured good, the market for which is depicted in Figure 20-1. The curves labeled *S* and *D* are the competitive supply and demand curves.

a. The equilibrium price is ______ and the equilibrium quantity is ______. Under perfect competition, the amount paid by demanders for the good would equal the area ______ and the total utility received by demanders would equal the area ______; therefore the total consumer surplus would equal ______. Under perfect competition, the producers' total revenue would equal ______ and their total costs would equal ______; therefore the total producer surplus would equal ______ and the sum of consumer and producer surplus would equal ______.

b. Suppose now that this competitive industry is nationalized. All private firms are taken over by the government, which becomes the sole producer of the good. Suppose that the marginal cost schedule is the same as before—namely, the supply curve *S*. Next, suppose that the government sells the good at the previous equilibrium price, *OG*. However, rather than producing the profit-maximizing

FIGURE 20-1

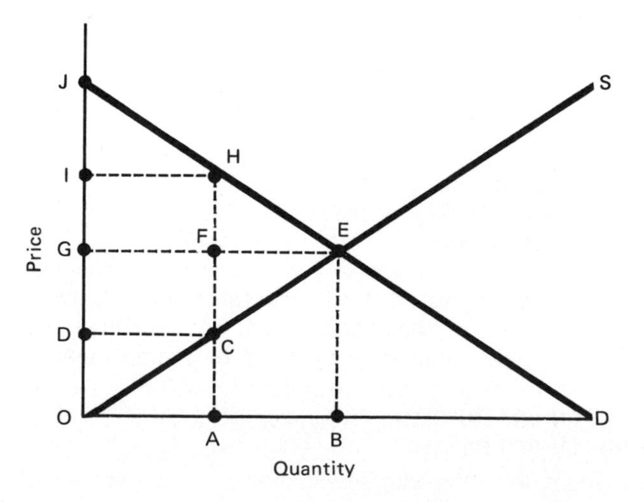

level of output generated by private firms, it produces only the amount OA. Then the amount paid by buyers will equal ______ and their total utility will equal ______. Therefore the total consumer surplus will equal ______.

c. The government's total revenue from producing the good will equal ______ and its total cost of producing the good will equal ______; thus its producer surplus will equal ______. In this situation, the sum of producer and consumer surplus will then equal ______, which is (more, less) than it was before the industry was nationalized by an amount equal to ______.

d. Suppose that, after the industry is nationalized, the government produces the amount OA, but that—instead of charging the previous equilibrium price—it charges the price OI. Then the amount paid by buyers will equal ______ and their total utility will equal ______. Therefore the total consumer surplus will equal ______. The government's total revenue from producing the good will equal ______ and its total cost of producing the good will equal ______; therefore its producer surplus will equal ______. In this situation, the sum of producer and consumer surplus will equal ______, which is (more, less) than it was before the industry was nationalized by the amount ______.

e. The efficiency loss created by the government's decision not to produce as much output as in the competitive equilibrium equals ______, which is (more, less, no different) than the change in the sum of consumer and producer surplus resulting from this decision when the government charges the previous equilibrium price. It is (more, less, no different) than the change in the sum of consumer and producer surplus resulting from the decision when the government charges the price OI.

2. Figure 20-2 shows the supply and demand for a particular grade of wheat in a particular year in a perfectly competitive market in Chicago.

a. The equilibrium price is ______, the equilibrium quantity is ______, the consumer surplus is ______, and the producer surplus is ______.

b. Now suppose that the government, instead of allowing the market to operate freely, buys all the wheat directly from the farmers, offering them a guaranteed price of OC. Therefore the amount supplied will be ______ and the producer surplus will be ______. As a result of this government intervention, producer surplus has gone (up, down) by the amount ______. Shade in this area in the figure.

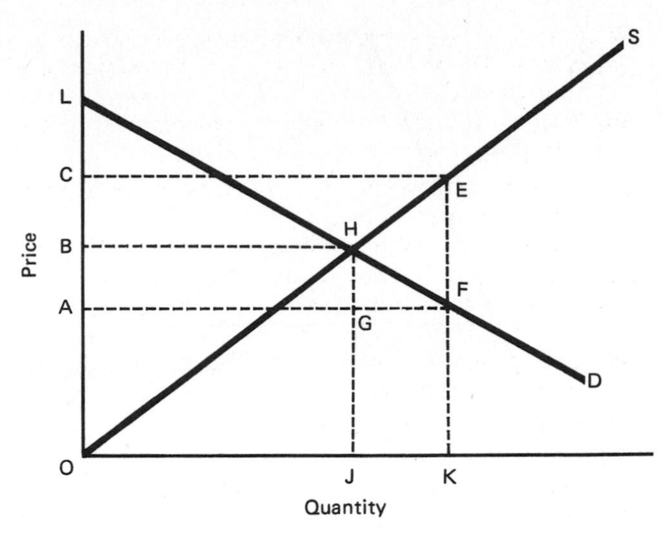

FIGURE 20-2

c. Suppose that the government, after buying this wheat, now sells it all on the market for whatever price it will fetch. This price will be ______; therefore the consumer surplus will be ______. As a result of this government intervention, consumer surplus has gone (up, down) by the amount ______. Shade in this area in the figure.

d. If we considered only the change in the sum of consumer and producer surplus (the two shaded areas), we would conclude that there has been a net gain to the economy as a result of the government's intervention. However, the government has suffered a loss on these wheat dealings, for which the taxpayers must pay. The total amount that the government paid for the wheat equals ______ and the total revenue that the government received for selling the wheat equals ______, so the loss equals ______. If we deduct this loss from the gain in consumer plus producer surplus, we conclude that the government's action resulted in a net (gain, loss) to the economy which equals ______. The standard measure of the efficiency loss from the action is ______.

3. The purpose of this exercise is to demonstrate the social benefit that can be produced by the existence of markets. Figures 20-3 and 20-4 represent the markets for a manufactured good in Florida and in Texas.

a. Suppose that initially there were no trade between the two states—that is, no market in which people from one state could trade with

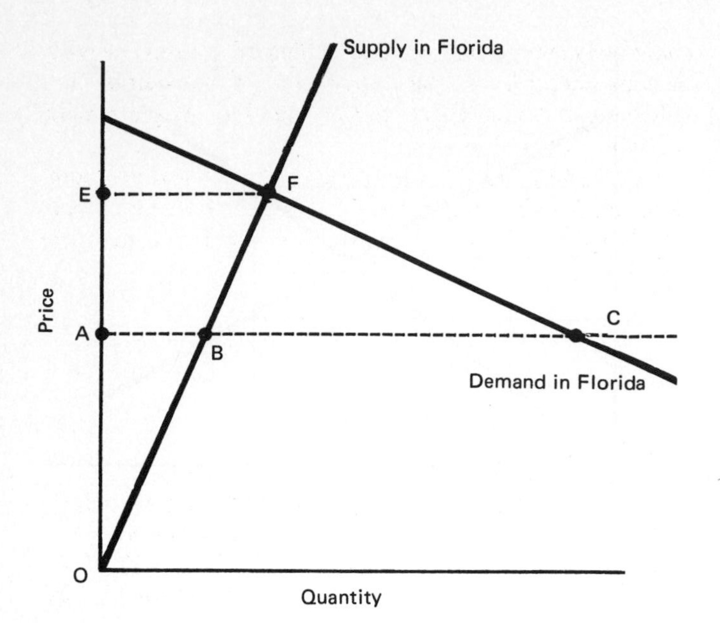

FIGURE 20-3

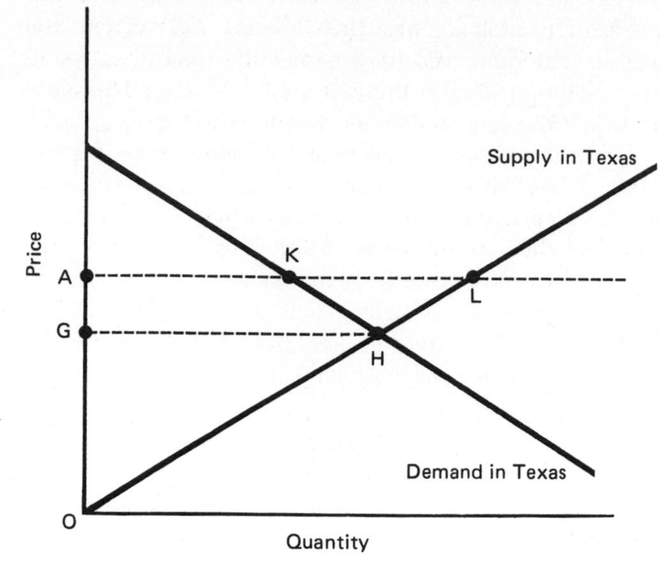

FIGURE 20-4

people from the other. Then the equilibrium price in Florida would be ______ and the equilibrium price in Texas would be ______.

b. Next, suppose that a group of traders organized a market in which Texans could trade with Floridians. Suppose that there were no transportation costs or any other kind of cost to separate the markets of the two states. Then there would, in fact, be only one market that included both states. A single equilibrium price would be established such that the total amount supplied in the two states was just equal to the total amount demanded in the two states (suppose no other states are involved). Therefore the excess of supply over demand in one state must equal the excess of demand over supply in the other. In the figures, this equilibrium price equals *OA*. At that price, Florida has an excess of (demand, supply) over (demand, supply) that is equal to ______, and Texas has an excess of (demand, supply) over (demand, supply) equal to ______. The reason why *OA* is an equilibrium price is that these two excesses are just equal to each other.

c. As a result of allowing trade between the two states, consumer surplus in Florida has gone (up, down) by the amount ______ and producer surplus in Florida has gone (up, down) by the amount ______; therefore the sum of consumer and producer surplus in Florida has gone ______ by the amount ______.

d. Consumer surplus in Texas has gone (up, down) by the amount ______, producer surplus in Texas has gone (up, down) by the amount ______, and the sum of consumer and producer surplus in Texas has gone (up, down) by the amount ______.

Essay Questions

1. According to the economist's theory of how markets work, butchers provide us with meat in an economically efficient manner not because they hate to see us go hungry but because they are interested in making as large a profit as possible. But if they are interested in maximizing their profit, will they not then be led to exploit consumers by charging a price far in excess of their costs? If they did this, would the results be economically efficient? Why would they be unable to do this under perfect competition? Does the invisible hand lead to an efficient level of output in the case of a good sold by a monopoly?

2. What general conclusion can you draw from Exercises 1 and 2 about the relationship between consumer and producer surplus on the one hand and our standard measure of economic efficiency on the other?

3. In Exercise 3, who would be the gainers and who would be the losers from the opening up of trade between the two states? What sorts of arguments do you suppose the losers might propose in favor of a government prohibition of such trade? How could these arguments be countered? Can you imagine any way in which the gainers might compensate the losers? Would the total gain in each state be enough so that, after such compensation, everyone could be a gainer?

4. Suppose someone were to argue that the excess of total benefit over total cost resulting from wheat production was far greater than the excess of total benefit over total cost in the production of household appliances but that, for efficiency, there should be an increase in the production of household appliances and not wheat. Is this possible? Explain why or why not with a diagram.

5. Show how a speculator who is also a poor forecaster will tend to amplify the fluctuations in the market price. Show why he or she won't stay in business long.

Answers

True-False Questions: 1 F 2 F 3 T 4 T 5 T 6 F 7 F 8 F 9 F 10 F

Multiple-Choice Questions: **1 d 2 d 3 d 4 a 5 a 6 b 7 e 8 b 9 a 10 d**

Exercises: **1a.** *OG*, *OB*, *OGEB*, *OJEB*, *GJE*, *OGEB*, *OEB*, *OGE*, *OJE;* **b.** OGFA, OJHA, GJHF; **c.** *OGFA*, *OCA*, *OGFC*, *OJHC*, less, *CHE;* **d.** *OIHA*, *OJHA*, *IJH*, *OIHA*, *OCA*, *OIHC*, *OJHC*, less, *CHE;* **e.** *CHE*, no different, no different.

2a. *OB*, *OJ*, *BLH*, *OBH;* **b.** *OK*, *OCE*, up, *BCEH;* **c.** *OA*, *ALF*, up, *ABHF;* **d.** *OCEK*, *OAFK*, *ACEF*, loss, *HEF*, *HEF*.

3a. *OE*, *OG;* **b.** demand, supply, *BC*, supply, demand, *KL;* **c.** up, *AEFC*, down, *AEFB*, up, *BFC;* **d.** down, *AKHG*, up, *ALHG*, up, *KLH*.

chapter 21 Monopoly

Learning Objectives

After you have studied this chapter in the textbook and the study guide, you should be able to

State four reasons why monopolies exist

Illustrate the situation of a natural monopoly in a diagram

Explain why the condition "marginal revenue = marginal cost" must be satisfied by the profit-maximizing monopolist

Show in a diagram that the monopolist generally produces less than the economically efficient level of output

List three types of government policy toward monopoly

Explain how marginal-cost pricing and average-cost pricing work

Explain why there is a natural instability in producers' associations because of the incentive to cheat

Show how price discrimination may sometimes be beneficial

CHAPTER HIGHLIGHTS

The last chapter discussed the ideal case of perfect competition. This one discusses the pathological case of monopoly—where there is just one seller. It deals with the questions of *(a)* why monopoly exists, *(b)* how a monopoly chooses price and quantity, *(c)* why monopoly is undesirable (usually!), *(d)* the effects of government policies directed toward monopoly, *(e)* how government agricultural policies can have the effect of allowing farmers to act as monopolists, and *(f)* how a monopoly may practice price discrimination.

Why Monopoly Exists

Monopolies exist for any or all of the following reasons: (1) the monopolist may possess something valuable that no potential competitor can acquire (for example, some talent, property, or patent); (2) the government may have created the monopoly by making competition illegal, as with the post office; (3) the existing sellers may have *colluded*—that is, agreed to act in cooperation rather than competition; or (4) there may be a *natural* monopoly.

The case of natural monopoly is perhaps the most important. It exists whenever there are economies of scale (recall this from Chapter 19) that would not be exhausted by a large number of firms in competition. In other words, a single firm's average cost curve might continue to fall even as its output became large enough to supply the entire industry (see Figure 21-1 in the text).

How a Monopoly Chooses its Price and Quantity

A monopoly, just like a perfectly competitive firm, maximizes profit by choosing the level of output where its marginal revenue (MR) equals its marginal cost (MC). But whereas the perfect competitor's MR equals the market price, the monopolist's MR is *less than* the market price. This is because the perfect competitor faces a horizontal demand curve but the monopolist's demand curve slopes downward to the right. When a perfect competitor sells one more unit, the price stays the same. The extra revenue is just the market price. When a monopolist sells one more unit, the price doesn't stay the same. It falls. Thus the monopolist's extra revenue (MR) is the market price that is received from selling an extra unit *minus* the loss incurred because selling an extra unit lowers the price that is received for all the other units.

In other words, the monopolist's MR curve lies below its demand curve; consequently, it intersects the MC curve at a lower level of output, as you can see in Figure 21-5*b* in the text. This lower output is how the monopoly exploits its advantage. By thus making the product scarce it keeps the price high.

As with the perfectly competitive firm, the marginal condition MR = MC only determines the monopolist's decision *provided* that the enterprise is able to cover its costs—that is, stay in business. This requires that the demand curve overlap the AC curve, as in Figure 21-4 in the text.

Why Monopoly Is (Usually!) Undesirable

Figure 21-5*b* in the text shows that the monopolist's profit-maximizing level of output (where MC = MR) is less than the efficient level (where MC = P). Thus a monopoly generates an efficiency loss. This loss is the main disadvantage of monopoly. But a complete verdict on any particular monopoly must also consider such other items as the transfer of income from the consumers to the monopolist. Whether this transfer is desirable or undesirable is largely a matter of value judgment. To repeat, there is no objective way of comparing one person's gain with another's loss.

Government Policies toward Monopoly

These policies generally take three forms: (1) controlling the monopolist's price, (2) nationalizing the industry (having the government buy it out), and (3) preventing any firm from monopolizing a new or existing industry. The first of these is analyzed in this chapter. The basic rule that guides price regulation is to set the price that would exist if the industry were perfectly competitive. Because the monopolistic firm must take this regulated price as given, it therefore acts like a perfect competitor—a price taker. The result is an efficient outcome. However, regulation may *(a)* reduce the firm's incentive to control costs (since higher MC will result in a higher regulated price) and *(b)* prevent the monopolist from making enough profit to stay in business. In case of *(b)*, Box 21-2 in the text shows how the efficiency loss of monopoly may be reduced by a compromise regulation that sets price equal to AC instead of MC or how the efficiency loss may be eliminated altogether if the MC rule is followed but the firm is given a subsidy to keep it in business.

Government Marketing Programs

These are aimed at keeping up producers' incomes in competitive industries. In agricultural markets, they attempt to deal with the problems discussed in Chapter 17. Many of these programs set producer quotas aimed at restricting output and thereby raising prices in the same way as a monopolist would do. The difficulty of any such program is that it is always in the individual producer's self-interest to cheat by producing more than the allotted quota. The quota system "works" (that is, raises producers' incomes) by raising price above MC. But as long as price exceeds MC, the individual producer will want to produce more. The *collective* interest of farmers is best served by quotas. But if everyone else obeyed the quotas, the *individual* interest of a farmer would best be served exceeding his or her quota.

Price Discrimination

So far we have assumed that the monopolistic firm charges a single price to all consumers. But such a firm will usually make more profits if different prices can be charged to different customers—that is, if a higher price is charged to those customers who are willing and able to pay it. Such price discrimination may be beneficial if it allows the monopoly to make

IMPORTANT TERMS

Natural monopoly A monopoly that exists because of economies of scale that could not be fully exploited by more than one firm in the industry.

Market power A firm has market power if it is able to influence the market price by changing its supply.

enough profits to stay in business when it would otherwise, if forced to charge a single price, go bankrupt.

Marginal revenue The change in revenue resulting from a unit increase in output. For the perfect competitor, marginal revenue (MR) equals price; for the monopolist, MR is less than price. Indeed, for the monopolist, MR may become negative if too much is produced.

****Theory of second best*** The theory of what constitutes an efficient level of output in one industry when the level of output in some of the other industries is not efficient because of, perhaps, monopoly in some of the other industries. (See Box 21-1 in the text.)

Price discrimination The practice of charging different prices to different customers for the same good. This is one method by which monopolists sometimes make supernormal profits.

Marginal-cost pricing The policy of regulating a monopolist's price by setting it at the level where the monopolist's MC curve intersects the market demand curve.

Average-cost pricing The policy of regulating a monopolist's price by setting it at the level when the monopolist's AC curve intersects the market demand curve.

Producers' association An organization designed to allow the firms in a perfectly competitive industry to behave collectively like a monopolist by setting quotas that restrict production. These associations tend to break down because of the incentive for individual firms to cheat by exceeding their assigned quotas.

True-False Questions

T F **1.** The term "monopoly" includes the situation in which the government operates the only firm in the industry.

T F **2.** The United States patent system provides one basis for the existence of monopolies.

T F **3.** One aim of producers' associations is to monopolize an industry.

T F **4.** A monopolist's marginal revenue can exceed the market price.

T F **5.** Whereas monopoly involves only one seller, oligopoly involves only one buyer.

T F **6.** Suppose that the equilibrium in a perfectly competitive industry occurred at a point where all firms' long-run AC curves were upward-sloping. With this demand and this cost structure, the industry might develop into a natural monopoly.

T F **7.** In the situation described in question 6, the industry might develop into a natural monopoly if total market demand were to increase.

T F **8.** In the situation described in question 6, the industry might develop into a natural monopoly if total market demand were to decrease.

T F **9.** A monopoly is free to charge any price and to sell any quantity that it wishes.

T F **10.** The elasticity of the monopolist's demand curve is less than that of the demand curve faced by the firm in perfect competition.

T F **11.** The monopoly exercises its monopoly power primarily by influencing the position of the demand schedule.

T F **12.** The monopolist's average-cost curve necessarily falls at the profit-maximizing output.

T F **13.** With no externalities, an unregulated monopolist will produce more than the economically efficient level of output.

T F **14.** When demand falls, the firm operating as an unregulated monopolist will not shut down in the short run, even if its AC curve lies to the right of the new demand curve, provided that the AVC curve overlaps the demand curve.

T F **15.** Marginal-cost pricing will always improve technical efficiency as well as allocative efficiency.

T F ***16.** According to the theory of the second best, if all other industries are unregulated monopolies, it may be efficient for this industry to produce less than the level of output that would exist under perfect competition.

T F **17.** If a monopolist suffers economic losses when forced to "marginal-cost" price, then a subsidy that allows the firm to stay in business will generate an efficiency loss.

T F **18.** The price-discriminating monopolist will make more profits than the single-price monopolist with the same costs and the same demand curve.

T F **19.** Average-cost pricing generally produces less of an efficiency gain than marginal-cost pricing.

T F **20.** Producers' associations tend to break down because firms tend to shut down and go out of business when quotas do not allow them to produce as much as they would like.

T F **21.** The desire by the owner of a firm to enjoy "a quiet life" rather than to maximize profits is more likely to play an important role in the case of monopoly than in that of perfect competition.

Multiple-Choice Questions

1. A successful voluntary producers' association would best be classified as
- **(a)** A monopoly arising from exclusive ownership of something
- **(b)** A legal monopoly
- **(c)** A natural monopoly
- **(d)** A collusive monopoly

2. The monopolist's marginal revenue is
- **(a)** Always positive
- **(b)** Always above average cost
- **(c)** Less than the marginal social benefit of producing the good (assuming no externalities)
- **(d)** More than the marginal social benefit of producing the good (assuming no externalities)

3. Which of the following is true of both the monopolist and the perfect competitor?
- **(a)** Price will be no greater than marginal cost.
- **(b)** Price will equal average cost.
- **(c)** Marginal revenue will equal marginal cost, regardless of average variable cost.
- **(d)** Marginal revenue will equal marginal cost as long as the price is not less than average variable cost.

4. Regardless of the number of other firms in the industry, a firm's demand curve indicates its
- **(a)** Marginal revenue
- **(b)** Marginal cost
- **(c)** Average revenue
- **(d)** Average cost

5. If a monopolist's marginal revenue exceeds marginal cost, the firm should
- **(a)** Decrease production
- **(b)** Increase production
- **(c)** Leave production unchanged
- **(d)** Close down

6. Which of the following makes the largest profit? (Assume that the monopolists are identical in all respects except those explicitly mentioned and that they all make enough profits to continue producing.)
- **(a)** The unregulated monopolist charging a single price
- **(b)** The unregulated, price-discriminating monopolist
- **(c)** The monopolist subject to a regulation that enforces marginal-cost pricing
- **(d)** The monopolist subject to a regulation that enforces average-cost pricing

7. Which of the following policies might allow a monopolist to stay in business whose average-cost curve was always to the right of its demand curve?
- **(a)** Average-cost pricing
- **(b)** Marginal-cost pricing, but only when combined with subsidization
- **(c)** Price discrimination
- **(d)** **(a)** and **(c)**
- **(e)** **(b)** and **(c)**

Exercises

1a. The monopolist described by Figure 21-1 will, if unregulated, produce the amount ______, charge the price ______, and make a profit equal to ______.

FIGURE 21-1

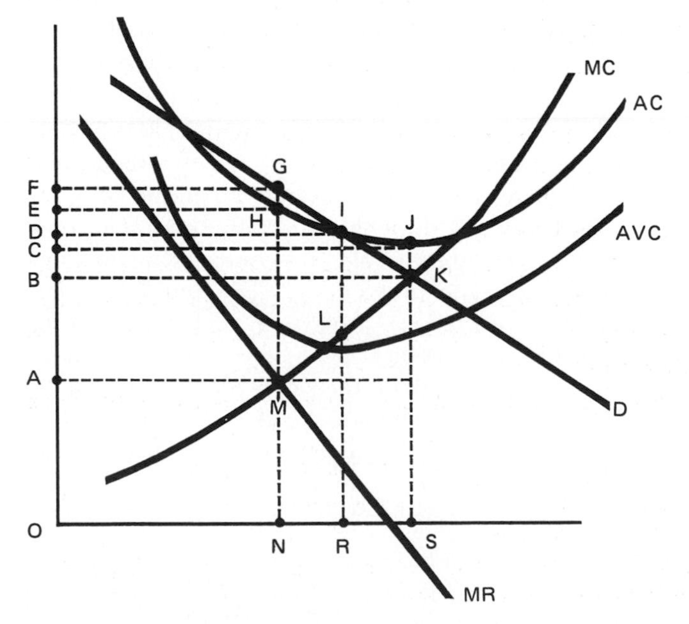

1b. The efficiency loss of this output level would be ______. If the monopolist firm were regulated according to an average-cost pricing scheme, its price would be ______, its output would be ______, and its profit would be ______. The efficiency loss of this level of output would be ______.

1c. If it were regulated according to a marginal-cost pricing scheme, its price would be ______, its output would be ______, its profit would be ______, and the minimum amount of lump-sum subsidy required to keep the monopolist in business would be ______. The efficiency loss of this level of output would be ______.

2. A monopolist produces subject to costs that depend upon the formula total cost $= 2 + Q^2$ (where Q is the monopolist's output level), and its demand curve obeys the formula $P = 10 - 2Q$, where P is, of course, the price at which the monopolist can sell the amount Q of output. Then if the monopolist sets $Q = 1$, total cost will equal $2 + (1)^2 = 3$, the price at which this amount of output can be sold will equal $10 - 2 \times 1 = 8$, and total revenue ($PQ = 8 \times 1$) will equal 8. Fill in the rest of Table 21-1, ignoring the last three columns for the time being.

Table 21-1

Q	*P*	Total revenue	Marginal revenue	Total cost	Average cost	Marginal cost	Profit	(1) Net profit with lump-sum tax	(2) Net total revenue with excise tax	(3) Net profit with excise tax
0	$____	$____	$ 0	$____	$ —	$ 0	$____	$____	$____	$____
1	8	8	____	3	____	____	____	____	____	____
2	____	____	____	____	____	____	____	____	____	____
3	____	____	____	____	____	____	____	____	____	____
4	____	____	____	____	____	____	____	____	____	____

a. The monopolist firm's fixed cost is ______. It will choose to produce a level of output equal to ______ and charge a price equal to ______. Its maximum attainable profit is ______.

b. Suppose that, in an attempt to capture some of this monopolist's profits for the general taxpayer's benefit, the government were to impose a lump-sum tax of $5. This tax may be regarded by the monopolist as a fixed cost, because he must pay it no matter how much he produces. After the imposition of this tax, the monopolist's fixed cost is ______. Fill in the third-to-last column (1) indicating the monopolist's after-tax profit. After the imposition of the tax the monopolist will choose to produce a level of output equal to ______ and to charge a price equal to ______; and its maximum attainable after-tax profit is ______.

c. Suppose that instead of a lump-sum tax the government decides to impose a 50 percent excise tax on the monopolist's output. In other words, the monopolist must now pay to the government 50 percent of its total (before tax) revenues. In this case, the monopolist's fixed cost is ______. Fill in the second-to-last column (2) showing the monopolist's net (after-tax) total revenue and the last column (3) showing the monopolist's net profit under the excise tax. In this case the monopolist will choose to produce a level of output equal to ______ and to charge a price equal to ______; its maximum attainable after-tax profit will be ______. The amount of excise tax collected from this monopolist will be ______.

d. From the point of view of economic efficiency the (lump-sum, excise) tax is preferable. From the point of view of maximizing the amount of tax revenue collected from the monopolist, the (lump-sum, excise) tax is preferable.

Essay Questions

1. Suppose that the government decides to prevent the merger of the only two firms in an industry, even though that merger would result in a reduction in costs of production in that industry because of the elimination of wasteful duplication. Defend the position that this government action is warranted on the grounds of economic efficiency. Defend the position that it is not warranted on the grounds of economic efficiency.

2. What do you suppose would happen to expenditure on research if the government always taxed away the monopoly profits that firms earn from their patented research results? In light of this, do you think that government should tax the profits of a natural monopoly differently from the profits of a monopoly based on the exclusive possession of patents?

3. Explain carefully what is wrong with the following statement. "If the industry demand curve lies to the left of a monopolist's average-cost curve, then—on the grounds of economic efficiency—it is a good thing for the monopolist to go out of business because demanders will not willingly pay enough for the good to cover the cost of producing it."

4. It has been argued by some that the American Medical Association operates the medical services industry as a collusive monopoly. By what method is the medical profession able to restrict the output of medical services? How does this affect the cost of medical services? What unfavorable consequences might there be if the government were to allow completely free entry into the medical profession—that is, if anyone could set up in a medical practice even with no medical training? In light of this, defend the position *(a)* that the medical profession's collusive monopoly has been beneficial to the economy and *(b)* that the medical profession's collusive monopoly has been harmful to the economy.

5. A monopolist might find it in his interest to expand output even if this had the effect of reducing the price at which he could sell his output and of increasing his costs per unit of output. How could this possibly make sense?

6. Recall our discussion of the elasticity of demand from Chapter 17. If a monopolist firm's demand function is elastic, what happens to its total revenue as output increases? In this case, what can be said about the monopolist's marginal revenue? In the case where the market demand function is inelastic, what can be said about marginal revenue? In light of this, explain why a monopolist firm that found its demand curve to be inelastic would want to change its output.

***7.** If the demand curve shifts to the right in a perfectly competitive market, the quantity produced in that industry will rise. Show how this might or might not be the case in a monopolistic industry depending upon how the shift in the demand curve affected the elasticity of demand.

***8.** If a monopolist were a *perfect* price discriminator, then for each unit sold she would charge the maximum attainable price. That is, she would charge a price so high for each unit that none of her consumers would be left with any consumer surplus whatsoever. Each customer would pay the maximum amount he would conceivably be willing to pay for each unit. What is this monopoly's MR? Its equilibrium price and quantity? Show that in this case the standard efficiency loss resulting from monopoly would actually disappear.

Answers

True-False Questions: **1** T **2** T **3** T **4** F **5** F **6** F **7** F **8** T **9** F **10** T **11** F **12** F **13** F **14** T **15** F **16** T **17** F **18** T **19** T **20** F **21** T

Multiple-Choice Questions: **1** d **2** c **3** d **4** c **5** b **6** b **7** e

Exercises: **1a.** *ON*, *OF*, *EFGH*; **b.** *GKM*, *OD*, *OR*, O, *ILK*; **c.** *OB*, *OS*, *−BCJK*, *BCJK*, O.

2.

Table 21-1

Q	*P*	Total revenue	Marginal revenue	Total cost	Average cost	Marginal cost	Profit	(1) Net profit with lump-sum tax	(2) Net total revenue with excise tax	(3) Net profit with excise tax
0	$10	$ 0	$ 0	$ 2	$ —	$0	$ −2	$ −7	$0	$ −2
1	8	8	8	3	3	1	5	0	4	1
2	6	12	4	6	3	3	6	1	6	0
3	4	12	0	11	3⅔	5	1	−4	6	−5
4	2	8	4	18	4½	7	−10	−15	4	−14

a. 2, 2, 6, 6; **b.** 7, 2, 6, 1; **c.** 2, 1, 8, 1, 4; **d.** lump sum, lump sum.

chapter 22 Markets Between Monopoly and Perfect Competition

Learning Objectives

After you have studied this chapter in the textbook and the study guide, you should be able to

Explain the distinction between oligopoly and monopolistic competition
Give two reasons why oligopoly may arise
Describe the kinked demand curve diagrammatically
Explain why the kinked demand curve would discourage an oligopolistic firm from changing its price frequently
Explain the concept of price leadership and its connection with collusion
Give three examples of non-price competition
List two possible barriers to entry
Summarize the cases for and against advertising
State four major problems connected with government policy toward oligopoly
List three major legislative acts aimed at reducing the problems of oligopoly and monopoly
Explain why the monopolistic competitor earns no supernormal profits in the long run

CHAPTER HIGHLIGHTS

The last two chapters dealt with the extreme cases of perfect competition (where all firms are price takers) and monopoly (where there is only one firm). This chapter deals with markets between these extremes, where firms are not price takers but there is more than one firm. There are two basic forms of such markets:

1. *Oligopoly*: the case of "few sellers." This is typical of much large-scale manufacturing that is dominated by giant corporations.

2. *Monopolistic competition*: In this case there are many sellers, but each firm can raise its price at least somewhat without losing all its sales to rivals. Because the firm's product is differentiated from those of its rivals, some customers will continue to buy the product even if it costs a little more. This is typical of many manufacturing industries in the United States that are not dominated by giant corporations.

This chapter discusses how these two forms of "imperfect competition" might come about, what principles govern the behavior of firms, why either form of market organization might be regarded as desirable or undesirable, and the effects on such markets of various government policies.

First, consider oligopoly. How many sellers is "a few"? This depends on the industry's concentration ratio—the fraction of sales going to the few (usually four) leading firms. Oligopoly exists if this concentration ratio is "high." An oligopoly can arise either because of natural oligopoly, where a small number of firms operating at minimum average cost can satisfy market demand, or because some firms grow large enough to obtain market power (some influence over price).

Because there are few clear-cut principles governing the behavior of oligopolists, the theoretical analysis in this chapter is much less straightforward than in earlier chapters. But the following points are important:

1. There is a tendency for oligopolists to collude—to act like a monopolist so as to maximize the total profits available to the industry as a whole. However, there is also a tendency for collusive arrangements to break down because of the incentive for members to violate these agreements. (Recall the last chapter's discussion of why collusive monopolies are unstable.) An example of this kind of arrangement is the OPEC oil cartel that succeeded in quadrupling world oil prices in 1973 and which by now would probably have collapsed if it were not for the very special circumstances outlined in this chapter.

2. When the oligopolist firm chooses its price and output, it must take into account the possible reaction of its rivals—a factor that need not even be considered by the monopolist (with no rivals) or the perfect competitor firm (whose rivals don't even notice it). This sort of complicated decision making is what makes the theory of oligopoly so difficult.

3. Some think that the typical oligopolistic firm faces a kinked demand curve. If it raises its prices, its rivals won't. Instead they'll hope to capture some of the oligopolist's sales. But if the firm in question lowers its price, the rivals *will* follow suit to avoid being undersold. As explained in Figure 22-5 of the text, this inhibits the oligopolist firm from changing its price except in extreme circumstances. However, many think that the kinked demand curve is not a very realistic theory.

4. Some oligopolies seem to operate by a pattern of *price leadership* in which one firm—on the understanding that other firms will follow suit—takes on the role of being the first to announce price changes. This sort of "gentleman's agreement" has often been criticized as a collusive arrangement. The price leader may set the price just like a monopolist would.

5. Rather than undertake potentially destructive price competition, many oligopolies favor various forms of non-price competition based on packaging, product differentiation, and advertising. But advertising may *(a)* involve wasteful competition, *(b)* distort people's values, and *(c)* mislead consumers. (In defense of advertising, it has been argued that it helps to make consumers well informed, that it supports the communications industry, and that it helps to promote product quality by making firms fearful of losing the goodwill that they achieve through advertising.)

6. Oligopolies often succeed in erecting barriers to entry against new competition. Advertising may serve as a barrier to entry by creating in customers' minds a favorable image of the existing firms, which is hard for new firms to overcome. But the most important barrier to entry is the natural one of the economies of scale that leave room for only a few firms in the industry. Since barriers to entry make it easier for oligopolists to collude, much of the United States government's efforts are directed against their erection.

In dealing with oligopoly, the government faces several problems: (1) It is hard to promote competition by more firms without at the same time giving up some of the economies of scale that may be enjoyed only when there is a small number of large firms in an industry. (2) The government is always confronted with reasonable-sounding arguments by oligopolists to the effect that potential competition is "unfair" or otherwise damaging (see Box 22-2 in the text). (3) Collusion, like any conspiracy, is hard to detect and even harder to prove in court. (4) Corporate mergers resulting in large "conglomerate" firms can create social and political problems because of their very size, even if no collusion or unfair barriers to entry are involved.

The main laws that underlie the government's antitrust policy are: (1) The Sherman Anti-Trust Act (1890), which made collusion illegal; (2) the Clayton Act (1914), which banned such specific acts as interlocking corporate directorships, the elimination of competition through corporate takeovers, and tie-in sales that force someone to buy a whole product line or nothing; and (3) the Federal Trade Commission (FTC) Act (1914), which established the FTC to prevent "unfair competition"—in particular, business mergers that would violate the Sherman or Clayton Acts. The text mentions the examples of the Robinson-Patman Act (1936) and the Miller-Tydings Act (1937) to show how some government laws actually work in *opposition to* the spirit of the antitrust legislation.

Monopolistic competition presents few of the problems that characterize oligopoly. The main problem is that monopolistically competitive firms quote prices that are somewhat above competitive prices. Like a monopolist, these firms face a downward-sloping demand curve. Thus they tend to quote a higher price and produce a lower output than a perfectly competitive firm. However, this does not necessarily imply inefficiency. The reason is that lower output by each firm means there will be more firms to satisfy total market demand. And since, in monopolistic competition, they are producing differentiated products, the consumer has a wider range of choice. Moreover, although the firm in monopolistic competition does have some influence over its price, it cannot use this market power in the long run to earn supernormal profits. The reason is that there is free entry of firms into this type of market. Thus, whenever existing firms start earning supernormal profits, new firms will enter and reduce the demand for existing firms' products. This process will continue until all supernormal profits have been eliminated. In other words, in the long run, the monopolistic competitor's demand curve will be just tangent to its AC curve (see Figure 22-6 in the text).

IMPORTANT TERMS

Oligopoly A market structure with few sellers.

Concentration ratio A measure of oligopoly—usually the proportion of an industry's sales going to the four largest firms.

Natural oligopoly One that arises because of economies of scale. It occurs when a firm producing at minimum average cost is large enough to satisfy a significant fraction of total market demand.

Product differentiation The ability of a firm to distinguish its product from those of its rivals. Such differentiation may be real or fancied.

Cartel Formal agreement among firms to collude in setting prices and/or in determining market shares.

Cutthroat competition The setting of price below average cost in order to drive rivals out of business.

OPEC The Organization of Petroleum Exporting Countries. This is the international oil cartel formed in late 1973.

Kinked demand curve The demand curve that some people think faces an oligopolist. It has a kink in it at the current price because rivals will respond to the oligopolist's price reduction by cutting their prices, but they will not respond to the oligopolist's price *increases* by raising their prices (see Figure 22-5 in the text).

Price leadership The practice in some oligopolistic industries of having one firm announce its price changes first, on the understanding that other firms will follow suit.

Barrier to entry Anything that makes it difficult for new firms to enter an industry to compete against existing firms. Some barriers, like advertising, are "created" (artificial); but others, like economies of scale, are natural.

Monopolistic competition A market in which *(a)* there are many firms and *(b)* each seller's product is differentiated from those of the others.

True-False Questions

T F **1.** The concentration ratio measures the amount of market power possessed by the largest single firm in an industry.

T F **2.** The minimum point on the AC curve lies further to the right for a natural monopoly than for a natural oligopoly (assuming the same market demand curve in each case).

T F **3.** A firm might want to expand its output beyond the point where MR = MC if by doing so it would increase its market power.

T F **4.** In monopolistic competition, there is always product differentiation.

T F **5.** The oligopolist firm's market power allows it to choose its price without having to worry about its rivals' reactions to its decision.

T F **6.** Collusion is legal in the United States.

T F **7.** Cutthroat competition is a common sequel to the breakdown of a cartel arrangement.

T F **8.** The OPEC oil cartel has not broken down, because oil constitutes such a large fraction of total costs in the industrialized nations of the world.

T F **9.** The kinked demand curve arises mainly in monopolistic competition.

T F 10. The theory of the kinked demand curve doesn't predict at which price the kink will occur.

T F 11. Price leadership is more common in monopolistic competition than in oligopoly.

T F 12. A price leader is often suspected of being the manager of a tacit cartel arrangement.

T F 13. Advertising often constitutes a natural barrier to entry in an industry.

T F 14. Economies of scale may constitute a natural barrier to entry in an industry.

T F 15. Barriers to entry are rare or nonexistent in monopolistically competitive industries.

T F 16. The monopolistic competitor typically has some market power.

T F 17. Conglomerate mergers create a problem for policy makers only if they result in more efficiency losses due to further restrictions of output.

T F 18. One of the purposes of the Sherman Act was to empower the FTC to prevent mergers that would reduce competition.

T F 19. The Miller-Tydings Act was intended to protect the interests of small businesses.

Multiple-Choice Questions

1. The concentration ratio usually measures the share of the industry sales going to the top
- **(a)** 3 firms
- **(b)** 4 firms
- **(c)** 6 firms
- **(d)** 10 firms

2. Product differentiation occurs
- **(a)** Never in perfect competition but always in monopolistic competition
- **(b)** Never in monopoly or monopolistic competition
- **(c)** Only in monopolistic competition
- **(d)** **(a)** and **(c)**
- **(e)** **(b)** and **(c)**

3. The oligopolist is sometimes referred to as a
- **(a)** Price taker
- **(b)** Price maker
- **(c)** Price searcher
- **(d)** Quantity taker

4. The efficiency loss that collusion imposes upon the nation results mainly from
- **(a)** The incentive for each firm to cheat by exceeding its quota
- **(b)** The transfer of income from customers to the sellers that collude
- **(c)** The resulting restriction in the industry's output
- **(d)** The unwillingness of other sellers to follow the price leader

5. According to the theory of the kinked demand curve
- **(a)** The kink is in the market demand curve, not the firm's individual demand curve.
- **(b)** The kink in one firm's demand curve will occur above the price being charged by other firms.
- **(c)** The firm believes that its rivals will follow suit if it lowers its price.
- **(d)** **(a)** and **(c)**.
- **(e)** **(b)** and **(c)**.

6. The practice of price leadership
- **(a)** Makes tacit collusion difficult to detect
- **(b)** Is most common in monopolistic competition
- **(c)** Does not occur in markets with differentiation
- **(d)** Is a device that is used in cutthroat competition

7. Non-price competition
- **(a)** Is often fostered by government price regulation in an industry
- **(b)** Is practiced by the firm in perfect competition
- **(c)** Is practiced only by monopolies
- **(d)** Is an effective way to stimulate aggregate demand during a recession

8. In the long run, the firm in a monopolistically competitive industry will
- **(a)** Make supernormal profits
- **(b)** Produce more than the amount that would minimize average cost
- **(c)** Produce less than the amount that would minimize average cost
- **(d)** Produce a quantity such that marginal revenue exceeds marginal cost

9. Of the following acts, which one has been regarded by economists as hindering the cause of dealing with the evils of imperfect competition?
- **(a)** The Sherman Antitrust Act
- **(b)** The Robinson-Patman Act
- **(c)** The Federal Trade Commission Act
- **(d)** The Clayton Act

Exercises

1. Figures 22-1, 22-2, and 22-3 depict three alternative short-run situations that might face a firm in monopolistic competition. The short-run cost curves (AC, AVC, MC) are identical in each situation, but the demand curves (D_1, D_2, D_3) and thus the marginal revenue curves (MR_1, MR_2, MR_3) are different in the three situations.

In Figure 22-1, the firm will produce the amount ______, charge the price ____________, and earn the amount of profits ________________________. In Fig-

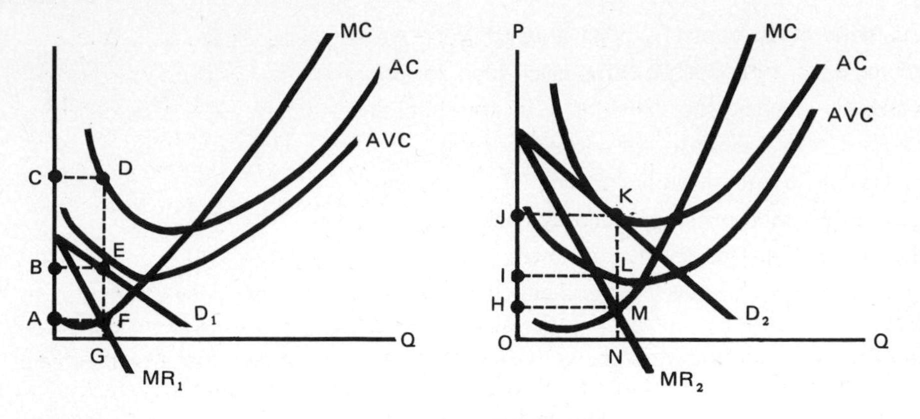

FIGURE 22-1

FIGURE 22-2

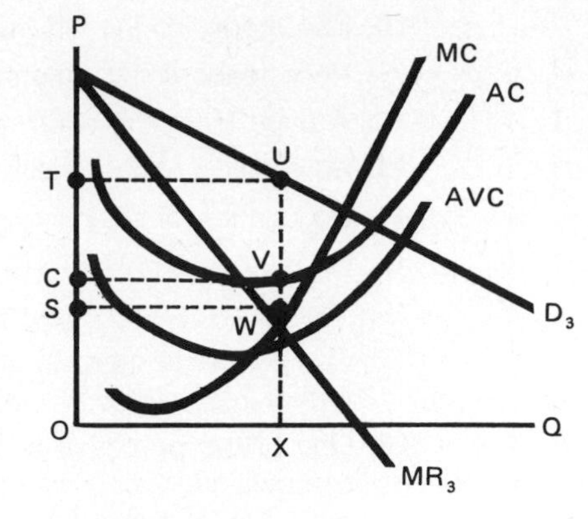

FIGURE 22-3

ure 22-2, the firm will produce the amount ______, charge the price ______, and earn the amount of profits ______. In Figure 22-3, the firm will produce the amount ______, charge the price ______, and earn the amount of profits ______. Of the three figures, the one that depicts a situation of long-run equilibrium in the industry is Figure ______.

2. In Figure 22-4, the oligopolist firm and all its rivals are currently charging the price *OP*, and the firm is currently producing the quantity *OQ*. It faces the kinked demand curve that consists of the segment of D_A above the price *OP* and the segment of D_B below the price *OP*. The respective marginal revenue curves are MR_A and MR_B.

a. If the firm under discussion increases its output beyond *OQ*, its MR curve follows (MR_A, MR_B). But if it decreases its output below *Q*, its MR curve follows (MR_A, MR_B). Therefore its complete MR curve is (MR_A, MR_B, *WXYZ*).

b. If its MC is MC_1, then it will charge a price that is (more than, less than, the same as) *OP*, and it will choose a quantity that is (more than, less than, the same as) *OQ*.

c. If its MC is MC_2, then it will charge a price that is (more than, less than, the same as) *OP*, and it will choose a quantity that is (more than, less than, the same as) *OQ*.

d. If its MC is MC_3, then it will charge a price that is (more than, less than, the same as) *OP*, and it will choose a quantity that is (more than, less than, the same as) *OQ*.

e. If MC is MC_2, we now see from a different point of view why the kinked demand curve results in a stable price. For if MC_2 shifted up but still intersected the horizontal segment *XY*, then the firm would (raise, lower, leave unchanged) its price. And if MC_2 shifted down, still intersecting *XY*, it would (raise, lower, leave unchanged) its price.

FIGURE 22-4

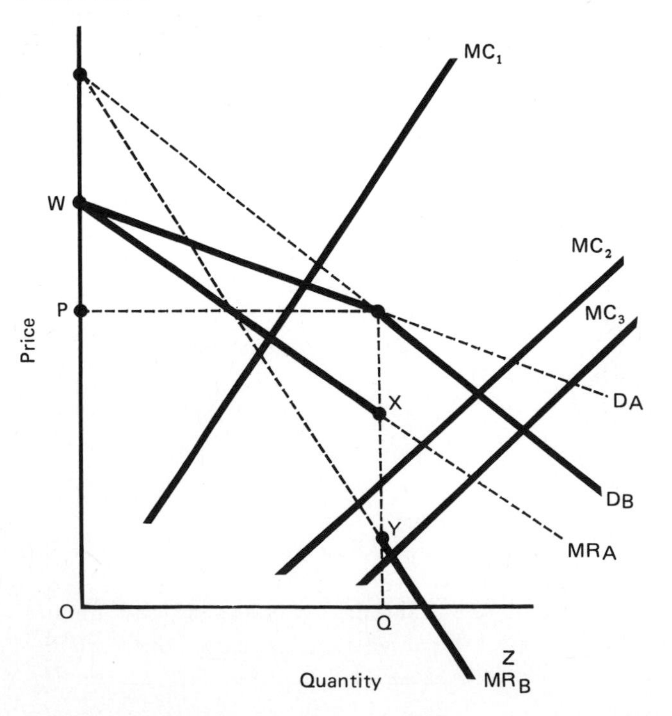

Essay Questions

1. How does the monopolist firm know what the market demand curve looks like? If it doesn't know already, how could it try to guess what it looks like? In what sense is this problem of estimating the firm's demand curve more difficult for an oligopolist than for a monopolist? Will a firm be more likely to keep its price stable if it can only guess its demand curve than if it *knows* its demand curve? Explain.

2. Suppose you observe an industry for a time and notice that, during any day, the price at which one firm is selling is identical to the price at which all the other firms are selling. Is this what you would expect to observe if the firms were acting competitively? Is it what you would expect to observe if they were acting collusively in a secret cartel? Can you therefore use this bit of evidence to support the argu-

ment that a cartel exists? What other sort of evidence would you look for in order to support such an argument? What sort of evidence would you look for in order to support the contrary argument that the firms are behaving competitively?

3. What sort of products would you expect to be advertised most heavily? In what sort of industries would you expect advertising to play the greatest role?

4. Some advertisements on television tell you absolutely nothing about the specific products being sold by a firm. Instead, they tell you why the people in the firm are likable or how the country would suffer if the firm didn't exist. Why do firms engage in such advertising? What would be the gains and what would be the losses to the economy as a whole if such advertising were prohibited by law?

5. Explain in words why an oligopolistic firm facing a kinked demand curve will be unlikely to change its price. (It may help to refer to Exercise 2 above.)

6. Would firms in an industry with a high concentration ratio be more likely or less likely to engage in collusive activity than those in an industry with a low concentration ratio? Why? In determining whether collusion is likely, what other factors would you take into consideration? How would you measure them?

7. In Chapter 20, we learned that competition is a good thing because it can, in ideal circumstances, lead each of us, as if by an invisible hand, to promote the well-being of others. Yet in this chapter we learned that the courts often prohibit competition because it is "unfair." In what sense can competition ever be harmful? Is cutthroat competition likely to aid the workings of the invisible hand?

***8.** Carefully criticize the following statement: "All industries are monopolistically competitive because *(a)* every firm's product is differentiated from every other firm's product at least a little bit and *(b)* no matter how much market power a firm has, its demand curve will be affected by the prices that are charged by other firms in the economy."

Answers

True-False Questions: **1** F **2** T **3** T **4** T **5** F **6** F **7** T **8** F **9** F **10** T **11** F **12** T **13** F **14** T **15** T **16** T **17** F **18** F **19** T

Multiple-Choice Questions: **1** b **2** a **3** c **4** c **5** c **6** a **7** a **8** c **9** b

Exercises: **1.** 0, undefined, minus the fixed cost, *ON*, *OJ*, O, *OX*, *OT*, *CTUV*, 22-2.

2a. MR_B, MR_A, *WXYZ*; **b.** more than, less than; **c.** the same as, the same as; **d.** less than, more than; **e.** leave unchanged, leave unchanged.

chapter 23
Problems of the Environment: Pollution and Congestion

Learning Objectives

After you have studied this chapter in the textbook and the study guide, you should be able to

Explain why perfect competition does not lead to efficiency when pollution is present

Measure diagrammatically the efficiency loss due to pollution, as in Figure 23-2 in the text

Show why the condition for economic efficiency is "marginal cost of having pollution = marginal cost of reducing pollution"

Show why we should not aim to eliminate pollution entirely

Explain why the tax on pollution should just equal the cost of pollution

Identify the two major legislative acts designed to control pollution in the United States

List six reasons why the United States government's antipollution policy has been unsatisfactory

Explain how recycling reduces the damage of pollution

State the reason why the problem of traffic congestion is similar to the problem of pollution

CHAPTER HIGHLIGHTS

You may think that environmental pollution has little to do with economics. But this chapter attempts to show that pollution can be seen as an economic problem—one that involves the same principles that you have already encountered in this book. The basic objectives of the chapter are to show you how economic analysis can shed light on the following questions: (1) What is pollution? (2) What is the damage caused by pollution and how can it be measured? (3) What policies can be used to deal with pollution? (4) What policies have actually been used in the United States, and how successful have they been? Let us deal with each of these questions in turn.

What Is Pollution?

Pollution is an externality; it is an external cost to society resulting from our economic activities of production and consumption. This cost is external because it isn't paid for by those responsible for it. For example, when someone's clothes are soiled by smoke from a factory chimney, the factory owner doesn't have to pay the cleaning bill.

The Damage of Pollution

When there is an externality like pollution, the classical analysis of the "invisible hand" is no longer valid. The proposition that perfect competition results in economic efficiency depends on the assumption that the marginal cost to producers equals the marginal cost to society. But when the production of some good causes pollution, the marginal cost to society includes a pollution cost as well as the cost paid by the producer. (This is illustrated in Figure 23-1 in the text.) Efficiency requires that the marginal benefit to society equal the marginal social cost to society (that is, at E_2 in Figure 23-2 in the text, where $MU_S = MC_S$). But the free competitive market does not generate this output, because firms equate MR with marginal *private* cost. (That is, equilibrium under perfect competition occurs at E_1 in Figure 23-2 in the text.) This means that level of output under perfect competition (Q_1 in Figure 23-2) exceeds the efficient level (Q_2 in Figure 23-2). The efficiency loss from this failure of the "invisible hand" can be estimated by the same sort of measurement that we used in Chapter 20: the triangle formed by the demand curve and the marginal social cost curve. In Chapter 20, we used the triangle formed by the demand curve and the *supply* curve, because the supply curve was, by assumption, the same as marginal social cost. Be sure you understand why this triangle measurement is used. It may help to refer back to the discussion surrounding Figure 20-4 in Chapter 20 of the text.

Antipollution Policies: Principles

The basic principle that *should* underlie any antipollution policy is that producers should be made to pay the external cost caused by their pollution. This does *not* mean that pollution should be eliminated entirely. Instead, it should be reduced to the point where further reductions would cost more than they would be worth.

Antipollution Policies: Our Experience

In the United States, the government has not taxed polluters. Instead, it has imposed limits on pollution. These limits have been set up largely by the Clean Air Act and the Water Pollution Control Act; they are enforced by the Environmental Protection Agency (EPA). The government has also relied upon another method—subsidizing the purchase of pollution-control equipment. On the whole, these programs have resulted in a great reduction in pollution, but most economists believe that the programs have not been successful in promoting efficiency, for the following reasons:

1. The limits in some cases have been too restrictive, in other cases too loose.

2. No satisfactory method has been found for allocating these limits among different firms. The idea that all firms should face the same restrictions has an immediate appeal, but it doesn't make much sense when reducing pollution may be much more expensive—and result in more unemployment—for some firms than for others.

3. The use of limits has encouraged many firms to engage the government in costly legal actions to try to gain exemption from the limits.

4. In some cases, the government has been forced to back down from its standards when firms claimed to be unable to meet them.

5. The government has failed to ensure that the pollution-control equipment it has subsidized is used effectively.

6. This pollution-control equipment has been of the "end-of-pipe" variety, which may have discouraged firms from finding more fundamental and perhaps more effective cures for pollution (like using inputs that are less polluting).

In addition, there are two other important ideas in this chapter. First, recycling can play a role in reducing the amount of pollution by converting what would otherwise be polluting wastes (such as empty beer cans) into usable commodities that don't pollute. This idea is illustrated by Figure 23-6 in the text. Next, you should understand that the problem of traffic congestion is similar to that of pollution. In congestion, as in pollution, there are external costs. When a driver decides to join the traffic on the highway, he or she does not take into account the cost of the extra congestion that the other drivers must face as a result. In other words, this cost to other drivers is an external one. Just as pollution problems can be dealt with by using taxes, so one way of dealing with congestion is to impose highway tolls during rush hours. But once again, as in the case of pollution, the problem of how big a tax or toll to charge is by no means easily solved.

IMPORTANT TERMS

Internal cost The cost that is considered by a firm or individual making decisions. Also called private cost.

External cost The cost not considered by a firm or individual because it is borne by someone else. Examples include costs of pollution and congestion.

The marginal cost of reducing pollution The cost of reducing pollution by one more unit.

Marginal cost of having pollution The cost that would result from allowing one more unit of pollution.

"End-of-pipe" treatment The policy of reducing pollution by capturing the polluting agents, such as smoke, just before they enter the environment, rather than undertaking more fundamental and perhaps more effective steps such as changing over to different production processes that produce less pollution in the first place.

Recycling Using materials again rather than throwing them away. This can reduce pollution and preserve natural resources.

True-False Questions

T F **1.** The costs of pollution are external costs only if the firm causing the pollution is taxed for them.

T F **2.** The costs of pollution are external costs if (*a*) the firm causing the pollution is taxed for them but (*b*) the extra taxes are really paid by consumers in the form of higher prices for the goods produced by these firms.

T F **3.** The main task of the Environmental Protection Agency is to collect the taxes that the government imposes to discourage pollution.

T F **4.** A policy of eliminating economic growth would probably reduce the rate at which pollution is increasing.

T F **5.** If pollution taxes accurately reflect the external costs of pollution, then legal limits on pollution activities are not also needed in order to achieve economic efficiency.

T F **6.** The efficiency losses from pollution arise only when markets are not perfectly competitive.

T F **7.** The use of taxes rather than limits as an antipollution policy allows the market to determine how much each firm will be permitted to pollute.

T F **8.** As a general rule, the marginal cost of having pollution can be estimated with greater certainty than can the marginal cost of preventing pollution.

T F **9.** One advantage of using taxes rather than limits to control pollution is that the appropriate tax on pollution can be determined even if the policy maker has no idea of the size of the marginal cost of having pollution.

T F **10.** The important similarity that economists recognize between pollution and congestion is that both are caused by automobiles.

T F **11.** Subsidizing the use of public transportation would be similar to taxing private transportation in the sense that both policies would raise the cost of using private transportation compared to public transportation.

Multiple-Choice Questions

1. The main provisions of the Clean Air Act
- **(a)** Set limits on the amount of output that can be produced by polluting firms
- **(b)** Set limits on the amount of pollution that can be caused by a firm or its products
- **(c)** Impose taxes on the output of polluting firms
- **(d)** Impose taxes on a firm depending upon the amount of pollution that it causes or that its products cause

2. The higher prices that we pay for products that must now meet tougher pollution standards
- **(a)** Constitute one of the external costs of pollution because they are paid for by consumers instead of by the producer
- **(b)** Would be avoided if the government relied upon taxes instead of limits to control pollution
- **(c)** Could not be avoided even if the government relied upon taxes instead of limits
- **(d)** **(a)** and **(b)**
- **(e)** **(a)** and **(c)**

3. If the production of some perfectly competitive good causes pollution, then
- **(a)** More than the economically efficient amount of the commodity will be produced.
- **(b)** The marginal benefit of the commodity will be more than the marginal social cost.
- **(c)** The marginal benefit of the commodity will be less than the marginal private cost.
- **(d)** **(a)** and **(b)**.
- **(e)** **(a)** and **(c)**.

4. The imposition of a tax on the output of firms in a polluting industry
- **(a)** Will always result in an economically efficient amount of output
- **(b)** Will result in an economically efficient amount of

output only if the tax rate is greater than the marginal private cost of production
- **(c)** Will result in an economically efficient amount of output only if the tax rate equals the marginal benefit of producing the commodity
- **(d)** Will result in an economically efficient amount of output only if the tax rate equals the marginal external cost of production

5. The efficiency loss from a polluting good
- **(a)** Is zero if the good is produced in a perfectly competitive market
- **(b)** Could conceivably be zero if the good was produced by a monopolist
- **(c)** Is measured by the "triangle" formed by industry demand and supply
- **(d)** Is always reduced by a limit on production, regardless of how severe that limit may be

6. The recycling of wastes
- **(a)** Can reduce the rate of depletion of natural resources
- **(b)** Will be attempted by private business firms only if taxes are imposed on the amount of waste that they produce
- **(c)** Is always economically efficient
- **(d)** **(a)** and **(b)**
- **(e)** **(a)** and **(c)**

7. Lower fares on a city's subway during rush hours than at other times might promote economic efficiency if its main effect were
- **(a)** To encourage subway users to travel during rush hours rather than at other times
- **(b)** To encourage people to use cars rather than the subway during the other hours
- **(c)** To encourage people to use the subway rather than cars during rush hours
- **(d)** Any of the above provided that the subsidy were large enough

8. Which of these is an external cost?
- **(a)** The extra gas that a motorist uses if he drives now rather than waiting until the road is less crowded
- **(b)** The extra gas that he causes others to use because the road will be more crowded if he drives now rather than waiting
- **(c)** The damage to his car if he gets into an accident because he is driving now rather than when the road is less crowded
- **(d)** The damage to his health that may be caused by exposure to more carbon monoxide from the other cars on the road than if he were to wait until there were fewer cars

Exercises

1. Figure 23-1 represents the market for a good the production of which causes pollution.

a. If the market is perfectly competitive, the level of output will equal ______, the market price will equal ______, the marginal social cost will equal ______, and the marginal external cost will equal ______.

b. If the commodity produces no external benefits, then the optimal level of output will equal ______. This output would be attained under perfect competition if the firms were faced with a tax rate equal to ______. Without this tax, the efficiency loss will equal ______. With this tax, the market price will equal ______.

c. Suppose that the good were produced by an unregulated monopolist. Then the level of output (with no tax) would equal ______, the market price would equal ______, and the efficiency loss would equal ______.

d. Assume that the marginal external cost is constant—i.e., that the lines MC_S and $MC_{industry}$ are parallel, with $LM = HK = IJ$. Then suppose that the government imposes the same tax on the monopolist that it earlier charged to the perfect competitors. In this case, the monopolist will produce an amount of output equal to ______, it will charge a price equal to ______, and the efficiency loss will be equal to ______. Thus a per-unit tax on a polluting *monopolist* (will, will not) necessarily lead to greater efficiency.

FIGURE 23-1

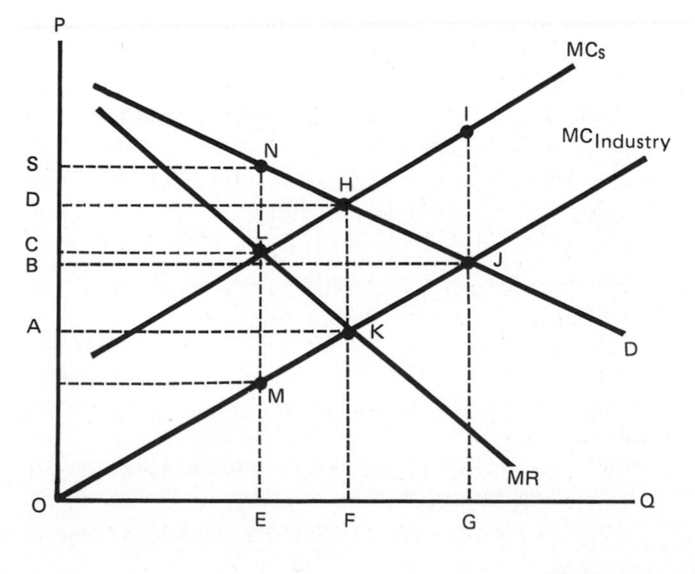

2. In Figure 23-2, the curve labeled MCR represents the marginal cost of reducing pollution, and the one labeled MCP_1 represents the marginal cost of hav-

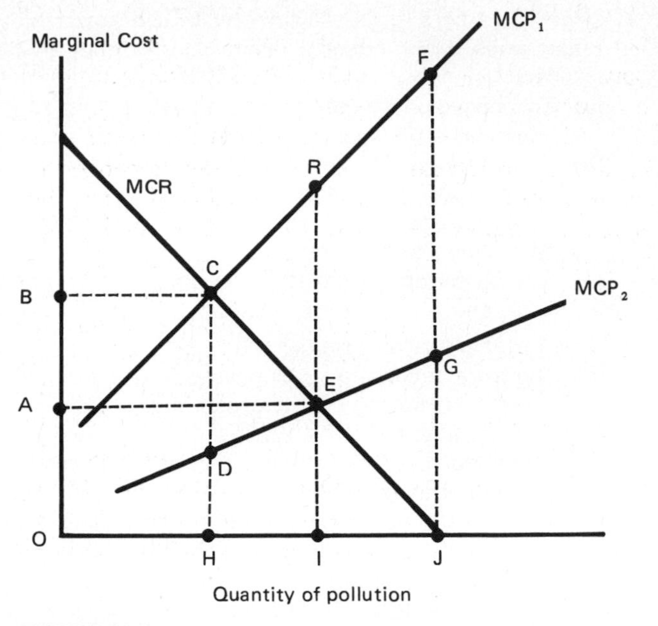

FIGURE 23-2

ing pollution. For the time being, you may ignore the one labeled MCP_2.

a. The economically efficient quantity of pollution equals ______. In the absence of any pollution tax, the quantity of pollution will equal ______, the value of MCR will equal ______, the value of MCP will equal ______, and the efficiency loss will equal ______. The economically efficient amount of pollution will result if firms are charged a tax equal to ______ per unit of pollution.

b. Now suppose that the marginal cost of having pollution is represented by MCP_2 instead of MCP_1. Then the economically efficient amount of pollution will result if firms are charged a tax equal to ______ per unit of pollution.

c. Suppose now that the marginal cost of having pollution is really represented by MCP_1 but that the government makes a mistake and estimates it to be represented by MCP_2. Suppose that the government sets the tax rate on pollution (calculated in the last paragraph), which is optimal if the pollution cost is MCP_2. Then the quantity of pollution will equal ______, which is (more, less) than the economically efficient amount; the MCR will equal ______; the true MCP will equal ______; and the efficiency loss will equal ______. Thus we (may, may not) conclude that, if the government underestimates the problem, it will take inadequate action to counter it (that is, set too low a pollution tax).

Essay Questions

1. One advantage of the use of taxes rather than limits to control pollution is that the former policy harnesses the forces of the marketplace to help find an efficient solution, whereas the latter policy does not. Explain this statement.

2. In some cities, there is a fine for smoking in elevators in a public building. Do you think that this is an example of the use of taxes or of limits to control pollution?

3. Some economists maintain that all external costs are a result of society's failure to assign property rights to individuals and to defend them. For example, if my factory pollutes the air above your house, then I am using a valuable commodity (namely, the air above your house) without having to pay for it, because it doesn't belong to you. If our laws were changed so that anyone who owned a house also owned all of the air above that house, then I would have to persuade you to sell me the right to use that property before I could pollute it. Explain how, if the law were changed in this way, the emission from my factory would no longer be pollution according to the definition that we have given in this chapter. Suppose that I had managed to persuade everyone in the neighborhood except you to sell me the right to pollute their air. Explain how that would put you in a position to take undue advantage of me when we were bargaining over what price I should pay for the right to pollute your air. What other problems can you imagine would arise if this solution to the problem of pollution were generally adopted? Show how this same analysis applies to the case of water pollution.

4. Explain how the concept of externality is illustrated by the following quotation from the nineteenth-century economist J. H. von Thunen: "In time of war we have no hesitation in sacrificing one hundred men in the bloom of their years to save one cannon. In a hundred men at least twenty times as much capital is lost as is lost in one cannon. But the production of the cannon is the cause of an expenditure of the state treasury, while human beings are again available for nothing by means of a simple conscription order. . . . When the statement was made to Napoleon, the founder of the conscription system, that a planned operation would cost too many men, he replied: 'That is nothing. The women produce more of them than I can use.' "

5. In recent years a large Canadian distillery has paid a subsidy to the Toronto Transit Commission, enabling anyone to travel free on the Toronto subway system on New Year's Eve. Explain carefully how this subsidy has helped to promote economic efficiency by internalizing an external cost. Why do you suppose that the subsidy was offered by a distillery rather than by a tobacco company?

6. What arguments can be made for government subsidies to support the use of public transportation? What arguments can be made against such subsidies? In what kinds of cities are the arguments for subsidies likely to be stronger than those against? In what sorts of cities are the arguments against likely to be stronger than the ones for?

7. In what sense is a policy of subsidizing firms for recycling materials equivalent to taxing firms according to the amount of waste that they produce?

8. Explain by reference to Figure 23-4 in the text under what circumstances economic efficiency would best be promoted by not levying any tax at all upon a particular kind of pollution. How would your answer be different if you took into account the costs involved in collecting the tax?

9. According to the analysis that has been developed in the present chapter, it could be argued that, in a perfectly competitive market system, the size of the deposit that people would pay on returnable beer bottles would be lower than that required to produce economic efficiency. Explain.

***10.** In the text it was mentioned that some cities have tried to reduce the problem of traffic congestion by reserving special fast lanes on throughways, but that this proposal produced very little benefit in the way of reducing congestion. Explain carefully what you think the costs of such a proposal might have been.

***11.** Defend or criticize the following statement, "If the government taxes the amount of wastes dumped by firms into a lake in order to control pollution, then some water pollution will still occur because some firms will still dump their wastes and pay the tax. If this happens, economic efficiency can be attained only if the government spends all the tax revenues it collects in this way on repairing the damage caused by these wastes."

Answers

True-False Questions: **1** F **2** F **3** F **4** T **5** T **6** F **7** T **8** F **9** F **10** F **11** T
Multiple-Choice Questions: **1 b** **2 c** **3 a** **4 d** **5 b** **6 a** **7 c** **8 b**
Exercises: **1a.** *OG*, *OB*, *GI*, *IJ*; **b.** *OF*, *KH*, *HIJ*, *OD*; **c.** *OF*, *OD*, O; **d.** *OE*, *OS*, *LNH*, will not.
2a. *OH*, *OJ*, O, *JF*, *CFJ*, *OB*; **b.** *OA*; **c.** *OI*, more, *IE*, *IR*, *CRE*, may.

chapter 24
Public Goods

Learning Objectives

After you have studied this chapter in the textbook and the study guide, you should be able to

Define "public good" and "pure public good," giving an example of each

Explain why perfect competition does not produce an efficient quantity of public goods

Measure, in a diagram, the efficiency loss resulting from the private provision of public goods, as in Figure 24-1 in the text

State two major difficulties involved in estimating the marginal social benefit of a public good

Show why efficiency requires that the rate of subsidy for producing a public good be set equal to the marginal external benefit

State two reasons why governments may spend too much

Construct the marginal social benefit curve in a diagram, starting with the individual marginal utility curves (*a*) for a pure public good and (*b*) for a pure private good

CHAPTER HIGHLIGHTS

The last chapter dealt with external *costs*. This chapter deals with external *benefits*; that is, benefits that are enjoyed by others, above and beyond the internal benefits enjoyed by the buyers of a good. (As you might expect, marginal social benefit is the sum of both external and internal benefits.) With external benefits, perfect competition will produce an inefficient outcome. Why? Because it will equate marginal cost to marginal private benefit (utility) rather than to marginal social benefit. As illustrated by Figure 24-1 in the text, the market will produce too little of such a good. A good that produces large external benefit is often called a public good. The main objective of this chapter is to address the following questions:

1. What is a public good?

2. Why can we not rely upon the private market to provide public goods?

3. What principles govern the design of effective government policies toward the provision of public goods?

4. How effective are the policies that have been pursued with respect to public goods in the United States?

What Is a Public Good?

As mentioned above, a public good is one whose use produces large external benefits. A *pure* public good is the extreme case where the amount of benefit that an individual gets from a good is just as great if someone else buys it as it is if he or she were to buy it. That is, the individual cannot be excluded from enjoying it. For example, you get the same benefit from cleaner air, whether or not you help to pay for antipollution measures. This is not true of a private good. You can't enjoy a movie or a restaurant meal unless you pay for it.

Inefficiency of Private Markets

Not all goods with external benefits are provided by the government. Some, such as home improvements, are produced privately. Even some goods with very large external benefits—those that can rightly be called public goods—may be provided privately. One example is a lighthouse. Yet private provision (or, more accurately, the lack of such provision) involves inefficiency which can be measured by the same sort of triangle that we have been using all along (see, for example, Figure 24-1 in the text). However, one difficulty encountered in drawing such diagrams is that it is extremely difficult to measure the marginal social benefit of a good. You can't just ask people how much benefit they would derive if a particular public good were to be provided. Even if someone was going to benefit greatly from it, he probably wouldn't tell you for fear of revealing himself as one of those who should be required to pay for it. You might try undertaking a benefit-cost analysis, in which you would estimate the benefit by first trying to predict what effect the provision of the good would have on different producers and consumers and then trying to put a dollar value on these effects. A big problem that is encountered by benefit-cost analysis of a public good—like a flood-control dam, for example—is that one of its effects may be to cause the saving (or the loss) of human lives. This forces you to face the extremely difficult problem of how to attach a dollar value to a human life.

Principles of Effective Policy

Despite these difficulties, decisions must be made. The principles governing effective government policies are almost the same as in the case of pollution: (1) The government may subsidize the private production of a public good up to the level of the external benefits it provides or (2) the government may undertake the production of the good itself, as with national defense. Economic efficiency will result if production consequently increases to the point where marginal cost equals marginal social benefit (including external benefit).

The Effectiveness of Actual Policies

Some people such as J. K. Galbraith think that the United States provides far too few public goods. Others think that too many are provided. Until someone discovers how to measure social benefits accurately, we will never really know who is right. But there are reasons for thinking that the government spends too much: (1) Managers in private business who cut back expenditures may be rewarded if they have thereby increased their firms' profits. But the manager in government who cuts back expenditures may be punished, because the citizens who are hurt by the cutback will complain. (2) Even if it makes no *economic* sense for the government to provide a good, it may make *political* sense. Those who benefit from a good will vote for the party that promises to provide it, while those who don't benefit seldom voice their displeasure by voting for the other party.

Figures 24-2 and 24-3 in the text illustrate how the marginal social benefit (MU_S) curve of a pure public good is derived from the individual marginal utility (MU) curves.

Remember that the MU_S curve for a pure public good is the *vertical* sum of the individual MU curves, whereas the MU_S curve for a pure private good (one with no external benefits) is the *horizontal* sum of the individual MU curves.

IMPORTANT TERMS

External benefit The benefit derived from a good by those who do not own it.

Public good Any good that produces a substantial external benefit.

Pure public good A good from which people derive the same amount of benefit, whether or not they own it.

Internal (private) benefit The benefit from a good derived by the person who owns that good. These are usually the only benefits that are considered by households and firms in making their decisions.

Benefit-cost analysis The technique of estimating the dollar value of the different costs and benefits that are likely to result from a particular government icy.

Option demand The demand to have a good not because you want to use it but because you want it available just in case you might want to use it in the future. This appears to be the nature of the demand for some public goods, such as the preservation of a particular wildlife species.

True-False Questions

T F **1.** External benefits are generated by reducing traffic congestion.

T F **2.** Generally speaking, the private market produces too large a quantity of public goods.

T F **3.** Generally speaking, the private production of a public good results in marginal cost being less than marginal social benefit.

T F **4.** To promote economic efficiency, the government could just as easily tax the use of a public good as subsidize its production.

T F **5.** If a monopolist were producing a public good with no subsidy and no external costs, then it might by accident produce an economically efficient quantity.

T F **6.** One problem with the private provision of public goods is that it leads to the internalization of external benefits.

T F **7.** The marginal social benefit curve of a pure public good can be constructed as the horizontal sum of the individual demand curves.

T F **8.** You cannot be excluded from enjoying the benefits of a pure public good even if someone else pays for it.

T F **9.** Those who advocate zero-base budgeting believe that the fact that a program is already in existence does not justify its continuance.

T F **10.** If you want to use benefit-cost analysis, you may have to choose some method for attaching a dollar value to human life.

T F **11.** J. K. Galbraith believes that the United States provides too many public goods.

T F **12.** If the use of a good creates an external cost, then its conservation must create an internal benefit.

Multiple-Choice Questions

1. Which of the following comes closest to being a pure public good?
- **(a)** National defense
- **(b)** Smoking in an elevator
- **(c)** Vaccination against smallpox
- **(d)** Coal

2. Which of the following comes closest to being a pure private good?
- **(a)** Home improvements
- **(b)** Coffee
- **(c)** Fresh air
- **(d)** Courtesy

3. Private provision of a public good may be efficient if
- **(a)** An unregulated monopoly produces the good.
- **(b)** The good is subsidized.
- **(c)** The good is taxed.
- **(d)** None of the above.

4. The marginal social benefit of a good with external benefits is
- **(a)** Greater than the marginal private benefit
- **(b)** Less than marginal private benefit
- **(c)** Equal to marginal private benefit
- **(d)** Any of the above, depending on the price

5. The marginal social benefit curve is the *vertical* sum of the individual marginal utility curves
- **(a)** Only in the case of a pure private good
- **(b)** Only in the case of a pure public good
- **(c)** In the case of any good with external benefits
- **(d)** In the case of any good, whether or not it produces external benefits

6. To achieve economic efficiency, the per-unit subsidy to a good with external benefits should equal the
- **(a)** Marginal social benefit of the good
- **(b)** Marginal private benefit of the good
- **(c)** Marginal social cost of the good
- **(d)** None of the above

7. If the government produces more than the economically efficient amount of a public good,
- **(a)** The marginal social benefit of that good will exceed the marginal social cost.
- **(b)** The marginal social benefit of that good may equal the marginal social cost.
- **(c)** The efficiency loss involved in producing that amount may be as much as the efficiency loss from

allowing the private market to provide the good.
(d) None of the above.

8. When the government subsidizes a public good,
(a) The efficiency of the outcome does not depend upon whether the subsidy is paid to the producers or to the consumers of the good.
(b) The amount of production of the good will be less than the economically efficient amount if the subsidy is too large.
(c) The same result could be achieved if the government were to put a limit on production of the good.
(d) **(a)** and **(c)**.
(e) **(b)** and **(c)**.

Exercise

Figure 24-1 describes a perfectly competitive market for a good that provides external benefits, with the supply curve *S* and the demand curve *D*.

a. In an unregulated market, the quantity that is produced is ______ and the market price is __________. If the marginal social benefit curve is MU_s and there are no external costs of producing the good (for the time being, ignore the curve labeled MC_s), then the economically efficient quantity is ______ and the marginal external benefit is ______.

b. The efficiency loss from relying upon the private market for the provision of this public good is ______. The government could eliminate this efficiency loss by offering, to producers of the good, a subsidy of the amount ______ per unit of the good.

c. Now suppose that the good involves external *costs* as well as external benefits. (For example, the good may be a flood-control dam that would damage the environment by creating an artificial, polluted lake.) Let the curve labeled MC_s represent the marginal social cost of producing the good. Then the efficient amount of production of the good would equal ______. At that level of production, the marginal external cost would equal ______ and the marginal external benefit would equal ______. With no tax or subsidy, the private market would produce (more, less) than the economically efficient amount and the efficiency loss would equal ______. This efficiency loss could be eliminated if the government were to (tax, subsidize) the production of the good at a rate equal to ______ per unit.

FIGURE 24-1

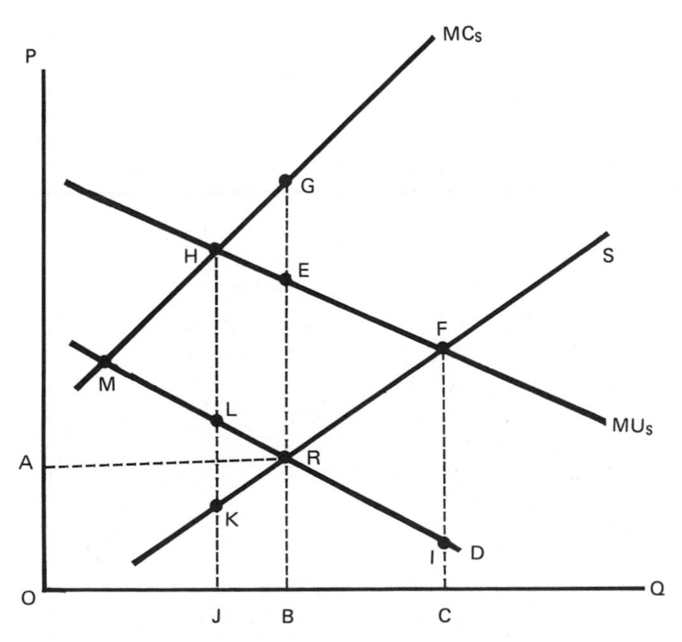

Essay Questions

1. Explain carefully why each of the following might be considered to be a public good. Would you consider any of them to be a pure public good?
a. The United States Olympic Team
b. Your telephone
c. Driver safety lessons
d. Television programs

2. In the text it was argued that if you asked people to reveal how much they would benefit from a public good, they would probably understate those benefits. If you asked them to reveal how much they would be damaged by the production of a good involving external costs, would they also tend to understate that damage? Why or why not?

3. Explain how the practice of a zero-base budgeting can help to keep down the cost of government expenditures.

4. Many industries pay people called lobbyists to argue on their behalf with regulatory agencies, congressional committees, and other government agencies and officials in Washington. These lobbyists spend much of their time arguing that their industry is a source of external benefits. Why would the firms in an industry pay lobbyists to spend their time this way?

5. What are the advantages and disadvantages of having the government provide public goods rather than subsidize private firms to provide them? Why is government provision of public goods more common than subsidization of private provision?

6. Explain what is wrong with the following statement: "You can rely upon the government to provide you with the goods you want at a reasonable price just as much as you can rely upon private business firms. The reason is that the party in power wants you to be pleased with what it provides so that you will vote for it in the next election, just as a private business firm wants you to be pleased with what it provides so that you will buy it again."

7. It has been argued that there is a tendency for government spending to grow too large because, every time the government spends more money, it provides a great deal of benefit to a very small number of people and a very small cost to a large number of people (namely, taxpayers). Explain how this might cause government spending to become too large.

***8.** In Essay Question 3 of the previous chapter, it was pointed out that, according to some economists, all external costs are the result of society's failure to allocate and enforce property rights. Using the same reasoning, could it be argued that this is also the source of all external benefits?

Answers

True-False Questions: 1 T 2 F 3 T 4 F 5 F 6 F 7 F 8 T 9 T 10 T 11 F 12 F
Multiple-Choice Questions: 1 a 2 b 3 b 4 a 5 b 6 d 7 c 8 a
Exercise **a.** *OB*, *OA*, *OC*, *IF*; **b.** *REF*, *IF*; **c.** *OJ*, *KH*, *LH*, more, *HGE*, tax, *KL*.

chapter 25
The Gains from International Trade

Learning Objectives

After you have studied this chapter in the textbook and the study guide, you should be able to

Identify the three main sources of gain from international trade

Give an example showing how international trade can result in an increase in the variety of available products

State the difference between comparative advantage and absolute advantage

Explain why countries export those commodities for which they have a comparative advantage

State two reasons why international trade is analogous to technological change

Measure diagrammatically the efficiency gain from international trade, as in Figures 25-6 and 25-7 in the text

Explain why this efficiency gain can be estimated by comparing the changes in producer surplus and consumer surplus that result from international trade

Identify who gains and who loses from international trade in a specific good

CHAPTER HIGHLIGHTS

The purpose of this chapter is to introduce some of the fundamentals of the theory of international trade. The chapter shows how the residents of a country may gain from being allowed to trade with residents of other countries. These gains arise from three principal sources: (1) increased competition, (2) economies of scale, and (3) comparative advantage.

Increased Competition

If there is no international trade, each producer sells in a market that includes only buyers in a single country. A market of this size may be a natural oligopoly. With international trade, each producer now sells in a much larger market that includes buyers all over the world; moreover, these sales are made in competition with other producers in other countries. Thus international trade moves us closer to the ideal of perfect competition. One of the reasons why we gain from international trade is that this move reduces the efficiency loss resulting from *im*perfect competition. This is illustrated in Figure 25-1 in the text.

Economies of Scale

We saw in Chapter 3 that, with economies of scale, the people in a country can gain if each specializes in the production of one or a few goods. The same principle applies to people in different countries. With no international trade, each country must produce a little of everything because it must be self-sufficient. With international trade, each country can produce large quantities of some things and purchase the rest of what it wants from other countries. The cost of the goods that we produce ourselves may be reduced through the economies of scale that result from large-scale production. Likewise, the price of the goods that we buy from other countries may be reduced because they, too, enjoy economies of scale.

Not only are costs reduced but variety may be increased. For example, if there were no international trade, then a New Zealander would be allowed to buy a car only if it was produced in New Zealand. Instead, because there is international trade, he or she can choose among Fords, Volkswagens, Datsuns, and many others that are produced elsewhere. Economies of scale make this increased variety available to the buyer. Without economies of scale, the manufacturer of each of these cars might set up a separate plant in New Zealand. If so, the New Zealander could buy any of them even without international trade. But with economies of scale, this doesn't happen. Because the market is so small (the population of New Zealand is just over 3 million), these manufacturers could not *all* sell enough cars there to cover their fixed costs. Since most varieties of cars are produced elsewhere, the New Zealander must be able to import them if he or she is to have a wide selection.

Comparative Advantage

To understand *comparative* advantage, you must first understand *absolute* advantage. To take an example, America has an absolute advantage over Europe in producing food if food can be produced using fewer inputs in America than in Europe. In the example of Table 25-2 in the text, food can be produced using only half as many inputs (workers) in America as in Europe. In other words, America has an absolute advantage in food if its *input* cost of food is lower. By contrast, America has a comparative advantage in food if its *opportunity* cost of food is lower; that is, if producing food requires a smaller sacrifice of other goods than it does in Europe. Both "absolute advantage" and "comparative advantage" refer to the cost of production. The difference is in how this cost is measured. For absolute advantage, you measure the cost in inputs. For comparative advantage, you measure it in other outputs.

Comparative advantage depends upon absolute advantage in the following way. America has a *comparative* advantage in food in three different cases:

1. If America has an absolute advantage in food and Europe has an absolute advantage in clothing

2. If America has an absolute advantage in both food and clothing but the absolute advantage is greater in food than in clothing

3. If Europe has an absolute advantage in both food and clothing but the absolute advantage is greater in clothing than in food

Case 1 is illustrated in Table 25-2 in the text. Europe's opportunity cost of food is 4 units of clothing. This is so because it takes one worker a given time to produce a unit of food, but that worker could have produced 4 units of clothing in the same time. On the other hand, America's opportunity cost of food is only 1½ units clothing, for to produce a unit of food in America requires only one-half worker (because each worker produces 2 units). But this "one-half worker" could have produced 1½ units of food (because each whole worker produces 3 units). Thus the opportunity cost of food is higher in Europe than in America. In other words, America has a comparative advantage in food. As an exercise, try going through the example of Table 25-3 to show why America also has a comparative advantage in food in case 2.

Even if there are no economies of scale but rather there are constant costs (i.e., average costs are constant), then each country will gain by specializing in producing those goods for which it has a comparative advantage. The gain arises because trade allows a country to acquire more cheaply the goods in which it does *not* have a comparative advantage. Why produce these goods at home, where their opportunity cost is high, when they can be purchased from another country where their opportunity cost is low? This gain from trade is illustrated by the examples of Tables 25-2 and 25-3 in the text.

Other than this, there is one analogy and one technique that you should learn from this chapter. The analogy, illustrated by Figure 25-5 in the text, is between international trade and technological change. Both allow a country to consume a combination of goods lying beyond its current production possibility curve, and both can be the source of troublesome unemployment that may have to be endured in the short run in order to realize gains in the long run.

The technique is that of measuring the efficiency gain from international trade in a commodity. To put it the other way around, this is also the efficiency loss from *not* permitting international trade in the commodity. The efficiency gain from exporting a commodity comes from being able to sell to foreigners at a price above the domestic cost of production (or above the domestic marginal utility of consumption). The gain from importing a commodity comes from being able to buy at a price below the domestic cost of production (or below the domestic marginal utility of consumption). Be sure that you understand why the "triangle" measures of Figures 25-6 and 25-7 of the text can be used to estimate these gains. Be sure, too, that you understand (in Figure 25-8) how this triangle measure is also exactly what we get if we compare changes in consumer and producer surplus that result from international trade. As a check on your understanding, you should be able to reproduce this same argument to confirm the triangular measure of benefit resulting from an export of wheat (first shown in Figure 25-6 of the text). This comparison of how producers and consumers are affected is important for understanding the conflict of interest between them in questions of international trade. In turn, this is important for understanding the problems that have hindered efforts in the United States to formulate sensible policies toward international trade.

IMPORTANT TERMS

Economies of scale A situation in which average cost falls as the amount produced rises. These constitute one source of the gains from international trade.

Comparative advantage Country A has a comparative advantage over country B in producing X if A's opportunity cost (the other goods that must be sacrificed in order to produce more X) is less than B's opportunity cost. This is another source of gain from international trade.

Absolute advantage Country A has an *absolute* advantage over country B in good X if the production of X requires fewer factors of production in country A. (Note that cost is measured in terms of factors of production required rather than in terms of other goods that must be sacrificed.)

True-False Questions

T F **1.** Over half of all exports from the United States are sold to Canada.

T F **2.** Some kinds of commodities are imported by the United States and also exported by the United States.

T F **3.** By allowing international trade in a commodity, we can possibly change a natural monopoly into a natural oligopoly.

T F **4.** Suppose that after the introduction of international trade, the producers of good X in the United States end up producing less than before because of the competition from foreign producers. Then, even if the United States gains from its international trade in *all* commodities, it loses from its trade in X.

T F **5.** If there are no economies of scale, international trade will not result in new products.

T F **6.** Even if a country has no absolute advantage, it will have some comparative advantage.

T F **7.** Even if a country has no comparative advantage, it will have some absolute advantage.

T F **8.** Economies of scale may exist even if production possibility curves are the same in all countries.

T F **9.** Where there are constant costs, then each country will, as a general rule, gain if it specializes in producing those goods in which it has an absolute advantage.

T F **10.** As a general rule, a country will gain from international trade if it exports those goods for which it has a relatively low opportunity cost of production.

T F **11.** If a country exports oranges, then consumers of oranges in that country lose from having international trade in oranges.

T F **12.** If a country imports oranges, then producers of oranges in that country gain from having international trade in oranges.

T F **13.** International trade allows a country to consume a combination of goods lying outside its current production possibility curve.

T F **14.** International trade allows a country to *produce* a combination of goods lying outside its current production possibility curve.

Multiple-Choice Questions

1. Which of the following items accounted for the largest fraction of total imports into the United States in 1976?
- **(a)** Machinery
- **(b)** Automobiles and parts
- **(c)** Oil and its products
- **(d)** Coffee, cocoa, and sugar

2. Which of the following is not a source of gains from international trade?
- **(a)** Comparative advantage
- **(b)** Absolute advantage
- **(c)** Economies of scale
- **(d)** Increased competition

3. If a country permits international trade in a good, then it will gain through the resulting increased competition unless, before the country was opened up to international trade, the good was sold in a market under
- **(a)** Monopoly
- **(b)** Oligopoly
- **(c)** Perfect competition
- **(d)** Any of the above

4. Suppose that, as a result of allowing international trade in a good, some producers in the United States are driven out of business. Then
- **(a)** There will be a loss to the United States as a whole because of the reduced competition that is caused by the elimination of those producers.
- **(b)** There will be a gain to consumers of the good in the United States.
- **(c)** There must be economies of scale in producing this good.
- **(d)** **(a)** and **(b)**.
- **(e)** **(b)** and **(c)**.

5. International trade results in an increased availability of goods only if
- **(a)** There are economies of scale.
- **(b)** International trade gives some producer a monopoly in the world market.
- **(c)** There are increasing costs in the long run.
- **(d)** National governments impose tariffs.

6. Suppose Canada and the United States produce only two goods, newsprint and machinery, and use only one factor of production, labor. Suppose that in both countries production is subject to constant costs and that the production possibilities are given by Table 25-1.

Then Canada has
- **(a)** A comparative advantage in machinery
- **(b)** A comparative advantage in newsprint
- **(c)** An absolute advantage in machinery
- **(d)** An absolute advantage in newsprint

7. In the situation described in the previous question, the United States has
- **(a)** A comparative advantage in machinery
- **(b)** A comparative advantage in newsprint
- **(c)** An absolute advantage in machinery
- **(d)** **(a)** and **(c)**
- **(e)** **(b)** and **(c)**

8. In question 6, suppose that international trade is allowed between Canada and the United States in machinery and newsprint, following a period in which no such trade has been permitted. Then unemployment may, in the short run, lead the industry to produce
- **(a)** Newsprint in the United States
- **(b)** Newsprint in Canada
- **(c)** Machinery in the United States
- **(d)** **(a)** and **(b)**
- **(e)** **(b)** and **(c)**

9. According to the theory of international trade discussed in this chapter,
- **(a)** Every American citizen gains from international trade.
- **(b)** As a general rule, international trade in a good will benefit both producers and consumers of that good.
- **(c)** As a general rule, producers of that good lose but consumers gain.
- **(d)** There is an efficiency gain to the United States from allowing international trade.

10. The triangular measure of the efficiency loss from preventing international trade
- **(a)** Is the same geometrical construction as the triangular measure of the efficiency loss from monopoly
- **(b)** Would not be a valid measure of the efficiency loss if the good created external benefits
- **(c)** Would be a valid measure of the efficiency loss even if the prevention of international trade created a monopoly in the domestic market
- **(d)** **(a)** and **(b)**
- **(e)** **(a)** and **(c)**

Table 25-1

	Output per worker in the United States	Output per worker in Canada
Machinery	7	5
Newsprint	8	4

Exercises

1. Suppose that Figures 25-1 and 25-2 represent the markets for shoes in England and Spain.

a. Without international trade, the price in England would equal ______ and the quantity produced in England would equal ______; the price in Spain would equal ______ and the quantity produced in Spain would equal ______.

b. With international trade (assuming that there are no other countries involved), the single price at which the total demand (English demand plus Spanish demand) equals the total supply is ______. At that price, English demand equals ______ and English supply equals ______; Spanish demand equals ______, and Spanish supply equals ______. In this situation, (Spain, England) will export the amount ______ of shoes.

2. In Figure 25-3, *D* is the demand curve for a good in the United States market alone; MR is the corresponding marginal revenue curve that a firm would face if it were able to monopolize this market. But for now, assume that this industry is perfectly competitive, with MC being its supply curve. Also assume that there are no externalities.

a. Suppose initially that there is no international trade in the good. Then the amount ______ will be produced and the market price will equal ______. Suppose now that international trade is introduced, and that it results in a price equal to *OC*. Then consumption of the good in the United States will equal ______, production of the good in the United States will equal ______, and the difference between these amounts will equal ______, which will be the amount of the good that the United States (exports, imports).

b. As a result of allowing international trade in this good, producer surplus in the United States has gone (up, down) by the amount ______ and consumer surplus in the United States has gone (up, down) by the amount ______; therefore the net efficiency (gain, loss) to the United States equals ______.

c. Suppose next that there is no international trade in the good and that the market in the United States is an unregulated monopoly. The monopolist will produce an amount of ______ and charge a price of ______. Suppose now that international trade is introduced and that, as a result, the firm that used to have a monopoly in the United States is forced to behave as a perfect competitor. Suppose as before that, with international trade, the market price will equal *OC*. Then consumption of the good in the United States will equal ______, production of the good in the United States will equal ______, and the difference between these two amounts will equal ______, which will be the amount of

FIGURE 25-1

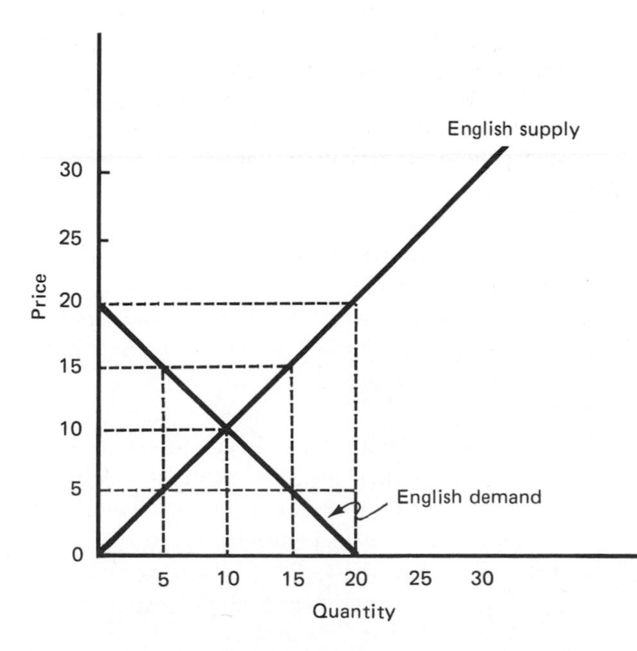

FIGURE 25-2

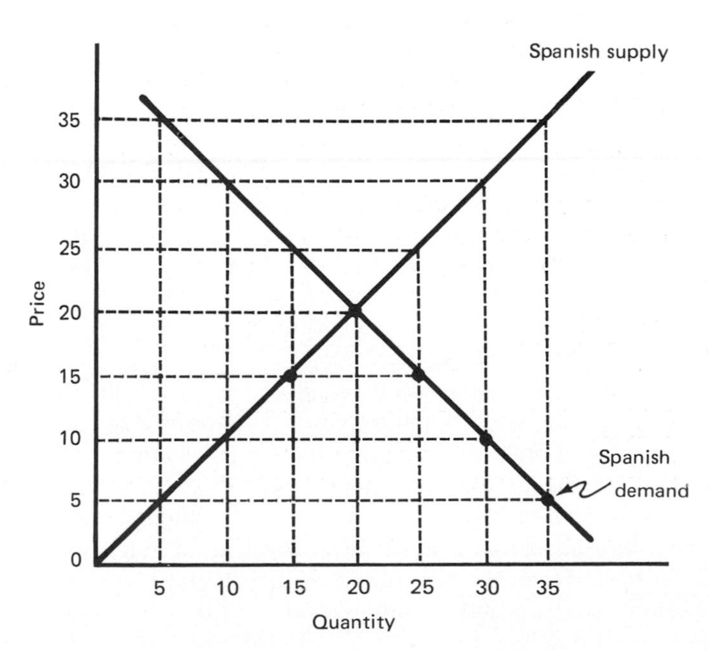

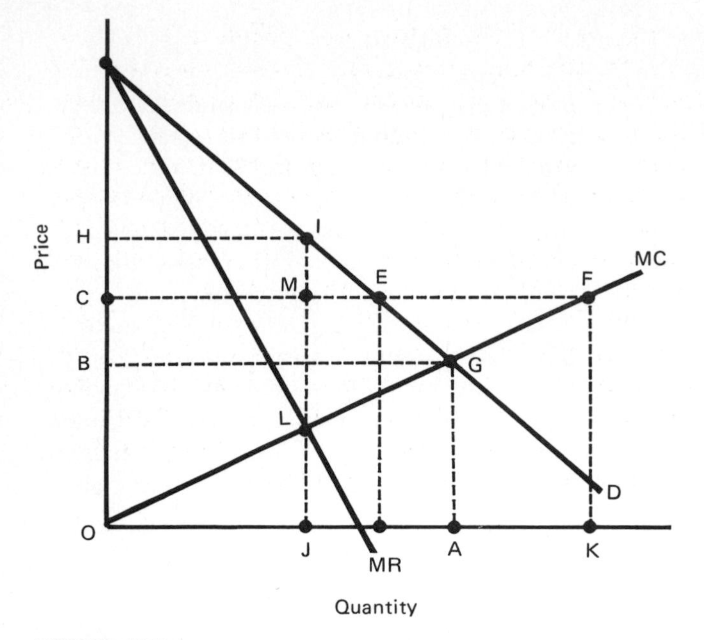

FIGURE 25-3

the good that the United States (exports, imports).

d. As a result of allowing international trade in this good, the total revenue received by the producer in the United States has gone from ________ to ________; therefore the net gain in total revenue equals the rectangle ______ minus the rectangle ________.

e. But the producer's cost increases by the four-sided figure ________; thus the net gain to the producer equals the triangle ________ minus the rectangle ________. At the same time, consumer surplus (rises, falls) by ______ __; thus the net gain to the country (the net gain to consumers plus the net gain to the producer) equals the area of the figure ______. Shade in this area.

f. Trade in this case brings two efficiency gains: the standard gain that results even in a world of perfect competition, shown by area ______ (like area *ABC* in Figure 25-6 in the text), *plus* a gain because trade ends monopoly abuse, shown by area ________ (like the red area in Figure 21-6*a*). Both gains make up the shaded area ________.

g. Does this illustrate a special case in which it is *possible* for international trade in a specific commodity to benefit both the consumers and the producers of that commodity?

3. Table 25-2 describes the production possibilities for clothing and food in the United States and Europe. Suppose, for simplicity, that there are no other countries and no other goods and that the goods

Table 25-2

	Output per worker in Europe	Output per worker in the United States
Food	3	4
Clothing	1	2

can both be produced under constant costs, with labor being the single factor of production.

Then (Europe, the United States) has an absolute advantage in food, and (Europe, the United States) has an absolute advantage in clothing. The opportunity cost of clothing is ______ units of food in Europe and ______ units of food in the United States. Therefore (Europe, the United States) has a comparative advantage in clothing. The opportunity cost of food is ____ units of clothing in Europe and ______ units of clothing in the United States. Therefore (Europe, the United States) has a comparative advantage in food.

Essay Questions

1. The United States imports a great number of cars each year, such as Hondas, Volkswagens, Toyotas, and so forth. Why do you suppose that so many of these cars are produced in other countries and shipped across the ocean, rather than being produced in the United States? Who in the United States gains from having these cars imported? Why? Who loses? Why?

2. "If the United States is to take full advantage of the gains from trade that arise from economies of scale, then it cannot hope to achieve the goal of self-sufficiency in all commodities. In fact, it must become dependent upon other countries." Explain why this is true. What are the costs to the United States of trying to become self-sufficient in satisfying its need for oil and other sources of energy? What are the benefits of self-sufficiency? Do you think, on the whole, that it is a good idea to pursue this goal? Do you think that *complete* self-sufficiency would be possible? If so, at what cost?

3. The figures in Table 25-1 in the text show that the United States imports a large volume of automobiles and parts, but it also exports a large volume of them. Why do you suppose it does both? How would your answer be different if the United States had not signed a free-trade agreement in automobiles with Canada?

4. Show how we may gain from international trade because it may induce firms to eliminate technical inefficiency. Is it true to say that this is "another efficiency gain from increased competition"?

5. In the text, it was argued that when we import a specific good, our consumers gain at the expense of our producers. Does this mean that all individuals gain at the expense of all business firms? Can you think of any reason why the leaders of the United Steelworkers of America, who represent the individuals working in the steel industry, argue so vigorously that the government should take steps to limit the amount of steel imported into the United States?

6. As a rule, producers of a good lose when it is imported and consumers of a good lose when it is exported. Yet Washington is full of professional lobbyists who argue in favor of government restrictions on imports, whereas hardly anyone ever argues in favor of government restrictions on exports. How do you suppose that this is connected with the basic fact that most of us earn our living in one particular industry but consume products from *most* industries?

***7.** Carefully evaluate the following statement: "If marginal costs rise with the amount produced, then there is no gain from engaging in international trade because the country that ends up exporting a good has to produce more of it. This means that its marginal cost—and therefore its price—must be higher than without international trade. In other words, international trade makes goods more expensive."

***8.** In the example given in Table 25-3 in the text, can you tell what the specific price of food will be in terms of clothing when these items are traded between Europe and America? What extra information would you need to answer this? What information *does* the table give you about this price?

Answers

True-False Questions: **1** F **2** T **3** T **4** F **5** T **6** T **7** F **8** T **9** F **10** T **11** T **12** F **13** T **14** F
Multiple-Choice Questions: **1** c **2** b **3** c **4** b **5** a **6** a **7** e **8** e **9** d **10** b
Exercises: **1a.** 10, 10, 20, 20; **b.** 15, 5, 15, 25, 15, England, 10.
2a. *OA*, *OB*, *CE*, *CF*, *EF*, exports; **b.** up, *BCFG*, down, *BCEG*, gain, *EFG*; **c.** *OJ*, *OH*, *CE*, *CF*, *EF*, exports; **d.** *OHIJ*, *OCFK*, *JMFK*, *CHIM*; **e.** *JLFK*, *LMF*, *CHIM*, rises, *CHIE*, *LIEF*; **f.** *EGF*, *ILG*, *IEFL*; **g.** yes, provided that the new price is less than the monopolist's old price.
3. The United States, the United States, 3, 2, the United States, 1/3, 1/2, Europe.

chapter 26
Tariffs and Other International Trade Issues

Learning Objectives

After you have studied this chapter in the textbook and the study guide, you should be able to

State the main political reason and the main military reason for having tariffs

State three fallacious economic arguments for protection, explaining why they are fallacious

State four economic arguments for protection that may sometimes be true

Explain the difficulties with the four "sometimes true" economic arguments for protection

List the three major events affecting the course of international trade that occurred in 1947, in the late 1950s, and in 1967

Give five reasons why multinational corporations (MNCs) exist

List three ways in which MNCs have benefited the world economy

CHAPTER HIGHLIGHTS

This chapter introduces the question of tariffs and other trade restrictions. It deals with (1) the arguments commonly made in favor of trade restrictions, (2) the history of trade policy in the United States and elsewhere, and (3) multinational corporations.

Arguments for Protection

Many trade restrictions exist for economic reasons. But often the reason is purely political. The loss that results from allowing a good to be imported is felt very heavily by the few people who specialize in producing that good and whose jobs are threatened by the competition of imports. These people will often vote for a politician who promises to restrict such imports. As we saw in the last chapter, the benefits from allowing a good to be imported are greater than the losses. But these benefits are typically spread among the many people who consume that good. Although every consumer benefits a little bit, few consumers gain benefit enough to vote against a politician who proposes to restrict such imports. Trade restrictions rarely make economic sense, but they often make political sense.

There is also a military reason for some trade restrictions. Some goods are vital to our national defense. Under free trade, these goods might not be produced in the United States. If so, the United States would be dependent upon foreign producers in time of war. Protection of such industries by tariffs enables us to supply our own military needs. It thereby contributes to our national security. The problem with this military reason is that it can easily be misused. Almost any industry can make the case that its products are vital for national defense.

The last chapter presented a strong economic argument against trade restriction (that is, for free trade). However, the following arguments have often been advanced in favor of trade restrictions. Some are fallacious, but others contain an element of truth and do merit serious consideration.

1. "Buy American because it keeps our money at home." This argument is fallacious. When you buy Japanese goods, your money does indeed go to the Japanese. But it comes back when the Japanese buy our exports. The Japanese want our goods, not our money.

2. "We can't compete with cheap foreign labor." This argument is also fallacious. Foreign labor may be less expensive because it is less productive. We can compete with cheap foreign labor in goods for which we have a comparative advantage. We can't compete when we don't have a comparative advantage.

3. "Tariffs should be tailored to equalize costs at home and abroad." This too is a fallacious argument. According to the theory of comparative advantage, we gain from international trade because of the *differences* in costs between different countries. Tailoring tariffs to equalize costs would just eliminate trade and all the gains it provides.

4. "If we buy cars from Detroit rather than Japan, employment will rise in Detroit rather than Japan." There is a grain of truth in this argument. Restricting imports of cars from Japan may stimulate employment in Detroit, at least in the short run. However, there are two problems. First, Japan may retaliate with her own restrictions, in which case everyone will be worse off for losing the gains from trade. Second, if we buy fewer cars from Japan, then the Japanese will have fewer United States dollars with which to buy American goods, which means that employment may decline in some of our exporting industries.

5. "Restricting trade will diversify a nation's economy." This may be true for some countries. Trade may lead a country to specialize in producing just a few goods. It may not be good for a country to have all its eggs in one basket. However, a country as large as the United States will always produce such a large variety of goods that lack of diversification is unlikely ever to become a serious problem.

6. "We need to protect our infant industries." This argument is sometimes valid. Without the motherly protection of trade restrictions, some of our industries may never reach the size where they can realize the economies of scale necessary to compete in world markets. The difficulties with this argument are threefold: *(a)* Even if the industry were to "grow up," it might still not be able to compete effectively. This is always difficult to determine in advance. *(b)* Infant industries never do seem to grow up. They typically continue to demand protection, and no government wants to lose votes by cutting the apron strings. *(c)* If the infant industry really does have a promising future, then the logical question is why it was unable to persuade private lenders to lend it enough money to enable it to survive to maturity.

7. "Restricting imports may reduce the price we have to pay for them." This may make sense if the United States demands so much of a good that it can significantly reduce the world price of that good by cutting back its demand. However, if other big countries see the United States doing this, they will likely take the same attitude and restrict their imports. If so, the gains from trade will shrink.

History of Trade Policy

The history of trade policy in the Western world has been one of falling tariffs. However, the fall has not been steady. The highlights of this history are illustrated in Figure 26-1 in the text. The most important events to remember are the following. In 1947, the United States and 22 other countries signed the GATT, in which they agreed to the idea of multilateral negotiations to lower tariffs. In the late 1950s, the European Economic Community (EEC) was formed to introduce free trade between all its members, to impose a common tariff against all goods coming in from outside the EEC, and to introduce other measures of economic cooperation. In 1967, the GATT countries completed the "Kennedy Round" of negotiations by agreeing to cut their tariffs, on average, by about 35 percent. In the 1970s there has been some backsliding from the spirit of the Kennedy Round. In particular, many countries have been raising non-tariff barriers, such as import quotas.

The Multinational Corporation (MNC)

The most important thing to understand about MNCs is the reasons for their existence. These are as follows:

1. By producing goods in the country in which they are being sold rather than producing them all in the United States and then shipping them abroad, the company can reduce transportation costs.

2. A company with operations in many different countries is in a position to realize the comparative advantages that go along with producing in those different countries.

3. A company with operations in many different countries is not so vulnerable to political pressure from any one country; that is, if the company feels that the government in one country is taxing it too heavily or imposing regulations that are too costly, then it can reduce these difficulties by switching some of its operations to other countries.

4. The multinational corporation is in a good position to exploit the economies of scale resulting from its large size; for example, the technological improvements it discovers in one country can be transferred easily to its operations in other countries.

5. One reason for producing goods in a foreign country (rather than in the United States and then exporting them to that foreign country) is the existence of tariffs in the foreign country. For example, a number of United States companies that have wanted to sell in Canada have set up branch plants to produce there and have thus avoided paying the Canadian tariff. (If they had, instead, produced in the United States and shipped to Canada, they would have had to pay the Canadian tariff at the border.)

The world economy has benefited from the development of the MNC in three ways: (1) The MNC has helped to reduce transportation costs; (2) it has promoted the gain to all countries from international trade by its ability to realize comparative advantages in different countries; and (3) it has promoted efficiency by its ability to exploit economies of scale. However, many people think that the multinationals now have too much power over governments. How this power can be abused is illustrated by the recent scandals in which executives in the MNCs have paid large bribes to government officials in other countries.

The two appendices to this chapter in the textbook show how the diagrammatic techniques of consumer and producer surplus (which we have been using since Chapter 17) can be used to measure (1) the efficiency loss from a tariff or quota that reduces imports and (2) the efficiency gains and losses that accrue to a country entering into a customs union like the EEC.

IMPORTANT TERMS

Tariff A tax that is levied on goods imported into a country.

Non-tariff barrier (NTB) Any other government regulation that restricts trade, such as a quota or a quality regulation that reduces the amount a country imports.

Quota A government regulation that prohibits the importation of more than a specified amount of some good into a country during a specified time period.

Trade restriction Any tariff or non-tariff barrier that reduces the volume of international trade.

Protection The policy of shielding the industries within a country from the competition of imports by means of trade restrictions.

"Beggar my neighbor" policy The policy of using trade restrictions to reduce unemployment. If such a policy is successful, it transfers the unemployment problem to another country.

Infant industry An industry that has not yet reached the size at which it can exploit enough economies of scale to compete in world markets.

Terms of trade The price in terms of our exported goods that we pay for our imported goods. Some people advocate the use of trade restrictions on some goods only—namely, those for which the United States demand is a large part of world demand, since this would improve our terms of trade.

Bilateral negotiations Negotiations involving only two countries, as opposed to multilateral negotiations, which involve many countries.

GATT The General Agreement on Tariffs and Trade. This was signed in 1947 by the United States and 22 other countries. It involves multilateral negotiations to reduce trade restrictions.

EEC The European Economic Community. It is the common market in Europe which was formed in the late 1950s by Germany, France, Italy, Holland, Belgium, and Luxembourg and was later joined by Britain, Ireland, and Denmark.

Kennedy Round The series of multilateral negotiations between GATT countries initiated by President Kennedy in the 1960s and concluded by the worldwide tariff reduction of 1967.

Multinational corporation (MNC) A large international corporation that operates in many countries.

True-False Questions

T F **1.** The level of tariffs in the Western world has fallen without interruption throughout the twentieth century.

T F **2.** The political pressure that is exerted upon governments to impose trade restrictions is mainly a pressure for import restriction rather than for export restriction.

T F **3.** The last chapter's arguments demonstrating the gains from international trade may also apply to trade in military equipment.

T F **4.** Most economists have concluded that trade restrictions make economic sense but that they are not adequately imposed because politicians are afraid of losing the votes of consumers.

T F **5.** The political pressure for tariffs might not be as great if every congressman and senator had to be elected by a nationwide vote rather than being elected by a particular geographical constituency like a congressional district or state.

T F **6.** One of the strongest arguments for trade restrictions is that they keep us from losing our United States dollars to foreigners.

T F **7.** If foreign labor is cheaper than American labor and if it is as efficient in producing textiles (which are quite labor-intensive), then American firms will find it difficult to compete in the American textile market without protective trade restrictions.

T F **8.** The gains from trade would be totally eliminated if tariffs were set so as to equalize costs at home and abroad.

T F **9.** By using fiscal and monetary policies to solve our unemployment problems, the government of the United States is pursuing a "beggar my neighbor" policy.

T F **10.** If the United States were to increase the tariff on imported cars, that would tend, at least in the short run, to increase unemployment in Japan.

T F **11.** If the United States were to increase the tariff on imported cars, that would also tend, at least in the short run, to stimulate employment in Detroit.

T F **12.** A country whose exports are heavily concentrated in one commodity (or a small number of commodities) is exposed to risk from adverse movements in its terms of trade.

T F **13.** Infant industries are easily identified as such.

T F **14.** Very few infant industries seem to attain successful adulthood without the support of protective trade restrictions.

T F **15.** The purpose of GATT is to provide for bilateral negotiations in which countries will agree to lower their tariffs.

T F **16.** If the United States were to enter into a customs union (like the EEC) with Canada and Mexico, then she might suffer a net loss if the goods that she then began to buy from Canada were produced at greater cost than those that she used to buy from Japan.

T F **17.** Stiff health standards that must be met by imported goods constitute a non-tariff barrier.

T F **18.** A company may go multinational for purely political reasons that have little to do with economic efficiency.

T F **19.** Canadian tariffs restrict the production of goods in Canada by branch plants of United States firms.

Multiple-Choice Questions

1. The most important reasons why we have tariffs
- **(a)** Are valid because our imports cause money to leave the country
- **(b)** Are political
- **(c)** Are valid because other countries do not retaliate against our trade restrictions
- **(d)** Will no longer be present once our infant industries have grown up

2. The main problem with the "national defense" argument for trade restriction is that
- **(a)** By waging war, we can always recover the money lost through international trade.
- **(b)** We have a comparative advantage in defending other countries as well as our own.
- **(c)** It is difficult in practice to tell which industries are vital for our defense and which aren't.
- **(d)** The standard argument proving the gains from trade does not apply to the case of military equipment.

3. The strongest political pressure for trade restrictions comes from
- **(a)** Producers lobbying for import restrictions
- **(b)** Producers lobbying for export restrictions
- **(c)** Consumers lobbying for import restrictions
- **(d)** Consumers lobbying for export restrictions

4. Because of specialization,
   (a) We are able to realize the gains from trade that arise from comparative advantage and economies of scale.
   (b) We tend to vote more as producers than as consumers.
   (c) The United States economy is widely diversified.
   (d) **(a)** and **(b)**.
   (e) **(a)** and **(c)**.

5. Which of the following arguments for protection contains at least a grain of economic truth?
   (a) Infant industries may warrant some tariff protection.
   (b) The competition of cheap foreign production makes tariff protection essential.
   (c) Tariffs should always be applied to prevent firms in the United States from being undersold.
   (d) Tariffs help us to keep our money from leaving the country.

6. We may reduce the price that we have to pay for imports by imposing tariffs on them, but
   (a) We need the imported goods more than we need the tariff revenue.
   (b) We cannot improve our terms of trade.
   (c) The lower price that we pay does us no good if our own producers are not able to compete at the lower price.
   (d) We may be worse off if our tariffs provoke other countries into doing the same thing.

7. The signing of GATT took place in
   (a) 1934 **(c)** 1959
   (b) 1947 **(d)** 1967

8. The Kennedy Round resulted in an average tariff reduction of
   (a) 5 percent **(c)** 25 percent
   (b) 15 percent **(d)** 35 percent

9. The members of the EEC have
   (a) No tariffs on imports from other members
   (b) No tariffs on imports from nonmembers
   (c) A common tariff on trade with nonmembers
   (d) **(a)** and **(b)**
   (e) **(a)** and **(c)**

10. Which of the following is not a reason why multinational corporations exist?
   (a) An MNC can arrange its production throughout the world so as to reduce transportation costs.
   (b) MNCs can avoid tariffs by producing in the countries in which they sell.
   (c) The United Nations provides protection to MNCs that is denied to producers in any single country.
   (d) MNCs are in a good position to exploit economies of scale.

11. The major problem posed by MNCs is that they
   (a) May acquire too much influence over political officials
   (b) Are unable to exploit the gains from comparative advantage
   (c) Do not have economies of scale
   (d) Incur large transportation costs

Exercise

(Parts of this exercise cover the same ground as the two appendices to the chapter. You will probably be able to do the exercise and will find it helpful even if you are not being asked to study the appendices. If you get stuck, you should refer to the appendices for help. Otherwise try to do the exercise on your own.) Figure 26-1 represents the domestic supply and demand for a good that is traded internationally.

a. Without international trade, the price would equal ______ and the quantity produced would equal ______. If international trade results in a price of *OA*, then domestic production will equal ______, domestic consumption will equal ______, and the country will (import, export) the amount ______. As a result of this international trade, consumer surplus will be (more, less) than without trade by the amount ______, and producer surplus will be (more, less) by the amount ________. The change in consumer surplus will be (more, less) than the change in producer surplus by the amount ______. Therefore, as a result of international trade, there will be a net efficiency (gain, loss) to the country of the amount ______.

b. Now suppose that the government imposes an import quota that restricts imports to no more

FIGURE 26-1

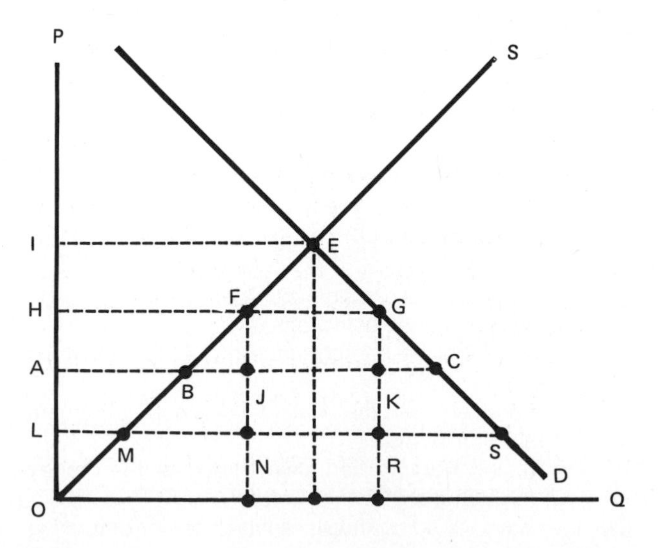

than the quantity FG. (Suppose this has no effect upon the world price of the good, which remains at OA.) Because of the quota, the price in the domestic market will rise to equal ______. At this price, domestic production will equal ______ and domestic consumption will equal ______. The quota will (increase, decrease) consumer surplus by the amount ______ and (increase, decrease) producer surplus by the amount ______. The difference between these two changes in surplus is the net (gain, loss) to the nation resulting from the quota, and it equals ______. The gain to the nation remaining from international trade after the quota is imposed equals ______.

c. Instead of a quota, suppose that the government imposes a tariff of the amount AH on the good. Suppose that this has no effect on the world price of the good. Because of the tariff, the domestic price will equal ______ and the quantity of imports will equal ______. As a result of the tariff, consumer surplus will be (more, less) than it would be with free trade by the amount ______, and producer surplus will be (more, less) than it would be with free trade by the amount ______. Moreover, the government collects revenues from this tariff, the total amount of which equals ______. Thus, when we take into account the loss to consumers and the gain to both producers *and* the treasury (taxpayers)—the net loss to the nation would be the two small triangles ______ and ______. This loss would be (more, less) than the loss from the quota studied in the previous paragraph by the amount ______.

d. The example of this exercise suggests the general rule that the efficiency loss to a nation from imposing a tariff is (more, less) than the efficiency loss of a quota that results in the same volume of trade, and the difference in these efficiency losses equals the amount of ______________.

Essay Questions

1. Why is it that United States Presidents have been more strongly in favor of free trade than have United States congressmen? What sorts of states do you think are likely to elect congressmen that favor free trade?

2. A physician coming from another country must often pass lengthy and difficult examinations before being permitted to practice medicine in the United States, even if she has already received a training in her own country that makes her more qualified than most of the doctors already practicing in the United States. In what sense does this type of regulation resemble a non-tariff barrier? The medical examinations involved are vigorously defended by American physicians, who claim that *(a)* they protect the public against unqualified physicians and *(b)* if we allowed free entry of qualified physicians from everywhere else in the world, there would be such an oversupply of physicians here that many of the young Americans graduating from medical school would be unable to find jobs in medicine. What do you think are the strengths and weaknesses of these arguments?

3. In the text it was argued that a country may improve its terms of trade by restricting *imports*. In 1973, the oil producing countries of OPEC managed to improve their terms of trade by restricting their *exports*. Explain carefully the similarities and differences between the "terms of trade" argument for restricting imports and that for restricting exports.

4. Throughout modern history, the big increases in trade restriction seem to have occurred during times in which many countries were suffering from a recession. Why do you suppose this has been so?

5. Explain carefully the following statement: "There may be a lot of political pressure on a government to protect an infant industry, but there is even more pressure on it to keep the protection going once it has been started."

6. People in many countries think that American-based multinational corporations should be discouraged from setting up operations in their countries because the big decisions that such companies make will be influenced by their American interests rather than the interests of the countries in which they are producing. Analyze the strengths and weakness of this argument.

7. Sometimes American industries demand protection from foreign competition because foreigners have been "dumping" their goods on the United States market. That is, foreigners have been selling their goods in the United States at a price below the price they are charging in their home markets. In what sense does this practice resemble the "cutthroat competition" that sometimes occurs in oligopolistic industries? What are the strengths and weaknesses of the argument that we need tariffs in order to protect our industries against the practice of dumping?

Answers

True-False Questions: **1** F **2** T **3** T **4** F **5** T **6** F **7** T **8** T **9** F **10** T **11** T **12** T **13** F **14** T **15** F **16** T **17** T **18** T **19** F

Multiple-Choice Questions: **1** b **2** c **3** a **4** d **5** a **6** d **7** b **8** d **9** e **10** c **11** a

Exercises: **a.** *OI*, *IE*, *AB*, *AC*, import, *BC*, more, *AIEC*, less, *AIEB*, more, *BEC*, gain, *BEC*.
b. *OH*, *HF*, *HG*, decrease, *AHGC*, increase, AHFB, loss, *BFGC*, *FEG*.
c. *OH*, *FG*, less, *AHGC*, more, *AHFB*, *JFGK*, *BFJ*, *KGC*, less, *JFGK*.
d. less, tariffs collected.

PART FIVE
MICROECONOMICS:
How Income Is Distributed

chapter 27
Wages in a Perfectly Competitive Economy

Learning Objectives

After you have studied this chapter in the textbook and the study guide, you should be able to

Explain why a perfectly competitive firm's demand-for-labor schedule is the same thing as its marginal productivity-of-labor schedule

State two reasons why the demand-for-labor curve might shift to the right

Explain why the height of the labor supply curve measures (approximately) the opportunity cost of labor in that market

Explain why the outcome of a competitive equilibrium in the labor market may be socially efficient

Measure diagrammatically the efficiency loss of departing from a perfectly competitive labor market equilibrium

List four reasons why one cannot jump, from the proposition that a perfectly competitive labor market may be socially efficient, to the conclusion that a perfectly competitive labor market is "best"

Measure in a diagram the total income of labor in a market and the total income of other factors in that market

Show diagrammatically four effects of introducing a minimum wage law into an otherwise perfectly competitive labor market with no externalities

State three important qualifications to this chapter's analysis of minimum wage laws

Show diagrammatically six likely effects of labor market discrimination against blacks

CHAPTER HIGHLIGHTS

This chapter deals with the question of how wages get determined under the assumption of perfectly competitive labor markets (*im*perfect labor markets are studied in the next chapter). This question can be addressed using the same tools of supply and demand that you are already familiar with. For our purposes, someone's wage is just the price of a commodity that is traded in the market. The commodity is labor, the demanders are employers, and the suppliers are workers. The chapter analyzes: (1) the demand for labor, (2) the supply of labor, (3) the efficiency of a perfectly competitive equilibrium and how to measure the efficiency loss if the equilibrium is disturbed, (4) the distribution of income between workers and other factors of production, (5) the effects of minimum wage legislation, and (6) labor market discrimination.

The Demand for Labor

The demand for labor depends on the marginal productivity of labor (MPL). Under the assumption that a firm sells its output in a perfectly competitive market, the firm's MPL is equal to the price of its output times the marginal physical product of labor. The profit-maximizing firm will demand labor up to the point where the MPL is just equal to the wage rate (W). (If MPL were greater than W, the firm could increase its profits by hiring more workers, and if MPL were less than W, the firm could increase its profits by hiring fewer workers.) Thus the MPL curve shows how much the firm will hire at each possible wage. In other words, the MPL curve *is the same thing* as the firm's labor demand curve. To understand this proposition, it may help to compare it with the proposition (explained in Chapter 18) that a consumer's marginal utility curve is the same thing as his or her demand curve.

A firm's demand-for-labor schedule slopes down because of diminishing returns (recall this concept from Chapter 19). As a firm hires more and more labor (with other factors fixed), it eventually finds that the marginal physical product of labor diminishes. Also, there are only two reasons why a firm's labor demand curve might shift: (1) If the price of the firm's output rises, this will increase the MPL for any given amount of employment—in other words, it will shift the demand curve to the right, and (2) anything that increases the marginal physical product of labor for a given amount of employment will also shift the demand curve to the right. This might occur, for example, because of *(a)* an increase in the amount of capital employed by the firm, which makes labor physically more productive by providing it with more machinery to work with, or *(b)* any technological improvement that allows a firm to get more physical output from its workers. (Generally speaking, increased capital equipment and technological change come together, but it is possible for one to occur without the other.)

The market demand curve for labor is just the horizontal sum of the individual firms' demand curves for labor. (Recall how this summation was done at the beginning of Chapter 18.)

The Supply of Labor

The labor supply curve for an industry is derived much like the supply curve for a commodity (as in Chapter 19). The height of the labor supply curve at any point indicates how much must be paid to attract one more worker into the industry. This is (roughly) the wage that the extra worker could earn in another industry. In other words, the height of the labor supply curve is just the opportunity cost faced by the additional worker. (In the early part of Chapter 19 in the text, the simplifying assumption is made that the labor supply schedule is vertical, but—generally speaking—it will have an upward slope.)

Efficiency

Social efficiency requires that labor be hired in an industry up to the point where its marginal social cost is just equal to its marginal social benefit. If there are no externalities, then the marginal social benefit equals the MPL (that is, the height of the demand curve) and the marginal social cost is the opportunity cost of labor (that is, the height of the supply curve). In this case, a competitive equilibrium, where supply equals demand, results in a socially efficient level of unemployment in an industry. This argument is summarized in Box 27-3; compare it to the similar argument in Chapter 20.

When a labor market has been shifted away from a perfectly competitive equilibrium, the efficiency loss can be measured by the triangle between the demand curve, the supply curve, and the vertical line at the actual quantity of employment, as in Figure 27-8 in the text. Remember that this measure is only valid under the twin assumptions of (1) perfect competition and (2) no externalities. If any of this is not clear, you should review your understanding of Chapter 20.

In summary, a perfectly competitive labor market *may* be socially efficient. However, for the following four reasons, we cannot go immediately to the conclusion that a free, unregulated labor market is "best": (1) In an unregulated market, employers may practice unfair discrimination (see the discussion under "Discrimination," below). (2) An unregulated market may not be perfectly competitive. (3) Even if it is, there may be externalities. (4) Even if none of these problems arise and an unregulated labor market is efficient, it may not provide a desirable distribution of income. (The problems involved in dealing with this issue are discussed in Chapter 31.)

The Distribution of Income

The total revenue in an industry is just the sum of the marginal productivities of each worker. In other words, total revenue is just the area to the left of the quantity of employment under the MPL curve for the industry. Of that revenue, the amount going to workers is the quantity of employment times the wage. In other words, in a perfectly competitive equilibrium, it is the quantity of employment times the MPL. In Figure 27-4 in the text, this is just the rectangular area 2, and the amount going to others (in the form of salaries, rent, interest, and profit) is the triangular area 1 above the equilibrium wage. Notice that this measure of "other" income is defined geometrically in the same sort of way as consumer surplus. It may help to review this measurement technique from Chapter 18.

Minimum Wages

When a competitive labor market is subjected to a minimum wage (above the equilibrium wage), there are, as illustrated in Figure 27-5 in the text, four important effects:

1. Employment is reduced.

2. The wage received by workers who are still employed rises, so that the overall effect on total labor income is uncertain. If the demand for labor is elastic, labor income will fall; and if the demand for labor is inelastic, it will rise.

3. The amount of income going to other factors of production will definitely decrease, because the triangle under the demand curve has shrunk.

4. There will be an overall efficiency loss. Generally speaking, this will be measured by a triangle, as in Figure 27-8 in the text; but when the supply of labor schedule is vertical, it is measured by the four-sided figure in Figure 27-5.

These four effects can be predicted from our theory. There is also an effect that experience has taught us: namely, that the unemployment created by minimum wage legislation falls most heavily on teenagers and nonwhites.

There are three important qualifications to this analysis: (1) Even if the minimum wage raises total labor income, workers may not feel that they benefit overall from the change. Even though jobs pay better now, they are harder to find. (2) The amount of unemployment created will depend upon the comprehensiveness of the minimum wage legislation. In the United States in 1965, 6 to 7 percent of the labor force were in jobs not covered by the minimum wage legislation. (3) The argument, as we shall see in the next chapter, depends crucially upon the assumption of perfect competition.

Discrimination

Figure 27-6 in the text analyzes the case of discrimination against black workers. Such discrimination removes the black workers from the main labor market, thereby restricting the quantity supplied in the main labor market and forcing the black workers to enter the less lucrative ghetto market. Make sure that you are able to demonstrate diagrammatically how the following effects result: (1) Black workers' income decreases. (2) White workers' income increases. (3) Income to other factors of production decreases. (4) When the second and third effects are considered together, there may be little overall effect on whites' incomes. (5) There is an efficiency loss. (6) The efficiency loss is borne mainly by blacks.

IMPORTANT TERMS

Derived demand Demand that exists because a good or service is used to produce something else. An example is the demand for labor to produce autos or steel.

Marginal physical product of labor The additional number of units of output that a firm can produce by hiring one more worker.

Marginal productivity of labor The additional revenue that a firm can earn by hiring one more worker.

Opportunity cost of labor In a particular industry, the amount that an additional worker could earn in another industry.

True-False Questions

T F **1.** The marginal physical product of labor in an industry increases whenever the price of the output in that industry increases.

T F **2.** The demand-for-labor schedule shifts to the right whenever the marginal productivity-of-labor schedule shifts to the right.

T F **3.** If a labor market is always in a competitive equilibrium, then a rightward shift in the labor supply schedule will increase the amount of employment and will reduce the marginal productivity of the last worker hired.

T F **4.** If the marginal productivity of labor is less than the wage, a perfectly competitive firm can increase its profits by hiring more labor.

T F 5. An increase in the quantity of capital employed by a firm will probably cause a rightward shift in the marginal productivity-of-labor schedule.

T F 6. The geometric measure of *labor* income using a labor demand curve is identical to the geometric measure of consumer surplus using a consumer demand curve.

T F 7. One likely effect of an increase in the minimum wage is a decrease in the total income going to factors of production other than labor.

T F 8. An increase in the minimum wage will not reduce economic efficiency if the demand for labor is elastic.

T F 9. The unemployment that is caused by minimum wage legislation falls mainly on the old.

T F 10. Discrimination against one group of workers in an otherwise perfectly competitive labor market causes an increase in total income received by the other workers in that market.

T F 11. The height of the labor supply curve is (approximately) equal to the opportunity cost of labor.

T F 12. If the labor supply schedule in a market becomes perfectly inelastic, then the geometric measure of the efficiency loss resulting from a departure from equilibrium is not a triangle.

T F 13. A rightward shift in the labor supply schedule in a market may eliminate the inefficiency resulting from a minimum wage in that market.

T F 14. A rightward shift in the labor demand schedule may eliminate the inefficiency resulting from a minimum wage in that market.

T F 15. If the output of a particular industry provides external benefits, then a perfectly competitive labor market in that industry will generate less than the socially efficient amount of employment.

T F 16. Our analysis of monopoly in Chapter 21 suggests that if there is a monopoly seller in a labor market (a union), then it will set the wage rate above the opportunity cost of labor.

Multiple-Choice Questions

1. A perfectly competitive firm's demand curve for labor slopes down because, as the firm hires more, there is
- **(a)** A decreasing wage
- **(b)** Decreasing marginal cost
- **(c)** Diminishing marginal utility
- **(d)** Diminishing marginal physical productivity

2. Which of the following events is most likely to cause a rightward shift in an industry's demand-for-labor schedule?
- **(a)** A decrease in the wage rate in that industry
- **(b)** A decrease in the amount of capital employed in that industry
- **(c)** An increase in the price of the output of that industry
- **(d)** An increase in the work force in that industry

3. If there are no externalities in a labor market and the market is in a perfectly competitive equilibrium, then the height of the labor demand curve at the existing quantity of employment equals
- **(a)** The marginal productivity of labor
- **(b)** The marginal social benefit of producing more output in the industry
- **(c)** The marginal social benefit of employing another worker in the industry
- **(d)** **(a)** and **(b)**
- **(e)** **(a)** and **(c)**

4. If the labor supply curve is vertical, then a technological improvement that increases the marginal physical product of labor will cause
- **(a)** An increase in the wage and no change in employment
- **(b)** An increase in both the wage and employment
- **(c)** An increase in employment and no change in the wage
- **(d)** A decrease in the wage and no change in employment

5. Whether or not externalities are present, the socially efficient amount of employment will occur in a labor market if the marginal social cost of employing labor equals
- **(a)** The marginal productivity of labor
- **(b)** The marginal social benefit of employing labor
- **(c)** The wage rate
- **(d)** **(a)** and **(b)**
- **(e)** **(a)** and **(c)**

6. The total area under an industry's demand-for-labor schedule to the left of the existing quantity of employment equals
- **(a)** The total revenue received in the industry
- **(b)** The total income of labor in the industry
- **(c)** Total profits in the industry
- **(d)** The quantity of other factors in the industry

7. Which of the following is not an effect of introducing a minimum wage law in a perfectly competitive labor market with no externalities?
- **(a)** The quantity of employment falls.
- **(b)** The wage received by employed workers rises.
- **(c)** The total income of labor rises if the demand for labor is elastic.
- **(d)** There will be an overall efficiency loss.

8. It has been commonly observed that the unemployment created by minimum wage legislation is particularly severe among
- **(a)** Teenagers

(b) White-collar workers
(c) Nonwhites
(d) (a) and (b)
(e) (a) and (c)

9. One result of discrimination against men in a perfectly competitive market for nurses' labor would probably be
(a) An efficiency loss
(b) An increase in the wages of female nurses
(c) A decrease in the income received by female nurses
(d) (a) and (b)
(e) (a) and (c)

10. The opportunity cost of labor in an industry
(a) Is approximately measured by the height of the labor demand schedule
(b) Is approximately measured by the height of the labor supply schedule
(c) Depends upon the level of employment in the industry
(d) (a) and (c)
(e) (b) and (c)

11. Suppose that a perfectly competitive firm's MPL schedule looks like the one in Figure 27-1. When the wage rate is *OW*, the firm will
(a) Demand the quantity ON_1 of labor
(b) Demand the quantity ON_2 of labor
(c) Be equally satisfied with the quantity ON_1 or the quantity ON_2 of labor
(d) Demand some quantity of labor between ON_1 and ON_2

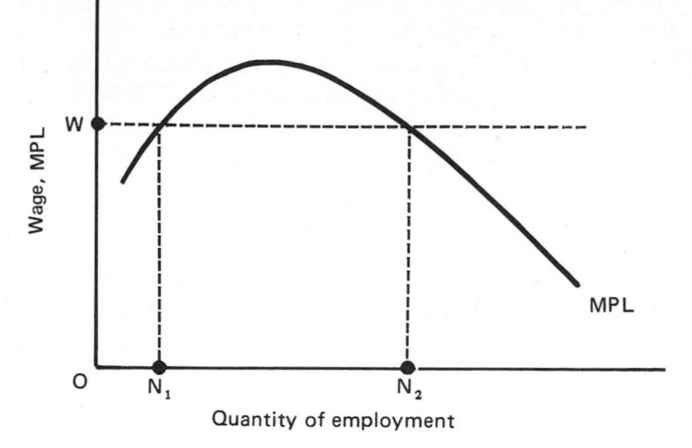

FIGURE 27-1

12. Which of the following is *not* one of the reasons why an economist cannot jump, from the proposition that a perfectly competitive equilibrium is efficient, to the conclusion that the best government policy with respect to labor markets is to leave them unregulated?
(a) Employers may practice unfair discrimination if left unregulated.
(b) The perfectly competitive outcome will always give workers too little income.
(c) The efficiency proposition is not valid except under the assumption of perfect competition.
(d) There may be externalities that invalidate the efficiency proposition.

Exercises

1. Fill in the missing data in Table 27-1 for a hypothetical firm with a given stock of capital and selling its output in a competitive market at a constant price.

If the wage rate is $55 per worker per day, then the firm will want to hire ______ workers when the price is $10 and ______ workers when the price is $15.

2. Fill in the missing data in Table 27-2 for another hypothetical firm in the same situation, assuming that the wage is $40 per worker per day and the price of output is $5.

The firm will be willing to hire no more than ______ workers. The income of other factors is maximized when the firm hires ______ workers. Plot the labor demand schedule of this firm in Figure 27-2. Draw a horizontal line at the wage rate $40 per worker per day and put a number 1 inside the measure of labor income. Put a 2 inside the measure of income going to other factors.

3. Figure 27-3 depicts a perfectly competitive labor market with no externalities. The equilibrium wage rate equals ______. The equilibrium quantity of

Table 27-1

Number of workers per day	Total physical output per day	Marginal physical output per day	Marginal productivity of labor when price of output equals $10 per unit	Marginal productivity of labor when price of output equals $15 per unit
0	0	—	—	—
1	12	______	______	______
2	19	______	______	______
3	24	______	______	______
4	28	______	______	______
5	30	______	______	______

Table 27-2

Number of workers	Total physical output	Marginal physical product	Marginal productivity of labor	Total revenue of industry	Total income of labor	Total income of other factors of production
0	0	—	—	____	____	____
1	____	10	____	____	____	____
2	____	9	____	____	____	____
3	____	8	____	____	____	____
4	____	7	____	____	____	____
5	____	6	____	____	____	____

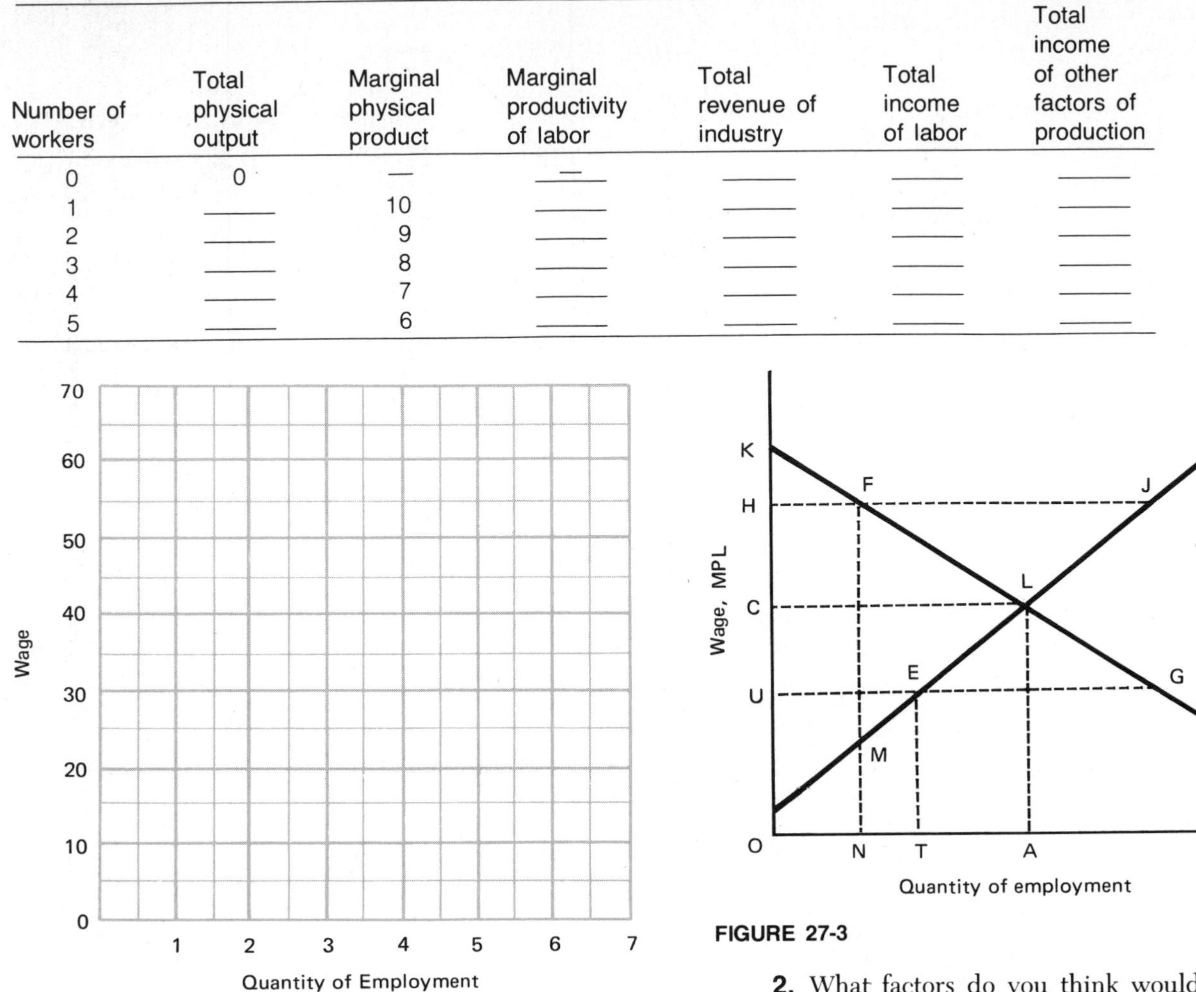

FIGURE 27-2

FIGURE 27-3

employment equals ______. Suppose the minimum wage equals *OU*. Then the actual quantity of employment will equal ______ and the difference between supply and demand will equal ______. Next, suppose the minimum wage equals *OH*. Then the actual quantity of employment will equal ______ and the difference between demand and supply will equal ______. Fill in Table 27-3.

Essay Questions

1. "The labor demand schedule slopes down for the same reason that the demand curve for a consumer good slopes down." Explain.

Table 27-3

	Efficiency loss	Total labor income	Income of other factors
No minimum wage	____	____	____
Minimum wage *OU*	____	____	____
Minimum wage *OH*	____	____	____

2. What factors do you think would be most important in determining the position of the labor supply curve in an industry? How would the position of this curve be affected by an increase in the generosity of payments under unemployment insurance?

3. Discuss the relationship between a firm's marginal physical product of labor schedule (MPPL) and its short-run marginal cost schedule (MC). Will a shift in MPPL shift MC? Why or why not? Is it true that if marginal physical productivity is increasing at first, then marginal cost must be decreasing at first? Why or why not?

4. Would you expect the supply curve for labor as a whole in the United States to be more or less elastic than the supply curve for labor in a particular industry? How would the elasticity of the supply of labor in a particular market be affected by a decrease in the cost of moving from one city to another?

5. See if you can list four factors affecting the elasticity of demand for labor that are analogous to the four factors affecting the demand for a consumer good discussed in Chapter 17.

6. Would you expect labor market discrimination to be more of a problem in a perfectly competitive industry or in a monopolistic industry? Why?

7. Show by means of a diagram how the effects in a labor market of a minimum wage law can be offset by an employment subsidy—that is, a policy of paying money to firms for hiring more workers. If you were to design such a policy, how would you go about doing it so as also to offset the effects of minimum wage laws in generating more unemployment among blacks and teenagers?

Answers

True-False Questions: **1 F 2 T 3 T 4 F 5 T 6 F 7 T 8 F 9 F 10 T 11 T 12 T 13 F 14 T 15 T 16 T**

Multiple-Choice Questions: **1 d 2 c 3 e 4 a 5 b 6 a 7 c 8 e 9 d 10 e 11 b 12 b**

Exercises: 1. Table 27-1

Number of workers per day	Total physical output per day	Marginal physical output per day	Marginal productivity of labor when price of output equals $10 per unit	Marginal productivity of labor when price of output equals $15 per unit
0	0	—	—	—
1	12	12	120	180
2	19	7	70	105
3	24	5	50	75
4	28	4	40	60
5	30	2	20	30

2, 4.

2. Table 27-2

Total physical output	Marginal productivity of labor	Total revenue of industry	Total income of labor	Total income of other factors of production
0	—	0	0	0
10	50	50	40	10
19	45	95	80	15
27	40	135	120	15
34	35	170	160	10
40	30	200	200	0

3, 2 or 3.

FIGURE 27-2 completed.

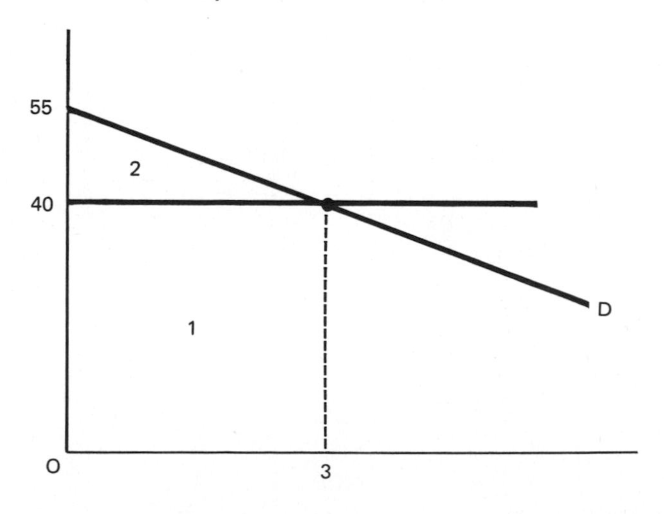

3. *OC*, *OA*, *OA*, O, *HF*, *FJ*.

Table 27-3

Efficiency loss	Total labor income	Income of other factors
0	OCLA	KLC
0	OCLA	KLC
FLM	OHFN	KFH

chapter 28
Wages in Imperfect Labor Markets

Learning Objectives

After you have studied this chapter in the textbook and the study guide, you should be able to

Describe how union membership has changed in three distinct periods of United States labor history

Identify three important laws in United States labor history and state their major provisions

Identify the four largest union organizations in the United States today

Show in a diagram the three main effects of introducing a union that succeeds in raising wages in an otherwise perfectly competitive labor market

Show in a diagram the three main effects of introducing a featherbedding agreement into an otherwise perfectly competitive labor market

Show in a diagram the three main effects of introducing a monopsony that reduces wages in an otherwise perfectly competitive labor market

Explain how the effects of introducing a union into an otherwise perfectly competitive labor market are reversed if the market is monopsonistic

Give two reasons why strikes occur even when no one really gains from them

Identify three ways of averting an imminent strike

State the distinctions between voluntary arbitration, compulsory arbitration, mediation, and conciliation

List four reasons why it might not be in the "public interest" to allow unions to develop in the public service

CHAPTER HIGHLIGHTS

In real life, many labor markets are not perfectly competitive. This chapter studies what happens in such instances. The issues discussed are (1) the history of the labor union movement in the United States, (2) the effects of introducing a union into an otherwise perfectly competitive labor market, (3) the effects of introducing a monopsony (single buyer) into an otherwise perfectly competitive labor market, (4) what happens in a labor market with bilateral monopoly—that is, a union bargaining with a monopsony, and (5) the special problems of the market for public service employees.

History

Figure 28-1 in the text shows that United States labor history may be divided into the following three distinct periods:

1. Prior to 1935, union membership was very low. The most important large union, the AFL, was mainly a craft union.

2. From 1935 to 1945, union membership grew very rapidly, aided by two major events:

- **a.** The founding in 1936 of the CIO, which favored the development of industrial unions
- **b.** The Wagner Act of 1935, which
  - **(1)** Made it clear that workers had the right to form a union
  - **(2)** Prohibited various unfair labor practices of employers
  - **(3)** Established the NLRB to control these unfair labor practices and to settle disputes between unions

3. Since 1945, union membership has fallen steadily as a proportion of total employment. There are four major reasons generally cited for this fall:

- **a.** Employment in heavy industry, which is highly unionized, has fallen as a proportion of total employment.
- **b.** Much heavy industry has also moved to the relatively nonunionized south.
- **c.** After the recovery from the massive unemployment of the Great Depression, unions no longer had such strong public sympathy and support.
- **d.** During World War II, many people felt that unions had used their newly gained power irresponsibly, which generated some public hostility toward unions.

You should be familiar with two major labor laws of this third period. The first is the Taft-Hartley Act of 1947, which

1. Outlawed closed shops in industries engaged in interstate commerce

2. Outlawed jurisdictional strikes

3. Outlawed the practice of checking off union fees

4. Imposed restrictions on union leaders designed to make them more responsible financially

5. Empowered the President to seek a court injunction forcing strikers to return to work for an 80-day "cooling off" period in the case of a strike that endangers national health or safety

6. In its famous section 14(b), declared that union shops are illegal in any state that decides to pass a right-to-work law.

The other major labor law is the Landrum-Griffin Act of 1959, which imposed even more financial restrictions upon union leaders and strengthened the power of union members to challenge their leaders in various ways.

In 1955, the AFL and CIO amalgamated. Today, therefore, the four largest union organizations in the United States are the AFL-CIO, the Teamsters, The United Mine Workers, and the United Auto Workers.

The Effects of Unions

The main objective of a union is to get high wages for its members. If a union is established and manages to raise the wage in an otherwise perfectly competitive labor market with no externalities, there are three main effects: (1) employment in that market falls, (2) incomes of other factors fall, and (3) an efficiency loss is created that can be measured by the usual geometric technique. Study Figure 28-2 in the text until you can demonstrate these three effects on your own.

Another objective of a union is to protect its members' jobs. This objective usually conflicts with that of obtaining higher wages. Just as any other monopolist must restrict the quantity supplied in order to raise its price, so the union must usually restrict the quantity of employment in order to raise wages. But a union can adopt two policies to protect jobs without depressing wages. First, it can negotiate a shorter work week. This restricts the supply of labor without necessarily reducing the number of jobs. Second, it can negotiate a featherbedding agreement. There are three main effects of introducing a featherbedding agreement into an otherwise perfectly competitive labor market with no externalities: (1) employment in that market increases, (2) an efficiency loss arises, not just for the usual reason that the quantity of employment differs from the competitive equilibrium quantity but also because, with featherbedding, workers may be employed at useless tasks instead of useful ones, and (3) job security of members of the union involved may be increased. However, common sense tells us that there are better ways of providing job security.

Monopsony

A monopsonist tries to exploit his or her market power by keeping wages below what they would be in perfect competition. If the monopsonist succeeds, the three main effects will be (1) to reduce employment in that market, (2) to create an efficiency loss, and (3) to increase the income going to factors of production other than labor. Study Figure 28-3 in the text until you can demonstrate these three effects on your own.

Bilateral Monopoly

In many labor markets, it is probably most realistic to assume bilateral monopoly. Unfortunately, this case is also the most difficult to analyze. This chapter discusses three issues concerning bilateral monopoly: (1) why the effects of introducing a union may be different when there is a monopsony than when the market is otherwise perfectly competitive, (2) the indeterminancy of the outcome with bilateral monopoly, and (3) the problem of strikes.

1. If a union succeeds in raising the wage in a monopsonistic market, the effects may be entirely different than those in the case of the competitive market that we have already studied (see "The Effects of Unions," above). In particular, suppose that, after the union has been introduced, the wage is still below what it would have been in a competitive market. In this case, the union will simply undo some of the effects of the monopsony. That is, it will *(a)* reduce the efficiency loss of monopsony, *(b)* increase employment, *(c)* increase the income going to labor, and *(d)* reduce the income going to other factors of production. This is illustrated in Figure 28-5 in the text.

2. However, there is no guarantee that a bilateral monopoly will produce a wage below the competitive wage. All we know for sure is that the wage will be no lower than the monopsony wage and no higher than the wage that would be set by a union in an otherwise competitive market. There is no way of predicting exactly where, between these two extremes, the wage will be. It depends mainly upon the bargaining power of each side. The bargaining power of the union depends largely upon the size of the union's strike fund. The bargaining power of the employer depends largely upon the size of its inventories of finished goods. The bargaining will also be influenced by the financial strength of the employer. A financially weak employer can often persuade its union to accept a relatively low wage by arguing that otherwise it will be forced out of business and the union members will therefore be out of work.

3. In a sense, nobody gains from a strike, for if work had proceeded during the period of the strike, the firm would then have more income (total revenue) to divide among the different factors of production. Thus, in principle, a settlement could have been reached that would have given more income to *both* sides than they received as a result of the strike. But strikes occur nevertheless because *(a)* each side sees a strike as a means of doing better than the other side's "final offer" and *(b)* each side, in order to improve its bargaining power next time around, may want to demonstrate that even a strike will not make it back down.

The main reason why strikes pose an important issue for public policy is that the costs of a strike may be much larger for people not involved in the bargaining than for the two sides directly involved, as when a coal strike causes layoffs in other industries. There are three main ways of averting a strike when the two sides are unable to reach agreement on their own: *(a)* The President may seek a Taft-Hartley injunction (see "History," above); the Federal Mediation Service may then help find an agreement during the cooling-off period. *(b)* Both sides may agree to voluntary arbitration, in which a third party decides upon a settlement that both sides agree in advance to accept. *(c)* If the two sides don't agree to voluntary arbitration, the government may force them to accept compulsory arbitration.

Public Service Employees

It has been argued that it would not be in the "public interest," for the following four reasons, to allow unions to develop in the public service:

1. Their strike weapon would be too strong because of the large spillover effects involved.

2. Politicians would find it too easy to give in to the unions, which would mean higher taxes to pay the wage bill.

3. A financially weak government does not have the same bargaining power as a financially weak private employer because it can't argue that a high wage settlement will force it out of business.

4. Because public service employees now constitute a large bloc of voters, there is an incentive for politicians to try to buy votes by offering them high wages.

IMPORTANT TERMS

Industrial union A union whose members all work in the same industry, although they may belong to different crafts or professions.

Craft union A union whose members all belong to the same craft or profession, although they may work in different industries.

Collective bargaining Negotiations between a union and an employer over wages, fringe benefits, hiring policies, job security, or working conditions.

AFL The American Federation of Labor, formed in the 1880s by Samuel Gompers.

National Labor Relations Act The Wagner Act of 1935.

CIO The Congress of Industrial Organizations, a big union organization formed by a group, led by John L. Lewis, that broke away from the AFL in 1936.

Closed shop A situation in which an employer can hire only union members.

Union shop A situation in which anyone hired by an employer must join the union within some specified period.

Open shop A situation in which employees do not have to join a union.

Right-to-work law A law making closed shops or union shops illegal.

Jurisdictional disputes Conflicts between unions over whose members will do specific jobs.

Checking off The practice of having employers collect union dues by deducting them from workers' paychecks.

Featherbedding Employing labor in superfluous jobs.

Monopsony A situation in which there is only one buyer in a market.

Strike fund A sum of money owned by a union for the purpose of supporting its members while on strike.

Injunction A court order compelling someone to refrain from a particular act, as when workers are compelled to end a strike.

Mediation The intervention of a third party—a mediator—to suggest a compromise settlement in a labor dispute; but the mediator cannot make any binding recommendations. Also called conciliation.

Arbitration The same as mediation, except that the recommendation of the arbitrator is binding upon both parties.

True-False Questions

T F **1.** Union members represented a higher proportion of total employees in the United States in 1945 than today.

T F **2.** In its early years, the AFL was mainly an industrial union.

T F **3.** The Wagner Act empowered the President to seek an injunction forcing strikers to return to work for an 80-day "cooling off" period in the case of a strike that endangers national health or safety.

T F **4.** One of the factors contributing to the decline in union membership since 1945 has been the decline in employment in heavy industry as a proportion of total employment.

T F **5.** The Taft-Hartley Act outlawed closed shops in industries engaged in interstate commerce.

T F **6.** The Landrum-Griffin Act is also called the National Labor Relations Act.

T F **7.** If a union succeeds in raising wages above what they would be in perfect competition and the demand curve for labor is elastic, this will raise the total income of labor in that market.

T F **8.** If a union manages to raise wages higher than they would otherwise be and there is a monopsonist employer, an efficiency loss may not ensue.

T F **9.** Negotiating for a shorter work week is one method whereby a union may attempt to protect jobs without depressing wages.

T F **10.** The efficiency loss from featherbedding in an otherwise perfectly competitive market with no externalities is probably smaller than indicated by the usual "triangle" measure.

T F **11.** A company near bankruptcy has less bargaining power and therefore will probably have to settle for a higher wage in negotiating with its union than a financially strong company.

T F **12.** Under voluntary arbitration, the recommendation of the arbitrator is not binding.

T F **13.** Section 14(b) of the Taft-Hartley Act allows states to make union shops illegal.

Multiple-Choice Questions

1. During which of the following four periods in the United States did union membership grow fastest as a proportion of total employment?

(a) 1915–1925 **(c)** 1935–1945

(b) 1925–1935 **(d)** 1945–1955

2. Which of the following came first?

(a) The founding of the CIO

(b) The Taft-Hartley Act

(c) The Landrum-Griffin Act

(d) The founding of the AFL

3. Which of the following statements about the Wagner Act is *in*correct?

(a) It outlawed jurisdictional strikes.

(b) It established that workers clearly had the right to form a union.

(c) It established the NLRB.

(d) It prohibited various unfair labor practices of employers.

4. Which of the following is *not* generally cited as a reason why union membership has fallen steadily as a proportion of total employment since 1945?

- **(a)** Employment in heavy industry has fallen as a proportion of total employment.
- **(b)** The AFL and CIO amalgamated in 1955.
- **(c)** Public support for unions declined when the massive unemployment of the Great Depression disappeared.
- **(d)** **(a)** and **(b)**.
- **(e)** **(a)** and **(c)**.

5. Which of the following acts outlawed closed shops in industries engaged in interstate commerce?

- **(a)** The Wagner Act
- **(b)** The Taft-Hartley Act
- **(c)** The Landrum-Griffin Act
- **(d)** None of the above

6. Which of the following is most likely to occur if a union is made illegal in an otherwise perfectly competitive labor market with no externalities?

- **(a)** Employment in that market will decrease.
- **(b)** Incomes of factors of production other than labor will increase.
- **(c)** An efficiency loss will be created.
- **(d)** Total income to labor will increase.

7. Which of the following is a device whereby unions restrict the supply of labor?

- **(a)** Negotiating for a shorter work week
- **(b)** Long apprenticeships
- **(c)** Lobbying for minimum wage laws in Congress
- **(d)** All of the above

8. Introducing a featherbedding agreement into an otherwise perfectly competitive labor market with no externalities creates an efficiency loss because

- **(a)** Job security of the members of the union may be reduced.
- **(b)** The quantity of employment differs from the competitive equilibrium quantity.
- **(c)** Workers may be employed at useless tasks instead of useful ones.
- **(d)** **(a)** and **(b)**.
- **(e)** **(b)** and **(c)**.

9. Which of the following conditions tends to make a high wage settlement more likely than a low wage settlement?

- **(a)** A large union strike fund
- **(b)** A large stock of inventories held by the employer
- **(c)** A near-bankrupt employer
- **(d)** A right-to-work law

10. Which of the following makes it *less* likely that a strike will occur?

- **(a)** The desire on the part of the union to demonstrate the credibility of its threats
- **(b)** A "final offer" by the employer involving a higher wage than the "final offer" of the union
- **(c)** A "final offer" of the employer involving a lower wage than the "final offer" of the union
- **(d)** **(a)** and **(b)**
- **(e)** **(a)** and **(c)**

11. Which of the following is *not* a reason that has been proposed why allowing unions to develop in the public sector would be against the "public interest"?

- **(a)** Their strike weapon would be too strong, because of the large spillover effects involved.
- **(b)** A financially weak government does not have the same bargaining power as a financially weak private employer because it can't invoke the threat of going out of business.
- **(c)** The government usually has less of an incentive to hold the line on wages than does a private employer.
- **(d)** Public servants should be motivated by a sense of duty to work for whatever wages the government can afford to pay.

Exercises

1a. Figure 28-1 depicts supply (S) and demand (D) in a perfectly competitive labor market with no externalities. The equilibrium wage equals ______ and the equilibrium quantity of employment equals ____. In perfect competition, the income of labor equals ________ and the income of other factors equals ____.

b. Suppose now that a union is formed, which increases the wage to equal OG. Then the quantity of employment will equal ______, the income going to labor will equal ______ ___, the income going to other factors will equal ______, and the efficiency loss will equal ______.

c. Now suppose that there is an externality. In particular, the marginal social cost of employment is really indicated by the curve labeled MSC rather than by the supply curve. Then the socially efficient quantity of employment will equal ______. In perfect competition, the wage will equal ______, the quantity of employment will equal ______, and the efficiency loss will equal ______.

d. With this externality, if a union is formed to raise wages to OG, then the quantity of employment will equal ______ and the efficiency loss will equal ______.

2a. Table 28-1 on the next page depicts the situation in the labor market of an industry with a given stock of capital. Column I indicates the number of workers per day and column II indicates total output of the industry. Fill in column III indicating the marginal physical product of labor and column IV indicat-

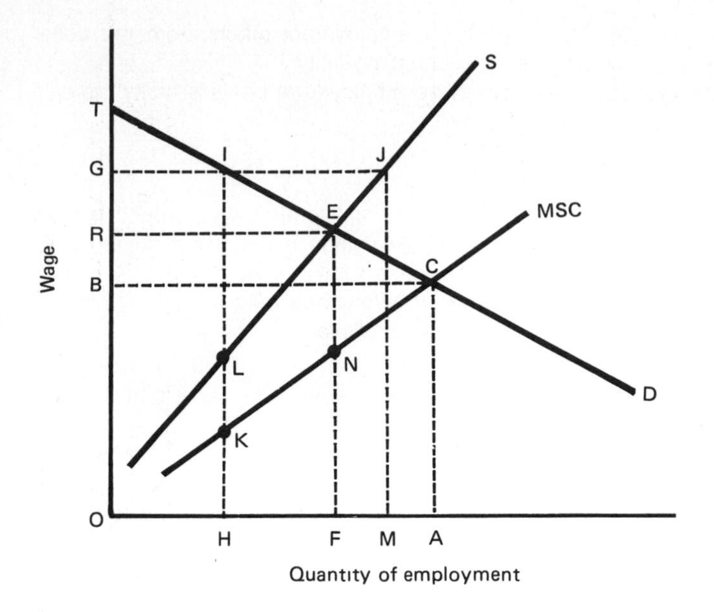

FIGURE 28-1

ing the marginal productivity of labor when the output price is $15 per unit. Column V indicates the wage on the labor supply curve. If the market is perfectly competitive, then the wage will equal ______, the amount of employment will equal ______ workers, the total revenue in the industry will be ______, the total income of labor in the industry will equal ______, and the total income of other factors will equal ______.

b. Now suppose that all the firms act in the labor market as a single monopsonist. The monopsonist realizes that whatever wage is offered, the total quantity of employment will be determined by the labor-supply curve and the output price is constant at $15 per unit. Fill in column VI indicating the monopsonist's total revenue, column VII indicating the total labor cost, and column VIII indicating the total amount of income to other factors. Suppose that the only other factor is "entrepreneurship." In other words, the income of other factors is all income to the monopsonist. If the monopsonist's firm wants to maximize its income, it will hire ______ workers at a wage of $______. The monopsonist's marginal factor cost of labor (MFC) is the amount by which the labor cost increases whenever one more worker is hired. Fill in column IX indicating the MFC. Compare columns IV and IX. What equilibrium condition does this suggest that governs the employment decision of the monopsonist? ______________.

Table 28-1

I	II	III	IV	V	VI	VII	VIII	IX
0	0	—	—	0	______	______	______	—
1	5	5	______	2	______	______	______	______
2	9	______	______	4	______	______	______	______
3	12	______	______	18	______	______	______	______
4	14	______	______	30	______	______	______	______
5	15	______	______	40	______	______	______	______

Essay Questions

1. Is it possible for a monopsonist to offer such a low wage that the firm's profit will actually be less than what it would be in a perfectly competitive industry?

2. Would you agree that a monopsonist "exploits" workers? Is there any reason to believe that workers "deserve" at least as much income as they would get in a perfectly competitive situation?

3. In Chapter 27, we showed how an increase in the minimum wage would reduce the amount of employment in a perfectly competitive labor market. Show by reference to Figure 28-3 in the text that, in a monopsonistic labor market, the effect of increasing the minimum wage may be to increase the amount of employment.

4. Why would a monopsonist prefer to operate in a market with an inelastic supply of labor rather than in one with an elastic supply of labor?

5. How would the bargaining power of a union be influenced by a reduction in the cost to its members of leaving town to get another job?

6. Argue the case that Congress tended to support the development of union power before 1945 but that Congressional actions have reduced union power since that time.

7. Argue the case that public service employees should be allowed to form unions and strike. Argue the opposite case.

8. Recall the problems of producers' associations discussed in Chapter 21. In what sense are these same problems shared by labor unions?

***9.** In what sense does a monopsonist not have a demand curve for labor?

Answers

True-False Questions: **1 T 2 F 3 F 4 T 5 T 6 F 7 F 8 T 9 T 10 F 11 F 12 F 13 T**
Multiple-Choice Questions: **1 c 2 d 3 a 4 b 5 b 6 b 7 d 8 e 9 a 10 b 11 d**
Exercises: **1a.** *OR, OF, OREF, TER*; **b.** *OH, OGIH, TIG, IEL*; **c.** *OA, OR, OF, ECN*; **d.** *OH, ICK.*
2. Table 28-1

I	II	III	IV	V	VI	VII	VIII	IX
0	0	—	—	0	0	0	0	—
1	5	5	75	2	75	2	73	2
2	9	4	60	4	135	8	127	6
3	12	3	45	18	180	54	126	46
4	14	2	30	30	210	120	90	66
5	15	1	15	40	225	200	25	80

a. 30, 4, 210, 120, 90; **b.** 2, 4, MPL equals MFC.

chapter 29
Other Incomes

Learning Objectives

After you have studied this chapter in the textbook and the study guide, you should be able to

Explain the different concepts of debt capital, equity capital, physical capital, and human capital

Explain why the marginal efficiency of investment (MEI) schedule is identical to the demand schedule for loanable funds

Show in a diagram three likely effects of imposing an interest-rate ceiling upon a perfectly competitive market for loanable funds

State two reasons why it is a fallacy to suppose that interest-rate ceilings necessarily help poor people

State three reasons for believing that investment in human capital may be less than the efficient amount

State two reasons for believing that investment in human capital may be more than the efficient amount

Give two possible reasons why the rate of return on investment in human capital has decreased since 1969

State six reasons why it is difficult to measure the rate of return on human capital

List five examples of economic rent

State the two basic roles played by factor prices in a market economy

CHAPTER HIGHLIGHTS

About one-quarter of national income in the United States does not go to labor. This chapter studies what determines those other incomes, mainly interest, profit, and rent. The specific issues discussed are (1) how the rate of interest is determined in the market for loanable funds, (2) the return to human capital, (3) the nature and significance of economic rent, and (4) the role of factor prices in the economic system.

The Rate of Interest

The rate of interest measures the rate at which present goods may be converted into future goods. This rate may be regarded as the price that clears the market for loanable funds. The demand for loanable funds is just the MEI schedule that we have already encountered in Chapter 12. The supply of loanable funds measures the willingness of savers to part with present income, which depends on the rate of interest that they can earn for doing so.

In practice, there is not one rate of interest but many. These differences are mainly accounted for by risk. The greater the risk that a borrower will be unable to repay a loan, the higher the rate of interest that this borrower will have to pay.

An important issue studied in this section is that of interest-rate ceilings. When the government imposes a ceiling on interest rates in a perfectly competitive loan market with no externalities, there are three main effects: (1) the quantity of loans decreases, (2) income is transferred from lenders to those borrowers who are still able to acquire loans, and (3) there is an efficiency loss which may be underestimated by the usual triangle (i.e., the borrowers who are rationed because of the ceiling may have been planning to invest in more profitable investment projects than those who are not rationed). Study Figure 29-3 in the text until you can demonstrate these three effects on your own. There are two reasons why it is a fallacy to suppose that interest-rate ceilings necessarily help poor people: (1) The borrowers that are helped by these ceilings may be quite rich. (2) Even if borrowers are poor, those who are rationed because of the ceiling are worse off as a result.

Normal profits (recall the definition from Chapter 19) are earned by owners of equity capital. Generally speaking, we estimate the amount of normal profit on equity capital as the amount of interest income that the owner could receive from lending this capital at the going rate of interest on risk-free loans plus an appropriate allowance for the riskiness of the equity capital.

Human Capital

There are two main forms of investment in human capital: (1) formal education and (2) apprenticeship or on-the-job training.

There are three reasons to believe that investment in human capital is less than the efficient amount:

1. Minimum wage laws tend to discourage employers from giving on-the-job training, because the employer cannot usually afford to offer an unskilled worker both the minimum wage *and* an education.

2. Employers are reluctant to provide on-the-job training because the trainee may quit and take his or her skills elsewhere.

3. There are external benefits from human capital, as when a scientist discovers a cure for a disease.

However, there are two reasons for thinking that there may be overinvestment in human capital. First, the government subsidizes education, and second, people often acquire an education not because it makes them more socially productive but because it gives them a "credential" that potential employers insist upon.

The concept of human capital also gives some insight into the problem of discrimination. A worker may not be able to invest in human capital through on-the-job training if discrimination prevents him from getting some jobs. He thus remains unskilled and is offered a lower wage than he would otherwise get, even by firms that do not practice unfair discrimination.

Statistical measurements of the rate of return on education in the United States show that it has fallen since 1969. There are two reasons commonly cited for this—first, that the supply of educated workers has shifted to the right since 1969, and second, that declining school enrollments have decreased the demand for teachers.

It is difficult to obtain precise measurements of the rate of return on human capital because

1. There is the problem of collinearity between training and skill.

2. It is difficult to measure the external benefits of education.

3. It is difficult to estimate the government subsidy to education.

4. It is difficult to tell whether education has increased a worker's productivity or simply given her a "credential."

5. Not all education is an investment in human capital; some of it is undoubtedly a consumption good.

6. Much of the return to education is in the form of a more satisfying job—a factor that is difficult to measure.

According to recent estimates, the private rate of return on an undergraduate education is between 8 and 10 percent, and the social rate of return may be as low as 4 percent. The private rate of return on a Ph.D. seems to be only about 2 percent.

Rent

Perhaps the most important thing to understand

about rent is that it does not apply only to land. The text gives five examples of economic rent:

1. The return to agricultural land because of differences in quality
2. The return to urban land because of differences in location
3. The income from owning mineral deposits with low extraction costs and high quality
4. Above-normal profits earned in an industry because of monopoly or innovation
5. The return to an individual's labor because of a scarce talent

A person's wage includes the basic wage, the return to his or her human capital, and the rent on the person's special talents. The opportunity cost of the worker's time is the sum of the first two items (minus the cost of any on-the-job training that is being provided by an employer).

The Role of Factor Prices

Factor prices do more than determine people's incomes. They also help to determine which factors of production will be allocated to which tasks. For example, when labor becomes more scarce and capital less scarce, wages rise and the cost of capital falls. As a result, firms are encouraged to substitute capital for labor. While this may be a painful process for the workers "displaced" by automation, it is also the source of most of our material progress since the industrial revolution.

IMPORTANT TERMS

Debt capital Funds that are lent to businesses (or others) to finance the purchase of machinery or the construction of new buildings.

Equity capital Funds that are used (without having to be borrowed) by the owners of businesses to purchase machinery or new buildings.

Human capital Skills, training, and education that are used for producing goods and services.

Affirmative action program A program designed to eliminate discrimination by favoring those who have been its victims in the past.

Economic rent The "surplus" return on any factor of production in excess of its opportunity cost.

Monopoly rent The excess profit accruing to any individual or business because of the possession of monopoly power.

True-False Questions

T F 1. In the United States, labor income is usually about three times as large as the rest of national income.

T F 2. Debt capital and equity capital are two forms of human capital.

T F 3. If the demand for loanable funds is highly elastic with respect to the rate of interest, then the MEI schedule is highly elastic.

T F 4. The efficiency loss of an interest-rate ceiling tends to be overestimated by the usual triangular measurement.

T F 5. Above-normal profit is an example of interest income.

T F 6. Government subsidization of higher education is one reason why more than the efficient amount of investment in human capital may occur.

T F 7. The fact that many of the benefits of investment in human capital are external is one reason why less than the efficient amount of investment in human capital may occur.

T F 8. Minimum wage laws tend to cause more of the investment in human capital to involve formal education rather than on-the-job training.

T F 9. According to most estimates, the social rate of return on investment in an undergraduate education is greater than the private return.

T F 10. The fact that workers may quit is one reason why less than the efficient amount of investment in human capital may occur.

T F 11. If a perfectly competitive market for apartment units is in a long-run equilibrium with free entry, then the income received by landlords would probably not be regarded as economic rent, except possibly for the income accruing to ownership of the land upon which the apartment buildings stand.

Multiple-Choice Questions

1. Investment in which of the following forms of capital yields an interest income?
- **(a)** Debt capital
- **(b)** Equity capital
- **(c)** Human capital
- **(d)** All of the above

2. A rightward shift of the MEI schedule would probably
- **(a)** Increase the rate of interest in a perfectly competitive market
- **(b)** Decrease the rate of interest in a perfectly competitive market
- **(c)** Reduce the efficiency loss imposed by a given interest-rate ceiling
- **(d)** **(a)** and **(c)**
- **(e)** **(b)** and **(c)**

3. Which of the following is the most likely result of an interest rate ceiling in a perfectly competitive market for loanable funds with no externalities?
- **(a)** A transfer of income from borrowers to some lenders
- **(b)** A transfer of income from rich to poor
- **(c)** A transfer of income from lenders to some borrowers
- **(d)** A reduction in the incidence of credit rationing

4. The normal profit received by a firm on its equity capital
- **(a)** Is usually greater than the interest income that the owners could receive from lending this capital at the risk-free rate of interest
- **(b)** Is usually less than the interest income that the owners could receive from lending this capital at the risk-free rate of interest
- **(c)** Is more than the interest income that the owners could receive from lending this capital if the firm is making above normal profits
- **(d)** Bears no relationship to the interest income that the owners could get from lending this capital

5. Which of the following is *not* a factor tending to result in less than the efficient amount of investment in human capital?
- **(a)** Minimum wage laws
- **(b)** The use of "credentials" as a screening device by employers
- **(c)** The fact that workers may quit voluntarily
- **(d)** The external benefits of investment in human capital

6. The rate of return on investment in human capital
- **(a)** Has been falling since 1969 partly because of the increase in supply of educated workers
- **(b)** Has been increased by the demographic factors that have slowed the growth in school enrollments in recent years
- **(c)** Is less for someone acquiring a Ph.D. than for someone acquiring an undergraduate degree
- **(d)** **(a)** and **(c)**
- **(e)** **(b)** and **(c)**

7. Which of the following is *not* a major problem encountered in trying to measure the rate of return on investment in human capital?
- **(a)** Going to school may be a consumption good.
- **(b)** The social rate of return on investment may be as low as 4 percent.
- **(c)** There are external benefits to investment in human capital.
- **(d)** It is difficult to distinguish the separate effects of skills and training.

8. Other things being equal, an individual will receive a higher wage if she
- **(a)** Has invested in human capital in the past
- **(b)** Possesses a rare talent
- **(c)** Is currently receiving on-the-job training
- **(d)** **(a)** and **(b)**
- **(e)** All of the above

9. Which of the following is *least* likely to be an economic rent?
- **(a)** The income from leasing cars
- **(b)** The return on high-quality land
- **(c)** The return on ownership of high-quality mineral deposits
- **(d)** The above-normal profits of a monopolist

Exercises

1a. Figure 29-1 depicts a perfectly competitive market for loanable funds with no externalities.

The equilibrium rate of interest in this market equals ______ and the equilibrium quantity of loans equals ______. In a competitive equilibrium, the interest income received by lenders would equal ________.

b. If the government imposes an interest-rate ceiling equal to OM, then the quantity of loans will equal ______, the MEI will equal ______, the excess demand for loans will equal ______, the interest income received by lenders will equal ________, and the size of the efficiency loss will probably be (more, less) than the area ______.

c. If the size of the interest ceiling is OJ, the size of the efficiency loss will be ______.

2a. Figure 29-2 depicts a perfectly competitive market for a factor of production, where D

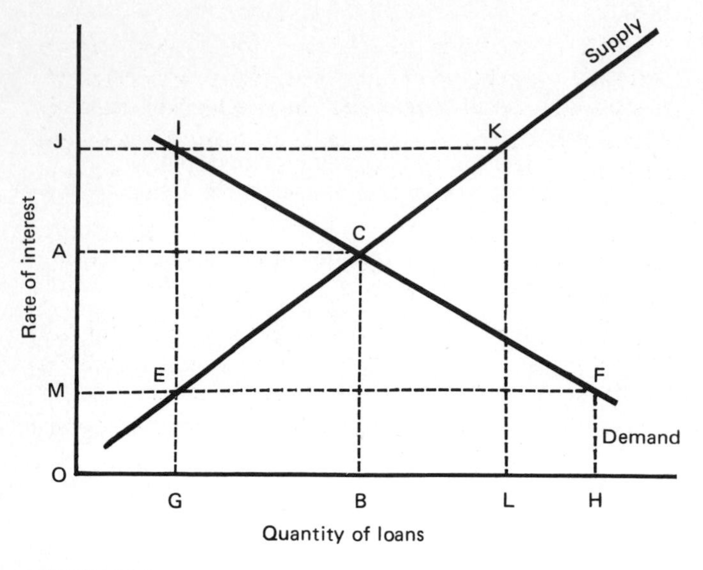

FIGURE 29-1

denotes the demand curve and S_1 denotes the supply curve. In a competitive equilibrium the factor price would equal ______ and the quantity of employment of the factor would equal ______. The income received by the factor would equal ______ and the income received by all other factors would equal ____.

b. Now suppose that a tax, equal in amount to EL per unit of employed factor, is imposed upon income received by this factor. This would shift the supply curve up vertically by the amount EL, so that the after-tax supply curve equals the one labeled S'_1. With the tax, the equilibrium price paid by the firms for the factor will equal ______; the equilibrium price received, after tax, by the owners of the factor will equal ______; the quantity of the factor employed will equal ______; the after-tax income accruing to owners of the factor will equal ______; the amount of the tax collected will equal ______; the income received by other factors will equal ______; and the size of the efficiency loss will equal ______.

FIGURE 29-2

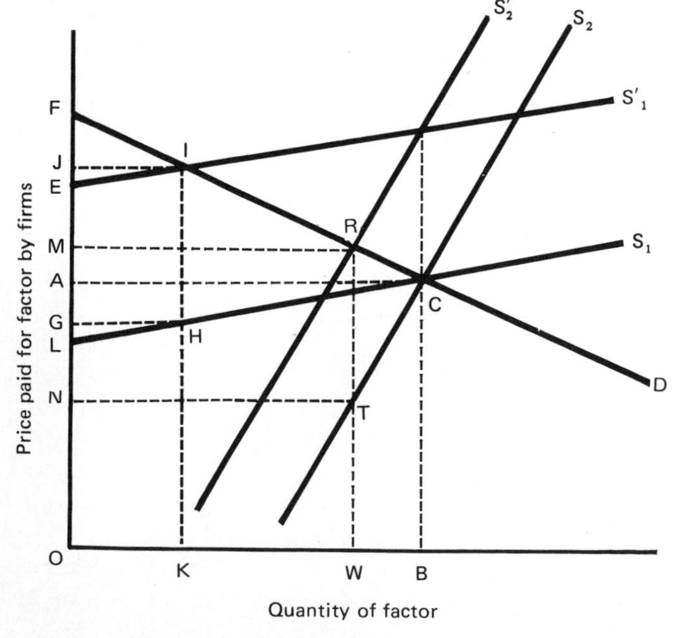

c. The supply curve labeled S_2 is (more, less) elastic than the one labeled S_1 at C. With supply curve S_2 and no tax, the equilibrium factor price will be (more, less, no different) than with S_1, and the equilibrium quantity of employment of the factor will be (more, less, no different) than with S_1.

d. With S_2, the tax will shift the supply curve vertically to the one labeled S'_2. With the tax, the equilibrium price paid by the firms for the factor will equal ______, the equilibrium price received after tax by owners of the factor will equal ______, the quantity of employment of the factor will equal ______, the after-tax income accruing to owners of the factor will equal ______, the amount of the tax collected will equal ______, the income received by other factors will equal ______, and the size of the efficiency loss will equal ______.

e. Of the two pretax supply curves S_1 and S_2, the one which generates the greater tax revenue is (S_1, S_2), the one that produces the smaller efficiency loss from the tax is (S_1, S_2), the one for which the tax generates the smaller reduction in employment is (S_1, S_2), the one for which the tax causes the larger reduction in the factor's after-tax price is (S_1, S_2), and the one for which the tax reduces other incomes by less is (S_1, S_2).

Essay Questions

1. The codiscoverers of insulin, Banting and Best, did not become millionaires as a result of their discovery, despite the fact that it has probably saved millions of human lives. What does this suggest about the private and social rates of return to human capital?

2. Show how the income of a surgeon is part wage, part interest, and part rent. Which of these components would be reduced if licensing requirements were relaxed so as to permit more people to practice as surgeons? Which would be increased by the surgeon's efforts to develop more advanced surgical techniques? By his decision to work longer hours?

3. Most on-the-job training is job-specific. That is, it is training that is useful only for a particular job, such as selling insurance or operating a crane. Some on-the-job training is also firm-specific. That is, it involves "learning the ropes" of a particular firm's operations. Does the fact that workers may quit tend to discourage job-specific on-the-job training more or less than it does firm-specific on-the-job training? Does the existence of a minimum wage tend to discourage either kind of on-the-job training more than the other?

4. Recall from Chapter 11 that as interest rates rise, the prices of assets fall. Bearing this in mind, show how a change in the rate of interest affects potential lenders differently from those who have already lent money, especially those who have bought marketable bonds. Show also how it affects potential borrowers differently from those who have already borrowed money.

5. When inflation increases, interest rates also tend to rise. Can you explain this in terms of the supply of and demand for loanable funds?

***6.** In the text, several reasons why it is difficult to measure the rate of return on investment in human capital were discussed. How many of these reasons also apply to measuring the rate of return on investment in physical capital?

Answers

True-False Questions: **1** T **2** F **3** T **4** F **5** F **6** T **7** T **8** T **9** F **10** T **11** T
Multiple-Choice Questions: **1** d **2** a **3** c **4** a **5** b **6** d **7** b **8** d **9** a
Exercises: **1a.** *OA, OB, OACB*; **b.** *OG, OJ* (or *GI*), *EF* (or *GH*), *OMEG*, more, *ICE*; **c.** 0.
2a. *OA, OB, OACB, FCA*; **b.** *OJ, OG, OK, OGHK, JIHG* (or *EIHL*), *FIJ, ICH*; **c.** less, no different, no different; **d.** *OM, ON, OW, ONTW, NMRT, MFR, RCT*; **e.** S_2, S_2, S_2, S_2, S_2.

chapter 30
Natural Resources, Conservation, and Growth

Learning Objectives

After you have studied this chapter in the textbook and the study guide, you should be able to

Explain how the demand curve for a natural resource is derived

State the two components of marginal cost that underlie the supply curve of a privately owned natural resource

Explain why only one of these components underlies the supply curve of a common-property natural resource

Explain why the outcome of a perfectly competitive market in a natural resource may be socially efficient if the resource is privately owned but not if it is a common-property resource

(Optional) Show what happens if more than the maximum sustainable yield is harvested from a population

(Optional) Show how, when the population grows beyond the point of maximum sustainable yield, more can be extracted both now and later.

Explain why simple projections of the use and availability of resources yield misleading predictions

List three special reasons why population growth continues to be rapid in less developed countries despite the scarcity of resources

State three arguments in favor of economic growth and two arguments against

Illustrate in a diagram the rationale given by OPEC countries for their 1973 to 1974 oil price increase

Illustrate in a diagram the criticism of this rationale

CHAPTER HIGHLIGHTS

This chapter shows how to apply economic analysis to some important issues concerning our use of the world's resources. These issues are (1) the efficient use of resources and how that may be accomplished by a competitive market, (2) the problems of a common-property resource, (3) the conservation of nonrenewable resources, (4) the pros and cons of economic growth, and (5) the efficiency and transfer effects of the OPEC increase in oil prices.

Efficiency

Consider the supply and demand for a natural resource that is privately owned. The demand curve for this resource will be the marginal productivity schedule of that resource, as with any other productive input. The supply curve is just the marginal cost of providing the resource. This marginal cost has two components: (1) the direct cost of harvesting or extracting the resource and (2) the cost incurred because of the fact that, if the resource is used up now, it will not be available in the future. The sum of these two components of marginal cost is also called the *reservation price* of the resource. In a perfectly competitive equilibrium, the marginal cost of providing the resource would just equal the marginal productivity of using the resource; this would be socially efficient. (This is explained in Figure 30-1 in the text.)

Common Property Resources

For the free competitive market to be socially efficient, it is important that the resource be privately owned. In the case of a common-property resource, such as fish, there is reason to suppose that overharvesting will occur in a competitive equilibrium. This is because the suppliers will take into account the direct harvesting cost but not the second component of marginal cost explained under "Efficiency," above. Figure 30-2 in the text shows how much harvesting will occur in this case and illustrates how a familiar triangle can be used to measure the efficiency loss. The tendency for a common-property resource to be overharvested is a reason given by some countries for wanting to extend their territorial rights to the waters within 200 miles of their land.

An optional section of this chapter deals with the concept of maximum sustainable yield. The population growth of a species can be described in terms of a sustainable yield curve, as in Figure 30-3 in the text, with the size of the population on the horizontal axis and the rate of increase in the population on the vertical axis. Generally speaking, there will be some size of population at which the annual increase is maximized. This maximal increase is called the *maximum sustainable yield*. It is the highest amount that could be harvested every year without reducing the size of the population. There are two important implications of this idea: (1) If more than the maximum sustainable yield is harvested, then the species will eventually become extinct because we will be extracting more from the population than is being replaced by natural reproduction. (2) If very little harvesting occurs, then the population will probably grow beyond the point of maximum sustainable yield. If this happens, it would be inefficient to extract only the sustainable yield. For if more were extracted now, the population would fall toward the point of maximum sustainable yield, which would also permit more to be extracted in the future; in other words, we could extract more now and more later.

Nonrenewable Resources

The big issue concerning nonrenewable resources is whether they will run out—and if so, what we can do then. Simple projections of present trends point to an eventual doomsday, when rising population overtakes our limited resources. But these simple projections cannot be trusted because they do not allow for the kind of adjustment that the economic system will produce. As a resource becomes more scarce, it will also become more expensive. This will create four kinds of adjustment: (1) substitution of other factors of production, (2) substitution of consumer goods that use less of that resource, (3) induced innovation that allows economizing on that resource, and (4) a reduction in the rate of growth of population because of the high cost of raising children. Critics of this economic argument point to the experience of less developed countries, where population growth has continued despite high poverty levels. However, the experience of the less developed countries can be explained by three special factors: (1) with so much poverty, people wan many children in order to support them in their old age, (2) recent dramatic advances in medicine have produced a sharp decrease in death rates in these countries, and (3) there are religious and social objections to birth control in many of these countries.

Economic Growth

The arguments in favor of economic growth are that it helps to relieve unemployment, to solve the problem of poverty, and to raise not only our incomes but also those of our children. The arguments against growth are that it depletes our natural resources and contributes to pollution. The main difficulty with the antigrowth argument is that the restriction of growth is too general a policy with which to attack these specific problems of resource depletion and pollution.

OPEC and Oil

In 1973 and 1974, the OPEC countries increased the price of oil from below $3 a barrel to above $10 a barrel. These countries argued that their new price was the appropriate reservation price and that a lower price would result in overextraction of this nonrenewable resource, despite the fact that the direct extraction costs were only about 25 cents a barrel. The critics of OPEC (mainly the oil-consuming nations) argued that the appropriate reservation price was closer to the old price than the new one, and that the main purpose of the price rise was to transfer income from the oil-consuming nations to the oil-producing nations. In fact, the increase in oil prices did succeed in transferring as much as 2 or 3 percent of oil-consuming nations' incomes to the OPEC countries. Both of these arguments are illustrated by Figure 30-6 in the text.

IMPORTANT TERMS

Reservation price The marginal cost of providing a resource. It includes (1) the cost of extraction and (2) the cost of not having the resource in the future.

Common property resource A resource that is not privately owned.

Sustainable yield curve (optional) The curve relating the population of a species to the natural annual increase in the species. This natural annual increase is the sustainable yield. It is the amount that can be extracted by humans with no change in the species' population.

Maximum sustainable yield (optional) The largest value of sustainable yield in the yield curve. This is the most that can be extracted each year without making the species extinct.

Induced innovations Innovations that result when people turn their minds to finding substitutes for increasingly expensive resources.

Renewable resource One that reproduces itself naturally or that can be reproduced by humans. One that cannot be reproduced is called a nonrenewable resource.

True-False Questions

T F **1.** The height of the supply curve of a privately owned natural resource is its reservation price.

T F **2.** The cost of extracting a resource is more than its reservation price.

T F **3.** The height of the supply curve of a common-property resource equals the marginal cost of extracting that resource.

T F **4.** A competitive equilibrium in the market for a privately owned natural resource is generally inefficient.

T F **5.** A competitive equilibrium in the market for a common-property natural resource is generally inefficient.

T F **6.** Extension of countries' territorial rights to a 200-mile limit would probably increase the size of the inefficiency resulting from the common-property nature of fishing.

T F **7.** Handing over a common-property resource to a monopolist would probably increase the amount of overharvesting of the resource.

T F **8.** Economists who criticize the simple projections of the "doomsday" approach point to the experience of the less developed countries as an example of how population growth rates are reduced automatically by the scarcity of resources.

T F **9.** The increase in oil prices in 1973–1974 can be attributed mainly to increases in the cost of extracting oil.

T F **10.** This rise in oil prices would have transferred less income to the OPEC countries if the demand for oil had been more elastic.

T F ***11.** If the population of a species falls below the point of maximum sustainable yield, it will become extinct unless human extraction is eliminated at least temporarily.

T F ***12.** If the population of a species is above the point of maximum sustainable yield and if people are presently extracting the sustainable yield associated with that size of population, then an increase in the size of the harvest now may allow people also to increase the size of the harvest in the future.

T F ***13.** If a species is completely unharvested, it will grow only up to the size of maximum sustainable yield.

*These questions are only for those who have studied the optional section on marginal sustainable yield.

Multiple-Choice Questions

1. Consider a natural resource with a given demand and a given cost of extraction. Which of the following will be higher if the resource is privately owned (and the market is perfectly competitive) than if it is a common property resource?
   - **(a)** The price of the resource
   - **(b)** The rate of extraction of the resource
   - **(c)** The size of the efficiency loss associated with extracting the resource
   - **(d)** **(a)** and **(b)**
   - **(e)** **(a)** and **(c)**

2. Which of the following is *not* a common property resource?
   - **(a)** Fish
   - **(b)** Lake water
   - **(c)** Mineral deposits in a privately owned mine
   - **(d)** Timber on unowned property

3. Which of the following is *not* an example of an adjustment that helps us to deal with the increasing scarcity of oil?
   - **(a)** The production of cars that use fuel more economically
   - **(b)** The increased rate of extraction of coal deposits
   - **(c)** The reduction in the price of oil for heating homes
   - **(d)** The move to lower room temperatures in homes

4. Which of the following is *not* an argument commonly used in favor of economic growth?
   - **(a)** Unemployment is likely to be less severe in a rapidly growing economy.
   - **(b)** Faster economic growth helps to economize on scarce natural resources.
   - **(c)** Growth makes it easier to solve the poverty problem.
   - **(d)** Growth increases not only our future incomes but also those of our children.

5. The main problem with the antigrowth argument is that
   - **(a)** We need to grow rapidly in order to keep ahead of our country's enemies.
   - **(b)** We need rapid economic growth in order to avoid inflation.
   - **(c)** Slowing growth is not a specific enough policy to cure any single specific problem.
   - **(d)** Growth helps to avoid the pollution problem.

6. The justification offered by the OPEC countries for their 1973–1974 oil price increase was that
   - **(a)** The marginal cost of extracting oil had increased.
   - **(b)** The demand for oil had shifted to the right.
   - **(c)** The supply of oil had shifted to the left.
   - **(d)** The old price was below the reservation price.

*7. The size of population of a species at which the maximum sustainable yield occurs is
   - **(a)** The largest possible population of the species
   - **(b)** The largest permanently sustainable size of population of the species
   - **(c)** The only population size at which people may begin extracting the maximum sustainable yield every year without eventually extinguishing the species
   - **(d)** The minimum population size at which people may begin extracting the maximum sustainable yield every year without extinguishing the species

Exercises

1a. Figure 30-1 depicts a perfectly competitive market for a natural resource. The demand curve is D, the marginal cost of extraction is given by the curve labeled S, and the full reservation price is given by the curve labeled S'.

The socially efficient quantity (assuming no external benefits) equals ______, and this quantity will be demanded if the price equals ______. If the resource is privately owned, the price will equal ______, the quantity extracted will equal ______, and the size of the efficiency loss will equal ______. This efficiency loss would be eliminated by a tax on extraction equal to ______ per unit.

b. If the resource is not privately owned, the price will equal ______, the quantity extracted will equal ______, and the size of the efficiency loss will equal ______. This efficiency loss would be eliminated by a tax on extraction equal to ______ per unit.

FIGURE 30-1

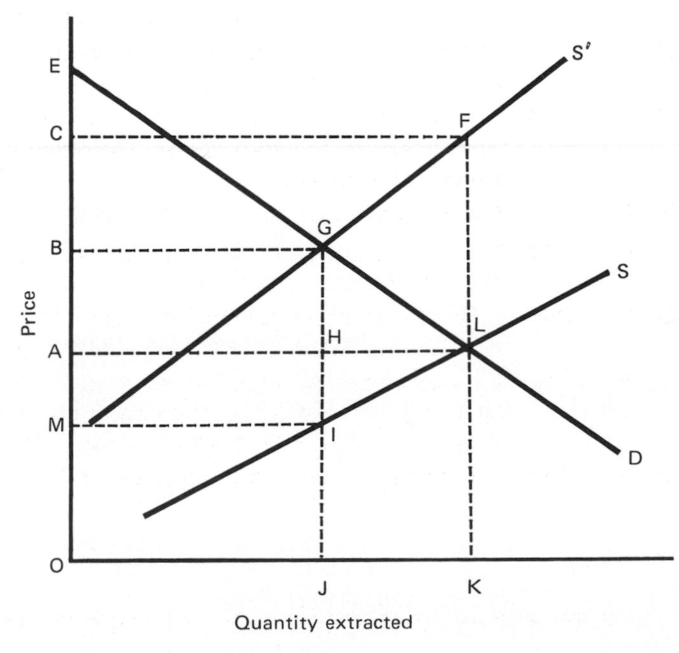

2a. In Figure 30-2, D represents the demand curve for a natural resource, S represents the marginal cost of extracting the resource, S' represents the reservation price of providing the resource, and MR represents the marginal revenue curve that would be faced by a monopolist in the market (recall this concept from Chapter 21). The efficient quantity of extraction (assuming no external benefits) equals ______, at which quantity the marginal productivity of the resource would equal ____. If the resource were a common property and the market were perfectly competitive, the price would equal ______, the quantity extracted would equal ______, the size of the efficiency loss would equal ______, and the amount paid for the resource by demanders would equal ______.

b. If the resource were now given to a monopolist who exploited her monopoly power to the fullest, she would extract a quantity equal to ______ and set a price equal to ______. The reservation price would equal ______. The size of the efficiency loss would equal ______ and the amount paid for the resource by demanders would equal ______.

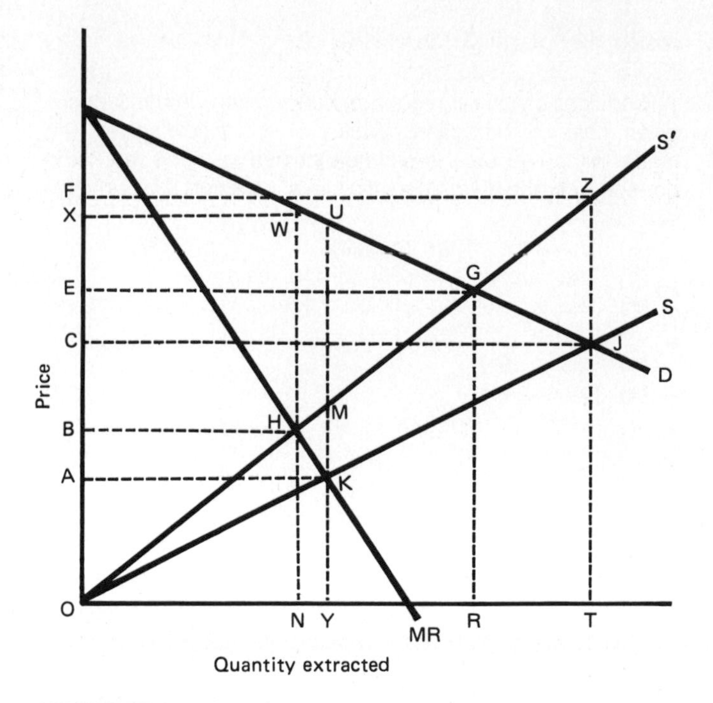

FIGURE 30-2

Essay Questions

1. Explain how the problem of a common-property resource is similar to the problem of environmental pollution.

2. Argue the case that the OPEC oil price increase reduced economic efficiency. Argue the case that it didn't.

3. In what sense have the miracles of modern medicine aggravated the problems of nonrenewable natural resources, especially in less developed countries?

4. Recall from Chapter 17 the difference between short- and long-run elasticities of demand. If the OPEC countries keep the price of oil constant (relative to the general price level), show what will happen over time to the size of the transfer from oil-consuming nations to oil-producing nations because of the changing elasticity of demand for oil and the changing elasticity of supply of substitutes for oil.

5. Current projections show that at present rates of use, the known reserves of oil in the world will be exhausted in a few years. Projections in the 1920s showed the same: that the known reserves would be used up by the 1940s. Why have there always been about the same "number of years" of oil supply in known reserves? Can this be true forever? (Remember that present rates of use will not be constant over time.)

***6.** By studying Figure 30-3 in the text, you can see that if the population of a species is initially above the point of maximum sustainable yield and if people are now harvesting at a rate just large enough to maintain a constant size of population, then by increasing the rate of extraction they can harvest more now *and* more in the future. Suppose the cost of extraction is zero. What is the opportunity cost of raising the rate of extraction in this situation? Is this a case of being able to get something for nothing?

Answers

True-False Questions: 1 T 2 F 3 T 4 F 5 T 6 F 7 F 8 F 9 F 10 T 11 F 12 T 13 F
Multiple-Choice Questions: 1 a 2 c 3 c 4 b 5 c 6 d 7 d
Exercises: **1a.** *OJ*, *OB*, *OB*, *OJ*, zero, zero; **b.** *OA*, *OK*, *FLG*, *GI*.
2a. *OR*, *OE*, *OC*, *OT*, *ZJG*, *OCJT*; **b.** *ON*, *OX*, *OB*, *WGH*, *OXWN*.

chapter 31
Income Inequality

Learning Objectives

After you have studied this chapter in the textbook and the study guide, you should be able to

List seven reasons why some people have more income than others

Explain how the Lorenz curve is constructed and in what sense it measures inequality

State why the Lorenz curve possibly overstates the degree of inequality

Identify four kinds of government policy that reduce income inequality and which of these accomplishes the most

State two reasons why the outcome of a free-market situation has no special claim to being fair

State four reasons why perfect equality of income distribution is not necessarily fair

Explain two principles for compromising between the extremes of a free market and perfect equality

Show why there exists a conflict between equity and efficiency

CHAPTER HIGHLIGHTS

There are four main issues dealt with in this chapter: (1) why income inequality exists; (2) how much of it exists in the United States; (3) how much of this inequality has been eliminated by government expenditures, transfers, and taxes; and (4) what constitutes a fair method of distributing income.

Why Inequality?

There are at least seven reasons why one person may be richer than another:

1. She may have invested more than the other in human capital.

2. She may be earning a rent on some innate ability.

3. She may possess greater financial wealth either because she saved it in the past or because she inherited it.

4. She may possess more market power because of her membership in a union or possession of some monopoly power.

5. She may have decided to work harder or longer hours.

6. The other may suffer more from discrimination in the labor market than she does.

7. She may simply be lucky in that her particular skills are more in demand than the other's.

All these reasons have been explained in the previous three chapters. Professor Jacob Mincer recently estimated that 60 percent of the differences in family incomes can be attributed to the first factor on this list—differences in human capital.

How Much Inequality?

In the United States, the poorest 20 percent of families receive less than one-third of 1 percent of all the income before taxes and transfers, whereas the richest 20 percent of families receive half of it. Facts like these are summarized in the Lorenz curve, an important diagrammatic construction that is shown in Figure 31-1 in the text. This curve shows what percent of total income is received by the poorest 10 percent of families, the poorest 20 percent, and so on. The degree of inequality can be measured by the area between the Lorenz-curve and the 45-degree line. The 45-degree line is called the *complete equality line*. If the Lorenz curve were to coincide with the complete equality line, then every family would receive exactly the same income. Thus the further away the actual Lorenz curve lies from the complete equality line, the further is the actual situation from the situation of complete equality. It is important to realize, however, that the Lorenz curve probably overstates the degree of inequality, because it measures current incomes rather than lifetime incomes. Families whose heads are retired, very young, or perhaps temporarily unemployed will have lower current incomes than those whose heads are in their peak earning years and fully employed, even if the families all have the same lifetime incomes.

The Effects of Taxes and Expenditures on Inequality

The Lorenz curve for family incomes *after* taxes and transfers (Figure 31-2 in the text) shows about one-third less inequality than before taxes and transfers. (That is, the area between the complete inequality line and the Lorenz curve is reduced by a third.) This reduction has been accomplished by (1) taxes, (2) transfers in kind, (3) cash transfers, and (4) social insurance. By far the largest reduction is accomplished by social insurance. Very little is accomplished by taxes because, as we saw in Chapter 5, our tax system is not very progressive. The degree of inequality after taxes and transfers has been falling steadily since the 1960s.

Fairness in Distributing Income

The problem of defining what is a "fair" way of distributing income is one that can never be answered with complete certainty, because it refers not to "what is" but to "what ought to be." Nevertheless, reasonable people can agree on two points: (1) The outcome of the free market situation has no special claim to being fair, because, first, there is no way of justifying huge profits to monopolists and, second, even with perfect competition and no externalities, we can say only that the market is efficient, not that it "divides the pie" fairly. (2) Complete equality would not be fair because some people work harder and longer than others, some have more dangerous or odious jobs than others, some have invested more in human capital than others, and some have saved more than others to build up their financial wealth.

The text suggests two principles for compromising between the extremes a free market and perfect equality: (1) The race should be fair. In other words, we should give equality of opportunity, not necessarily equality of rewards. For example, we should ensure that no one is denied the opportunity of a formal education because of unfair discrimination, but this doesn't mean that everyone should be awarded a college degree—that should depend on what they are able to make of their opportunity. (2) We should modify the rewards of the game, so that even those at the bottom of the heap are still tolerably well off.

All these problems of pinning down an acceptable notion of equity would exist even if there were no conflict between equity and efficiency. But in fact this conflict does exist, and it is very important. To take the extreme case, if everyone were guaranteed an equal income through a system of taxes and transfers, who would want to fight fires or work the long hours of the corporation executive?

The ideas of Prof. John Rawls are discussed in Box 31-2. Rawls argues that the way to arrive at an objective definition of equity is (1) to put everyone in an "original position" in which no one knows what his or her particular income will be and then (2) to ask what kind of income distribution a reasonable person would choose from behind this "veil of ignorance," knowing that after each individual had chosen a distribution of income, that person would then be assigned by chance to one of the rungs on his or her own ladder. Rawls argues that everyone would then agree to the "difference principle" that there should be complete equality in the distribution of income unless there happens to be an unequal distribution that leaves everyone better off. But he gets this conclusion by supposing that everyone would choose according to a "maximin" principle. In other words, everyone would figure that luck might well place him or her on the lowest rung of the ladder, so he or she would choose whichever distribution of income gave the most to the poorest person.

IMPORTANT TERMS

Lorenz curve The curve that shows what percentage, measured on the vertical axis, of total national income is received by the poorest 10 percent of families in a country, by the poorest 20 percent of families in a country, and so forth, where these percentages of families are measured on the horizontal axis.

Complete equality line The straight line in the Lorenz curve diagram with a slope of 45 degrees. The Lorenz curve would coincide with the complete equality line only if all families received exactly the same income.

Social insurance Any government-run scheme (like unemployment insurance or social security) where large groups of people are forced to contribute insurance premiums but receive the benefits in the event that they become unemployed or retire.

Transfers in kind Any transfer payments made by the government not of cash but of claims to particular commodities, as in the case of food stamps.

****Original position*** A situation in which no one knows what his or her income will be—only what the overall distribution of income will be. According to Rawls, one must put oneself in this original position in order to arrive at an acceptable definition of equity.

****Difference principle*** The principle that income should be equally distributed unless there is some other distribution that makes everyone better off.

****Maximin principle*** The principle of choosing the income distribution that maximizes the minimum income. According to Rawls' argument, this principle implies the difference principle.

True-False Questions

T F **1.** The poorest 20 percent of families in the United States earn less than 1 percent of national income before taxes and transfers.

T F **2.** According to recent studies, the most important factor in explaining income differences is market power.

T F **3.** The Lorenz curve for current income is probably less bowed out than that for lifetime income.

T F **4.** Government expenditures, transfers, and taxes have reduced income inequality in the United States by about a third.

T F **5.** Income inequality in the United States has been steadily increasing since the early 1960s.

T F **6.** One of the reasons that the free-market solution to distributing income is not necessarily fair is the possibility that monopolies may exist.

T F **7.** One problem with the ideal of perfect equality of income distribution is that it conflicts with the objective of efficiency.

T F **8.** The free-market system under ideal conditions will maximize the total income pie and will also achieve a fair distribution of that pie.

T F ***9.** In Rawls' original position, you can tell the shape of the Lorenz curve but not your own position on the curve.

T F ***10.** According to Rawls' difference principle, there should always be exact equality in the distribution of income.

Multiple-Choice Questions

1. According to the study by Jacob Mincer, which of the following is the most important factor in explaining income differentials?
- **(a)** Rents earned on innate ability
- **(b)** Financial wealth
- **(c)** Luck
- **(d)** Human capital
- **(e)** Discrimination

2. In the United States, the richest 20 percent of families

*These terms are important only for those who have studied Box 31-3.

get about what percentage of the total national income before taxes and transfers?

(a) 20 percent (c) 50 percent
(b) 35 percent (d) 65 percent

3. If the Lorenz curve were a straight line,

(a) There would be more inequality of income than there is in the United States at present.
(b) There would be complete equality of income.
(c) There would be an equitable distribution of income.
(d) None of the above.

4. The Lorenz curve as usually drawn probably overstates the degree of inequality in income distribution because

(a) It measures inequality in current income rather than in lifetime income.
(b) It measures income rather than financial wealth.
(c) It refers to the incomes of individuals rather than the incomes of families.
(d) It shows that the poorest 20 percent of families get only 20 percent of national income.

5. Which of the following accounts for the largest reduction in income inequality in the United States?

(a) Taxes **(c)** Cash transfers
(b) Transfers in kind **(d)** Social insurance

6. Which of the following is a reason why the free-market solution may not be fair?

(a) Some people work harder than others.
(b) Some people have more market power than others.
(c) Some people's jobs are more hazardous than those of others.
(d) Some people have invested more than others in human capital.

7. Recall from Chapter 2 the distinction between positive and normative economics. Which of the following statements is true?

(a) Equity and equality are both positive concepts.
(b) Equity and equality are both normative concepts.
(c) Equity is a positive concept and equality is a normative concept.
(d) Equity is a normative concept and equality is a positive concept.

***8.** According to Rawls' maximin criterion, which of the following income distributions is best?

(a) Everyone gets $3,000 per year.
(b) Everyone but one person gets $5,000 per year and the other person gets $3,100 per year.
(c) Half the people get $10,000 per year and the other half get $1,000 per year.
(d) Everyone but one person gets $20,000 per year and the other person gets $2,900 per year.

Exercises

1. Table 31-1 gives the income distribution of a hypothetical economy, as in panel *a* of Table 31-1 in the text. Fill in the cumulative income distribution in Table 31-2, as in panel *b* of Table 31-1 in the text.

Plot the Lorenz curve in Figure 31-1 and label it L_1. Suppose that the government then taxed away half the income of every family in the top 20 percent of the income distribution and gave it in equal amounts to every family in the lowest 60 percent of the distribution. Fill in the resulting income distribution in Table 31-3 and the resulting *cumulative* income distribution in Table 31-4.

Table 31-1

	Lowest 20%	Second 20%	Third 20%	Fourth 20%	Highest 20%
Percent of income	4	6	10	20	60

Table 31-2

	Lowest 20%	Lowest 40%	Lowest 60%	Lowest 80%	Total
Percent of income					

Table 31-3

	Lowest 20%	Second 20%	Third 20%	Fourth 20%	Highest 20%
Percent of income					

Table 31-4

	Lowest 20%	Lowest 40%	Lowest 60%	Lowest 80%	Total
Percent of income					

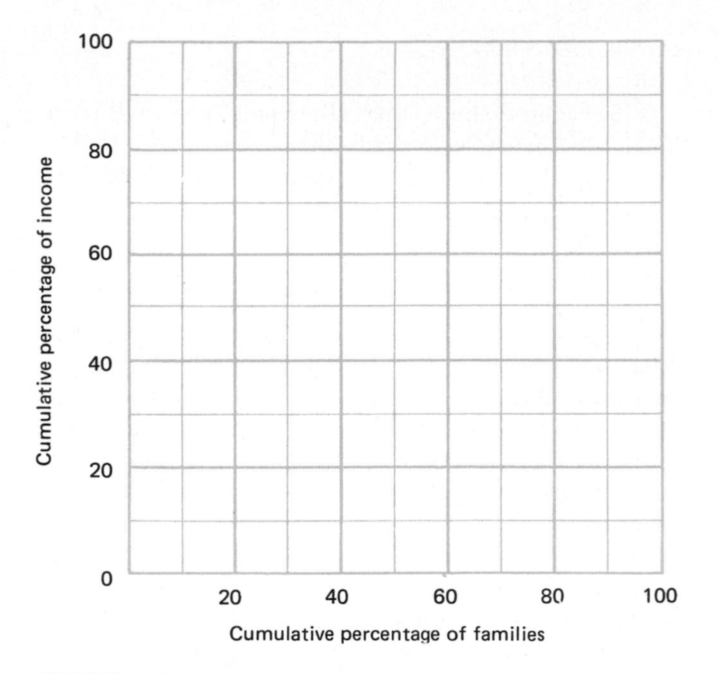

FIGURE 31-1

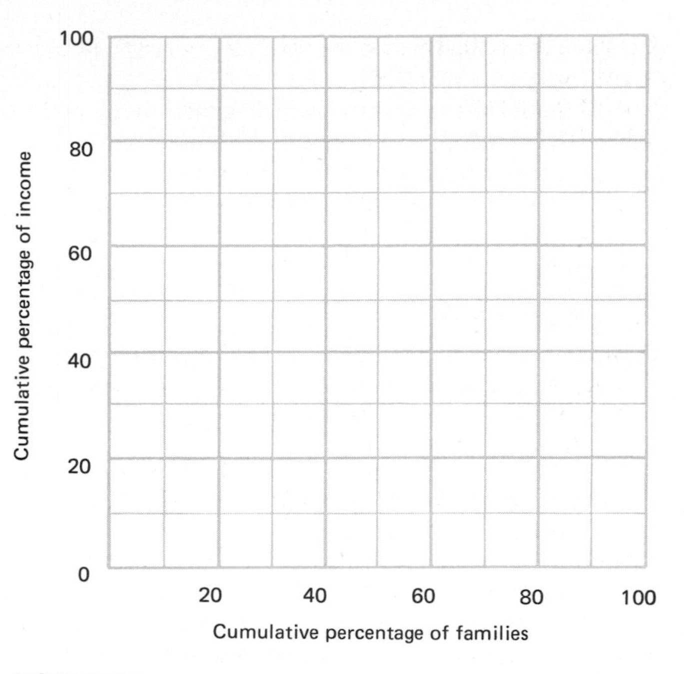

FIGURE 31-2

Plot the Lorenz curve for income after taxes and transfers in Figure 31-1 and label it L_2.

2. Suppose that income can be distributed among the five families in an economy according to each of the following distributions:

a. Four families receive $1,100 per year each and the fifth receives $600 per year.

b. Four families receive $500 per year each and the fifth receives $3,000 per year.

c. Each family receives $500 per year.

d. Four families receive $1,100 per year each and the fifth receives $5,600.

e. Four families receive $5,000 per year each and the fifth receives nothing.

Fill in Table 31-5, giving the total national income according to each distribution:

Table 31-5

Distribution	Total national income
a	_____
b	_____
c	_____
d	_____
e	_____

Fill in Table 31-6 for each of the distributions, showing the cumulative percentages as in panel *b* of Table 31-1 in the text.

Table 31-6

	Lowest 20%	Lowest 40%	Lowest 60%	Lowest 80%	Total
Percent of income—*a*	_____	_____	_____	_____	_____
Percent of income—*b*	_____	_____	_____	_____	_____
Percent of income—*c*	_____	_____	_____	_____	_____
Percent of income—*d*	_____	_____	_____	_____	_____
Percent of income—*e*	_____	_____	_____	_____	_____

Draw and label the Lorenz curve for each distribution in Figure 31-2. *Indicate in Table 31-7 the way that these distributions would be ranked according to Rawls' maximin criterion. According to this ranking, does the best distribution have the largest total income? _____. Does it have the lease inequality as measured by the Lorenz curve? _____.

Table 31-7

Rank	Distribution
First	_____
Second	_____
Third	_____
Fourth	_____
Fifth	_____

*The remaining questions in this paragraph are only for those who have studied Box 31-3.

Essay Questions

1. Some of the ways in which government policy affects the distribution of income are not so obvious as taxes and transfers. How do you suppose that the shape of the Lorenz curve is affected by *(a)* government's support of higher education, *(b)* the farm subsidy programs, and *(c)* the government's support of restrictions to entry into the medical profession?

2. Recall from Chapter 1 the distinction between poverty and inequality. What can you learn about poverty just from studying the Lorenz curve? Explain.

3. Some people feel that no matter how rich we become as a society, "the poor will always be with us." Do you think this statement best refers to inequality or poverty? Do you agree or disagree with the statement? Why?

4. The government is able to affect the distribution of income through its taxes and transfers, and we all have an equal vote in choosing the government. In that sense, we all have equal opportunity to determine the distribution of income. Why do some people argue that we need more equality of opportunity?

5. Some believe that all people are "self-made men," but most have made themselves poor. If they had wanted to make themselves rich, they could have done so by saving or by investing in human capital. In what sense is this view correct? In what sense is it misleading?

6. Marxists believe in the principle "To each according to his needs, from each according to his abilities." Do you agree or disagree? Why or why not? Do you think that this principle would lead to a straight-line Lorenz curve? Why or why not? Explain how a government that tried to put this principle into effect would run into the conflict between equity and efficiency.

***7.** Is the income distribution which is best according to Rawls' maximin criterion necessarily the one that maximizes total income? Is it necessarily the one that minimizes inequality according to the Lorenz curve? Can it be the one with both the least total income and the greatest inequality? (Hint: refer to Exercise 2 above.)

Answers

True-False Questions: **1 T 2 F 3 F 4 T 5 F 6 T 7 T 8 F 9 T 10 F**
Multiple-Choice Questions: **1 d 2 c 3 b 4 a 5 d 6 b 7 d 8 b**
Exercises: 1. Table 31-2: 4, 10, 20, 40, 100.
Table 31-3: 14, 16, 20, 20, 30.
Table 31-4: 14, 30, 50, 70, 100.

2. Table 31-5

Distribution	Total national income
a	$ 5,000
b	$ 5,000
c	$ 2,500
d	$10,000
e	$20,000

Table 31-6

	20	40	60	80	Total
a	12	34	56	78	100
b	10	20	30	40	100
c	20	40	60	80	100
d	11	22	33	44	100
e	0	25	50	75	100

Table 31-7

Rank	Distribution
First	*d*
Second	*a*
Third	*b*
Fourth	*c*
Fifth	*e*

no, no.

FIGURE 31-2 completed.

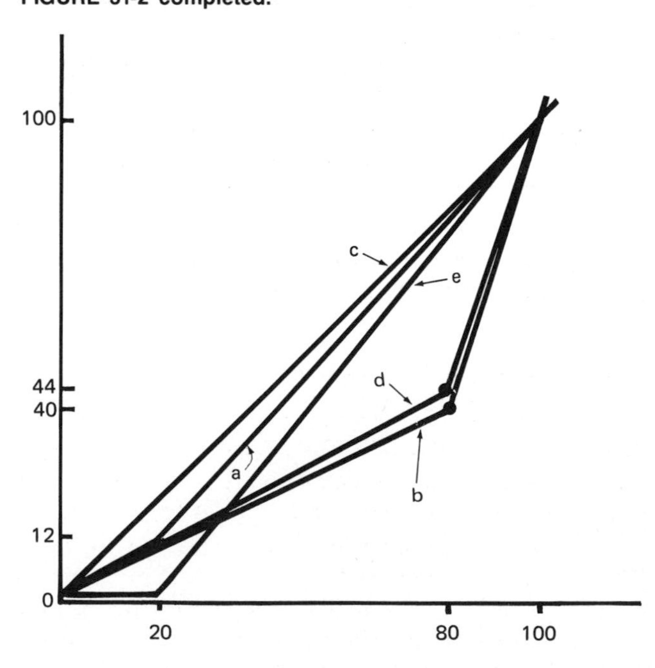

chapter 32
Government Policies to Reduce Inequality

Learning Objectives

After you have studied this chapter in the textbook and the study guide, you should be able to

Explain how the poverty line is defined
State two reasons why the poverty line has been rising over the years
List six factors that increase the likelihood of a family's being poor
Describe four kinds of government policy attacking the causes of poverty
Describe three kinds of government policy attacking the symptoms of poverty
State three reasons why some believe that government welfare programs have been unsuccessful
Describe how a negative income tax program would work
Explain why a negative income tax could not simultaneously provide everyone with an acceptable minimum income, preserve incentives, and keep costs down
List five advantages of a negative income tax program

CHAPTER HIGHLIGHTS

The problem of inequality can exist even if everyone is rich, as long as some aren't as rich as others. But in fact not everyone is rich in the United States; we also face the problem of poverty. This chapter discusses (1) the meaning of poverty, (2) the nature of government policies aimed at reducing poverty in the United States, (3) how successful these policies have been, and (4) the proposal for a negative income tax.

The Meaning of Poverty

The Department of Agriculture estimates the lowest possible cost of feeding a family of any given size with a reasonable diet that meets minimal nutrition standards. It then defines the "poverty line" as three times the cost of this diet. Thus a family is poor by this standard if it has to pay more than a third of its income just for food. In 1976 the poverty line was $5,700 for an urban family of four (lower for a rural family). This poverty line keeps rising every year, for two reasons: (1) inflation makes a given diet cost more each year and (2) our idea of what constitutes poverty changes over the years.

Studies indicate that a family is more likely to be poor if it is (1) nonwhite, (2) from the South, (3) large, (4) not well educated, (5) living in the core of a big city, or (6) fatherless. Make sure that you can use economic analysis (and common sense) to explain why each of these factors contributes to poverty.

Government Programs

Probably the most significant aspect of government welfare programs is their size. From 1965 to 1975, the cost of these programs at all levels of government quadrupled. By 1975, this cost was 20 percent of GNP.

There are four kinds of government programs that attack the *causes* (as opposed to the symptoms) of poverty: (1) those that subsidize investment in human capital, such as *(a)* free elementary and secondary schooling, *(b)* low-interest loans to college students, *(c)* the MDTA program (recall this from Chapter 13), and *(d)* the JOBS program; (2) those that aim to reduce unemployment and disability, such as *(a)* monetary and fiscal policies, and *(b)* the OSHA program; (3) laws that aim to reduce labor-market discrimination, such as the Equal Pay Act of 1963 and the Civil Rights Act of 1964; and (4) other programs, such as WIN.

There are three kinds of programs that attack the *symptoms* of poverty: (1) social security, which helps to relieve poverty even though it also pays benefits to the rich; (2) Aid to Families with Dependent Children (AFDC), which has the unfortunate side effect of encouraging fathers to leave home so that their families will qualify; and (3) transfers in kind, such as food stamps and public housing.

Successes and Failures of Welfare Programs

Poverty has been greatly reduced in the twentieth century. The poverty line of 1976 (adjusted for inflation) was the average income of 1929. But many believe that government programs have not contributed much to this reduction in poverty, for three broad reasons:

The current array of programs has generated ill will among several groups because some recipients are helped much less than others, some welfare recipients actually receive more income than some taxpayers, recipients sometimes complain of the arbitrary use of power by welfare workers, and the welfare workers themselves complain about the tangle of bureaucratic rules they must contend with.

The programs have generated much economic inefficiency, through (1) the disincentive effects on taxpayers, who are discouraged by high taxes from working (although this effect is probably not large) and encouraged to seek tax loopholes, (2) the disincentive effects on recipients, who are discouraged from working by the "implicit tax" they must pay for working (when they earn their own income, they lose welfare support), and (3) the effect of encouraging people whom the program wasn't intended to support to quit work in order to qualify for benefits. Figure 32-2 in the text shows how effects (1) and (2) operate.

Associated with these economic costs are two severe social problems: first, the incentive for fathers to leave home so that their families may qualify for AFDC, which is altering the family structure of the nation's poor, and, second, the incentive for a family to quit work and go on welfare, which can lead to a weakening of pride and self-respect. It has been suggested that it is more difficult for some families to get off welfare once they have become accustomed to the "culture of poverty."

Negative Income Tax

Many economists have suggested that it would be best to replace the whole array of existing programs with a negative income tax scheme like the one illustrated in Figure 32-3 in the text. You should understand how this scheme works, the major problems of the scheme, and the economic arguments in favor of it.

The negative income tax scheme works like this: To begin with, the government gives every family of four a subsidy of, say, $5,000 per year (more to larger families, less to rural families). For every dollar of income that the family earns above this, it must pay back 50 cents in taxes. Thus a family earning $10,000 would just break even; its tax (half of $10,000) would just cancel out the initial subsidy. A family earning more than $10,000 would pay a net tax, but one earning less than $10,000 would receive a net subsidy—that is, a negative tax. Study Figure 32-3 in the text until this is clear to you.

Like any other antipoverty program, the negative income tax scheme cannot simultaneously attain the three conflicting goals of (1) providing an acceptable minimum income for everyone, (2) preserving the incentive for people to work, and (3) keeping costs down. A negative income tax would have a disincentive effect because it would replace the current implicit taxes with an explicit tax of 50 percent. If it guarantees a minimum of $5,000 per annum, then, as we have seen, it must also pay a net subsidy to the nonpoor earning between $5,000 and $10,000, and it would reduce the taxes paid by some earning even more than $10,000. All this could be costly for those at the upper end of the income distribution.

There are five main advantages to a negative income tax:

1. Experimental projects have shown that the disincentive effect of the scheme is not as great as originally feared.

2. The scheme would probably eliminate many of the inequities of existing programs.

3. The scheme has the selling point for currently disgruntled taxpayers that it will not allow anyone to increase his or her income by quitting work.

4. It would guarantee that no one was below the poverty line. (Indeed, considerable cost could be saved by setting the guaranteed income below the poverty line and dealing separately with the special case of the disabled.)

5. It would give a big break to the taxpayers now earning between $5,000 and $10,000 per year.

IMPORTANT TERMS

Poverty Inadequate income to buy the necessities of life.

Poverty-line An income equal to three times the minimum cost of an adequate diet, as determined by the Department of Agriculture. In 1976, this was about $5,700 for an urban family of four.

JOBS The Job Opportunities in the Business Sector program, which provides subsidies for on-the-job training of workers who suffer from some disadvantage.

EPA The Equal Pay Act of 1963, which requires that women be paid the same as men for equal work.

Civil Rights Act of 1964 An act outlawing discrimination in hiring, firing, and other employment practices.

OSHA The Occupational Safety and Health Administration, which is responsible for maintaining adequate safety standards in the workplace.

WIN The Work Incentive Program, which subsidizes the training and employment of people on welfare and also—by providing day-care facilities for children—makes it possible for parents to take jobs.

AFDC Aid to Families with Dependent Children, a program under which welfare is paid to families not headed by an able-bodied male.

Food stamps Vouchers that can be bought by the poor at a price that depends upon the purchaser's income and that can be used only for buying food.

Public housing A program under which the federal government pays local governments to clear slums, build houses, and rent these houses to low-income tenants who pay 25 percent of their income in rent, with the federal government paying the rest.

Implicit tax The implicit tax built into a welfare program is measured by the amount of subsidy lost when a family earns another dollar of income.

Culture of poverty A phrase describing the increasing dependency of welfare recipients on their welfare payments.

Guaranteed income A program in which the government subsidizes income to ensure that no one earns less than a certain amount.

Negative income tax A program for guaranteeing a minimum income without also imposing a 100 percent implicit tax on earnings.

True-False Questions

T F **1.** In 1976, one American family in twelve was below the poverty line.

T F **2.** The poverty line of 1976 (adjusted for inflation) was well below the average real income of 1929.

T F **3.** The rise in the poverty-line from year to year is due entirely to inflation.

T F **4.** Families living in the core areas of big cities are more likely to be below the poverty line than those living in suburbs.

T F **5.** In 1975, Americans were spending about 20 percent of GNP on social welfare programs.

T F **6.** None of the federal government's programs attack the causes of poverty; they all merely attack the symptoms.

T F **7.** Giving food stamps to a family may not increase that family's consumption of food, even though it uses the stamps.

T F **8.** A subsidy program that gave $3,000 a year to families that earned no income and nothing to families that earned some income, no matter how small, would involve an implicit tax of over 100 percent.

T F **9.** Under the public housing program, low-income tenants pay 25 percent of their income in rent.

T F **10.** If everyone were guaranteed a $5,000 per year minimum income but a 100 percent implicit tax were imposed on earned income up to $5,000 per year, then the true economic cost of the program would be no more than $5,000 per recipient of a subsidy.

T F **11.** The negative income tax proposal would work only if existing welfare programs were also kept intact.

Multiple-Choice Questions

1. In 1976, the annual poverty-line income for a *rural* family of four was
- **(a)** Less than $5,700
- **(b)** $5,700
- **(c)** Between $5,700 and $6,400
- **(d)** $6,400
- **(e)** Above $6,400

2. The poverty line has risen considerably since the 1920s because
- **(a)** Inflation has occurred.
- **(b)** Our standards of what constitutes an adequate diet have risen.
- **(c)** Government welfare programs have been reduced.
- **(d)** **(a)** and **(b)**.
- **(e)** **(a)** and **(c)**.

3. Which of the following factors would make it more likely that a family was *above* the poverty line?
- **(a)** The father has deserted the family.
- **(b)** The family lives in the North.
- **(c)** The family is large.
- **(d)** The family is nonwhite.

4. By 1975, welfare expenditures by all levels of government in the United States were how many times larger than in 1965?
- **(a)** Two
- **(b)** Three
- **(c)** Four
- **(d)** Five

5. Which of the following kinds of government programs relieve only the symptoms of poverty?
- **(a)** Those that subsidize investment in human capital
- **(b)** Aid to Families with Dependent Children
- **(c)** Antidiscrimination policies
- **(d)** Policies to reduce unemployment and disability

6. Which of the following government programs is designed to attack the causes of poverty?
- **(a)** WIN
- **(b)** Social security
- **(c)** Food stamps
- **(d)** Public housing

7. Suppose that when a family earns another dollar, its welfare benefits are reduced by 25 cents. The implicit tax of this welfare program is
- **(a)** 20 percent
- **(b)** 25 percent
- **(c)** 75 percent
- **(d)** 80 percent

8. Which of the following is an example of in-kind assistance?
- **(a)** Public housing
- **(b)** Food stamps
- **(c)** Unemployment insurance
- **(d)** **(a)** and **(b)**
- **(e)** All of the above

9. Of the following, the most common criticism of the negative income tax is that it would
- **(a)** Increase the inequity of the government's welfare program
- **(b)** Increase the implicit tax on work
- **(c)** Require many of the existing welfare programs to be expanded
- **(d)** Be very costly if it is designed to keep everyone above the poverty line

10. One of the advantages of the negative income tax is that it would
- **(a)** Completely eliminate disincentive effects
- **(b)** Ensure that no one could earn more by not working than by working
- **(c)** Allow unhappy fathers to leave home
- **(d)** Allow us to eliminate poverty at a cost of less than 1 percent of GNP

Exercise

1. Consider the four following tax-subsidy programs:

- **a.** Every family earning less than $5,000 receives enough subsidy to give it an income of $5,000 after taxes and subsidies. For every dollar earned over $5,000, a family must pay 20 cents tax.
- **b.** Every family receives a subsidy of $5,000 but then pays a tax of 50 cents for *every* dollar earned.
- **c.** Every family receives a subsidy of $3,000 but then pays a tax of 30 cents for *every* dollar earned.
- **d.** Every family receives a subsidy of $3,000 but then pays a tax of 50 cents for *every* dollar earned.

In Figure 32-1, plot the line for each program, showing a family's income after taxes and subsidies as a function of its income before taxes and subsidies.

Indicate in Table 32-1 the marginal tax rates for each program on income earned below $5,000 and on income earned above $5,000.

Suppose that the income distribution in the economy is given by Table 32-2. In Table 32-3, fill in the net tax (i.e., tax minus subsidy) paid by each family under each of the programs.

Table 32-1

Program	Marginal tax rate on income earned above $5,000	Marginal tax rate on income earned below $5,000
a		
b		
c		
d		

Table 32-2

Annual income before taxes and transfers (thousands of dollars)	0	3	5	6	10	15	20	50
Number of families earning this income	1	2	4	4	3	2	1	1

Table 32-3

	Income (in thousands of dollars)							
	0	3	5	6	10	15	20	50
Net tax of family under program *a*	____	____	____	____	____	____	____	____
Net tax of family under program *b*	____	____	____	____	____	____	____	____
Net tax of family under program *c*	____	____	____	____	____	____	____	____
Net tax of family under program *d*	____	____	____	____	____	____	____	____

FIGURE 32-1

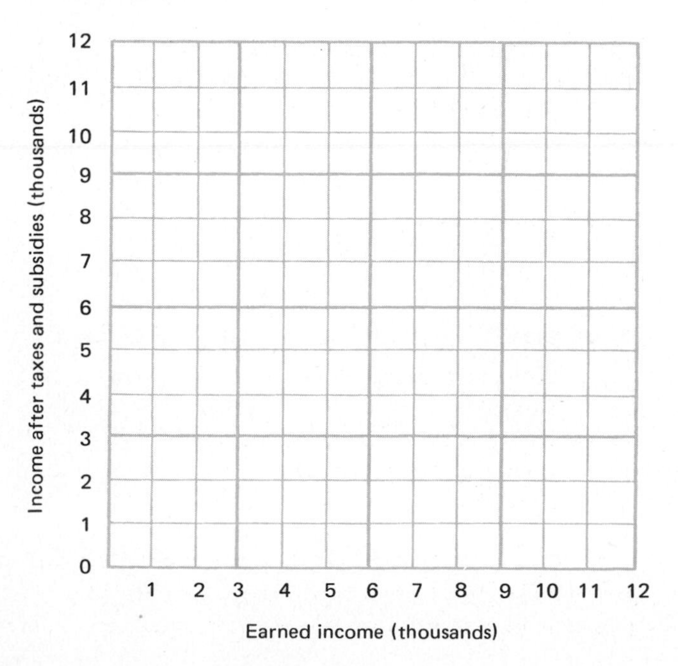

In Table 32-4, show the total net taxes collected—that is, total taxes collected minus total subsidy paid, under the assumption that each family *earns* the same income under one program as under another.

Table 32-4

Programs	Total net taxes
a	____
b	____
c	____
d	____

Essay Questions

1. At one point in his unsuccessful presidential campaign in 1972, Senator McGovern proposed sending out a check for $50 to every individual in the country. If this program had been carried out, even with no other change in government programs, in what sense would this have accomplished, at least to some extent, the benefits of a negative income tax? What would it have done to the federal government's deficit? What would the government eventually have to do in order to make up for this effect on its deficit, and in what sense would this undo the effects of the initial $50 per person?

2. If the main ill effect of AFDC is to encourage fathers to leave their families so that they may qualify, wouldn't it be best to maintain the program but disqualify any family whose father has abandoned them?

3. Do you think that a negative income tax program would reduce inequality of incomes after taxes and transfers? Do you think it would reduce inequality of incomes before taxes and subsidies?

4. If the government gave equivalent cash transfers instead of assistance in kind, would the recipients be better off? Why? Why does the government not do so?

5. Why cannot the disincentive effects of welfare programs be overcome simply by requiring welfare recipients to work unless they are disabled?

6. In the text, it was mentioned that the 1976 poverty line was actually the 1929 average income. In what sense is the person on the poverty line in 1976 better off than the person receiving the average income in 1929? In what sense is he or she worse off?

7. Our usual definition of the poverty line depends mainly upon the biological fact of life that we need food to live. Argue the case that poverty has little to do with such biological requirements.

Answers

True-False Questions: 1 T 2 F 3 F 4 T 5 T 6 F 7 T 8 T 9 T 10 F 11 T
Multiple-Choice Questions: 1 a 2 d 3 b 4 c 5 b 6 a 7 b 8 d 9 d 10 b
Exercise:

FIGURE 32-1 completed.

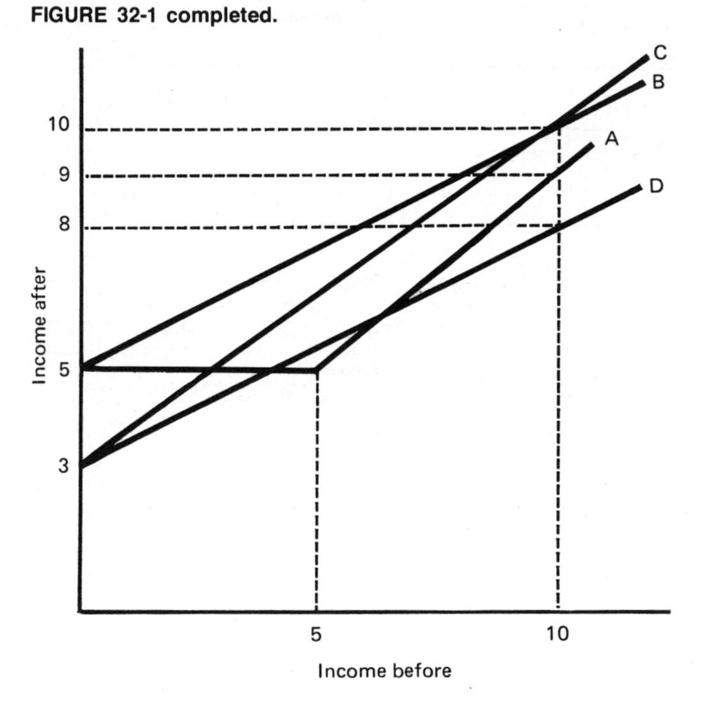

Table 32-1

Marginal tax rate on income earned above $5,000	Marginal tax rate on income earned below $5,000
20%	100%
50%	50%
30%	30%
50%	50%

Table 32-3

Income (in thousands of dollars)							
0	3	5	6	10	15	20	50
$-5,000	$-2,000	$ 0	$ 200	$1,000	$2,000	$3,000	$ 9,000
-5,000	-3,500	-2,500	-2,000	0	2,500	5,000	20,000
-3,000	-2,100	-1,500	-1,200	0	1,500	3,000	12,000
-3,000	-1,500	- 500	0	2,000	4,500	7,000	22,000

Table 32-4

Total net taxes
$10,800
0
0
36,000

chapter 33
Marxism and the Systems of the Soviet Union and Yugoslavia

Learning objectives

After you have studied this chapter in the textbook and the study guide, you should be able to

Describe the labor theory of value
Explain why, according to Marxism, workers are exploited
State two predictions of Marxism that have not been verified by history
Explain the Marxist solution for raising capital and three problems with it
Describe three major difficulties with central planning
State why and by how much the Soviet economy grew faster than the American economy in the 1960s and '70s
State two reasons for believing that the Soviet and American economic systems are becoming increasingly similar
List three specific effects of the Liberman reforms in the Soviet Union
State two differences between the Soviet and Yugoslavian economic systems
Describe four ways in which the government exerts a great deal of centralized control over the Yugoslavian economy
Explain why workers' incomes tend to be more unstable and less evenly distributed in Yugoslavia than in the Soviet Union

CHAPTER HIGHLIGHTS

This chapter discusses three closely related topics: (1) the theory of Marxism, (2) the economic system of the Soviet Union, and (3) the economic system of Yugoslavia. Under these topics, the chapter discusses what a socialist economic system is like, the Marxists' arguments in favor of a socialist system and against our own capitalist system, and the capitalist critique of these Marxist arguments and of their practical applications in the Soviet Union and Yugoslavia.

The Theory of Marxism

Marxism is based upon the labor theory of value and the subsistence theory of wages. It claims that workers are exploited under capitalism because, instead of enjoying all the fruits of their labor, they receive just enough to subsist, the rest going in the form of "surplus value" to the capitalists. According to Marx, the only way of resolving this class struggle is a revolution—in which workers forcibly seize the ownership of physical capital from their exploiters—followed by a dictatorship of the proletariat and the eventual state of communism.

One criticism of Marxist theory is that its predictions have not been borne out by history. To begin with, the dictatorship of the proletariat, rather than withering away, has remained powerful in Marxist states. Furthermore, under capitalism, workers have enjoyed rising real incomes rather than the increasing misery predicted by Marx.

Another criticism of Marxist theory is that if capitalists are eliminated, some other way must be found of generating physical capital for production. The Marxist solution is to generate capital by taxation rather than by personal saving. But (1) taxes can be burdensome, (2) governments typically lack the inventiveness of private capitalists, and (3) some substitute must be found for the profit motive as a means of allocating capital among different industries.

The question of profit raises an important issue in the debate between capitalism and Marxism. Supporters of Marxism and capitalism alike generally agree that monopoly profits should not go unchecked. Capitalist supporters argue that this can be done through government regulation under a basically capitalist system. Marxists argue that regulation is ineffective because big-business interests are so powerful that they end up controlling their own regulators. A capitalist response to this criticism is that big-business interests have even greater power in a Marxist state because they themselves *are* the government.

The Soviet System

The two important features of a socialist system are that (1) physical capital is owned by the state rather than by private individuals and (2) decisions concerning how much of various goods to produce and how much to invest in different industries are made by a central government rather than through the interplay of market forces. In the Soviet Union, these centralized decisions are based on 5-year plans, administered by the agency called GOSPLAN. These plans set yearly production targets, or quotas, for the managers of different firms. There are three major difficulties with central planning of this sort:

1. It is difficult for the government to determine a set of consistent quotas. For example, if steel producers are to meet their quota, this requires so many machines to be produced, which, in turn, requires the use of so much steel, and so forth. As a result of this difficulty, bottlenecks are common in the Soviet economy.

2. Consumers' wants tend to be ignored in the Soviet system, because each firm's manager tends to concentrate on satisfying the firm's quota rather than producing the type and variety of goods that consumers most want. The big advantage of central planning is that it produces very little measured unemployment. However, critics point out that if someone is working to produce unwanted goods, this really constitutes "disguised" unemployment.

3. Critics also argue that central planning could not work without a repressive political dictatorship, as in the Soviet Union. Marxists counter by saying that our freedom is enjoyed only by the rich and powerful.

The 5-year plans of the Soviet Union have emphasized rapid growth. For example, from 1960 to 1974, the average annual rate of growth was 4.9 percent in the Soviet Union as compared with 3.8 percent in the United States. To accomplish this, investment in the Soviet Union is about 30 percent of GNP, compared with 15 percent in the United States. This investment is financed by taxes on consumer goods, which amount to about one-third of the price of the typical good. One reason for using this kind of tax is that it can be made progressive by taxing luxury items more heavily than necessities.

However, there are two reasons for thinking that the Soviet and United States systems are converging toward one another: (1) Rapid growth in welfare programs in the United States has been reducing income inequalities while at the same time diminishing economic incentives. Meanwhile, Soviet workers are being given more incentives in the form of wage differentials and bonuses in order to encourage efficiency, with the result that income inequalities are probably growing in the Soviet Union. (2) In the United States, the government is becoming more and more involved in production decisions, while—largely as a result of the Liberman reforms—production decisions are becoming more responsive to the market in the Soviet Union. The Liberman reforms have *(a)* allowed managers of firms to take orders for particular kinds of goods from their customers, *(b)* imposed penalties on managers unable to produce goods that will sell at a "reasonable" price, and *(c)* allowed managers some scope in changing their prices.

The System of Yugoslavia

In Yugoslavia as in the Soviet Union, the state owns most physical capital. But production decisions are much less centralized in Yugoslavia. Firms there are operated by workers, who elect a manager. This manager attempts, like the manager of a capitalist enterprise, to maximize profits, which are then distributed to the workers.

However, the government still exerts a great deal of centralized control upon the economy:

1. Although most firms are allowed to change their prices, they do so only within fixed limits.

2. As in the Soviet Union, the government diverts one-third of annual GNP into the production of investment goods.

3. The allocation of these investment goods into different sectors of the economy is also determined by the central government.

4. The government sets out 5-year plans as in the Soviet Union (although these plans are not strictly enforced).

There are three special problems that the Yugoslav system has encountered:

1. Some of the "worker enterprises" have a monopoly position, which their managers have exploited by restricting output.

2. Because workers receive the firm's profits and because these profits fluctuate with market conditions, workers' incomes are not as stable as in the Soviet Union and tend to be more unevenly distributed than in the Soviet Union.

3. The system allows no incentive to create a new firm. Thus many existing firms do not face even the threat of competition.

IMPORTANT TERMS

Capitalism An economic system in which most physical capital is privately owned.

Socialism An economic system in which physical capital (and land) is owned by the state.

Communism In Marxist theory, this is the ideal system in which all means of production and other forms of property are owned by the community as a whole and the central government has "withered away." In capitalist countries, the term "communism" refers to the present economic and political systems of countries like the Soviet Union. However, these countries do not consider themselves to have achieved communism.

Labor theory of value The theory that the value of any good is determined solely by the amount of labor that goes into producing it. Notice that this labor includes not just the labor directly involved in producing the good but also the labor embodied in the capital used to produce the good.

Subsistence wage theory The theory that in a capitalist economy workers' wages can never rise except temporarily above a socially defined subsistence level.

Surplus value In Marxist theory, the difference between the total value of output (all of which "belongs" to labor) and the wages actually received by labor.

Exploitation The Marxist description of any system in which the workers themselves do not receive the surplus value.

GOSPLAN The central planning agency in the Soviet Union.

5-year plan A plan drawn up in a Marxist country every 5 years, setting production and investment targets for each industry. In practice, these plans are revised from year to year.

Proletariat The Marxist term for the working class.

Bourgeoisie The Marxist term for the capitalist class.

Dictatorship of the proletariat According to Marxist theory, this is the transition stage after the workers' revolution and before the government withers away and the ideal state of communism is achieved.

Disguised unemployment Disguised unemployment exists if people are employed at useless tasks. This might be regarded as the Soviet equivalent of featherbedding.

Liberman reforms The reforms carried out in the early '60s in the Soviet Union, inspired by the ideas of Professor Liberman, which made Soviet firms more responsive to market forces.

True-False Questions

T F **1.** According to Marxist theory, only the owners of human capital are called capitalists.

T F **2.** The government of the Soviet Union does not regard itself as having achieved communism.

T F **3.** The labor theory of value attempts primarily to explain the wages received by workers.

T F **4.** Surplus value is the difference between the value of output and the total income of workers.

T F **5.** According to Marxist theory, exploitation occurs because workers do not receive even subsistence wages.

T F **6.** Marx advocated the achievement of communism through nonviolent methods rather than through revolution.

T F 7. Marxist theory predicts that the state will eventually "wither away" after the dictatorshop of the proletariat is achieved.

T F 8. Marx regarded as surplus value only above-normal profits, not normal profits.

T F 9. Five-year plans are not drawn up in Yugoslavia.

T F 10. Marxists argue that our political freedom is illusory because politicians are really controlled by big-business interests.

T F 11. One of the problems of the Soviet system is that, because the capitalist class has been abolished, there is not enough investment.

T F 12. One of the problems of the Soviet system is that consumer goods are not produced in as much variety as in a capitalist system.

T F 13. The Soviet Union has experienced a higher growth rate in the 1960s and '70s than Japan.

T F 14. The Soviet Union has experienced a higher growth rate in the 1960s and '70s than the United States.

T F 15. One advantage of central planning is that it succeeds in eliminating disguised unemployment.

T F 16. Most people agree that, in recent years, capitalist and Marxist systems have become increasingly similar.

T F 17. In Yugoslavia, workers face less uncertainty about their income than they do in the Soviet Union.

T F 18. In Yugoslavia, the manager of a firm is elected by the workers.

T F 19. In Yugoslavia, the state exerts no direct control over the amount of investment every year.

Multiple-Choice Questions

1. Investment in the Soviet Union constitutes how large a percentage of GNP?
- **(a)** 15 percent
- **(b)** 30 percent
- **(c)** 45 percent
- **(d)** Any amount, depending upon interest rates

2. Which of the following is true about the experience of the past two decades?
- **(a)** Soviet growth rates have been higher than those in the United States.
- **(b)** The differences between the Soviet and American systems have been widening.
- **(c)** The Soviets have been investing twice as high a proportion of GNP as the United States.
- **(d)** **(a)** and **(b)**.
- **(e)** **(a)** and **(c)**.

3. Marx believed that under capitalism, the workers
- **(a)** Would and should revolt
- **(b)** Would revolt but shouldn't
- **(c)** Wouldn't revolt but should
- **(d)** Wouldn't and shouldn't revolt

4. Which of the following is *not* a commonly acknowledged defect of the Soviet system?
- **(a)** Bottlenecks are common in the Soviet economy.
- **(b)** The variety of consumer goods is less than in the United States.
- **(c)** The Soviet government has not been as innovative in its investment decisions as the private capitalists in Western economies.
- **(d)** Measured unemployment tends to be higher in the Soviet Union than in Western countries.

5. In Figure 33-1, the curve labeled MPL denotes the marginal productivity of labor in a perfectly competitive industry, where the wage equals *OW*. According to Marxist theory, the area of the triangle *ABW* measures
- **(a)** The subsistence wage
- **(b)** The amount of labor embodied in the output of the industry
- **(c)** Surplus value
- **(d)** The total income of workers

6. In the Soviet Union, investment is financed mainly through
- **(a)** Government borrowing
- **(b)** Income taxes
- **(c)** Taxes on investment goods
- **(d)** Taxes on consumer goods

7. One reason why it has been argued that the economic systems of the United States and the Soviet Union are becoming increasingly similar is that
- **(a)** The Soviets have been allowing greater scope for market forces in production decisions than in the past.
- **(b)** The Soviet government is relying more heavily upon its 5-year plans.
- **(c)** The United States government is becoming increasingly involved in production decisions.
- **(d)** **(a)** and **(b)**.
- **(e)** **(a)** and **(c)**.

8. The purpose of the Liberman reforms was to
- **(a)** Increase efficiency in production
- **(b)** Impose stricter quotas on managers
- **(c)** Allow workers to own their own firms
- **(d)** Increase the fraction of GNP going to investment every year

9. Which of the following is *not* true about the economic system of Yugoslavia?
- **(a)** The managers of firms are restricted in their freedom to change prices.
- **(b)** The government allows the total volume of investment each year to be determined by market forces.

(c) The government issues 5-year plans.
(d) The government allows workers to elect the managers of their firms.

10. The Liberman reforms did *not*
(a) Allow managers to accept special orders from their customers
(b) Penalize managers whose output did not sell well
(c) Allow workers to elect their managers
(d) Give some freedom to managers to change prices

Essay Questions

1. The text pointed out that while Soviet-style central planning reduces measured unemployment, it often replaces this with disguised unemployment. Likewise, the Soviet system does not appear to suffer from inflation as ours does. In what sense do you think it might be true that the Soviets have also replaced measured inflation with a less obvious kind? (Hint: Is the value of your money really constant if prices remain the same but, due to increasingly severe bottlenecks, goods are becoming harder to find?)

2. If you lived in the Soviet Union, would you have more or less of an incentive to save than you do living in the United States? In view of this, what do you think the consumption function looks like in the Soviet Union?

3. Most workers in the United States save toward their retirement. Much of this saving takes the form, either directly or through pension funds, of investment in shares in corporations. Do you think it is true, then, that most workers in the United States are also capitalists? Why or why not? Likewise, very few people in the United States earn a living without doing work of one sort or another. Is it true, then, that most capitalists are also workers? Why or why not? Argue the case either for or against the proposition that Marxist theory is based upon a class struggle that doesn't really exist.

4. Construct an argument in support of the following statement: "Because the Soviet system has abolished traditional capitalism, it is going overboard in support of the system of human capitalism, thus creating a new bourgeoisie of those who possess large quantities of human capital."

5. "The reason why economic growth has been faster in the Soviet Union than in the United States is that in the Soviet Union peoples' efforts are devoted toward the common good, whereas in the United States peoples' efforts are devoted toward their own self-interest." Do you agree or disagree? Explain.

6. Review your understanding, from Chapter 29, of why land has value. How does the labor theory of value run into trouble in trying to explain the value of land?

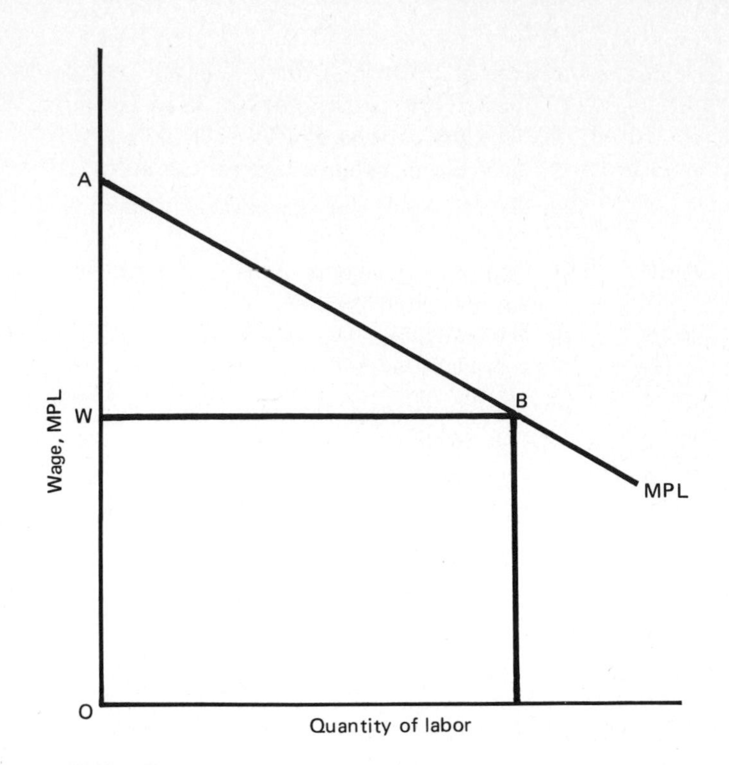

FIGURE 33-1

7. Recall from Chapter 32 the difficulties of finding the poverty line. Do these difficulties also apply to defining "subsistence wage"?

8. The text pointed out two predictions of Marxism that have not been verified by history. How do you suppose the development of labor unions in the United States and other capitalist countries has helped to undermine Marxist predictions?

9. Why has economic growth been more rapid in the Soviet Union than in the United States? Do you think it would be desirable for the government of the United States to raise taxes on consumer goods and increase subsidies on investment activities in order to bring our rate of growth up to the Soviet level? Who would gain from such a policy? Who would lose? What political problems do you think there would be with such a policy?

10. In his famous *General Theory*, Keynes said, "The ideas of economists and political philosophers, both when they are right and when they are wrong, are more powerful than is commonly understood. Indeed the world is ruled by little else. Practical men, who believe themselves to be quite exempt from any intellectual influences, are usually the slaves of some defunct economist. Madmen in authority, who hear voices in the air, are distilling their frenzy from some academic scribbler of a few years back. I am sure that the power of vested interests is vastly exaggerated compared with the gradual encroachment of ideas . . . soon or late, it is ideas, not vested interests, which are dangerous for good or evil." In what sense does the history of Marxism and Marxist states tend to bear out this opinion? In what sense does it tend to contradict the opinion?

Answers

True-False Questions: 1 F 2 T 3 F 4 T 5 F 6 F 7 T 8 F 9 F 10 T 11 F 12 T 13 F 14 T 15 F 16 T 17 F 18 T 19 F
Multiple-Choice Questions: 1 b 2 e 3 a 4 d 5 c 6 d 7 e 8 a 9 b 10 c

A